South University Library
Richmond Campus
2151 Old Brick Road
Glen Allen, Va 23060

MAR 1 3 2018

Workplace Bullying and Mobbing in the United States

Workplace Bullying and Mobbing in the United States

Volume 2

Maureen Duffy and David C. Yamada, Editors

Foreword by Gary Namie

An Imprint of ABC-CLIO, LLC
Santa Barbara, California • Denver, Colorado

Copyright © 2018 by ABC-CLIO, LLC

All rights reserved. No part of this publication may be reproduced, stored in a retrieval system, or transmitted, in any form or by any means, electronic, mechanical, photocopying, recording, or otherwise, except for the inclusion of brief quotations in a review, without prior permission in writing from the publisher.

Library of Congress Cataloging-in-Publication Data

Names: Duffy, Maureen P., editor. | Yamada, David C., editor.
Title: Workplace bullying and mobbing in the United States / Maureen Duffy
   and David C. Yamada, editors ; foreword by Gary Namie.
Description: Santa Barbara, California : Praeger, 2018. | Includes
   bibliographical references and index.
Identifiers: LCCN 2017013247 (print) | LCCN 2017031060 (ebook) |
   ISBN 9781440850240 (ebook) | ISBN 9781440850233 (set : alk. paper) |
   ISBN 9781440850257 (volume 1) | ISBN 9781440850264 (volume 2)
Subjects: LCSH: Bullying in the workplace—United States. | Harassment—United States.
Classification: LCC HF5549.5.E43 (ebook) | LCC HF5549.5.E43 W67168 2018 (print) |
   DDC 331.25/6—dc23
LC record available at https://lccn.loc.gov/2017013247

ISBN: 978-1-4408-5023-3 (set)
       978-1-4408-5025-7 (vol. 1)
       978-1-4408-5026-4 (vol. 2)
       978-1-4408-5024-0 (ebook)

22 21 20 19 18   1 2 3 4 5

This book is also available as an eBook.

Praeger
An Imprint of ABC-CLIO, LLC

ABC-CLIO, LLC
130 Cremona Drive, P.O. Box 1911
Santa Barbara, California 93116-1911
www.abc-clio.com

This book is printed on acid-free paper ∞

Manufactured in the United States of America

Contents

VOLUME 1

Foreword   ix
Gary Namie

Preface   xiii
Maureen Duffy and David C. Yamada

PART I: UNDERSTANDING WORKPLACE BULLYING AND MOBBING

1. Workplace Bullying and Mobbing: Definitions, Terms, and When They Matter   3
   David C. Yamada, Maureen Duffy, and Peggy Ann Berry

2. Prevalence of Workplace Bullying and Mobbing among U.S. Working Adults: What Do the Numbers Mean?   25
   Loraleigh Keashly

3. Risk Factors for Becoming a Target of Workplace Bullying and Mobbing   53
   Gary Namie and Ruth Namie

4. Organizational Risk Factors: An Integrative Model for Understanding, Treating, and Preventing Mobbing and Bullying in the Workplace   75
   Len Sperry

PART II: EXAMINING THE IMPACT OF WORKPLACE BULLYING AND MOBBING

5 Workplace Bullying and Mobbing and the Health of Targets ... 101
    Melody M. Kawamoto

6 The Psychosocial Impact of Workplace Bullying and Mobbing on Targets ... 131
    Maureen Duffy

7 Workplace Bullying and Mobbing: A Neuropsychotherapeutic Perspective ... 151
    Pieter J. Rossouw

8 Vicarious and Secondary Victimization in Adult Bullying and Mobbing: Coworkers, Target-Partners, Children, and Friends ... 171
    Pamela Lutgen-Sandvik

9 When Workplace Bullying and Mobbing Occur: The Impact on Organizations ... 201
    Renee L. Cowan

PART III: PREVENTION OF WORKPLACE BULLYING AND MOBBING

10 How Awareness and Education Can Help with Recognition of Workplace Bullying and Mobbing ... 221
    Gary Namie, Ruth Namie, and Carol Fehner

11 The Role of Human Resources in Bullying and Mobbing Prevention Efforts ... 235
    Teresa A. Daniel

12 Innovative Practices in Workplace Conflict Resolution ... 265
    John-Robert Curtin

VOLUME 2

PART IV: UTILIZING EFFECTIVE INTERVENTIONS IN RESPONDING TO WORKPLACE BULLYING AND MOBBING

13 Best Practices in Psychotherapy for Targets of Workplace Bullying and Mobbing   291
   Maureen Duffy and Jessi Eden Brown

14 Best Practices in Coaching for Targets of Workplace Bullying and Mobbing   315
   Jessi Eden Brown and Maureen Duffy

15 Best Practices in Coaching for Aggressors and Offenders in Workplace Bullying and Mobbing   335
   Benjamin M. Walsh

16 The Role of the Consultant in Assessing and Preventing Workplace Bullying and Mobbing   357
   Gary Namie and Ruth Namie

17 The Role of the Ombuds in Addressing Workplace Bullying and Mobbing   387
   Tony Belak

PART V: THE LEGAL LANDSCAPE IN THE UNITED STATES FOR WORKPLACE BULLYING AND MOBBING

18 The American Legal Landscape: Potential Redress and Liability for Workplace Bullying and Mobbing   413
   David C. Yamada

19 Comparing and Contrasting Workplace Bullying and Mobbing Laws in Other Countries with the American Legal Landscape   435
   Ellen Pinkos Cobb

PART VI: WORKPLACE BULLYING AND MOBBING WITHIN SPECIFIC EMPLOYMENT SECTORS

20 Workplace Bullying and Mobbing in the Health Care Sector   457
    Susan Johnson

21 Workplace Bullying and Mobbing in K–12 Settings:
    School Principal Mistreatment and Abuse of Teachers   481
    Jo Blase and Joseph Blase

22 Workplace Bullying and Mobbing in U.S. Higher Education   507
    Loraleigh Keashly and Joel H. Neuman

23 Workplace Bullying and Mobbing in the Public Service
    Sector and the Role of Unions   539
    Gregory Sorozan

24 Workplace Bullying and Mobbing in the Corporate Sector   561
    Kelly H. Kolb and Mary Beth Ricke

25 Workplace Bullying and Mobbing in the Nonprofit Sector   589
    Vega Subramaniam

Epilogue: An Agenda for Moving Forward   611
David C. Yamada and Maureen Duffy

About the Editors and Contributors   619

Index   627

PART IV

Utilizing Effective Interventions in Responding to Workplace Bullying and Mobbing

13

Best Practices in Psychotherapy for Targets of Workplace Bullying and Mobbing

Maureen Duffy and Jessi Eden Brown

In this chapter and in chapter 14, we examine counseling and coaching strategies for working with targets and survivors of workplace bullying and mobbing. In the current chapter, we focus on best practices in counseling and psychotherapy and provide a detailed overview of the concept of trauma-informed care. In chapter 14, we extend the application of trauma-informed care to the practice of professional coaching with targets of workplace bullying and mobbing. In both chapters, we will use the terms *professional counseling* and *psychotherapy* synonymously to refer to the provision of professional mental health care services. Professional coaching is distinct from counseling and psychotherapy, and that distinction will be described in the next chapter, which focuses specifically on professional coaching.

By definition, bullying and mobbing are health-harming processes (Duffy & Sperry, 2007, 2012, 2014; Namie & Namie, 2011). The health-harming effects can be both physical and psychological and may include the aggravation of preexisting health problems or the development of new health problems during and after bullying and mobbing episodes (Duffy & Sperry, 2007, 2012, 2014). A thorough review of these health effects, both physical and psychological, can be found in chapter 5. Because we are looking at counseling and coaching interventions for targets and survivors in this and the following chapter, our focus is primarily on the negative psychological consequences of bullying and mobbing while acknowledging that stress impacts a person's overall health, including physical health (Duffy & Sperry, 2007; Kivimaki et al., 2003).

The psychological negative consequences associated with bullying and mobbing include full clinical syndromes and disorders meeting psychiatric diagnostic criteria as well as subclinical syndromes that do not meet full diagnostic criteria but result in significant emotional and psychosocial distress.

Understanding the clinical diagnoses and subclinical syndromes associated with workplace bullying and mobbing is important because it is for these conditions that targets, survivors, and family members are most likely to seek help and treatment. Existing research supports a strong association between bullying and mobbing and certain health conditions and subclinical syndromes.

Workplace bullying and mobbing have been found to be associated with clinical diagnoses of depression (Cassitto & Gilioli, 2003; Hansen et al., 2006; Leymann & Gustafsson, 1998; Niedhammer et al., 2006; Pompili et al., 2008; Punzi, Cassito, Castellini, Costa, & Gilioli, 2007); anxiety (Brousse et al., 2008; Cassitto & Gilioli, 2003; Chen, Hwu, Kung, Chiu, & Wang, 2008; Hansen et al., 2006; Tomei et al., 2007); post-traumatic stress disorder (PTSD) or post-traumatic stress disorder symptoms (Balducci, Alfano, & Fraccaroli, 2009; Hoel, Faragher, & Cooper, 2004; Leymann & Gustafsson, 1996; Matthiesen, & Einarsen, 2004; Mikkelsen & Einarsen, 2002; Nielsen, Matthiesen & Einarsen, 2005; Nielsen, Tangen, Idsoe, Matthiesen, & Magerøy, 2015; Rodríguez-Muñoz, Moreno-Jiménez, Vergel, & Garrosa Hernández, 2010; Tehrani, 2004) and misuse of alcohol and drugs (Richman, Flaherty, & Rospenda, 1996; Rospenda, Richman, Wolff, & Burke, 2013; Traweger, Kinzl, Traweger-Ravanelli, & Fiala, 2004). Results from the National Health Interview Survey (Khubchandi & Price, 2015), which included 17,524 U.S. adults, indicated workplace harassment to be associated with "significantly higher rates of serious mental illnesses, disrupted sleep patterns, and psychosocial distress symptoms" (p. 559).

THE QUESTION OF POST-TRAUMATIC STRESS DISORDER (PTSD)

From the above brief review of mental health diagnoses associated with workplace bullying and mobbing, it is clear that depression, anxiety, and PTSD have repeatedly been diagnosed in targets and survivors of workplace bullying and mobbing. PTSD has been assigned as a diagnosis for targets and survivors of bullying and mobbing since Leymann's original clinical work in the 1980s and 1990s (Leymann & Gustafsson, 1996) and has continued as an assigned diagnosis to the present day. For those who provide clinical mental health services for targets of bullying and mobbing and their family members, it is no surprise that PTSD is a frequently considered or assigned diagnosis. Westhues (2004) referred to workplace mobbing as the "stressor to beat all stressors" (p. 4), and the renowned traumatologist Dr. Robert Scaer (2005) described the workplace as a common site of traumatic experiences. Scaer said that "almost any social setting where control is lost and relative helplessness is part of the environment can easily progress to a traumatic experience. Perhaps the most obvious and pervasive source of this insidious societal trauma is in the workplace" (p. 132). Yet, whether the diagnosis of PTSD can appropriately be applied to targets and survivors of workplace bullying and mobbing remains a topic of debate.

The *Diagnostic and Statistical Manual of Mental Disorders* (5th ed.; *DSM-5*; American Psychiatric Association (APA), 2013) is the most widely used system of classification of mental disorders by clinicians and researchers globally. How a diagnosis is defined and explained in the *DSM* has theoretical, clinical, legal, and practical implications, including whether reimbursement for treatment is likely to be available and for how long and whether a person is eligible for benefits such as workers' compensation and Social Security disability insurance.

PTSD is now included in the *DSM-5* (APA, 2013) in a new section under the heading "Trauma and Stressor-Related Disorders" and not under the heading "Anxiety Disorders," as in past editions. As a diagnosis for targets and survivors of workplace bullying and mobbing, PTSD raises particular issues. On the one hand, clinicians and survivors frequently identify PTSD as the most appropriate mental health diagnosis for many targets and survivors, given the traumatic nature of the experience of workplace bullying and mobbing and the resulting symptom set. On the other hand, the *DSM-5* (APA, 2013) criteria necessary to accurately make the diagnosis of post-traumatic stress disorder present some specific problems for clinicians who wish to use the diagnosis for targets and survivors presenting with a cluster of traumatic stress symptoms.

Criteria for Making Diagnosis of PTSD

The *DSM-5* (APA, 2013) lists eight sets of criteria (Criterion A through Criterion H) required for the diagnosis of PTSD to be accurately made. Criterion A describes the nature of the initiating traumatic stressor necessary before a diagnosis of PTSD can be rendered, and it is this criterion that is most problematic for clinicians working with targets and survivors of workplace bullying and mobbing. The criterion requires direct exposure or witnessing to actual or threatened death, actual or threatened serious injury, or actual or threatened sexual violence. Indirect exposure through learning that a significant other was exposed to this same set of traumatic events is acceptable for the diagnosis provided that, in the case of indirect exposure to death or threatened death, the death was violent or accidental. Repeated exposure to extremely unpleasant details of the triggering event, often in the course of discharging occupational or professional responsibilities (for example, first responders, child abuse investigators), also can satisfy Criterion A.

Criterion B explains the requirement that intrusive and repetitive memories, thoughts, and feelings are present in the symptomatic person. These thoughts and feelings are forms of traumatic reexperiencing, such as nightmares, flashbacks, and unwanted images of the events surrounding the initiating traumatic stressor. Criterion C describes symptoms of avoidance necessary to make the diagnosis of PTSD. These avoidant symptoms can be avoidance of actual thoughts, memories, or feelings about the initiating stressor or avoidance of persons, places, things, conversations, or any other reminders of the initiating stressor.

Criterion D outlines negative changes in thought or mood that either began or got worse after the initiating traumatic stressor. These negative changes in thought or mood include the inability to remember key details of the traumatic stressor, a persistent and often distorted sense of blame of self or others for the traumatic event and for its consequences, persistent and strong negative emotions related to the initiating traumatic event, persistent and often distorted beliefs and expectations about the world and oneself, diminished interest in activities once found to be pleasurable or a source of satisfaction, a sense of detachment from others, and a persistent inability to experience positive emotions.

Criterion E describes arousal symptoms either beginning or worsening after exposure to the initiating traumatic stressor. These arousal symptoms include irritable, aggressive, reckless, or self-destructive behavior; hypervigilance (excessive watchfulness or scanning the environment for threats); problems with focus or concentration; and sleep disturbances. Criterion F specifies that the symptoms in Criteria B, C, D, and E must have lasted longer than a month. Criterion G specifies that these symptoms must have resulted in significant subjective feelings of distress or impairment in functioning. And, finally, Criterion H specifies that these symptom sets must not be due to illness, medications, or substances. The full, detailed diagnostic criteria with respect to the number of symptoms that must be present in each cluster and other explanatory details may be found in the *DSM-5* (APA, 2013).

Difficulties with Criterion A

If we return to Criterion A, the qualifying stressor for a diagnosis of PTSD, it is debatable whether exposure to workplace bulling or mobbing satisfies the criteria for a diagnosis. For some and perhaps many bullying and mobbing targets, the threat of job loss, with all its attendant financial implications and associated loss of personal and professional identity, is directly experienced as an actual (if job loss is the outcome) or threatened serious injury and, therefore, arguably is a qualifying stressor. There is a seldom-discussed bias in the *DSM* toward overemphasizing the precipitating stressor as representing a threat to *physical* injury or death and underemphasizing the *psychological* threat and terror accompanying a range of human experiences that typically do not result in physical injury or death but that equally trigger intense psychological reactions consistent with the remainder of the criteria for establishing a diagnosis of PTSD.

A notable exception is the work of Roberts et al. (2012), who, in their study, used data from the PTSD subsample of the Nurses' Health Study II consisting of over 3,000 nurse subjects. They concluded that subthreshold stressors (i.e., those stressors not meeting the life-threatening criteria of the *DSM*) also resulted in PTSD symptoms as significant as those from the diagnostic life-threatening stressors. Their overall conclusion is that PTSD may be a severe, nonspecific stress response syndrome and that a range of stressors, both life-threatening and non-life-threatening, can operate as precipitating events.

Another area of controversy surrounding Criterion A is the diagnostic legitimacy of pairing a narrowly defined precipitating event with a set of psychological reactions or sequelae (Breslau & Davis, 1987a; Roberts et al., 2012). Almost all other diagnoses in the *DSM* are based only on symptoms and do not connect a precipitating factor as imputed cause, as does the diagnosis of PTSD. Additionally, the professional literature has amply documented the presence of PTSD in the absence of a Criterion A (life-threatening) stressor (Brewin, Lanius, Novac, Schnyder, & Galea, 2009; McNally, 2003, 2009; Roberts et al., 2012, Rosen & Lilienfeld, 2008, Scott & Stradling, 1994). Severe financial and legal problems; marital problems; job loss; sexual harassment; divorce (Roberts et al., 2012); caring for a partner with a life-threatening condition; workplace harassment (Scott & Stradling, 1994); being stalked (Pathe & Mullen 1997); and chronic stress experienced by military personnel (Breslau & Davis, 1987b) are among the examples of subthreshold stressors associated with the subsequent development of PTSD. With specific reference to workplace bullying, Matthiesen and Einarsen (2004) found a very high level of post-traumatic stress symptoms among the workplace bullying targets whom they studied.

It is worth noting that most of these subthreshold, non-life-threatening stressors associated with the subsequent onset of PTSD involved the experience of prolonged periods of stress, as is the case in workplace bullying and mobbing. From a clinical and treatment perspective, therefore, an individual who experienced workplace bullying and mobbing and who presents with symptoms of reexperiencing, avoidance, arousal, emotional numbing, or other changes in thoughts or mood should be assessed for PTSD irrespective of the ambiguity and controversy over Criterion A.

Not Everyone Who Is Bullied or Mobbed Develops Post-Traumatic Stress Symptoms

Not everyone who is exposed to life-altering or chronic stressors such as bullying and mobbing develops PTSD or post-traumatic symptoms. Individuals exposed to significant life stress can experience long-term traumatic responses, short-term traumatic responses, or none at all (Breslau, 2009).

Recent research sheds some interesting light on factors associated with more severe and long-lasting traumatic responses. Those factors include previous exposure to a range of different types of traumatic stress, suggesting that cumulative trauma exposure is related to poorer outcomes, and interpersonal trauma marked by high betrayal is likewise associated with poorer outcomes (Martin, Cromer, DePrince, & Freyd, 2013). Severity and duration of the trauma exposure are also directly related to symptom development (Martin et al., 2013). By definition, bullying and mobbing are experiences that go on over a protracted period of time, from months to even years. It should also not escape our attention that many workplace bullying and mobbing targets feel betrayed by coworkers whom they previously trusted and may have counted as friends. Additionally, other risk factors, such as inadequate family or social support systems, other health or mental health problems, and financial pressures, are likely to increase the risk of a traumatic response to workplace bullying or mobbing. Risk information is important for counselors and coaches in planning the best treatment strategies in collaboration with their clients.

TRAUMA-INFORMED CARE

Effective counseling or coaching for targets of workplace bullying and mobbing and their families is an important step in recovery for many survivors. Research has yet to be conducted about what kinds of interventions work best for targets and is certainly needed. In the meantime, targets of workplace bullying and mobbing, their families, and mental health and coaching professionals need to have some framework for selecting and structuring counseling and coaching services.

Keeping in mind the research about the psychological and emotional health effects of bullying and mobbing summarized above and the frequency with which either PTSD or post-traumatic stress symptoms are identified in the literature as an associated outcome, we support earlier recommendations (Duffy & Sperry, 2012, 2014) that counseling and coaching services for targets of workplace bullying and mobbing be provided within the framework of trauma-informed care. The Substance Abuse and Mental Health Services Administration (SAMHSA) of the United States is the federal agency in charge of public health efforts to promote the behavioral and mental health of the country and has taken a leadership role in promoting the incorporation of trauma-informed models of care in mental health education and intervention. A growing emphasis in the United States on the importance of trauma-informed models of care is based on the fact that trauma is a common experience as opposed to an uncommon experience, as was once thought

(El-Gabalawy, 2012; Kessler et al., 1999), and on the belief that trauma has actual and potentially far-reaching and enduring effects on the health, well-being, lives, and relationships of those who have experienced it (Substance Abuse and Mental Health Services Administration, 2014a, 2014b). SAMHSA has described the basic elements, or three Rs, of trauma-informed models of care as "(1) *realizing* the prevalence of trauma; (2) *recognizing* how trauma affects all individuals involved with the program, organization, or system, including its own workforce; and (3) *responding* by putting this knowledge into practice" (2012, p. 4).

Two primary ethical principles underlie models of trauma-informed care. Those principles are nonmaleficence and beneficence. Nonmaleficence is the principle of "do no harm," and beneficence is the principle of doing good for others. When working with trauma victims and survivors, nonmaleficence requires that mental health care professionals are aware of the pervasive effects of traumatization and that they work proactively to avoid retraumatizing a client. In the case of workplace bullying or mobbing, examples of harmful counseling or coaching actions would include target or victim-blaming, minimizing or dismissing the impact of the negative workplace situation on the client, or suggesting that it is all or mostly on the target's shoulders to improve the situation at work. Trauma-informed professionals would be aware of the harm that such misguided actions could produce and would work consciously to practice from a perspective that is trauma-informed and that avoids retraumatization.

In clinical mental health practice, beneficence is the obligation to work to improve the welfare of one's clients. In the case of workplace bullying and mobbing, the principle of beneficence requires, for example, that clinical professionals who work with targets become knowledgeable about the nature of workplace bullying and mobbing and its negative health impacts and about the nature and impact of trauma, especially interpersonal trauma. Putting that knowledge into action would include, for example, beneficent actions such as helping a client to develop a personal support group for the grief and recovery period after bullying or mobbing or helping a client to give voice to the values and strengths that his or her unique response to being bullied or mobbed signifies.

Principles of Trauma-Informed Care

For mental health and coaching professionals, it is not enough to understand the principles of trauma-informed care. These principles must be translated into professional practices that give expression to their full meaning. Ten basic trauma-informed principles (Elliot, Bjelajac, Fallot, Markoff, &

Reed, 2005; SAMHSA, 2014b) are listed here and are expanded below in terms of how these principles might be translated in clinical or coaching work with clients:

1. Recognizing the importance of trauma awareness
2. Thinking of trauma-related symptoms and behaviors as forms of adaptation to traumatic events and experiences
3. Viewing trauma in relation to the unique life histories and circumstances of individual clients
4. Minimizing the risk of retraumatization or of reproducing trauma dynamics
5. Creating a safe and secure environment
6. Identifying recovery from trauma as a primary goal
7. Supporting client autonomy, choice, and control
8. Building collaborative and supportive relationships
9. Familiarizing clients with trauma-informed services
10. Utilizing a sociocultural lens through which to view trauma

These trauma-informed principles in health care function similarly to universal precautions in infection control. Utilizing universal precautions means treating all blood and body fluids as if they were infectious to prevent and reduce actual infection and cross-contamination. Putting trauma-informed principles into practice requires treating all clients as if they have been exposed to trauma in their lives and thereby minimizes the risk of retraumatization for those who have experienced trauma. These principles are designed to maximize client psychological and emotional safety without having to know any details of previous or current traumas or psychological injuries.

Translating Trauma-Informed Principles into Practice with Bullying and Mobbing Clients

Principle #1: Recognizing the importance of trauma awareness

Counselors and coaches are proactive and responsible in thinking through the therapeutic or coaching context for their bullying and mobbing clients so that clients experience safe and secure environments with minimum risk of retraumatization. From the initial contact with the client, it is important that counselors and coaches are welcoming and supportive. Bullying and mobbing clients have routinely been characterized as incompetent, difficult to get along with, or the cause of workplace problems, so a mistrust of authority figures, including counselors and coaches, should not be surprising. Frequently checking in with clients about how they are reacting to the counseling or coaching sessions, what they find helpful or not helpful, and what topics they feel they need to spend more or less time on are examples of ways of interacting that recognize the importance of trauma awareness.

Principle #2: Thinking of trauma-related symptoms and behaviors as forms of adaptation to traumatic events and experiences

Counselors and coaches work hard to understand the behaviors and symptoms of their bullying and mobbing clients as forms of adaptation to the experience of being bullied or mobbed rather than as instances of pathological behavior that must be diagnosed and labeled. Counselors and coaches avoid pathologizing and labeling the emotional and behavioral responses of bullying and mobbing clients. Their clients' behavior is best understood as a set of solution attempts to cope with the negative experiences of being bullied or mobbed—even if the solution attempts are not working. For example, the behavior of bullying and mobbing clients who are mistrustful of authority and who isolate themselves socially from contacts with others is understandable when considering that the client(s) felt betrayed by coworkers who did not stand up for them at work when they were under attack from supervisors or other coworkers. For the clients, it may be safer to remain skeptical of the motives of others or to mistrust them and to reduce contact with others who could end up betraying them again. Mistrusting most other people and isolating may be easier and less exhausting for the bullying or mobbing client than trying to figure out who is safe to trust.

Principle #3: Viewing trauma in relation to the unique life histories and circumstances of individual clients

Counselors and coaches take a relational and contextual perspective when working with their bullying and mobbing clients. They understand the cumulative nature of trauma (Martin et al., 2013) and its influence on client responses to current trauma. They also understand that what clients bring to the table in terms of strengths, social support, and other resources is one of the two largest factors in determining counseling outcome—the other being the relationship between the counselor and client (Hubble, Duncan, & Miller, 1999). Therefore, counselors, but not necessarily coaches, gently inquire, without pressure or coercion, about any previous trauma exposure.

Counselors and coaches also seek information about the level of social support that their bullying and mobbing clients have in their lives and about the presence or absence of other resources, including educational, career, financial, spiritual resources, and the role of family and friends. Counselors and coaches recognize that understanding the contextual and relational backdrop of a bullying or mobbing client will help them to assess whether the client is more or less vulnerable in a particular situation and will enable them to utilize client strengths and resources in a proactive way. The fewer the resources and social support that a bullying or mobbing client has, the more at risk that client is likely to be.

A contextual factor central in bullying and mobbing cases is the organizational context within which the bullying or mobbing occurred. What were the structure, climate and culture, and leadership of the organization in question? What kind of power dynamics operated between supervisors and subordinates within the workplace? Were there antibullying policies in place? Did the organization have procedures for addressing allegations of workplace harassment? Did the organization have a history of harassment claims to the Equal Employment Opportunity Commission (EEOC) or reports in the news media or elsewhere? What kind of reputation did the organization have as a place to work?

For many bullying and mobbing clients, developing a wider perspective about their organization and workplace can be useful in helping them to make sense of their experiences and to locate those experiences within their developing narrative of what happened and its impact on them. Such conversations about their organization and workplace, like other conversations about difficult topics related to their trauma exposure, should only be conducted if and when the bullying or mobbing client expresses a desire to participate in them and with the advance understanding that the client is in charge of the direction of the conversation and when to stop.

Principle #4: Minimizing the risk of retraumatization or of reproducing trauma dynamics

Counselors and coaches who work with bullying and mobbing clients are aware of the risks of retriggering traumatic experiences, thoughts, and feelings, and they work cooperatively with their clients to minimize the risk of retraumatization. By its nature, trauma is associated with powerlessness and, often, helplessness. Expert or authoritarian standpoints in counseling and coaching risk reproducing in a different context the unequal power dynamics of interpersonal trauma such as bullying and mobbing and, therefore, must be avoided to minimize the risk of retraumatization.

Think about what it would be like for a client who was bullied by a boss or supervisor to be in a counseling or coaching relationship with a professional who followed his or her own agenda rather than the client's. The bullying or mobbing client must be in charge of what to talk about, how much to talk about, and pausing or ending conversations. Paying careful attention to timing, pacing, and leading in counseling and coaching is necessary to avoid retraumatization. Details of the bullying or mobbing may be very difficult for the client to talk about, especially early on in the counseling or coaching process, and any pressure to elicit details is inadvisable and contrary to trauma-informed best practices.

Counselors and coaches working with bullying and mobbing clients make explicit at the beginning of their work with clients that ensuring psychological safety and comfort is paramount. They frequently check in with their clients and invite feedback about how the session is going and what they, as the counselor or coach, might do to make the session even more helpful. This check-in process happens throughout the session, not just at the end. Regular checking in puts the client at the center of the counseling or coaching process and gives the client control over the topics and the depth of clinical and coaching conversations, thereby reducing the risk of retraumatization.

Principle #5: Creating a safe and secure environment

Counselors and coaches communicate to their bullying and mobbing clients that their well-being and psychological safety and security are top priorities. They adopt an approach that is client-centered and convey positive regard and warmth to their clients. The process for scheduling appointments is not cumbersome, and counselors and coaches convey to their clients that they will work with them to facilitate their recovery and will make referrals, as needed. Counselors and coaches also let their clients know that they are not made uncomfortable by the expression of strong emotion and that they have confidence that their clients can also successfully manage strong emotion. A safe and secure environment for clients is reinforced by honesty and transparency. For example, if a counselor is unsure about whether a particular topic is helpful for the client to focus on in a session, the counselor increases psychological safety for the client by expressing that uncertainty to the client, sharing the rationale for it, and soliciting the thoughts and ideas of the client about the topic. Acknowledging and apologizing for any errors or mistakes that may arise also increases psychological safety. Many bullying and mobbing clients, like other trauma-exposed clients, may be hypervigilant to perceived threats in their environment, and they respond best when afforded the respect of honesty and transparency.

Principle #6: Identifying recovery from trauma as a primary goal

Counselors and coaches who work with bullying and mobbing targets identify recovery from trauma as a primary goal and instill hope that recovery is a realistic goal. Common factors research (Hubble et al., 1999; Wampold, 2010) demonstrates the therapeutic importance of harnessing hope and positive expectations as a primary common factor in successful clinical outcomes. While it may be difficult and take time and professional support, recovering from trauma involves acknowledging that trauma happened and recognizing its impact on current functioning. Targets of bullying and mobbing are frequently in a state of disbelief about what has happened to them, especially in the initial stages of the process of bullying or mobbing. It is common for them to have a very hard time accepting that they could have been bullied or mobbed given their commitment and conscientiousness to their jobs. When they realize that they have been bullied or mobbed, they typically respond with both sadness and anger and then begin to look at the losses they have incurred as a result of being on the receiving end of bullying or mobbing.

Naming (Smith, 2012) what happened at work, its effects on one's life and relationships, and its meaning for a bullying or mobbing target is a primary part of the recovery process and provides a framework through which to develop realistic and positive goals for one's future. Naming does not mean the elicitation of details that can retrigger traumatic memories and feelings. It simply means an acknowledgment that negative events directed toward the client occurred at the workplace in the context of carrying out one's job.

Looking at the effects of bullying or mobbing on a client's life and health is not a one-session process; it takes place over time and with the client always in charge of whether or not to discuss particular topics. In our collective clinical experience, bullying and mobbing targets want the opportunity to discuss what happened to them and its meaning in their lives with professionals who are knowledgeable about bullying and mobbing. For targets, such knowledgeable professionals can be hard to find.

Principle #7: Supporting client autonomy, choice, and control

Counselors and coaches who work with bullying and mobbing clients embrace a collaborative and supportive standpoint in therapy and coaching and, consistent with trauma-informed best practices, reject acting from an authoritarian standpoint. Counselors and coaches encourage their bullying and mobbing clients to make decisions in their own best interests, including decisions about how counseling or coaching should proceed. In counseling and coaching, the moment-by-moment practice of respect, open dialogue, and promoting clients' abilities to make choices and exercise control over their decision making reduces feelings of powerlessness and helplessness and replaces those with actual in-session experiences of choice and control—essential elements of empowerment. A word about techniques associated with specific clinical counseling models is in order here. Supporting client autonomy, choice, and control is not consistent with the use of some confrontational counseling techniques that place the counselor in a "one-up" more powerful position than the client and in which the counselor acts from an "I know best" point of view.

Principle #8: Building collaborative and supportive relationships

Counselors and coaches value collaborative and supportive relationships with their bullying and mobbing clients and work to build collaborative relationships with other professionals whose services may be needed to help clients fully recover. The importance of collaboration as an antidote to a bullying or mobbing client's experience of the misuse of power in a work setting has been discussed at length in this section. There are other important reasons for counselors and coaches to think in a collaborative and multidisciplinary way when working with bullying and mobbing clients. The effects of bullying and mobbing can lead to multiple losses and problems in many domains of life (Duffy & Sperry, 2012, 2014). Physical and mental health problems, family problems, financial problems, career problems, and legal problems are some of the major ones. Hence, bullying and mobbing clients may need to obtain professional services from a range of physicians and health care providers, mental health providers, career counselors, marriage and family therapists, employment attorneys, and insurance and credit counselors. Counselors and coaches who have links to other professional service providers in the community, especially to providers who are familiar with bullying and mobbing, can facilitate the process of making necessary referrals for their clients or simply the process of obtaining needed information.

Principle #9: Familiarizing clients with trauma-informed services

Counselors and coaches understand that trauma-informed care is an established framework for providing physical and mental health services to victims and survivors of trauma within a context of maximum safety and security. The trauma-informed care framework takes into account common psychological and emotional reactions of persons who have experienced trauma and also emphasizes the importance of minimizing the risk of retraumatization. The core principles of trauma-informed care are based on best practices from research evidence, clinical experience, and stakeholder input and preferences (SAMHSA, 2012, 2014a, 2014b). By explaining to bullying and mobbing clients that a framework for trauma-informed care exists to safeguard clients who have experienced trauma in their lives, clients will have more information about the nature and context of services available to them and will be able to make more informed decisions. At a minimum, bullying and mobbing clients will be able to ask whether the treatment services and context are trauma-informed. If the provider or program never heard of trauma-informed care, then that is important information for clients to factor into their decision making about potential services and treatment.

Principle #10: Utilizing a sociocultural lens through which to view trauma

Counselors and coaches take a broad view when considering the meaning of trauma and make every effort to situate their understanding of trauma within the contextual framework of a client's family, community, and culture. For example, when counselors and coaches work with clients who have been bullied or mobbed, it is important to develop an understanding of how work and conflict at work were viewed within the client's family. What did a client learn from his or her family about what it means to do a good job at work, about conflict at work, about job loss and unemployment, about standing up for oneself at work, or about being treated poorly in the workplace? Such information can be invaluable for counselors and coaches and helps to locate a client's response to being bullied or mobbed within a broader relational system.

Likewise, information about the values of a client's community and culture about work, employment, unemployment, conflict, and mistreatment helps to situate a client's perspective about workplace bullying and mobbing within a broader community and cultural framework. Similarly, how individuals respond to trauma is situated within this broader sociocultural system. Clients, when responding to trauma, are influenced and shaped by the values, experiences, and customs of their families, communities, and cultures. Knowing some of these influences opens up a window for clinical conversations about whether the values and experiences about work that have shaped the client, upon reflection and within professional dialogue, are ways of thinking and acting that continue to make sense or that perhaps would be better if revised. Taking a sociocultural perspective encourages clients to think about the profoundly shaping values, beliefs, and experiences of their families and cultures and also gives openings for clients to talk back to those values, beliefs, and experiences if they do not fit or do not help to make sense of current experience. Families, communities, and cultures have had much to say about the topic of work. Clients who have been bullied or mobbed can benefit immensely from counselors and coaches who are skilled at initiating conversations about the influence of family and culture in understanding and responding to having been bullied or mobbed.

Case Illustration: Lisa

Lisa sought counseling at the end of a very difficult year as a librarian in a new middle school where she had transferred so that she could be closer to home. She was a midcareer professional who had spent most of her career in middle and high schools, both as a language teacher and then as a librarian. In her roles as a language teacher and librarian at her previous schools, she had easily accepted leadership positions and had excelled in them, based on the feedback of her peers and principals. She was recognized as a leader and innovator in community and team building and was often asked by parent associations throughout her district to speak to parent groups about community and team building.

At her new school, Lisa's principal started to criticize her about everything from the layout of the tables and chairs to the book displays and bulletin board exhibits in the library. Some of the criticism was private, but a lot of it took place at full faculty meetings in front of all the other faculty members. Lisa was humiliated, and she also became angry over what she saw as the principal's continued interference and hostile comments about her open-door policy for the teachers and the way in which she conducted her classes with the kids. At the beginning, other teachers were supportive of Lisa, but by the end of the year, most had backed off from supporting her and many had stopped talking to her altogether except about essential work matters. Lisa figured that the other teachers really liked her but were scared that what they saw happening to her would happen to them if the principal saw them engaging with her.

When it came time for Lisa's performance review, she was shocked to see the disparaging comments that her principal had written about her and included in her permanent record. Lisa felt helpless and was told by her union leader that this principal had a bad reputation and seemed to pick on a particular teacher every year and this year it was Lisa's turn. Lisa became increasingly distraught and told the counselor that she would blow up over the simplest things that went wrong and that this had been going on for months. She also told the counselor that she had quit socializing with people from work and with her friends outside of work and had turned down all of her recent invitations to talk at parents' groups about community and team building. Lisa didn't want to risk anybody else turning away from her and not supporting her, so she reduced her contacts with other people across the board. She also started to doubt whether she was a likeable person.

One of the first things that Lisa's counselor did was to suggest that Lisa take her time about deciding whether the counseling was helpful or not and encourage her to ask each and every question that she had about the counseling process and the counselor. The counselor checked in with Lisa frequently during each session to see whether the conversations were helpful for her, whether Lisa had topics other than the one they were talking about that she wanted to get in before a session ended, and whether there were questions that the counselor had not asked that Lisa wished the counselor would ask. The counselor was mindful from the outset to respect Lisa's understandable difficulties with trusting others and to counteract Lisa's perceived powerlessness in her work situation by acting to support Lisa's personal agency and autonomy in their counseling relationship.

Over time, these basic trauma-informed practices made a positive difference for Lisa, who felt increasingly secure within the counseling relationship. Lisa's growing sense of psychological safety and autonomy in counseling made it possible for her to explore with her counselor the effects of being bullied on her personal and professional identities and on her relationships with coworkers and others.

SPECIFIC TREATMENT MODALITIES FOR TRAUMA

The general trauma-informed principles discussed above provide a framework for counselors and coaches who practice from a variety of helping models to incorporate best practices in their work, irrespective of their preferred treatment modality. To a large extent, counseling practice and the selection of a preferred treatment model is a function of professional training. Counselors tend to practice from the models in which they received formal professional training. This makes sense because counselors cannot ethically practice from models in which they were not trained. Professional counseling training takes place in graduate school and then is extended through postgraduate training and continuing education, including self-learning.

The general trauma-informed principles for working with survivors of trauma can be mapped on to a counselor's preferred treatment paradigm for good general practice. Nonetheless, there are likely to be times when counselors and coaches need to refer to clinicians who have more specialized training in the treatment of trauma or when clients want practitioners who are trauma specialists. The models briefly described here have either been developed for the treatment of trauma or have some quantitative or qualitative evidence to support their use as primary interventions for the psychological treatment of trauma. The list is intended to be representative rather than exhaustive.

Cognitive Behavioral Therapy (CBT)

Cognitive behavioral therapy focuses on changing unhelpful or counterproductive thinking and acting to reduce traumatic symptoms. It has been utilized with a range of populations who have been exposed to various traumatic stimuli. Its efficacy as an intervention model for PTSD has been extensively studied and reviewed (Najavits et al., 2009; Rothbaum, Meadows, Resick, & Foy, 2000).

Exposure Therapy

Exposure therapy is a form of cognitive behavioral therapy that combines relaxation techniques with in vivo exposure or imagined recall of traumatic events, situations, stimuli, or related memories to reduce the avoidance and fear associated with post-traumatic stress symptoms. Clinician training and skill in the use of this treatment modality is essential to avoid client retraumatization. Exposure therapy in the treatment of trauma is well studied and has demonstrated efficacy (Watts et al., 2013).

Eye Movement Desensitization and Reprocessing (EMDR)

Eye movement desensitization and reprocessing (EMDR) is an information-processing therapy developed to relieve distress associated with traumatic experiences and memories. Clients focus on bilateral external stimuli, for example, hand tapping or tracking the therapist's finger movements while attending for short periods at a time to internal memories of the distressing experiences. Traumatic memories stored in the brain are thought to be accessed and processed and then linked to new associational networks in the brain that are more adaptive. Its effectiveness as a treatment for PTSD has been widely studied and supported (Lee, Gavriel, Drummond, Richards & Greenwald, 2002; Seidler & Wagner, 2006).

Mindfulness and Meditation Practice

Mindfulness practice is focused and intentional awareness of the present moment together with nonjudgmental acceptance of accompanying thoughts and emotions. These practices can be used by clients without the need of a counselor or coach once the techniques have been learned. While mindfulness and meditation may or may not be sufficient as a primary treatment for post-traumatic stress symptoms, there is evidence that they may be useful in relapse prevention (Segal, Williams, & Teasdale, 2002), and there is growing interest in their general use with PTSD survivors (Vujanovic, Youngwirth, Johnson, & Zvolensky, 2009).

Relaxation Therapy

Relaxation and breathing training are a set of techniques for regulating and relaxing various parts of the body as a way of reducing anxiety and stress. Clients learn to recognize internal cues and sensations indicating stress and anxiety and to respond by using relaxation methods. Relaxation therapy is a self-help strategy that has fairly robust evidence to support its use in clients who are anxious (Manzoni, Pagnini, Castelnuovo, & Molinari, 2008).

Narrative Therapy

Narrative therapy is an approach centered on the development of clients' stories and narratives about key events and situations in their lives, the ongoing processes of sensemaking and meaning-making about those events, and the identification of unique responses to those events that have helped them move forward in life (White, 2007). Centers of narrative training are encouraging more effectiveness research. A pilot study using narrative therapy with PTSD survivors showed promising results (Erbes, Stillman, Wieling, Bera, & Leskela, 2014).

Neurofeedback

Neurofeedback is a form of biofeedback that gives clients real-time information about the state of their brain in terms of frequencies and amplitudes displayed visually and with sound on a computer using neurofeedback software. Through these visual and auditory stimuli, brain frequencies and amplitudes in desired ranges are rewarded, and brain wave activity outside of the desired range is inhibited. Neurofeedback can be used, depending on the clinical goals, to both increase alertness and deepen relaxation. Empirical research into the efficacy of neurofeedback for PTSD is limited, but some early evidence suggests it can be effective (Hammond, 2005; Peniston & Kulkosky, 1991).

Sensorimotor Psychotherapy

Sensorimotor psychotherapy is one of a number of psychotherapies developed for the treatment of trauma (Ogden & Fisher, 2015). Like other body-based approaches, sensorimotor psychotherapy is based on the understanding that traumatic memories are stored in the body as well as in the mind. The approach utilizes methods like movement, as well as emotional and cognitive processing, to help clients deal with unassimilated sensorimotor reactions to trauma. The approach taken by sensorimotor practitioners is highly regarded by a number of trauma and attachment specialists. Effectiveness research is ongoing in London, Toronto, and Oslo.

Somatic Experiencing

Somatic experiencing is a body- and mind-based approach for releasing what is referred to as *trauma residue* that can remain in the body in the wake of traumatic experiences that have not been fully discharged or processed (Levine & Frederick, 1997). This approach utilizes supportive methods for helping trauma clients to complete interrupted or unfinished traumatic fight, flight, or freeze responses, thereby restoring physiological systems that may have been overwhelmed and dysregulated by the trauma response. Some effectiveness data exists (Leitch, 2007). Proponents of the model identify its assumptions as in accordance with basic principles in trauma, attachment, and neuroscience (Payne, Levine, & Crane-Godreau, 2015).

The above descriptions of a variety of specific treatment modalities for PTSD and post-traumatic stress symptoms include such well-known approaches as cognitive-behavioral therapy and newer body-based approaches such as sensorimotor psychotherapy and somatic experiencing. Most of the modalities listed require professional counselor facilitation. Some however, such as mindfulness practices and relaxation strategies, can be used by clients themselves after training in the methods, without the presence of a mental health professional or coach. For symptomatic clients struggling with the effects of post-traumatic exposure, professional mental health intervention is usually necessary to facilitate recovery (Taylor et al., 2003).

CONCLUSION

Workplace bullying and mobbing are associated with a range of negative psychological consequences and conditions, among them anxiety, depression, alcohol and substance misuse, and PTSD and post-traumatic stress symptoms. Targets of workplace bullying and mobbing and their family members look to professional psychotherapists, counselors, and coaches to receive help for these often severe and life-altering negative consequences and symptoms. At present, there is no body of outcome research identifying best psychotherapeutic, counseling, and coaching models and strategies for working with targets and their families. Nonetheless, given workplace bullying and mobbing prevalence rates, targets and their families will continue to seek counseling and coaching services to obtain relief for their symptoms and help in planning for life after bullying and mobbing.

In the United States, SAMHSA has taken the lead in promoting trauma-informed care as a model of general principles and practices for health care professionals. These principles and practices are based on the view that trauma is a common, as opposed to a rare, phenomenon, and that many clients, mental health workers, and other personnel have been exposed to trauma in their lives. This view of trauma as a common experience for people is counter to the older view of trauma as relatively uncommon. The trauma-informed care model provides a way of working with trauma clients that recognizes the pervasiveness of traumatic experiences and that avoids retraumatization during treatment.

Given the high frequency of diagnoses of PTSD and post-traumatic stress symptoms in workplace bullying and mobbing targets, described above, we strongly endorse the adoption of a trauma-informed model of care for psychotherapists, counselors, and coaches who provide professionals services to workplace bullying and mobbing targets. In combination with specific training and study about workplace bullying and mobbing and the health impact and psychosocial effects on targets and their families, the trauma-informed care model provides the basis of current best practices in treating targets and their families.

In this chapter, we described the psychological health impact of workplace bullying and mobbing and provided a robust overview of the trauma-informed model of care for psychotherapists and counselors working with targets and their families. In the next chapter, we will extend the trauma-informed model of care and apply it to the provision of professional coaching services.

REFERENCES

American Psychiatric Association (APA). (2013). *Diagnostic and statistical manual of mental disorders* (5th ed.). Washington, D.C.: American Psychiatric Association.

Balducci, C., Alfano, V., & Fraccaroli, F. (2009). Relationships between mobbing at work and MMPI-2 personality profile, posttraumatic stress symptoms, and suicidal ideation and behavior. *Violence and Victims, 24*(1), 52–67.

Breslau, N. (2009). The epidemiology of trauma, PTSD, and other posttrauma disorders. *Trauma, Violence, & Abuse, 10*, 198–210. doi:10.1177/1524838009334448

Breslau, N., & Davis, G. C. (1987a). Posttraumatic stress disorder: The stressor criterion. *Journal of Nervous and Mental Disease, 175*(5), 255–264.

Breslau, N., & Davis, G. C. (1987b). Posttraumatic stress disorder: The etiologic specificity of wartime stressors. *American Journal of Psychiatry, 144*(5), 578–583.

Brewin, C. R., Lanius, R. A., Novac, A., Schnyder, U., & Galea, S. (2009). Reformulating PTSD for DSM-V: Life after Criterion A. *Journal of Traumatic Stress, 22*(5), 366–373. doi:10.1002/jts.20443

Brousse, G., Fontana, L., Ouchchane, L., Boisson, C., Gerbaud, L., Bourguet, D., & Chamoux, A. (2008). Psychopathological features of a patient population of targets of workplace bullying. *Occupational Medicine, 58*(2), 122–128.

Cassitto, M. G., & Gilioli, R. (2003). Emerging aspects of occupational stress. *La Medicina del Lavoro, 94*(1), 108–113.

Chen, W-C., Hwu, H-G., Kung, S-M., Chiu, H-J., & Wang, J-D. (2008). Prevalence and determinants of workplace violence of health care workers in a psychiatric hospital in Taiwan. *Journal of Occupational Health, 50*(3), 288–293.

Duffy, M., & Sperry, L. (2007). Workplace mobbing: Individual and family health consequences. *The Family Journal, 15*(4), 398–404.

Duffy, M., & Sperry, L. (2012). *Mobbing: Causes, consequences, and solutions.* New York: Oxford University Press.

Duffy, M., & Sperry, L. (2014). *Overcoming mobbing: A recovery guide for workplace aggression and bullying.* New York: Oxford University Press.

El-Gabalawy, R. (2012). *Association between traumatic experiences and physical health conditions in a nationally representative sample* [PDF document]. Retrieved from http://www.adaa.org/sites/default/files/El-Gabalawy%20331.pdf

Elliot, D. E., Bjelajac, P., Fallot, R. D., Markoff, L. S., & Reed, B. G. (2005). Trauma-informed or trauma-denied: Principles and implementation of trauma-informed services for women. *Journal of Community Psychology, 33*(4), 461–477.

Erbes, C. R., Stillman, J. R., Wieling, E., Bera, W., & Leskela, J. (2014). A pilot examination of the use of narrative therapy with individuals diagnosed with PTSD. *Journal of Traumatic Stress, 27*(6), 730–733. doi:10.1002/jts.21966

Hammond, D. C. (2005). Neurofeedback with affective and anxiety disorders. *Child and Adolescent Psychiatric Clinics of North America, 14*(1), 105–123.

Hansen, A. M., Hogh, A., Persson, R., Karlson, B., Garde, A. H., & Ørbaeck, P. (2006). Bullying at work, health outcomes, and physiological stress response. *Journal of Psychosomatic Research, 60*(1), 63–72.

Hoel, H., Faragher, B., & Cooper, C. L. (2004). Bullying is detrimental to health, but all bullying behaviors are not necessarily equally damaging. *British Journal of Guidance and Counselling, 32*(3), 367–387.

Hubble, M. A., Duncan, B. L., & Miller, S. D. (1999). Introduction. In M. A. Hubble, B. L. Duncan, & S. D. Miller (Eds.), *The heart and soul of change: What works in therapy* (pp. 1–19). Washington, D.C.: American Psychological Association.

Kessler, R. C., Sonnega, A., Bromet, E., Hughes, M., Nelson, C. B., & Breslau, N. N. (1999). Epidemiological risk factors for trauma and PTSD. In R. Yehuda (Ed.), *Risk factors for PTSD* (pp. 23–59). Washington, D.C.: American Psychiatric Press.

Khubchandi, J., & Price, J. H. (2015). Workplace harassment and morbidity among US adults: Results from the National Health Interview Survey. *Journal of Community Health, 40*(3), 550–563.

Kivimaki, M., Virtanen, M., Vartia, M., Elovainio, M., Vahtera, J., & Keltikangas-Järvinen, L. (2003). Workplace bullying and the risk of cardiovascular disease and depression. *Occupational and Environmental Medicine, 60*(10), 779–783.

Lee, C., Gavriel, H., Drummond, P., Richards, J., & Greenwald, R. (2002). Treatment of post-traumatic stress disorder: A comparison of stress inoculation training with prolonged exposure and eye movement desensitisation and reprocessing. *Journal of Clinical Psychology, 58*, 1071–1089.

Leitch, L. (2007). Somatic experiencing treatment with tsunami survivors in Thailand: Broadening the scope of early intervention. *Traumatology, 13*(3), 11–20. doi:10.1177/1534765607305439

Levine, P., & Frederick, A. (1997). *Walking the tiger: Healing trauma*. Berkeley, CA: North Atlantic Books.

Leymann, H., & Gustafsson, A. (1996). Mobbing at work and the development of post-traumatic stress disorders. *European Journal of Work and Organizational Psychology, 5*(2), 251–275.

Leymann, H., & Gustafsson, A. (1998). *Suicides due to mobbing/bullying—about nurses' high risks in the labour market* [Unpublished internal report]. World Health Organization (WHO).

Manzoni, G. M., Pagnini, F., Castelnuovo, G., & Molinari, E. (2008). Relaxation training for anxiety: A ten-years systematic review with meta-analysis. *BMC Psychiatry, 8*(41). doi:10.1186/1471-244X-8-41

Martin, C. G., Cromer, L. D., DePrince, A. P., & Freyd, J. J. (2013). The role of cumulative trauma, betrayal, and appraisals in understanding trauma symptomatology. *Psychological Trauma: Theory, Research, Practice and Policy, 52*(2), 110–118. doi:10.1037/a0025686

Matthiesen, S. B., & Einarsen, S. (2004). Psychiatric distress and symptoms of PTSD among victims of bullying at work. *British Journal of Guidance and Counselling, 32*(3), 335–356.

McNally, R. J. (2003). Progress and controversy in the study of posttraumatic stress disorder. *Annual Review of Psychology, 54*(1), 229–252. doi:10.1146/annurev. psych.54.101601.145112

McNally, R. J. (2009). Can we fix PTSD in DSM-V? *Depression and Anxiety, 26*(7), 597–600. doi:10.1002/da.20586

Mikkelsen, E. G., & Einarsen, S. (2002). Basic assumptions and symptoms of post-traumatic stress among victims of bullying at work. *European Journal of Work and Organizational Psychology, 11*(1), 87–11.

Najavits, L. M., Ryngala, D., Back, S. E., Bolton, E., Mueser, K. T., & Brady, K. T. (2009). Treatment of PTSD and comorbid disorders. In E. B. Foa, T. M. Keane, M. J. Friedman, & J. A. Cohen (Eds.), *Effective treatments for PTSD: Practice guidelines from the International Society for Traumatic Stress Studies* (2nd ed., pp. 508–535). New York: Guilford Press.

Namie, G., & Namie, R. F. (2011). *The bully-free workplace: Stop jerks, weasels, and snakes from killing your organization*. Hoboken, NJ: John Wiley & Sons.

Niedhammer, I., David, S., Degioanni, S., & 143 occupational physicians. (2006). Association between workplace bullying and depressive symptoms in the French working population. *Journal of Psychosomatic Research, 61*(2), 251–259.

Nielsen, M.B., Matthiesen, S.B., & Einarsen, S. (2005). Ledelse og personkonflikter: Symptomer på posttraumatisk stress blant ofre for mobbing fra ledere [Leadership and interpersonal conflicts: Symptoms of posttraumatic stress among targets of bullying from supervisors]. *Nordisk Psykologi, 57*(4), 391–415.

Nielsen, M. B., Tangen, T., Idsoe, T., Matthiesen, S. B., & Magerøy, N. (2015). Post-traumatic stress disorder as a consequence of bullying at work and school. A literature review and meta-analysis. *Aggression and Violent Behavior, 21,* 17–24.

Ogden, P., & Fisher, J. (2015). *Sensorimotor psychotherapy: Interventions for trauma and attachment*. New York: Norton.

Pathe, M., & Mullen, P. E. (1997). The impact of stalkers on their victims. *British Journal of Psychiatry, 170*(1), 12–17.

Payne, P., Levine, P. A., & Crane-Godreau, M. A. (2015). Corrigendum: Somatic experiencing: Using interoception and proprioception as core elements of trauma therapy. *Frontiers in Psychology, 6,* 423. doi:10.3389/fpsyg.2015.00423

Peniston, E. G., & Kulkosky, P. J. (1991). Alpha-theta brainwave neuro-feedback therapy for Vietnam veterans with combat-related post-traumatic stress disorder. *Medical Psychotherapy, 4*(1), 47–60.

Pompili, M., Lester, D., Innamorati, M., De Pisa, E., Iliceto, P., Puccinno, M., . . . Girardi, P. (2008). Suicide risk and exposure to mobbing. *Work, 31*(2), 237–243.

Punzi, S., Cassito, M. G., Castellini, G., Costa, G., & Gilioli, R. (2007). Mobbing and its effects on health: The experience of the "Clinica del Lavoro Luigi Devoto" in Milan. *La Medicina del Lavoro, 98*(4), 267–283.

Richman, J. A., Flaherty, J. A., & Rospenda, K. M. (1996). Perceived work-place harassment experiences and problem drinking among physicians: Broadening the stress/alienation paradigm. *Addiction, 91*(3), 391–403.

Roberts, A. L., Dohrenwend, B. P., Aiello, A. E., Wright, R. J., Maercker, A., Galea, S., & Koenen, K. C. (2012). The stressor criterion for posttraumatic stress disorder: Does it matter? *Journal of Clinical Psychiatry, 73*(2), e264–e270. doi:10.4088/JCP.11m07054

Rodríguez-Muñoz, A., Moreno-Jiménez, B., Vergel, A. I. S., & Garrosa Hernández, E. (2010). Post-traumatic symptoms among victims of workplace bullying: Exploring gender differences and shattered assumptions. *Journal of Applied Social Psychology, 40*(10), 2616–2635. doi:10.1111/j.1559-1816.2010.00673.x

Rosen, G. M., & Lilienfeld, S. O. (2008). Posttraumatic stress disorder: An empirical evaluation of core assumptions. *Clinical Psychology Review, 28*(5), 837–868. doi:10.1016/j.cpr.2007.12.002

Rospenda, K. M., Richman, J. A., Wolff, J. M., & Burke, L. A. (2013). Bullying victimization among college students: Negative consequences for alcohol use. *Journal of Addictive Diseases, 32*(4), doi:10.1080/10550887.2013.849971

Rothbaum, B. O., Meadows, E. A., Resick, P., & Foy, D. W. (2000). Cognitive-behavioral therapy. In E. B. Foa & T. M. Keane (Eds.), *Effective treatments for PTSD: Practice guidelines from the International Society for Traumatic Stress Studies* (pp. 60–83). New York: Guilford Press.

Scaer, R. (2005). *The trauma spectrum: Hidden wounds and human resiliency.* New York: Norton.

Scott, M. J., & Stradling, S. G. (1994). Posttraumatic stress disorder without the trauma. *British Journal of Clinical Psychology, 33*(1), 71–74.

Segal, Z. V., Williams, J. M. G., & Teasdale, J. D. (2002). *Mindfulness-based cognitive therapy for depression: A new approach to preventing relapse.* New York: Guilford Press.

Seidler, G. H. & Wagner, F. E. (2006). Comparing the efficacy of EMDR and trauma-focused cognitive-behavioral therapy in the treatment of PTSD: A meta-analytic study. *Psychological Medicine, 36*(11), 1515–1522.

Smith, G. (2012). *Working with trauma: Systemic approaches.* London, England: Palgrave Macmillan.

Substance Abuse and Mental Health Services Administration (SAMHSA). (2012). *SAMHSA's working definition of trauma and principles and guidance for a trauma-informed approach* [Draft]. Rockville, MD: SAMHSA.

Substance Abuse and Mental Health Services Administration (SAMHSA). (2014a). *SAMHSA's concept of trauma and guidance for a trauma-informed approach* (HHS Publication No. SMA 14-4884). Rockville, MD: SAMHSA.

Substance Abuse and Mental Health Services Administration (SAMHSA). (2014b). *Trauma-informed care in behavioral health services.* Treatment Improvement Protocol (TIP) Series 57 (HHS Publication No. SMA 13-4801). Rockville, MD: SAMHSA.

Taylor, S., Thordarson, D. S., Maxfield, L., Federoff, I. C., Lovell, K., & Ogrodniczuk, J. (2003). Comparative efficacy, speed, and adverse effects of three PTSD treatments: Exposure therapy, EMDR, and relaxation training. *Journal of Consulting and Clinical Psychology, 71*(2), 330–338.

Tehrani, N. (2004). Bullying: A source of chronic post traumatic stress? *British Journal of Guidance and Counselling, 32*(3), 357–366.

Tomei, G., Cinti, M. E., Sancini, A., Cerrati, D., Pimpinella, B., Ciarrocca, M., . . . Fioravanti, M. (2007). Evidence based medicine and mobbing. *Giornale Italiano di Medicina del Lavoro ed Ergonomia, 29*(2), 149–157.

Traweger, C., Kinzl, J. F., Traweger-Ravanelli, B., & Fiala, M. (2004). Psychosocial factors at the workplace—Do they affect substance use? Evidence from the Tyrolean workplace study. *Pharmacoepidemiology and Drug Safety, 13*(6), 399–403.

Vujanovic, A. A., Youngwirth, N. E., Johnson, K. A., & Zvolensky, M. J. (2009). Mindfulness-based acceptance and posttraumatic stress symptoms among trauma-exposed adults without axis I psychopathology. *Journal of Anxiety Disorders, 23*(2), 297–303.

Wampold, B. E. (2010). The research evidence for the common factor models: A historically situated perspective. In B. L. Duncan, S. D. Miller, B. E. Wampold, & M. A. Hubble (Eds.), *The heart and soul of change: Delivering what works in therapy* (2nd ed., pp. 49–82). Washington, D.C.: American Psychological Association. doi:10.1037/12075-002

Watts, B. V., Schnurr, P. P., Mayo, L., Young-Xu, Y., Weeks, W. B., & Friedman, M. J. (2013). Meta-analysis of the efficacy of treatments for posttraumatic stress disorder. *Journal of Clinical Psychiatry, 74*(6), e541–e550.

Westhues, K. (2004). *Workplace mobbing in academe: Reports from twenty universities.* Lewiston, NY: Edwin Mellen Press.

White, M. (2007). *Maps of narrative practice.* New York: Norton.

14

Best Practices in Coaching for Targets of Workplace Bullying and Mobbing

Jessi Eden Brown and Maureen Duffy

Target-victims of workplace bullying and mobbing need helping professionals who are well versed in trauma-informed principles and practices. Normally, practitioners are only able to accurately determine the role and extent of trauma experienced by a client *after* services have been initiated. The basic tenets of trauma-informed care, as outlined in chapter 13, help to create a sense of safety. By incorporating trauma-informed practices from the first point of contact with a bullied individual, we can be sure we are creating the best possible conditions for exploration, understanding, and healing. In this chapter, we discuss coaching as an intervention for targets of workplace bullying and mobbing and overlay principles of trauma-informed care onto coaching practices.

HOW COACHING DIFFERS FROM PSYCHOTHERAPY FOR TARGET-VICTIMS OF WORKPLACE BULLYING AND MOBBING

Coaching and psychotherapy are separate and unique modalities for supporting targets of workplace bullying and mobbing. This chapter outlines the ways in which coaching assists bullied targets by creating a road map for achieving goals and addressing well-defined problems. Admittedly, there is some overlap between coaching and psychotherapy; both modalities are goal-directed approaches aimed at increasing clients' understanding of their concerns and exploring possible solutions (Biswas-Diener, 2009; Green, Oades, & Grant, 2006; Hart, Blattner, & Leipsic, 2001). However, coaching is not diagnostically driven and cannot be effectively or ethically utilized to treat psychological issues or mental illness (Grant & Cavanaugh, 2007). Coaching is a forward-focused, nonclinical approach that is more akin to a working partnership between the helping professional and the client (Ives & Cox, 2012). The International Coach Federation (ICF) emphasizes that the coaching relationship stresses accountability and action. Coaching builds opportunities for discovery, clarity, responsibility, and brainstorming of client-driven solutions and strategies (ICF, 2016).

As compared to psychotherapy, the coaching client may perceive the process as being more directed, shorter-term, and more singularly focused on a particular goal or set of goals (Hart et al., 2001). Although coaching may produce some mild emotional upset in a client, it never aims to push the individual into a state of chaos (Cavanagh, 2006). Most coaches are neither trained nor experienced in the skills necessary to contain and appropriately deal with acute levels of emotional distress (Hart et al., 2001). Williams (2004), a life coach and author, summarizes the differences between coaching and psychotherapy: "While therapy and coaching may share a common background, their differences are vast. Therapy is vital for those with psychological problems—what we call pathology. Coaching is for those who are healthy and already self-motivated. Both fields have their place and should not be confused" (p. 39).

Coaches must possess an ability to quickly triage the situation and assess the client's level of functioning (Buckley & Buckley, 2012; Grant, 2006). Bullied workers often present with significant levels of emotional distress. The coaching process will be ineffective (and could inflict additional harm) if applied to individuals with considerable psychological injury or impairment, particularly if the coach lacks advanced education and training in mental health treatment. In these cases, the coach must encourage the client to seek the assistance of a qualified local mental health or medical practitioner (Buckley & Buckley, 2012; Cavanagh & Buckley, 2014; Grant & Cavanagh, 2007).

It may be possible for a client to engage in coaching and psychotherapy concurrently (via different providers), but this decision should be determined on a case-by-case basis and defined by the individual's needs, goals, and current health state. Counselors and coaches working in concert must pay close attention to any legal and ethical concerns, including matters related to clarifying roles and responsibilities, obtaining informed consent, managing confidential information, and maintaining professional boundaries. When multiple professionals simultaneously support an individual, collaboration and coordination of those efforts is valuable and likely to produce the best possible outcomes (Fewster-Thuente & Velsor-Friedrich, 2008).

Advantages of Coaching

One advantage is that the options or modes for service delivery are often more flexible in coaching than they are in psychotherapy (Hart et al., 2001).

For example, coaching sessions might take place in person, by telephone, through video chat, via e-mail, or through other communication platforms. The profession of psychotherapy, on the other hand, is regulated in every U.S. state and territory. The psychotherapist is bound by laws that influence how services can be delivered, and many states specifically restrict or limit the practice of telemedicine (Shifflett, 2016).

Likewise, the route to becoming a professional coach has fewer educational and experiential hurdles. There is no nationally accepted educational standard as an entry point into this profession (Grant & Cavanaugh, 2007; Grant, 2006). By contrast, state licensing boards maintain stringent requirements regarding the formal education, practical training, and documented clinical experience of psychotherapists. In addition to an advanced academic degree in the field of psychology, most states and U.S. territories require thousands of hours of post-master's supervised clinical experience and passing scores on national board examinations prior to eligibility for licensure (Shifflett, 2016).

State licensing boards also enforce laws pertaining to confidentiality, record keeping, informed consent, mandated reporting, and other practices related to the occupation of psychotherapy. The coaching profession is not regulated in this way, thereby simplifying matters of documentation and compliance for the practitioner (Biswas-Diener, 2009). However, it should be noted that the majority of organizations offering training and certification in coaching do create and enforce their own standards. As well, most certifying bodies ask coaches to abide by ethical codes of conduct, which often address topics such as confidentiality and professionalism (Association for Coaching, 2016; European Mentoring & Coaching Council, 2016; ICF, 2015).

Limitations of Coaching

Professional coaching is a relatively young profession. Despite the growing popularity of coaching, there has been little rigorous research into its effectiveness or outcomes. Coaching, as a helping modality, lacks the empirically based evidence and theoretical underpinnings of psychotherapy and other more developed practices (Ives & Cox, 2012). Elliott (2003) pointed out that without foundations in behavioral science, coaches are more likely to rely on popular motivational approaches that have not been validated.

Whereas, in psychotherapy, the consumer can be assured that licensed professionals with distinguishable credentials have met the minimum state standards in terms of education, clinical instruction, supervision, and board examination, coaches hail from a wide variety of educational and experiential backgrounds. While that diversity undeniably brings unique perspectives, it may also make the selection process more difficult for consumers attempting to understand and synthesize varied information about a coach's training or qualifications (Grant, 2006). It is worth restating here, as an additional limitation, that coaches without clinical training are not qualified to work with clients experiencing significant psychological distress. This is especially important because clients may purposely seek out coaching because they perceive it as being a less threatening form of help.

At the time of this writing, the health insurance community does not recognize professional coaching as a qualifying medical expense. Prior to processing or paying a claim, insurance companies require procedural codes, diagnostic codes, and other medical billing details. There is no medical billing code for coaching, and the vast majority of coaches are not qualified or legally permitted to make clinical diagnoses. Therefore, the client is unlikely to be able to access his or her insurance benefits when seeking coaching services, even if the goals and nature of the work are entirely health-focused.

Another area of concern about coaching with providers who do not have clinical psychotherapy training involves boundary issues. In psychotherapy, clinicians are trained to protect the welfare of clients by continually maintaining professional boundaries. Codes of ethics published by the American Psychological Association (APA, 2010) and the American Counseling Association (ACA, 2014) require practitioners to safeguard the integrity of the therapeutic relationship by establishing clear boundaries, avoiding all nonprofessional contact, and thoroughly documenting any extension of a relationship outside of the treatment setting. Crossing these lines may lead to legal action and sanctions against a provider from the licensing board. Coaches are not subjected to the same stringent guidelines and oversight. As stated by Hart et al. (2001), "Looser boundaries allow the coach much more latitude than the therapist" (p. 232). Some may see this as a good thing, but there is also reason for concern, especially as coaching lacks a unified professional body to collect and respond to consumer complaints, including complaints about practitioners who practice outside of their areas of competence or those who blur boundaries in ways that potentially exploit or harm the client.

THE COACHING PROCESS

The first step in initiating a coaching relationship is to define and clarify the partnership, including the roles of participants and the nature of the work to be accomplished (Peltier, 2011). This may involve teaching the client what to expect from the process, stating the risks and benefits associated with coaching, discussing how information will be documented and stored, and covering other details about the coach's practice. It is recommended that coaches create contracts and define their terms of service (in written and verbal formats) to help ensure that clients comprehend the scope of the work and give appropriate consent (Buckley & Buckley, 2012). The coach must assess for full client understanding before initiating the relationship.

Very early in the process, the trauma-informed bullying coach will inquire about the client's comfort level in remembering and discussing details of the bullying experience as well as its impact on various areas of the client's life. In our clinical and coaching experience, most target-victims want to talk with someone knowledgeable about bullying and mobbing. They actively seek out practitioners who understand the phenomena and the associated negative health outcomes. Most target-victims with whom we have had contact express fairly intense frustration about the lack of knowledgeable professionals, thus restricting their opportunities for obtaining well-informed, secure support for coping with bullying and mobbing in the workplace.

Nonetheless, the trauma-informed bullying coach recognizes that not every target-victim may wish to talk about the details of the bullying experience early on in the coaching process, and the coach is mindful about not exerting any pressure whatsoever on a client to do so. If the client indicates, after being asked, a desire to talk about the details of the bullying or mobbing experience, the coach will then ask the client to share his or her experience as a target of workplace bullying and mobbing—complete with before, during, and after the bullying details of how he or she has been affected. The trauma-informed coach is at all times cognizant of the fact that target-victims vary in their comfort levels and willingness to bring up distressing details. If the client does want to talk about the bullying experience and its aftermath, it is useful to discuss what he or she has tried so far to resolve the matters of concern and to ascertain the outcomes of those attempts. In the less common event, in our experience, that the client does not want to review the bullying and its impact, the coach will ask the client to identify what aspects of life he or she wishes to focus on at this stage of the coaching process. These conversations lay the course for goal setting.

Goal Setting and Strategic Planning

Next, the coach and client outline and identify realistic goals to steer their efforts toward positive change (Palmer, 2007). Coaches should encourage bullied individuals to explore desired outcomes regarding their situations at work. Sometimes, a goal identified by the target may be impractical or unfitting (e.g., turning others against the bully, publically humiliating the bully or his or her managers, etc.). These exchanges are teachable moments where coaches can assist clients with contemplating barriers (and possible repercussions) to pursuing particular aims. They may also be opportunities to stimulate deeper reflection on paths toward resolution.

Many targets of workplace bullying and mobbing outline goals consistent with common and foreseeable themes (e.g., seeking justice, exposing the abuse, restoring personal health, protecting coworkers from the same fate, etc.). The coach promotes a reframing of any unrealistic goals by exploring the higher-order themes that emerge from reflection and discussion of unrealistic goals. Having discarded unrealistic goals in favor of realistic goals as a result of this reflection and discussion, the coach and client are free to brainstorm strategies for accomplishing the reframed goals and objectives.

The coach serves as a sounding board while encouraging the client to explore possible solutions to problems. With the initial goals laid out, the coach and client work together to develop strategic plans (Palmer, 2007). They dedicate time to mapping out specific steps and establishing measureable outcomes to assess the client's progress. At this point, the coach might choose to share relevant resources and information to guide the client along the way of discovery and transformation.

The coach provides accountability by maintaining a consistent focus on the stated goals and encouraging the client to evaluate results on a session-to-session basis, which is a trauma-informed consistent practice (Biswas-Diener, 2009; Ives & Cox, 2012). It is the coach's role to facilitate clarification of the client's objectives as needed. The coach may assist with generating ideas and solutions for accomplishing identified aims, but this is primarily a task for the client (ICF, 2015). It is also the client's responsibility to implement any plans born from the process.

Strengths-Based Approach

Coaches should strive to take a strengths-based approach when partnering with targets of workplace bullying and mobbing. During each session, the coach must carefully listen to the client's words to pick up on his assets, strengths, and evidence of past success (Biswas-Diener, 2010). Coaches actively seek out opportunities to engage the client's potential as a means of challenging him based on personal attributes, strengths, and ambitions. According to the ICF (2016), these challenges serve to expose blind spots, reveal new perspectives, and promote the creation of alternate solutions. Focusing on client strengths and resources is at the heart of trauma-informed practice for both coaching and counseling.

Effective coaches find ways to keep the workplace bullying client tethered to his strengths, which promotes self-esteem and self-efficacy (Biswas-Diener, 2010). Furthermore, coaches and clients should actively weave recognized assets into the strategies and solutions they implement (Biswas-Diener, 2009). Building on what already works well creates an important touchstone for the client and provides a useful springboard toward positive change (Gelso & Woodhouse, 2003).

Planning from the Beginning for the Termination of the Coaching Relationship

The coaching process continues session-by-session with the coach and client evaluating progress, breaking down steps as necessary, and problem-solving to achieve desired outcomes (Biswas-Diener, 2009). Keeping the goals in the forefront guides the work and also allows the coach and client to identify when their efforts should come to a conclusion. It is important to incorporate a discussion of how and when the coaching work will end (Cox, 2010). As the last session nears, the coach and client will take time to examine their results, with an emphasis on highlighting the skills and tools used to achieve success. This should include a conversation about how these skills can carry forward and help the client in any future situations involving workplace bullying or mobbing.

Examples of Coaching-Related Inquiries, Interventions, and Interest Areas

- Using a trauma-informed approach, consistent with the client's preferences and comfort level, ask deepening and open questions to learn about the client's bullying experience.
- Teach the client about the phenomenon of workplace bullying and mobbing to provide context and to deepen understanding.
- Review what strategies have been attempted by the client. Were they effective? Why or why not?
- Challenge the client to answer his or her own questions—after all, he or she is the "resident expert" on his or her workplace and bullying experiences.
- Assuage the client's shame (e.g., from assaults on personal or professional identity or from false characterizations of the target as a worthless person) and guilt (e.g., for not having countered the bullying when first assaulted).
- Clarify and validate emotions. Normalize thoughts and feelings common to targets of workplace bullying and mobbing.
- Help the client discover ways to rally support from professionals, family members, friends, or carefully chosen coworkers.
- Educate the client about typical defensive (bully-protecting) tactics employers use that have the potential to derail target-initiated actions.

- Share known outcomes from other workplace bullying clients (without any personal or identifying information). This may aid the client with idea generation, while also decreasing a sense of isolation.
- For clients who face an imminent confrontation or meeting with the employer, provide tips for protecting oneself in meetings, especially where representation by advocates is forbidden.
- For clients who have lost their jobs, advise them on alternative approaches to employment interviews that may identify and avoid potential toxic work environments.

Helping the Client Understand the Health Impacts

Throughout the coaching process, coaches can normalize the client's feelings (anger, shame, guilt, confusion, fear, etc.) as they teach about the phenomenon of workplace bullying and mobbing. Bullied workers report symptoms of hypervigilance, a waning sense of trust in others, self-doubt and eroded confidence, and other reactions common to trauma (Keashly & Neuman, 2005; Lutgen-Sandvik, 2008). Many targets feel traumatized by a bully's repeated attacks in conjunction with the unrelenting and prolonged exposure to stress at work.

Without delving into the world of psychotherapy, a coach might educate targets, in general terms, about trauma reactions to provide context and understanding. Workplace bullying and mobbing has been linked to posttraumatic stress disorder, depression, anxiety, panic attacks, substance abuse, and other forms of mental illness (Duffy & Sperry, 2007; Leymann, 1990; Leymann & Gustafsson, 1996; Matthiesen & Einarsen, 2004; Namie, 2012; Nielsen & Einarsen, 2012; Simpson, Byrne, Gabbay, & Rannard, 2015; Tehrani, 2004). As previously mentioned, targets may find that working with a local counselor will be important for addressing the psychological effects and consequences.

Likewise, the coach can help the client recognize the physical and cognitive components of the stress response. As the client describes his experiences with the bullying, the coach listens for symptoms and complaints stemming from the abuse. Occupational stress, including stress from workplace bullying, has been linked to cardiovascular problems, gastrointestinal issues, sleep disorders, musculoskeletal complications, headaches, skin conditions, and other medical concerns (Di Rosa et al., 2009; Kivimäki et al., 2003; Namie, 2012; Ray, Chang, & Asfaw, 2014; Vedaa et al., 2016). Cognitive effects of occupational stress include difficulties with concentration and focus, distraction, indecisiveness, and mental fatigue; these cognitive effects can impair memory, increase the likelihood for making errors, and increase the risk of job burnout (Allen, Holland, & Reynolds, 2015; Farley, Coyne, Sprigg, Axtell,

& Subramanian, 2015; Namie, 2012; Ray et al., 2014). Coaches should urge affected workers to promptly seek medical treatment to address health-related symptoms associated with bullying, mobbing, and general occupational stress.

Life outside of work is also affected. The Workplace Bullying Institute (WBI) conducted an online study of targets in 2010 to examine the effect of the bullying on the target's primary support relationship (e.g., spouse, parent, child, best friend, etc.). The majority of respondents (76%) reported negative consequences, indicating the relationship was marked by more conflict and stress or had been completely dissolved since the onset of the bullying (Brown, 2010). Coaches can encourage clients to expand their social support networks to help distribute this type of strain.

PRACTITIONER SKILLS REQUIRED FOR EFFECTIVE COACHING FOR TARGETS OF WORKPLACE BULLYING AND MOBBING

Boundary Setting

Coaching targets of workplace bullying requires well-honed skills of boundary setting and maintenance (Buckley & Buckley, 2012). Coaches must draw clear lines to avoid shifting into territory and topics more appropriate for psychotherapy, medical treatment, or legal counsel (Hart et al., 2001). The coach and client may need to revisit and reestablish boundaries as necessary over the course of the working relationship, depending on the nature and intensity of their work.

Listening

Listening skills are paramount. As a sounding board, the coach must be able to truly hear the client's concerns while conveying empathy and understanding (Biswas-Diener, 2009). Targets report significant isolation associated with the bullying that contributes to feeling unheard (Lutgen-Sandvik, 2008). Targets protest that even when they do speak up about the bullying, they are often not believed (Hallberg & Strandmark, 2006; Namie, 2014). Strong listening skills not only foster safety and build rapport for the coaching process, but they also offer targets of workplace bullying a much-needed chance to feel heard and believed. Providing opportunities for target-victims to reclaim their own voices and agency is an integral part of trauma-informed practice.

Practice and Feedback

As clients begin to take steps toward change, it is beneficial for them to have a safe place to experiment with new responses or behaviors to address the bullying. The coach and client may choose to work together to identify and solve common situations at work. The client can explain, role-play, and rehearse alternative strategies with the coach prior to applying them in the workplace. The client receives immediate feedback from the coach and works through any issues or concerns before settling on an implementation plan.

Patience

Coaching targets of workplace bullying and mobbing requires patience. The client's level of distress may dictate a slower, more methodical approach. Coaches have to carefully consider the client's available reserves (e.g., physical energy, time, money, emotional resilience, etc.) during the formation of goals and action plans (Biswas-Diener & Dean, 2010). A skilled and effective coach assesses and mobilizes the client's resources without unduly taxing him or her or adding to his or her current strain and distress. A coach that cannot recognize and appropriately deal with a client's real limitations risks inflicting serious harm and complicating the healing process for the bullied target.

Resources and Referrals

Knowledge of reading materials, dedicated Web sites and apps, relevant research articles, and other tailored items are valuable coaching tools. Coaches can accumulate a library of information specifically aimed at understanding and addressing workplace bullying and mobbing. Recommended reading lists and other references aid coaches in educating clients and enhancing the work done during and between coaching sessions (ICF, 2015).

Coaches should also have a familiarity with available services and experts in the field of workplace bullying and mobbing. This knowledge allows the coach to provide appropriate referrals when necessary in support of client goals. Coaching often requires good networking skills and an ability to cultivate relationships with other professionals to ensure the best possible outcomes for clients (Nash & Sproule, 2009; Sperry, 1993).

Coaches with specializations in workplace bullying must have basic knowledge about a wide variety of resources appropriate for their clients. One of the most essential roles a coach can play is to assist target-victims with identifying and triaging current needs and then addressing those needs by offering valuable, dedicated resources. For example, coaches can help educate and advocate for clients by sharing information related to the following:

- How to obtain legal assistance and prepare to meet with an employment attorney.
- How to solicit involvement from the labor union (when applicable).

- Considerations in reporting issues to HR or management.
- How to locate qualified counselors or medical practitioners.
- Where to get additional support or counseling for career-related concerns.
- How and when to apply for unemployment benefits.
- How to find and utilize common job-seeker resources (e.g., job boards, recruiting firms, professionally focused social media sites, resume writing services, etc.).

Specialized Knowledge and Training in Workplace Bullying and Mobbing

Finally, and most importantly, coaches who choose to partner with targets of workplace bullying are duty bound to firmly educate themselves on the phenomenon. Workplace bullying and mobbing are complex and multifaceted systemic problems. There are rarely simple or straightforward solutions to the issues clients face. Coaches can receive specialized professional training, read books and research published on the topic, and draw from personal experience as they delve into the subject.

Of special note, when coaches are former targets themselves, they must be far enough removed from their own exposure to bullying to be effective and to avoid becoming triggered by the stories of clients. They must not allow their own experiences to impede their abilities to focus fully on their clients and deliver objective, professional support. This may require receiving counseling to work through personal trauma, as well as the passage of time and other hallmarks of distance from targethood.

LEGAL AND REGULATORY ISSUES ASSOCIATED WITH COACHING TARGET-VICTIMS OF WORKPLACE BULLYING AND MOBBING

Although the coaching profession is not currently regulated, coaches should seek out education, training, and accountability for their work (Grant & Cavanaugh, 2007). Career seekers may choose to obtain specialized instruction or certification in coaching practices. Coaching is a talent that is rehearsed and acutely honed over time. Professional development and education is important for keeping skills current and ensuring the use of sound, evidence-based practices (Grant, 2006; Williams & Davis, 2002).

Coaches who are licensed professionals in other fields (e.g., counselors, social workers, physicians, attorneys, etc.) must use extreme caution when delineating their coaching work from their licensed profession. The onus falls on the coach to ensure that the client is clear about the coach's role as well as the nature and scope of coaching as a helping modality (Williams & Davis,

2002). Coaches who blur these lines incur risk, including potentially breaking laws, violating ethical codes of conduct, jeopardizing their professional licenses, and compromising malpractice insurance coverage. An intentional lack of clarity or overstepping of bounds does a profound disservice to clients and the helping professions as a whole.

Duty to warn issues may come up for coaches who are also licensed or certified in other fields (e.g., health care providers, educators, law enforcement, certain public servants, etc.). These professionals are responsible for informing coaching clients, prior to initiating services, of the circumstances and conditions under which information will be disclosed to protect the lives or rights of others. Duty to warn statutes differ by state, but, in general, they require disclosure when a client makes a threat of self-harm or communicates an intent to harm an identifiable other or others.

Coaches may consider carrying professional liability insurance to cover their practice. For those with licenses in other areas, who already have malpractice insurance, it is advisable to carefully examine the terms and limitations of the policy. Many liability insurance companies sell add-on policies to cover activities performed outside the licensed area of practice. Coaching is likely to be an area of practice falling outside of licensed, regulated activity, although, as mentioned, licensed professionals are always bound by the ethical codes of their professions no matter what professional activity they are performing.

Regardless of the coach's background, he or she must work with clients only within established areas of competence. It is essential for a coach to consult with other professionals or obtain supervision, as needed, under more experienced practitioners to ensure responsible and ethical behavior in all coaching-related interactions (Hart et al., 2001).

CASE ILLUSTRATION: JENNIFER

Jennifer, a 53-year-old woman, contacts a professional coach with expertise in workplace bullying and mobbing after realizing her work-related stress stems from interactions with her boss. After reviewing the coaching process and ensuring the client understands the nature of the work (including the terms of service), the coach and client begin.

> **Coach:** Jennifer, why don't you give me a little background on the situation at work. What are your most significant concerns right now?
> **Jennifer:** I'm worried I might be fired at any moment. My boss is always angry and quick to jump on every mistake I make. When my work is excellent—which it often is because I care about my job immensely—my

boss simply makes up an issue or blames me for another employee's mistake. I feel like I can't win! Why do I even try anymore? I've attempted many approaches to dealing with this problem, including putting in more hours and effort at work, avoiding my boss whenever possible, asking a trusted colleague for ideas, searching the staff handbook for guidance, and so much more. I even talked to an attorney, but I learned I don't have any legal options for making her stop. It's upsetting because my boss is so well liked by the district manager and the VP of operations that I doubt anyone would even believe she is treating me this way.

Jennifer continues her story by offering examples of bullying incidents and detailing some of the ways the situation at work has compromised her well-being. Note: For brevity's sake, we've indicated Jennifer looked into many resources and solutions prior to initiating coaching. In reality, most coaches will find they spend a great deal of time helping the client brainstorm and explore initial options for addressing bullying and mobbing.

Coach: I imagine the whole ordeal has been confusing, frustrating, and very painful. I can tell you've given the matter significant thought and have been looking for answers for some time.
Jennifer: I really have! I want to keep my job, and I do love the work. I feel like I could thrive there—if only I had a different boss.
Coach: Yes, your passion for the work certainly comes through in your story. I believe I have some ideas for addressing your concerns. But first, let's break this down a bit and see if we can identify a few concrete goals for our work together.

Jennifer and the coach analyze possible areas for goal setting. The coach frequently checks in to ensure Jennifer remains comfortable with the coaching method and is not becoming triggered when discussing distressing details. As needed, the coach teaches Jennifer more about the phenomena of workplace bullying and mobbing. In the process, they generate a list of outcomes Jennifer wants and then decide to categorize the aims into two primary areas that fit well into the coaching model.

Coach: Nice job! To summarize, you identified two main areas to focus our work. First, you stated you are looking for ways to build up your support network, hoping this will improve your ability to cope with the stress. Second, you said you're interested in searching for opportunities to stay with the company but get away from your boss.
Jennifer: Yes, exactly! Where do we start?

Jennifer and her coach then dig deeper into these goals to outline the initial steps and establish measures for their progress. They break her goals down into week-by-week objectives so they will have clear checkpoints for their sessions. This creates direction and accountability for their efforts.

At the end of the first session, it becomes clear to the coach that while Jennifer has some coping mechanisms, she would likely benefit from working with a therapist to learn additional self-care techniques. The coach suggests the idea, and Jennifer contacts her doctor for a referral—armed with helpful information supplied by the coach (e.g., the different types of mental health practitioners, the importance of seeking out a clinician experienced in trauma-informed care, who is either well versed in workplace bullying and mobbing or is willing to learn more about the phenomena to effectively treat the client, etc.). Jennifer begins meeting with a therapist. She signs a release of information that allows her coach and therapist to collaborate and coordinate on any overlapping goals.

Coach: This is our third session, and I want us to begin, as always, by checking in. Tell me, how have things been going at work?

Jennifer: Unfortunately, not much has changed with my boss. Just this week, she failed to tell me about an important meeting; so, of course, I didn't show up. Later, she tracked me down to ask where I was and why I "didn't find it important enough to grace the team with my presence." I was completely shocked! She confronted me in front of my colleagues, and I'm pretty sure her boss overheard it as well. I told her I didn't know about the meeting, and she quickly countered, "Oh, Jennifer, that's not true. I told you yesterday to be there." She lied! Again. I just can't take this anymore!

Coach: Oh no! I can understand why you'd feel incredibly angry about that. I imagine it feels like a setup.

Jennifer: Yes, absolutely!

Coach: So, how did you deal with it?

Jennifer: I calmly stated that there must be some misunderstanding because I had not been informed, but that I would like to get caught up on what took place at the meeting ASAP. I then took a short break from my desk, used the self-soothing skills my therapist taught me, and documented the incident in my own notes. For me, this was the last straw! When I went home that night, I talked with my husband, my sister, and my best friend about the possibility of seeking an immediate transfer to another department.

Coach: I'm so glad you reached out to your support network! I'm also really happy to hear you are incorporating more self-care skills into stressful situations as they come up at work.

Jennifer: Yes, thanks! Everyone has been really understanding and patient with me. I only wish I'd opened up to them sooner. The incident with my boss this week was also the spark I needed to mobilize our idea to try to stay with the company by getting a safer position under a different supervisor.

Coach: Excellent. So, what are the next steps?

Jennifer and her coach map out the next steps. The coach offers materials and information to prepare Jennifer for approaching HR about a transfer. Jennifer plans what she wants to say to justify the request. She practices it on the coach and gets feedback. It is through this dyadic process of revision that Jennifer finalizes her message and strategy. They discuss potential pitfalls, and the coach asks Jennifer to outline how she will engage her support network, her self-care skills, and other resources they've covered to accomplish the task.

Jennifer successfully persuades HR and management to grant an expedited transfer. She and her coach decide they will continue to meet while Jennifer makes the transition to the new position at work. As they approach the end of their work together, they define how they will wrap up the process. During the last coaching session, they recap Jennifer's progress.

Coach: It has been a real treat watching you work so hard and achieve your goals, Jennifer! You courageously opened up to family and trusted friends about your problems at work. You established an effective support network you will be able to rely on now and in the future. You put a lot of effort into exploring solutions for the false accusations and bullying you experienced at the hands of your boss. You made an excellent, compelling case to HR and management for a transfer. You remained focused and never gave up. You did it, Jennifer! I'm relieved to know you feel safer at work and no longer have contact with your former boss. I'm proud of what you accomplished and how you applied your strengths to overcome such a painful and difficult situation.

Jennifer: It has been quite the journey! While I miss aspects of the old position, I'm so much happier at work now. I no longer feel nauseous going into the office each morning. I feel like my work is finally recognized and appreciated. It is almost like I've rediscovered myself! Most importantly, I've learned to use my support at home and with my friends when I'm stressed out. Thank you for your guidance, knowledge, and encouragement. I'm glad you were there to help me make this all happen.

Coach: You are very welcome, Jennifer. As we discussed, this marks the end of our coaching relationship for now. However, if you felt this process was useful, you are invited to contact me again in the future should you want assistance with setting and achieving other work- or stress-related goals.

CONCLUSION

Psychotherapists and coaches choosing to work with bullied individuals must first educate themselves. The information in this chapter is not a substitute for obtaining thorough professional training on the topic of workplace bullying and mobbing. Workplace bullying and mobbing are complex and destructive phenomena that have been associated with serious health harm for targeted individuals. Unremitting exposure to stress at work has been linked to debilitating physical, relational, economic, and psychological injuries. Target-victims of workplace bullying and mobbing need knowledgeable, supportive, and skilled psychotherapists and coaches to navigate this terrain.

Coaching and psychotherapy are separate and unique modalities for supporting bullied workers. Both modalities, when anchored in trauma-informed principles and practices, are effective methods for helping target-victims understand their experiences and begin to heal from abuses they have suffered in the workplace. Psychotherapy is better suited for responding to acute situations and for treating the mental illnesses or injuries associated with work trauma. Coaching is a short-term, forward-focused approach designed to help clients address specific goals related to their bullying experiences. Not infrequently, a combination of psychotherapy and coaching works best for target-victims of workplace bullying and mobbing.

Public interest about workplace bullying and mobbing has been growing in the United States over the past couple of decades. Employers, legislators, legal professionals, health care providers, and other workplace stakeholders increasingly view workplace bullying and mobbing as a significant problem. It is hoped this trend of inquiry continues and that it produces much-needed empirical, outcomes-focused research into effective psychotherapeutic treatments and coaching approaches for targets of workplace bullying and mobbing.

REFERENCES

Allen, B. C., Holland, P., & Reynolds, R. (2015). The effect of bullying on burnout in nurses: The moderating role of psychological detachment. *Journal of Advanced Nursing, 71*(2), 381–390.

American Counseling Association (ACA). (2014). *ACA Code of Ethics*. Alexandria, VA: American Counseling Association.

American Psychological Association (APA). (2010). *Ethical principles of psychologists and code of conduct including 2010 amendments*. Retrieved from http://www.apa.org/ethics/code

Association for Coaching. (2016). *Global code of ethics for coaches and mentors*. Retrieved from http://www.associationforcoaching.com/pages/about/code-ethics-good-practice

Biswas-Diener, R. (2009). Personal coaching as a positive intervention. *Journal of Clinical Psychology, 65*(5), 544–553.

Biswas-Diener, R. (2010). A positive way of addressing negatives: Using strengths-based interventions in coaching and therapy. In G. Burns (Ed.), *Happiness, healing and enhancement: Your casebook collection for applying positive psychology in therapy* (pp. 291–302). Hoboken, NJ: John Wiley & Sons.

Biswas-Diener, R., & Dean, B. (2010). *Positive psychology coaching: Putting the science of happiness to work for your clients*. Hoboken, NJ: John Wiley & Sons.

Brown, J. E. (2010, September 30). *Workplace bullying strains relationships*. Retrieved from http://www.workplacebullying.org/2010/09/30/relat-strain

Buckley, A., & Buckley, C. (2012). *A guide to coaching and mental health: The recognition and management of psychological issues*. London, England: Routledge.

Cavanagh, M. (2006). Coaching from a systemic perspective: A complex adaptive conversation. In A. M. Grant & D. R. Stober (Eds.), *Evidence based coaching handbook: Putting best practices to work for your clients* (pp. 313–354). Hoboken, NJ: John Wiley & Sons.

Cavanagh, M., & Buckley, A. (2014). Coaching and mental health. In E. Cox, T. Bachkirova, & D. A. Clutterbuck (Eds.), *The complete handbook of coaching* (pp. 405–417). Thousand Oaks, CA: Sage.

Cox, E. (2010). Last things first: Ending well in the coaching relationship. In S. Palmer & A. McDowall (Eds.), *The coaching relationship: Putting people first* (pp. 159–181). London, England: Routledge.

Di Rosa, A. E., Gangemi, S., Cristani, M., Fenga, C., Saitta, S., Abenavoli, E., . . . Abbate, S. (2009). Serum levels of carbonylated and nitrosylated proteins in mobbing victims with workplace adjustment disorders. *Biological Psychology, 82*(3), 308–311.

Duffy, M., & Sperry, L. (2007). Workplace mobbing: Individual and family health consequences. *Family Journal, 15*(4), 398–404.

Elliott, R. (2003, February). The state of the coaching industry. *In-Psych*, 20–21.

European Mentoring & Coaching Council. (2016). *The EMCC code of ethics*. Retrieved from http://www.emccouncil.org/webimages/EMCC/Global_Code_of_Ethics.pdf

Farley, S., Coyne, I., Sprigg, C., Axtell, C., & Subramanian, G. (2015). Exploring the impact of workplace cyberbullying on trainee doctors. *Medical Education, 49*(4), 436–443.

Fewster-Thuente, L., & Velsor-Friedrich, B. (2008). Interdisciplinary collaboration for healthcare professionals. *Nursing Administration Quarterly, 32*(1), 40–48.

Gelso, C. J., & Woodhouse, S. (2003). Toward a positive psychotherapy: Focus on human strength. In W. B. Walsh (Ed.), *Counseling psychology and optimal human functioning* (pp. 171–197). London, England: Routledge.

Grant, A. M. (2006). A personal perspective on professional coaching and the development of coaching psychology. *International Coaching Psychology Review, 1*(1), 12–22.

Grant, A. M., & Cavanagh, M. J. (2007). Evidence-based coaching: Flourishing or languishing? *Australian Psychologist, 42*(4), 239–254.

Green, L. S., Oades, L. G., & Grant, A. M. (2006). Cognitive-behavioral, solution-focused life coaching: Enhancing goal striving, well-being, and hope. *Journal of Positive Psychology, 1*(3), 142–149.

Hallberg, L. R., & Strandmark, M. K. (2006). Health consequences of workplace bullying: Experiences from the perspective of employees in the public service sector. *International Journal of Qualitative Studies on Health and Well-being, 1*(2), 109–119.

Hart, V., Blattner, J., & Leipsic, S. (2001). Coaching versus therapy: A perspective. *Consulting Psychology Journal: Practice and Research, 53*(4), 229–237.

International Coach Federation (ICF). (2015). *Code of ethics.* Retrieved from http://coachfederation.org/about/ethics.aspx?ItemNumber=854

International Coach Federation (ICF). (2016). Retrieved from www.coachfederation.org

Ives, Y., & Cox, E. (2012). *Goal-focused coaching: Theory and practice.* London, England: Routledge.

Keashly, L., & Neuman, J. H. (2005). Bullying in the workplace: Its impact and management. *Employee Rights and Employment Policy Journal, 8,* 335–373.

Kivimäki, M., Virtanen, M., Vartia, M., Elovainio, M., Vahtera, J., & Keltikangas-Järvinen, L. (2003). Workplace bullying and the risk of cardiovascular disease and depression. *Occupational and Environmental Medicine, 60*(10), 779–783.

Leymann, H. (1990). Mobbing and psychological terror at workplaces. *Violence and Victims, 5*(2), 119–126.

Leymann, H., & Gustafsson, A. (1996). Mobbing at work and the development of post-traumatic stress disorders. *European Journal of Work and Organizational Psychology, 5*(2), 251–275.

Lutgen-Sandvik, P. (2008). Intensive remedial identity work: Responses to workplace bullying trauma and stigmatization. *Organization, 15*(1), 97–119.

Matthiesen, S. B., & Einarsen, S. (2004). Psychiatric distress and symptoms of PTSD among victims of bullying at work. *British Journal of Guidance & Counselling, 32*(3), 335–356.

Namie, G. (2012). *The WBI website 2012 instant poll-d: Impact of workplace bullying on individuals' health.* Retrieved from http://www.workplacebullying.org/multi/pdf/WBI-2012-IP-D.pdf

Namie, G. (2014). *The WBI website 2014 instant poll-c: The many ways workplace bullying offends its targets.* Retrieved from http://www.workplacebullying.org/multi/pdf/WBI-2014-IP-C.pdf

Nash, C. S., & Sproule, J. (2009). Career development of expert coaches. *International Journal of Sports Science & Coaching, 4*(1), 121–138.

Nielsen, M. B., & Einarsen, S. (2012). Outcomes of exposure to workplace bullying: A meta-analytic review. *Work & Stress, 26*(4), 309–332.

Palmer, S. (2007). PRACTICE: A model suitable for coaching, counselling, psychotherapy and stress management. *Coaching Psychologist, 3*(2), 71–77.

Peltier, B. (2011). *The psychology of executive coaching: Theory and application.* Abingdon, England: Taylor & Francis.

Ray, T. K., Chang, C. C., & Asfaw, A. (2014). Workplace mistreatment and health-related quality of life (HRQL): Results from the 2010 National Health Interview Survey (NHIS). *Journal of Behavioral Health, 3*(1), 9–16.

Shifflett, E. T. (Ed.). (2016). *Licensure requirements for professional counselors: A state-by-state report*. Alexandria, VA: American Counseling Association.

Simpson, G. W., Byrne, P., Gabbay, M. B., & Rannard, A. (2015). Understanding illness experiences of employees with common mental health disorders. *Occupational Medicine*, 65, 367–372.

Sperry, L. (1993). Working with executives: Consulting, counseling, and coaching. *Individual Psychology: Journal of Adlerian Theory, Research & Practice*, 49(2), 257–266.

Tehrani, N. (2004). Bullying: A source of chronic post traumatic stress? *British Journal of Guidance & Counselling*, 32(3), 357–366.

Vedaa, Ø., Krossbakken, E., Grimsrud, I. D., Bjorvatn, B., Sivertsen, B., Magerøy, N., . . . Pallesen, S. (2016). Prospective study of predictors and consequences of insomnia: personality, lifestyle, mental health and work-related stressors. *Sleep Medicine*, 20, 51–58.

Williams, P. (2004). Coaching vs. psychotherapy: The great debate. *Choice* 2(1), 38–39.

Williams, P., & Davis, D. C. (2002). *Therapist as life coach: Transforming your practice*. New York: W. W. Norton.

15

Best Practices in Coaching for Aggressors and Offenders in Workplace Bullying and Mobbing

Benjamin M. Walsh

Workplace bullying represents a form of interpersonal workplace mistreatment that is destructive not only to targets but also to the organizations within which it occurs (Hershcovis, 2011). Consequently, organizations must engage in efforts to prevent and address the occurrence of workplace bullying (Saam, 2010). Many tactics are encouraged by researchers and practitioners, such as the development of zero-tolerance policies on workplace bullying (Namie & Namie, 2009); regular antibullying training for all workers (Fox & Stallworth, 2009); and utilizing systems designed to effectively manage workplace conflict (Saam, 2010), among others. An additional tactic recommended is the use of *coaching* (e.g., executive, managerial, leadership) for aggressors of workplace bullying (Crawshaw, 2007, 2010; Ferris, 2009; Fox & Freeman, 2011; Kets de Vries, 2014), specifically, and to improve interactions between supervisors and subordinates and prevent manager derailment (Kelloway & Barling, 2010; Mackey, Frieder, Brees, & Martinko, 2015; Nelson & Hogan, 2009; Wasylyshyn, Shorey, & Chaffin, 2012), more generally.

The goal of this chapter is to review what is known from both research and practice about utilizing coaching with aggressors of workplace bullying and mobbing to reduce and prevent problematic and abusive workplace behavior. First, given the focus specifically on coaching as a means of intervention, coaching is defined, and research on the effectiveness of coaching is briefly summarized. Second, literature on coaching for bullying (and related topics) is discussed. Third, following a review of the literature on coaching, a model for the application of coaching for aggressors of workplace bullying is presented. Finally, as will be seen, although frameworks exist for the use of coaching for aggressors of bullying (e.g., Crawshaw, 2010; Fox & Freeman,

2011), empirical research evaluating the effectiveness of these frameworks is sparse.

Thus, the chapter concludes with a call for research to evaluate the effectiveness of coaching for aggressors of bullying, with the goal of developing evidence-based best practices. Various perspectives are considered, including the client's (aggressor's), his or her employer's, and the coach's. To supplement the discussion of literature on the topic, throughout I summarize themes derived from semistructured phone interviews conducted with five subject matter experts (SMEs). Four are active in the practice of executive coaching with doctoral-level training, and all have worked with clients who are aggressors of workplace bullying, ranging from a low of 6 clients and a high of 460 clients. The fifth SME is a registered social worker who has worked with perpetrators of domestic violence and has observed that the abusive behavior of the clients often extends into the workplace, hence the relevance to the present topic. Questions were structured around the steps in the model presented in figure 15.1, and interviews lasted approximately 60 minutes.

What Is Coaching?

Given our focus on organizations and the use of coaching for aggressors of bullying, it is important to first define what exactly coaching entails. Indeed, many definitions of coaching appear in the literature (e.g., Feldman & Lankau, 2005; Hall, Otazo, & Hollenbeck, 1999; Kilburg, 1996). For example, the International Coach Federation (ICF) defines coaching as "partnering with clients in a thought-provoking and creative process that inspires them to maximize their personal and professional potential" (ICF, 2016). An oft-cited definition is offered by Kilburg (1996), who defines coaching as "a helping relationship formed between a client who has managerial authority and responsibility in an organization and a consultant who uses a wide variety of behavioral techniques and methods to help the client achieve a mutually identified set of goals to improve his or her professional performance and personal satisfaction and, consequently, to improve the effectiveness of the client's organization within a formally defined coaching agreement" (p. 142). Gregory, Levy, and Jeffers (2008) highlight four components of Kilburg's conceptualization of coaching that align with other conceptualizations. These features include that coaching is a collaborative one-on-one relationship, involves the collection of data on the client's behavior and other factors (e.g., personality), relies on goal setting that is guided by the collected data, and involves using and delivering feedback.

Coaching shares characteristics with other comparable working relationships, such as counseling or mentoring, as well as therapy (Hart, Blattner, & Leipsic, 2001). Some individuals emphasize the differences between coaching and therapy (e.g., Feldman & Lankau, 2005). For example, Feldman and

Lankau (2005) state that coaching is more short-term in its focus on behavior change, whereas therapy is more long-term in its focus. The length of therapy is also a function of how well the client responds, whereas coaching is defined by a contract with a set number of sessions. Feldman and Lankau (2005) also assert that therapy is usually reserved for those with some fundamental problem, whereas coaching is for healthy clients.

Others perceive a close connection and considerable overlap between coaching and therapy (e.g., Kets de Vries, 2014; McKenna & Davis, 2009; Nelson & Hogan, 2009). Gebhardt (2016) reiterates that the basis for coaching lies in clinical psychology and highlights the trend of psychologists, including those with clinical training turning toward work as a coach. The lines between coaching and therapy appear particularly blurred when focusing on its application for aggressors of workplace bullying, given that bullying (and potentially its root causes) is a problem to be addressed. Kets de Vries (2014) relies on both coaching and therapy, when appropriate, to address toxic leaders. As discussed in greater detail below, Fox and Freeman (2011) propose a coaching intervention for aggressors of bullying that is grounded in cognitive behavioral therapy. Thus, given the nature of workplace bullying, the line between coaching and therapy does appear blurred.

Research on Coaching Effectiveness

Although limited in number, research from primary studies suggests that coaching is effective for driving change on various criteria. Grant, Curtayne, and Burton (2009) conducted a randomized controlled study with executives in a public health agency and found that coaching increased goal attainment, resilience, and workplace well-being and lowered depression and stress when compared with the control group. McGonagle, Beatty, and Joffe (2014) tested the effectiveness of a coaching intervention among workers with chronic illness and observed improved work ability, exhaustion, core self-evaluations, and resilience among those in the coaching group when compared with the wait-list control group. Reviews and meta-analyses suggest promising benefits from coaching (Feldman & Lankau, 2005; Jones, Woods, & Guillaume, 2016; Sonesh et al., 2015; Theeboom, Beersma, & van Vianen, 2014). For instance, Jones et al. (2016) conducted a meta-analysis of the effectiveness of coaching on various outcomes and found evidence for positive effects of coaching on affective outcomes, skill-based outcomes, and individual-level results outcomes. However, there was evidence for some moderators, suggesting variability in coaching effectiveness, and empirical evidence for the effectiveness of coaching, especially those using experimental methods, is limited. This suggests that it may be too tentative to speak to "best practices" in coaching for aggressors of bullying, in particular.

A Model for the Application of Coaching for Aggressors of Workplace Bullying

While there is evidence for the effectiveness of coaching, generally, evidence specifically on the effectiveness of coaching for aggressors of workplace bullying is especially limited. Following a review of the literature and request for information to listservs, I am aware of no systematic empirical research on the effectiveness of coaching for aggressors of bullying. Nonetheless, some frameworks for coaching bullies exist, such as Crawshaw's (2005, 2010, 2012) and Fox and Freeman's (2011) approaches, which will be summarized in a subsequent section. Likewise, coaches are engaging in this work, as is evident from various case studies (e.g., Sargent, 2011; Schlatter & McDowall, 2014); the literature on manager derailment (e.g., Hogan, Hogan, & Kaiser, 2010), for which abusive and bullying behavior is one of several reasons for manager failure; and in discussions with the SMEs.

To provide guidance on utilizing coaching with aggressors of workplace bullying, I developed a model by drawing on the literature on coaching (general), coaching for workplace bullies (and related terms such as abusive supervision and aggression), and related literatures on multirater feedback and management derailment. The model developed by Gregory et al. (2008) of the feedback process in executive coaching served as the basis and was adapted for the model presented herein. Indeed, Gregory et al. (2008) note, "Coaching, feedback, and development should be considered in concert, as opposed to isolated practices" (p. 43). Below, I describe steps in the model, highlight key decisions through the process, and summarize themes derived from the aforementioned SMEs.

The model presented in figure 15.1 provides a framework for the application of coaching for aggressors of workplace bullying. Although the model distinguishes between the various steps, in practice there may be considerable overlap. For example, assessing and building client motivation to change through coaching is an ongoing process. It is important to emphasize that the model assumes the presence of a workplace climate or culture that is intolerant of mistreatment (Yang, Caughlin, Gazica, Truxillo, & Spector, 2014). That is, coaching is assumed to be effective only when the workplace climate indicates that mistreatment such as bullying is not tolerated, as evidenced by the presence and enforcement of policies, practices, and procedures intended to deter mistreatment.

In this context, coaching would be merely one tactic among many to address bullying. SMEs were clear in conveying that the key for effective coaching for aggressors of workplace bullying is such a climate or culture, and it starts first with the behavior modeled and held accountable by senior leaders; without the presence of a climate that is clear in its intolerance of

Best Practices in Coaching for Aggressors and Offenders 339

Workplace Mistreatment Climate
- Anti-mistreatment policies (e.g., anti-bullying policy)
- Anti-mistreatment practices (e.g., anti-bullying training)
- Anti-mistreatment procedures (e.g., bullying reporting protocol)

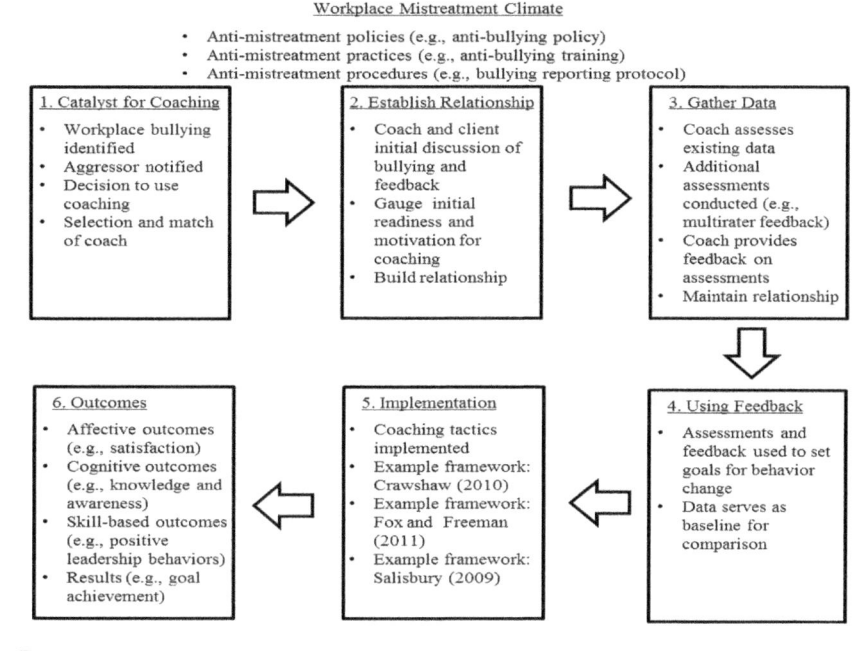

1. Catalyst for Coaching	2. Establish Relationship	3. Gather Data
• Workplace bullying identified • Aggressor notified • Decision to use coaching • Selection and match of coach	• Coach and client initial discussion of bullying and feedback • Gauge initial readiness and motivation for coaching • Build relationship	• Coach assesses existing data • Additional assessments conducted (e.g., multirater feedback) • Coach provides feedback on assessments • Maintain relationship

6. Outcomes	5. Implementation	4. Using Feedback
• Affective outcomes (e.g., satisfaction) • Cognitive outcomes (e.g., knowledge and awareness) • Skill-based outcomes (e.g., positive leadership behaviors) • Results (e.g., goal achievement)	• Coaching tactics implemented • Example framework: Crawshaw (2010) • Example framework: Fox and Freeman (2011) • Example framework: Salisbury (2009)	• Assessments and feedback used to set goals for behavior change • Data serves as baseline for comparison

Figure 15.1

workplace mistreatment, coaching is likely to be ineffective. In a workplace where bullying is tolerated, such behavior may even be seen as strategic, reinforced, and instrumental for performance (Ferris, Zinko, Brouer, Buckley, & Harvey, 2007; Fox & Freeman, 2011). Upon returning to such a work environment following coaching, it is likely that clients would simply revert to their abusive ways, if the context is one in which abusive behavior is tolerated or, even worse, accepted and expected. Moreover, although a systematic managerial coaching program may even be used as a means of preventing workplace bullying, the focus of the model is largely on coaching for identified aggressors of bullying, once bullying has occurred.

Catalyst for coaching

The catalyst for coaching means that the impetus for coaching—workplace bullying—has been identified (Gregory et al., 2008). To identify workplace bullying, an organization first has to understand what it is and what it is not by establishing an antibullying and respectful workplace policy and communicating this information to its employees (Fox & Stallworth, 2009; Namie & Namie, 2009). SMEs agreed that identifying bullying will be easier in a climate intolerant of workplace mistreatment, where an established policy, regular employee training on bullying, and surveying practices are used to define workplace bullying, build awareness of the problem, and measure its incidence and prevalence, respectively.

Just what exactly is workplace bullying? The academic literature on workplace mistreatment is fragmented (Hershcovis, 2011) and ranges from low-level rudeness and workplace incivilities (Andersson & Pearson, 1999) to more intense behaviors such as aggression and bullying where intent to harm is clear (Neuman & Baron, 1998). For the purposes of this chapter, the definition of bullying provided by Fox and Cowan (2015) is used; they considered input from human resource professionals to put forth a revised definition of workplace bullying: "Actions and practices that a 'reasonable person' would find abusive, occur repeatedly or persistently, and result in adverse economic, psychological, or physical outcomes to the target and/or a hostile work environment" (p. 124).[1] Although their conceptualization differs from researcher definitions (e.g., Leymann, 1990), it nonetheless may be a useful definition for inclusion in organizational policies to guide the identification of bullying in practice, given its development based on input from human resource professionals. Likewise, this definition clearly distinguishes bullying from an intermittent rude remark made by a manager having a stressful day or employee that may, from time to time, be a little tough on their colleagues. Although such incivilities are inappropriate and are not to be condoned, they are not bullying. Bullying, per Fox and Cowan (2015), is repeated and persistent abuse that results in harm.

After bullying is defined, such behaviors can be monitored through surveying and reporting processes. Measurement of workplace bullying can be done in regular employee surveys, using such measures as the Workplace Bullying Checklist (Fox & Cowan, 2015), which aligns with the aforementioned definition of workplace bullying. Moreover, it is important that all employees as well as organizational outsiders (e.g., customers, where applicable) be empowered to report bullying when it occurs (Swiggart, Dewey, Hickson, Finlayson, & Spickard, 2009).

Once bullying is identified, intervention with the aggressor is necessary. If the focus of the organizational climate is one of intolerance of bullying, and the decision to use coaching implies a desire to develop one's employees, then ensuring justice in this process is critical. Without a sense of justice and fairness, aggressors of bullying may feel alienated and rejected by their employers. Jenkins, Winefield, and Sarris (2011) surveyed and interviewed managers accused of workplace bullying to learn about their experiences, including in the accusation of bullying and the investigation conducted by their employer. The authors found that those accused of bullying often experienced a lack of fairness and justice following the accusation, in particular in the way the process was handled by their organizations. Thus, organizations must ensure that basic principles of procedural justice—the fairness of the process used to conduct the investigation into alleged workplace bullying—are followed. Basic components of procedural justice would include allowing the alleged aggressor to express their views concerning the allegations, consistently applying these procedures, ensuring that the process is free of bias, and ensuring that the process allows accurate information to be gathered, among others (Colquitt, 2001).

It is at this stage that the decision to use coaching is made (Gregory et al., 2008). Does coaching always have to mean a formal contracted engagement with an external coach? Although this approach is the primary focus of this chapter, SMEs generally agreed that informal intervention is generally preferred over more formal approaches. Graduated intervention from informal to formal is preferred. Along these lines, it may be possible to intervene early when a colleague engages in incivility, prior to the behaviors manifesting as bullying. One such program that aligns with this model is the Cup of Coffee program in the Vanderbilt Center for Patient and Professional Advocacy ("Cup of Coffee program," n.d.). It is designed to make a colleague aware of their unprofessional behavior in a nonjudgmental, more informal fashion, prior to relying on more involved interventions, such as external intervention from a coach. Several SMEs suggested that, ideally, it is the manager or supervisor of the aggressor that should be empowered and trained to intervene following reports of disrespectful behavior. One SME emphasized that bullying is ultimately about power, which aligns with academic conceptualizations of bullying such that an imbalance of power exists between perpetrator and target (Einarsen, 2000). The SME noted that it is important to have someone in a position of greater authority and legitimate power to address the issue early on, such as the person's manager.

Although informal intervention may inhibit bullying, a formal contracted agreement with an external coach may be necessary. Assuming that the work environment is one in which mistreatment is not tolerated, it may be that the bullying stems from internal (e.g., prior experience, personality) as opposed to external (e.g., a climate that tolerates mistreatment) factors, and hence coaching may be effective. Research suggests that a number of individual differences are predictive of bullying and aggression, more generally. For example, individuals that lack self-control may be more aggressive (Douglas & Martinko, 2001). Bullying may be a reaction to threats to self-esteem and to one's competence (Fast & Chen, 2009; Fox & Freeman, 2011; Zapf & Einarsen, 2003), which aligns with what Crawshaw (2010, 2012) argues are reasons for the abusive behavior she sees in the leaders she coaches. Bullying may also stem from a lack of self-awareness, perspective taking, empathy, and emotional intelligence (Fox & Freeman, 2011; Martinko, Harvey, Brees, & Mackey, 2013; Zapf & Einarsen, 2003), problems that are also highlighted in Crawshaw's (2010, 2012) abusive clients and others (Salisbury, 2009).

An inability to effectively cope with work stress may also trigger bullying (Wheeler, Halbesleben, & Shanine, 2010). Thus, given the connection between theory and research on individual differences that are predictive of aggression, and the aims of coaching, there is reason to believe that coaching may be effective for addressing bullying behavior. However, some argue that coaching may not be an effective strategy. For example, Kets de Vries (2014) argues that some toxic leaders are impossible to change. This concern regarding client motivation for coaching will be revisited.

What experience and background are needed to effectively coach aggressors of bullying? Gregory et al. (2008) suggest the need to select a coach with expertise in the area of the problem, workplace bullying in the present case. Given the nature of workplace bullying and the fact that such behavior may stem from issues of personality such as narcissism (e.g., Fox & Freeman, 2011) or other dark side personality traits (Goldman, 2006; Hogan et al., 2010), selecting coaches with psychological (e.g., clinical psychology, counseling psychology, social work) graduate training may also be helpful in coaching aggressors of bullying. SMEs largely agreed that coaches doing work with aggressors of workplace bullying need to be experienced (i.e., this work is not for a new graduate); have an understanding of the phenomenon of bullying; and may benefit from a clinical background so as to effectively understand human behavior. One SME also noted that coaches must model the behaviors the clients need to develop, including compassion and capacity for empathy.

Establish relationship

In the second stage, the coach and client have an initial discussion of the reason for coaching, and an assessment of readiness and motivation for coaching is conducted. The focus needs to be on building the coach-client relationship (Gregory et al., 2008). Although Gregory et al. (2008) point to a coach-client meeting, several SMEs emphasized that their initial meeting include three parties: the coach, the client, and the organization. This is particularly important with aggressors of workplace bullying for several reasons. As one SME pointed out, it is the organization that is seeking assistance and relief from suffering, and very often the entity from whom the request for coaching is made. There may also be differences in the perspectives held by the client and his or her employer concerning the facts surrounding the bullying.

This meeting is a time in which the coaching agreement can be set and informed consent can be provided and obtained from the client (Gebhardt, 2016). Informed consent would be required of those with clinical training, such as by coaches with training as psychologists (American Psychological Association (APA), 2010), but it is a recommended ethical practice regardless of one's training, and also aligns generally with recommendations in the International Coach Federation's code of ethics concerning the content of coaching agreements (ICF, 2015). An informed consent would present such details as the roles, rights, and responsibilities of the coach, client, and organization; the number of coaching sessions to be held; the types of feedback provided by the coach to the client (and organization, if applicable); steps taken to ensure confidentiality of gathered data; and any consequences for the client that are associated with not participating in or terminating the coaching, among others. Indeed, the organization may require that participation in coaching is a condition of continued employment, but it is critical that such requirements be specified in detail and understood up front, prior to initiating coaching. This coach-client-organization meeting is critical to ensure that all parties have the same information and are on the same page, so to speak, before moving forward.

As noted, it is most likely that the organization (as opposed to the client) will be the impetus for coaching aggressors of bullying (Jenkins et al., 2011; Salisbury, 2009). Hence, motivation for the coaching will, at least initially, stem from external as opposed to internal factors. Thus, the client will likely react negatively to the initial reason (bullying) for the coaching (Salisbury, 2009). This is consistent with the experience described by Crawshaw (2010, 2012) when working with abrasive leaders, such that they often dismiss or deny there is a problem in the first place.

Various theories and research highlight the importance of perceiving that there is a need to change one's behavior as being critical for individual behavior change, such as Prochaska's transtheoretical model of change (Prochaska et al., 1994). In the training literature, motivation to learn before training predicts such training outcomes as knowledge and skill acquisition (Colquitt, LePine, & Noe, 2000). Coaches of bullies likely have a challenge ahead of them in building such motivation and awareness of the need to change, yet this is critical for coaching to be beneficial. Wasylyshyn et al. (2012) note, "Leaders with predominately toxic behaviours warrant particular scrutiny at the needs assessment stage for they may or may not be viable coaching candidates" (p. 74). This may be the stage at which it is concluded that coaching is not a viable option given a lack of client motivation.

Gregory et al. (2008) as well as others (e.g., McKenna & Davis, 2009; Salisbury, 2009) highlight the need to build a trusting relationship between the coach and client in this second stage. Research shows that the coach-client relationship predicts coaching outcomes, including client self-efficacy (Baron & Morin, 2009). When coaching aggressors of bullying, SMEs completely agreed and emphasized that building and establishing trust between coach and client is of paramount importance. Crawshaw (2010, 2012) provides guidance on how to build this trusting relationship with aggressors.

For example, she notes the fundamental need to treat clients as capable of change, at least until there is reason to believe this is not the case. The basic fact that one's continued employment may be contingent on engaging in coaching may facilitate greater motivation. In addition, ensuring confidentiality concerning the collected data is critical for building trust. Several SMEs also stressed that aggressors of bullying are often vilified. They want to convey to the client that they are there to help them be successful and that it is their bullying behavior that is hindering their ability to be successful. By partnering with the client in this way, and framing their disrespectful behavior as a problem standing in the way of professional growth, coaches may be able to help build the readiness the client needs to grow from the coaching.

SMEs conveyed that gauging readiness and motivation for coaching was an ongoing and iterative process. One SME establishes a three-month trial when he sets up a contract, within which he expects to see improvement; another expects to see improvement within the first three sessions. SMEs have avoided working with clients exhibiting a lack of motivation to change. If a coach deems the client incapable of change or simply unmotivated to change, early on or in subsequent sessions, then it is up to the organization to determine the appropriate consequences and discipline, up to and including termination. Ideally such consequences were already agreed upon during the initial meeting. If and when such issues arise, to maintain the confidentiality of the coaching process, one SME noted that she redirects any questions from the referring organization to the client so that the client is ultimately responsible for his or her behavior and confidentiality is not breached by the coach.

Gather data

This stage focuses on gathering data to inform the coaching, providing feedback to the client, and working to solidify the coach-client relationship (Gregory et al., 2008). Continuing to build motivation for the coaching during this stage may also occur and may be aided by feedback provided via collected data.

There are several places from which existing data may be gathered. Organizations with a strong intolerance of workplace mistreatment are likely to engage in proactive monitoring of workplace bullying via their own survey data collections, such as with the Workplace Bullying Checklist (Fox & Cowan, 2015) referenced earlier. However, such data may lack important identifiers to specifically link the bullying behavior to the client in question. More specific information may be derived from an investigative report provided by the organization, should one be available. One SME requests the letter or investigative report prepared by the organization to get a baseline assessment of the nature of the problem, and often relies only on this report before moving forward with the coaching.

Collecting additional types of data is also likely to be helpful. It may be helpful to collect data multirater feedback (e.g., 360-degree feedback) specifically on bullying behaviors (e.g., client report of bullying behaviors and subordinate reports of bullying behaviors). Coaching and multirater feedback are often used in conjunction with one another (Hooijberg & Lane, 2009; Luthans & Peterson, 2003), and if at least part of the problem stems from a lack of awareness of one's behavior and its impact (Crawshaw, 2007; Salisbury, 2009), then comparing self (client) and other (subordinate) ratings of the client's behavior may aid in demonstrating the nature of the problem and building readiness and motivation for coaching. This data need not be exclusively quantitative in nature. For example, Crawshaw (2007, 2010, 2012) collects qualitative data (after ensuring confidentiality of the data) from the client's coworkers regarding the abusive behavior and its impact and then shares this data with the leader so as to build insight into the problem.

Several SMEs also rely only on qualitative data when working with aggressors of workplace bullying. For example, one SME collects qualitative data via interviews with five to seven key people working right around the client (e.g., peers, direct reports), noting that the interview is the best way to gain insight on the context surrounding the mistreatment (e.g., exactly what kinds of bullying behaviors, when the bullying behavior occurs, and who is targeted). If such data is captured, it is incumbent on the coach to ensure the confidentiality and anonymity of the data.

Coaches may also find value in including personality and individual difference assessments (e.g., dark side personality, emotional intelligence) in the multirater feedback instrument, as is recommended in the literature on manager derailment (Nelson & Hogan, 2009). With respect to emotional intelligence, research shows emotional intelligence is predictive of performance among managers above and beyond other factors (Iliescu, Ilie, Ispas, & Ion, 2012) and ties in conceptually with potential reasons for bullying described above (e.g., lacking empathy). One SME commented that they often rely on an emotional intelligence assessment, given that it is helpful in diagnosing the underlying reasons for the bullying behavior. Other SMEs noted that they generally do not rely on assessments beyond the organization's investigative report and (qualitative) data collected from coworkers regarding the client's bullying. If the plan is to gather such data, it is important that the client be provided with the opportunity to refuse to undergo such testing, as would occur in the ongoing process of informed consent, while simultaneously ensuring that the client appreciates the potential consequences associated with failure to participate as stated in the coaching agreement (e.g., termination).

Once data is collected, feedback must be provided to the client. Feedback during this stage will focus on highlighting gaps between self-other perception of bullying behavior (and potentially dark side personality if conducted). Hogan et al. (2010) argue that "the key to development is self-awareness" (p. 17), and, similarly, Nelson and Hogan (2009) assert that leaders need to develop "strategic self-awareness" (p. 14). Research suggests that leaders very often do not see themselves as others do (i.e., self-other disagreement; Fleenor, Smither, Atwater, Braddy, & Sturm, 2010; Gentry, Hannum, Ekelund, & de Jong, 2007), and self-other rating discrepancies are associated with ineffective leader behavior (Kaiser, LeBreton, & Hogan, 2015).

Crawshaw (2007, 2010, 2012) and others (e.g., Salisbury, 2009) highlight that abusive leaders lack awareness of their behavior or its impact: "these individuals were *clueless*; they were profoundly lacking in psychological insight into the impact of their behavior" (Crawshaw, 2010, p. 62). Providing feedback at this stage may help to reinforce that there is indeed a problem, which may further aid in driving motivation to resolve bullying behavior.

With that said, it is plausible that not all workplace bullying stems from a lack of awareness of one's own behavior and its impact. Some aggressors of workplace bullying may be acutely aware of their behavior and use such aggression as a means to an end. Schwartz (2015) says as much about some of the most well-known leaders of our time, such as Steve Jobs, Elon Musk, and Jeff Bezos. Jobs was sensitive and aware, yet he still engaged in regular displays of hostility toward his employees. For such individuals, attempting to build self-awareness may be fruitless, and coaching, more generally, may be equally futile. Two SMEs remarked that for such examples of predatory bullying, coaching is likely to be ineffective; instead, clinical intervention (i.e., therapy), rather than coaching, may be necessary. This is a complex issue, as it suggests the possibility that not all clients will be capable of true behavior change (Kets de Vries, 2014), at least through the use of coaching alone.

Using feedback

In the feedback stage, the coach and client work together to set goals and identify areas for improvement for the coaching intervention (Gregory et al., 2008). No matter the reason for coaching, the use of goal setting is an inherent component of effective coaching (Grant et al., 2009; Gregory et al., 2008; Kilburg, 1996; Stern, 2004). Gregory et al. (2008) emphasize that a fundamental role of the coach is to aid the client in establishing goals and then assisting the client in meeting the set goals. Thus, the exact goals set will likely vary depending on the client in question.

Plausible goals for coaching aggressors of workplace bullying may include increasing self-awareness, which could ultimately be measured via a reduction in the gap between self-other reports from multirater feedback, assuming such data is gathered. Goals may also relate to one or more of the various plausible reasons for bullying behaviors, such as increasing self-control, increasing emotional intelligence and empathy, increasing coping strategies to effectively manage work stress, decreasing bullying behavior (and hence improving employee well-being), and building more productive leadership behaviors. Salisbury (2009) provides an example of goals and tactics for one client, which included (a) learn to listen and coach (e.g., practice active listening); (b) communicate respectfully at all times (e.g., delay responses to situations when aware of one's own frustration and anger); and (c) create an inclusive teamwork environment (e.g., identify ways to build relationships among team members).

SMEs were consistent in expressing that *their* ultimate goal as a coach is for their client to be successful. One SME noted that he essentially wants to help create a better human being, one that is capable of returning to the workplace and repairing relationships that have been damaged. To do so, SMEs were also clear that increasing self-awareness and insight into one's own behavior is merely one goal to be met. Clients also need to build the skills they need, such as in the examples provided above (e.g., coping skills, self-control, active listening), to effectively work with others and help meet what is arguably the ultimate goal of coaching aggressors of workplace bullying: decreasing the client's bullying behavior.

Implementation

This stage was added to Gregory et al.'s (2008) modified model so as to elaborate on the approach taken in existing frameworks for coaching aggressors of bullying. Several frameworks for coaching have been discussed in the literature, although empirical research on their effectiveness is lacking. Nonetheless, given their theoretical alignment with identified predictors of bullying, they do show promise. These frameworks are summarized next.

One framework for coaching aggressors of workplace bullying is presented by Crawshaw (2005, 2007, 2010, 2012). She defines abrasive leaders "as any individual charged with managerial authority whose interpersonal behavior causes emotional distress in coworkers sufficient to disrupt organizational functioning" (Crawshaw, 2010, p. 60). Although it is possible that not all abrasive leaders meet the definition of workplace bullying presented earlier, they do engage in behaviors that have the potential to harm, including overcontrol, threats, public humiliation, condescension, and overreaction (Crawshaw, 2007). Crawshaw presents an action-research framework that rests on the theory that abrasive leaders are unaware of their behavior and its impact on others and that their bullying behavior is fundamentally the result of perceived threats to their competence (e.g., including poor-performing employees that are perceived by the manager as a threat to his or her own competence). Such threats are theorized to provoke anxiety and defensive reactions in the leader, where such reactions can manifest in the aforementioned bullying behaviors.

Crawshaw (2010) relies on an action-research model to build self-awareness and empathy in abrasive leaders, including planning, action, and fact finding. The planning stage involves gathering data from coworker interviews (i.e., to collect evidence of bullying behavior); analysis and feedback of results to the client (i.e., to build awareness in the client of the problem); preliminary diagnosis (i.e., negative perceptions held by coworkers of the client); and collaborative action planning (i.e., where more positive management tactics are identified). In the action stage, which occurs after awareness of the destructive impact of the client's behavior is achieved, action is taken by having the client implement more productive leader behaviors and tactics. Crawshaw employs the client to test a hypothesis that by engaging in these more productive behaviors, clients will be able to eradicate the negative perceptions previously held by coworkers.

Finally, in fact-finding, data are gathered again from coworkers to examine the degree to which behavior has changed. This pattern is iterative, and repeated cycles are conducted until behavior change is achieved. Crawshaw is in the practice of distributing this method of coaching to individuals and organizations (Boss Whispering Institute, 2016), for which continuing coach education is offered through the International Coach Federation.

Another approach for coaching aggressors of workplace bullying is presented by Fox and Freeman (2011). They link the theory of planned behavior (Ajzen, 2002) and the stressor-emotion-control model of counterproductive work behavior (Fox & Spector, 2006) to reasons for client bullying. They argue that bullying may be proactive, or instrumental bullying, based on the theory of planned behavior, wherein clients hold a positive attitude toward bullying (e.g., bullying is productive); perceive a subjective norm supportive of bullying (e.g., the client keeps getting promoted with this behavior); and perceive control to engage in bullying (e.g., there is a lack of punishment for bullying). In addition, they argue based on the stressor-emotion-control model that bullying may be reactive. In this case, bullying is a reaction to perceived stressors, such as a perceived threat to one's identity.

Fox and Freeman (2011) propose a cognitive behavioral therapy-based coaching for narcissistic leaders, in particular, given their lack of empathy. They provide the basis for a cognitive behavioral therapy approach to coaching, where the "objective is to change the coachee's behavior through changing cognitions regarding the *instrumental value* and *social acceptance* of bullying" (Fox & Freeman, 2011, p. 178). They also note that their approach may be applied not only to clients (i.e., aggressors of workplace bullying) but also to targets and others. The goals of the coaching align with general goals of cognitive behavioral therapy, and for aggressors of workplace bullying, the goals include being able to "recognize, transform, [and] channel dysfunctional cognitions and behaviors" and "bring[ing] out the positive, creative, engaged behaviors that adaptive narcissism can facilitate" (Fox & Freeman, 2011, p. 184). Their focus on cognitive behavioral therapy also highlights the blurred line between coaching and therapy when addressing aggressors of bullying.

A third example is outlined by Salisbury (2009), for which the focus is on coaching for respectful leadership by increasing emotional intelligence. Salisbury emphasizes that workplace bullying is not the intended focus of coaching for respectful leadership, asserting, "More often than not, these behaviors result in termination and are not likely to change through a coaching process" (p. 184). Yet, I discuss the framework here given the comparable focus on improving client behavior and because it shares some similarities with the aforementioned frameworks.

Salisbury's (2009) framework rests on a series of stages. In stage I, Salisbury collects data from employees concerning the basis of disrespect and its impact and shares this data with the client. She notes that threat reactions from clients are likely when presented with this data, yet also that this stage is critical before moving to subsequent stages. In stage II, the reasons for disrespectful behavior are explored, and Salisbury comments that a primary reason is lack of awareness of the impact of the client's behavior on others. Then in stages III, IV, and V, goals and a plan for change through the coaching process are defined; the coach uses various methods to assist the client in acquiring more positive leader behaviors (e.g., developing empathy); and transformations are sustained, respectively. Salisbury (2009) notes that not all stages may be needed for all clients and also that coaching may fail, for example, due to the client's denial of feedback or lack of motivation to engage in the coaching process.

Thus, several frameworks exist to facilitate the implementation of coaching for aggressors of workplace bullying. It is evident from these frameworks that although there are differences, there are also many similarities, such as the possibility that bullying stems in part from perceived threats and that clients lack awareness of their behavior and its impact on employees and coworkers. The frameworks also reinforce the individualized nature of coaching and how specific strategies, tactics, and goals may differ depending on the reason for the bullying, as noted by others (e.g., Kets de Vries, 2014; Wasylyshyn et al., 2012). Ultimately, though, research is needed to examine their effectiveness.

Outcomes

In the final stage, the coaching is concluded once defined goals and outcomes are obtained or the coaching is deemed ineffective (Gregory et al., 2008). Effectively evaluating coaching for aggressors of workplace bullying requires attention to various outcome criteria as well as methods of measurement. Jones et al. (2016) provide a framework for differentiating among outcomes of coaching, generally, that may also provide guidance for evaluating the effectiveness of coaching for aggressors of workplace bullying, more specifically. In particular, Jones et al. (2016) draw on the training outcomes literature (e.g., Kirkpatrick, 1967; Kraiger, Ford, & Salas, 1993), given the connection between coaching and training. Specifically, they differentiate between affective outcomes, cognitive outcomes, skill-based outcomes, and results (Jones et al., 2016).

Affective outcomes capture client attitudes about the coaching (e.g., satisfaction) and variables related to motivation, such as motivation to use knowledge gained from coaching after the contract ends. Cognitive outcomes relate to knowledge acquisition (e.g., declarative and procedural knowledge). Skill-based outcomes pertain to the acquisition and use of skills from coaching, such as leadership skills. Finally, results include factors related to performance, be that for the client, team, or organization.

With some tailoring, Jones et al.'s (2016) framework is useful for conceptualizing outcomes of coaching for aggressors of workplace bullying, which can then be used to understand and measure the effectiveness of such coaching. For aggressors of bullying, affective outcomes could include client satisfaction with the coaching process. Affective outcomes could be readily assessed via self-report surveys collected from the client. Cognitive outcomes could include such variables as knowledge and self-awareness of one's bullying behavior and its impact on employees.

Such knowledge could also be assessed via self-report assessments as well as multirater feedback systems. Skill-based outcomes for aggressors of bullying could include the use of more positive and productive leadership behaviors rather than bullying behaviors. Rather than relying on the client to self-report such skill-based outcomes, skill acquisition and use could be assessed via reports from others that work directly with the client (e.g., employees, coworkers) to minimize any bias in reporting. In addition, cognitive and skill-based outcomes can be measured prior to and after coaching to provide data for a stronger test of coaching effectiveness as it relates to these criteria. Results are the final step and generally align with organizational performance and goals being achieved.

In the case of coaching for aggressors of workplace bullying, results would be achieved if the initial goals made at the outset of coaching (e.g., reduced bullying behavior) are achieved. As suggested previously, keep in mind that the specific goals of coaching for aggressors of bullying may vary depending on the client in question, although the elimination of bullying behavior may be a common goal across aggressors of bullying. Additional results may also be realized given the harm associated with bullying, such as increased health and well-being of employees and increased retention. Ultimately, the coaching intervention should conclude when goals are met and when the organization is satisfied with the results. To maintain confidentiality in the coaching process, one SME stated that it is up to the organization to determine whether the results are satisfactory by using their own definition and measurement (e.g. lack of complaints to human resources).

It may also be that the coaching is ineffective in the sense that one or more of the aforementioned coaching outcomes is not met, with reduced client bullying seemingly being the outcome of greatest importance. Wasylyshyn et al. (2012) emphasize that coaching for executives displaying toxic behaviors (i.e., bullying) is "not successful generally" (p. 78), and a similar message is conveyed by Salisbury (2009). Crawshaw (2012) acknowledges that coaching may not be effective. In these cases, the leader may be terminated, but in this case, it can still be beneficial because the bullying behavior will be stopped. Although SMEs saw a role for coaching aggressors of bullying, some also conveyed skepticism that coaching alone could address workplace bullying. This theme harkens back to the role of the organization in creating a work climate and culture that truly does not tolerate workplace mistreatment from top to bottom.

CONCLUSION AND A CALL FOR EMPIRICAL RESEARCH

Coaching for aggressors of workplace bullying is an intriguing tool to use to address bullying in organizations. On the one hand, many coaches work with clients engaged in bullying behavior, and, as described in this chapter, several frameworks exist with which to guide the coaching process. Yet, there is reason for some skepticism regarding its effectiveness; while some may respond well to such coaching, others may not. Ultimately, what is needed is systematic empirical research to inform best practices regarding the effectiveness of coaching for aggressors of bullying.

Crawshaw (2012) acknowledges the need for empirical research, and Fox and Freeman (2011) call for such research as well. Important research questions abound: For example, which process for coaching aggressors of workplace bullying is most effective, and for which coaching outcomes? What percentage of clients fail to experience positive outcomes from coaching? Is coaching more effective for clients engaged in incivility as opposed to workplace bullying? What factors explain the link between coaching and effectiveness? And how do characteristics of the client and coach impact these relationships? These and other questions will be important to address to guide the ongoing practice of coaching aggressors of workplace bullying.

NOTE

1. Fox and Cowan's (2015) definition of workplace bullying was presented to SMEs prior to initiating the semistructured interviews.

REFERENCES

Ajzen, I. (2002). Perceived behavioral control, self-efficacy, locus of control, and the theory of planned behavior. *Journal of Applied Social Psychology, 32*(4), 665–683.

American Psychological Association (APA). (2010). *Ethical principles of psychologists and code of conduct.* Retrieved from http://www.apa.org/ethics/code/index.aspx

Andersson, L. M., & Pearson, C. M. (1999). Tit for tat? The spiraling effect of incivility in the workplace. *Academy of Management Review, 24*(3), 452–471.

Baron, L., & Morin, L. (2009). The coach-coachee relationship in executive coaching: A field study. *Human Resource Development Quarterly, 20*(1), 85–106.

Boss Whispering Institute. (2016). Retrieved from http://www.bosswhispering.com

Colquitt, J. A. (2001). On the dimensionality of organizational justice: A construct validation of a measure. *Journal of Applied Psychology, 86*(3), 386–400.

Colquitt, J. A., LePine, J. A., & Noe, R. A. (2000). Toward an integrative theory of training motivation: A meta-analytic path analysis of 20 years of research. *Journal of Applied Psychology, 85*(5), 678–707.

Crawshaw, L. (2005). *Coaching abrasive executives: Exploring the use of empathy in constructing less destructive interpersonal management strategies* (Unpublished doctoral dissertation). Fielding Graduate University, Santa Barbara, California.

Crawshaw, L. (2007). *Taming the abrasive manager: How to end unnecessary roughness in the workplace.* San Francisco, CA: Jossey-Bass.

Crawshaw, L. (2010). Coaching abrasive leaders: Using action research to reduce suffering and increase productivity in organizations. *International Journal of Coaching in Organizations, 29*(8), 60–77.

Crawshaw, L. (2012). Coaching abrasive leaders: Contradictory tales of the big bad wolf. In N. Tehrani (Ed.), *Workplace bullying: Symptoms and solutions* (pp. 132–148). New York: Routledge.

Cup of Coffee program. (n.d.). Vanderbilt Center for Patient and Professional Advocacy. Retrieved from http://www.mc.vanderbilt.edu/root/vumc.php?site=cppa

Douglas, S. C., & Martinko, M. J. (2001). Exploring the role of individual differences in the prediction of workplace aggression. *Journal of Applied Psychology, 86*(4), 547–559.

Einarsen, S. (2000). Harassment and bullying at work: A review of the Scandinavian approach. *Aggression and Violent Behavior, 5*(4), 379–401.

Fast, N. J., & Chen, S. (2009). When the boss feels inadequate: Power, incompetence, and aggression. *Psychological Science, 20*(11), 1406–1413.

Feldman, D. C., & Lankau, M. J. (2005). Executive coaching: A review and agenda for future research. *Journal of Management, 31*(6), 829–848.

Ferris, P. A. (2009). The role of the consulting psychologist in the prevention, detection, and correction of bullying and mobbing in the workplace. *Consulting Psychology Journal: Practice and Research, 61*(3), 169–189.

Ferris, G. R., Zinko, R., Brouer, R. L., Buckley, M. R., & Harvey, M. G. (2007). Strategic bullying as a supplementary, balanced perspective on destructive leadership. *Leadership Quarterly, 18*(3), 195–206.

Fleenor, J. W., Smither, J. W., Atwater, L. E., Braddy, P. W., & Sturm, R. E. (2010). Self-other rating agreement in leadership: A review. *Leadership Quarterly, 21*(6), 1005–1034.

Fox, S., & Cowan, R. L. (2015). Revision of the workplace bullying checklist: The importance of human resource management's role in defining and addressing workplace bullying. *Human Resource Management Journal, 25*(1), 116–130.

Fox, S., & Freeman, A. (2011). Narcissism and the deviant citizen: A common thread in CWB and OCB. In P. L. Perrewé & D. C. Ganster (Eds.), *The role of individual differences in occupational stress and well being* (Research in occupational stress and well being, Vol. 9, pp. 151–196). Bingley, England: Emerald.

Fox, S., & Spector, P. E. (2006). The many roles of control in a stressor-emotion theory of counterproductive work behavior. In P. L. Perrewé & D. C. Ganster (Eds.), *Employee health, coping, and methodologies* (Research in occupational stress and well being, Vol. 5, pp. 171–201). San Diego, CA: Elsevier.

Fox, S., & Stallworth, L. E. (2009). Building a framework for two internal organizational approaches to resolving and preventing workplace bullying: Alternative dispute resolution and training. *Consulting Psychology Journal: Practice and Research, 61*(3), 220–241.

Gebhardt, J. A. (2016). Quagmires for clinical psychology and executive coaching? Ethical considerations and practical challenges. *American Psychologist, 71*(3), 216–235.

Gentry, W. A., Hannum, K. M., Ekelund, B. Z., & de Jong, A. (2007). A study of the discrepancy between self- and observer-ratings on managerial derailment characteristics of European managers. *European Journal of Work and Organizational Psychology, 16*(3), 295–325.

Goldman, A. (2006). High toxicity leadership: Borderline personality disorder and the dysfunctional organization. *Journal of Managerial Psychology, 21*(8), 733–746.

Grant, A. M., Curtayne, L., & Burton, G. (2009). Executive coaching enhances goal attainment, resilience and workplace well-being: A randomized controlled study. *Journal of Positive Psychology, 4*(5), 396–407.

Gregory, J. B., Levy, P. E., & Jeffers, M. (2008). Development of a model of the feedback process within executive coaching. *Consulting Psychology Journal: Practice and Research, 60*(1), 42–56.

Hall, D. T., Otazo, K. I., & Hollenbeck, G. P. (1999). Behind closed doors: What really happens in executive coaching. *Organizational Dynamics, 27*(3), 39–53.

Hart, V., Blattner, J., & Leipsic, S. (2001). Coaching versus therapy: A perspective. *Consulting Psychology Journal: Practice and Research, 53*(4), 229–237.

Hershcovis, M. S. (2011). "Incivility, social undermining, bullying . . . oh my!": A call to reconcile constructs within workplace aggression research. *Journal of Organizational Behavior, 32*(3), 499–519.

Hogan, J., Hogan, R., & Kaiser, R. B. (2010). Management derailment. In S. Zedeck (Ed.), *American Psychological Association handbook of industrial and organizational psychology* (Vol. 3, pp. 555–575). Washington, D.C.: American Psychological Association.

Hooijberg, R., & Lane, N. (2009). Using multisource feedback coaching effectively in executive education. *Academy of Management Learning & Education, 8*(4), 483–493.

Iliescu, D., Ilie, A., Ispas, D., & Ion, A. (2012). Emotional intelligence in personnel selection: Applicant reactions, criterion, and incremental validity. *International Journal of Selection and Assessment, 20*(3), 347–358.

International Coach Federation (ICF). (2015). *Code of ethics.* Retrieved from www.coachfederation.org

International Coach Federation (ICF). (2016). *How does ICF define coaching?* Retrieved from www.coachfederation.org

Jenkins, M., Winefield, H., & Sarris, A. (2011). Consequences of being accused of workplace bullying: An exploratory study. *International Journal of Workplace Health Management, 4*(1), 33–47.

Jones, R. J., Woods, S. A., & Guillaume, Y. R. F. (2016). The effectiveness of workplace coaching: A meta-analysis of learning and performance outcomes from coaching. *Journal of Occupational and Organizational Psychology, 89,* 249–277.

Kaiser, R. B., LeBreton, J. M., & Hogan, J. (2015). The dark side of personality and extreme leader behavior. *Applied Psychology: An International Review, 64*(1), 55–92.

Kelloway, E. K., & Barling, J. (2010). Leadership development as an intervention in occupational health psychology. *Work & Stress, 24*(3), 260–279.

Kets de Vries, M. F. R. (2014). Coaching the toxic leader. *Harvard Business Review, 92*(4), 100–109.

Kilburg, R. R. (1996). Toward a conceptual understanding and definition of executive coaching. *Consulting Psychology Journal: Practice and Research, 48*(2), 134–144.

Kirkpatrick, D. L. (1967). Evaluation of training. In R. L. Craig & L. R. Bittel (Eds.), *Training and development handbook* (pp. 87–112). New York: McGraw-Hill.

Kraiger, K., Ford, J. K., & Salas, E. D. (1993). Application of cognitive, skill-based, and affective theories of learning outcomes to new methods of training evaluation. *Journal of Applied Psychology, 78*(2), 311–328.

Leymann, H. (1990). Mobbing and psychological terror at workplaces. *Violence and Victims, 5*(2), 119–126.

Luthans, F., & Peterson, S. J. (2003). 360-degree feedback with systematic coaching: Empirical analysis suggests a winning combination. *Human Resource Management, 42*(3), 243–256.

Mackey, J. D., Frieder, R. E., Brees, J. R., & Martinko, M. J. (2015). Abusive supervision: A meta-analysis and empirical review. *Journal of Management.* Advanced online publication. doi:10.1177/0149206315573997

Martinko, M. J., Harvey, P., Brees, J. R., & Mackey, J. (2013). A review of abusive supervision research. *Journal of Organizational Behavior, 34*(S1), S120–S137.

McGonagle, A. K., Beatty, J. E., & Joffe, R. (2014). Coaching for workers with chronic illness: Evaluating an intervention. *Journal of Occupational Health Psychology, 19*(3), 385–398.

McKenna, D. D., & Davis, S. L. (2009). Hidden in plain sight: The active ingredients of executive coaching. *Industrial and Organizational Psychology, 2*(3), 244–260.

Namie, G., & Namie, R. (2009). U.S. workplace bullying: Some basic considerations and consultation interventions. *Consulting Psychology Journal: Practice and Research, 61*(3), 202–219.

Nelson, E., & Hogan, R. (2009). Coaching on the dark side. *International Coaching Psychology Review, 4*(1), 7–19.

Neuman, J. H., & Baron, R. A. (1998). Workplace violence and workplace aggression: Evidence concerning specific forms, potential causes, and preferred targets. *Journal of Management, 24*(3), 391–419.

Prochaska, J. O., Velicer, W. F., Rossi, J. S., Goldstein, M. G., Marcus, B. H., Rakowski, W., ... Rossi, S. R. (1994). Stages of change and decisional balance for 12 problem behaviors. *Health Psychology, 13*(1), 39–46.

Saam, N. J. (2010). Interventions in workplace bullying: A multilevel approach. *European Journal of Work and Organizational Psychology, 19*(1), 51–75.

Salisbury, J. (2009). Coaching for respectful leadership. In E. Biech (Ed.), *The 2009 Pfeiffer Annual: Consulting* (pp. 183–197). San Francisco, CA: Pfeiffer.

Sargent, N. (2011). What's happening in the coaching conversation with an executive at risk of derailing? *International Journal of Evidence Based Coaching and Mentoring, S5*, 28–38.

Schlatter, N., & McDowall, A. (2014). Evidence-based EI coaching: A case study in the mining industry. *Coaching: An International Journal of Theory, Research and Practice, 7*(2), 144–151.

Schwartz, T. (2015, June 26). The bad behavior of visionary leaders. *New York Times.* Retrieved from www.nytimes.com

Sonesh, S. C., Coultas, C. W., Lacerenza, C. N., Marlow, S. L., Benishek, L. E., & Salas, E. (2015). The power of coaching: A meta-analytic investigation. *Coaching: An International Journal of Theory, Research and Practice, 8*(2), 73–95.

Stern, L. R. (2004). Executive coaching: A working definition. *Consulting Psychology Journal: Practice and Research, 56*(3), 154–162.

Swiggart, W. H., Dewey, C. M., Hickson, G. B., Finlayson, A. J. R., & Spickard, W. A., Jr. (2009). A plan for identification, treatment, and remediation of disruptive behaviors in physicians. *Frontiers of Health Services Management, 25*(4), 3–12.

Theeboom, T., Beersma, B., & van Vianen, A. E. M. (2014). Does coaching work? A meta-analysis on the effects of coaching on individual level outcomes in an organizational context. *Journal of Positive Psychology, 9*(1), 1–18.

Wasylyshyn, K. M., Shorey, H. S., & Chaffin, J. S. (2012). Patterns of leadership behaviour: Implications for successful executive coaching outcomes. *Coaching Psychologist, 8*(2), 74–85.

Wheeler, A. R., Halbesleben, J. R. B., & Shanine, K. (2010). Eating their cake and everyone else's cake, too: Resources as the main ingredient to workplace bullying. *Business Horizons, 53*(6), 553–560.

Yang, L., Caughlin, D. E., Gazica, M. W., Truxillo, D. M., & Spector, P. E. (2014). Workplace mistreatment climate and potential employee and organizational outcomes: A meta-analytic review from the target's perspective. *Journal of Occupational Health Psychology, 19*(3), 315–335.

Zapf, D., & Einarsen, S. (2003). Individual antecedents of bullying: Victims and perpetrators. In S. Einarsen, H. Hoel, D. Zapf, & C. L. Cooper (Eds.), *Bullying and emotional abuse in the workplace: International perspectives in research and practice* (pp. 165–184). London, England: Taylor & Francis.

16

The Role of the Consultant in Assessing and Preventing Workplace Bullying and Mobbing

Gary Namie and Ruth Namie

This chapter first considers factors that can convince public and private sector American organizations to adopt methods to mitigate internal bullying and mobbing. Current employer attitudes are gleaned from responses of executives to a survey about bullying. They are contrasted with perceptions of the public and individuals who have been targeted for bullying.

Given that employers are not widely open to comprehensive solutions, we review the partial steps employers are willing to take. There is some agreement that policies, codes, or behavioral expectations prohibiting abusive conduct are required. Essential components of an ideal policy are discussed.

There have been employers who have embraced systemic approaches. One such program is outlined. However, the majority of programs are, at best, incomplete endeavors. Though it often takes months or years to build interest in and executive support for an antibullying initiative, commitment can be instantly withdrawn. Successes are fragile. Suggestions to make programs sustainable are shared. In the absence of strong employer demand for consulting, American unions have taken steps to protect the health of their bullied members.

Finally, we discuss the authors' experience with educating courts about workplace bullying and mobbing, though no legal standard yet exists. The record began with the nation's "first bullying trial" in 2005. Helping plaintiffs as well as defending good employers that terminated abusive employees are both discussed.

ANTECEDENTS TO TRADITIONAL CONSULTING

The authors began consulting with organizations in 1985, offering services for executives, managers and work teams on a host of human resources (HR)–related themes. We have watched, and participated in, "fad of the year" consulting programs that rose swiftly in popularity and then faded as the novelty wore off. A few substantive programs, such as Six Sigma, have stood the test of time. The timeless initiatives yield results that client organizations seek. What is less well understood is that leaders of those organizations had recognized their needs and voluntarily sought solutions to the identified problems.

We define a market as mature when leaders (1) are willing to gauge the scope of problems, (2) actively seek solutions, and (3) design and implement programs that directly confront the problems to improve the organization. The current American workplace bullying market is immature with respect to all three criteria. In 2010, a writer for *Bloomberg Businessweek* magazine credited us, the founders of the Workplace Bullying Institute (WBI), with originating the workplace bullying consulting specialization (Morgan, 2010). The writer exaggerated the field's development.

In 1998, we limited our consulting practice to workplace bullying. The work of WBI primarily focused on educating and helping bullied targets. So, we dropped all former consulting processes. Everything we did flowed from, and supported, the emerging social justice movement around workplace bullying. Our consulting principles, too, became target-centric.

American employers have a general aversion to being early adopters of consulting practices in new areas. Workplace bullying qualifies as new, even though researchers have been plumbing its depths since the 1980s (Leymann, 1990). Employers traditionally wait for others to experiment and prove the worth of interventions. But in the case of bullying, leaders are not yet ready to admit or assess the prevalence of bullying within their organizations. We rely on anecdotal evidence to prove the point.

WBI conducts its online research using a proprietary data collection Web site. In 2013, we offered a free online prevalence survey for organizations of any size wishing to assess bullying through a survey of employees (Namie, 2013), and 112 showed interest. We were contacted by representatives from government agencies, medium-size for-profit enterprises, and several large nonprofit organizations. All we required was a signature from a member of their senior leadership team approving the project. Not one contact person, typically in an HR role, was able to win approval! Executives did not want to know the size of the problem, if any, that existed within their ranks.

In fact, the only organizations willing to subject themselves to assessment of bullying prevalence were two public school districts. We attribute their willingness to the fact that they are perhaps the institutions most familiar with being measured and tested in the country.

Leaders rarely seek solutions. That is done by middle-ranking staff who see the harm bullying inflicts on employees. However, if they cannot win either active endorsement or a promise to not interfere from senior leaders, consulting initiatives will fail or have to be partial solutions, at best. This was the theme of our book (Namie & Namie, 2011) that was written to guide well-intentioned internal champions. They face many internal hurdles just to gain acknowledgment that a problem exists.

In 2009, there were two very different depictions of national marketplaces for bullying and mobbing consulting. The German consulting industry was by then well developed with several consulting options available for employers. Practitioners were either focused on mediation, individual coaching, or organization development (Saam, 2009). By comparison, the United States trailed behind German consultants (Namie & Namie, 2009).

In this immature consulting marketplace, consultants themselves must manufacture the need for their services. Executives have to be convinced that it is in their best interests to acknowledge that bullying occurs naturally in nearly every organization without an explicit plan to minimize it. Here are some of the interest-based perspectives used by bullying consultants.

Making the Business Case

The "business" case centers on loss prevention or mitigation. Bullying leads to talent flight by the most-skilled employees. They flee for their health's sake and so do witnesses, the ones who vicariously experience bullying. A review of patterns will spotlight certain units or divisions with disproportionate turnover rates. Those spots are where bullying is most likely occurring. Costs of turnover can be estimated using HR formulas for recruitment and replacement rates (typically a multiple of the displaced person's compensation). Absenteeism costs are easily calculated when attributable to bullying. Increases in insurance premiums for employment practices liability (EPLI), workers' compensation, and disability accompany bullying. Finally, there are legal expenses—mounting case defenses, settlements, damages—that should convince employers that bullies are too expensive to retain.

Of course, the business case assumes that employers are rational actors. Executives, representing employers, should want to minimize losses and maximize profits (or balance limited budgets in cash-strapped government agencies). We have found that few employers are rational in this way. Executives tend to give greater weight to their personal bonds with accused perpetrators than to fiscal matters. That is, the business case falls on mostly deaf ears. It is the duty of the consultant to identify high-ranking individuals in organizations who take their fiduciary responsibility seriously. Risk managers are important allies to consultants in that they know well the losses for which bullies are responsible.

Promoting Health and Safety

Another interest-based appeal is based on the damage bullying causes employee health. Stress-related diseases can develop from long exposure to frequent bullying incidents. Perpetrators' misconduct is a stressor for bullied targets. Therefore, one approach is to identify individuals in organizations responsible for health and safety. Good employers should care.

American employers can be shown that safety is not limited to Occupational Safety and Health Administration (OSHA)–relevant physical safety standards. Employers must comply with regulations related to minimizing employee exposure to hazardous materials (MSDS information sheets must be posted describing the risks of chemical exposure and remedies for exposure). Though no U.S. ergonomic standards were promulgated, employers are familiar with repetitive stress injuries and the need to heal those injuries. Workers' compensation programs readily address broken bones from falls on the job. However, there is a multistate legislative initiative by employers to eliminate job stress as a compensable workers' compensation injury. A 2002 South Australian workplace bullying conference was sponsored by the state workers' compensation board. A board representative opened the conference by reminding attendees that stress claims in that Australian state were uncontested. Quite a contrast.

Bullying-related safety is "psychological safety" (Edmondson, 1999). Workers need to feel free to express themselves without ridicule, threat, or humiliation. Psychological safety involves an equality of participation, allowing colleagues to take risks ("conversational turn taking"), and a high level of social sensitivity to the needs of others. Specifically, psychological safety depends on a workplace climate of interpersonal trust and mutual respect. It is a key ingredient to successful teams in innovative organizations (Duhigg, 2016).

American employers are not accustomed to considering psychological aspects of work. Enlightened European and Australian counterparts have a "duty of care" obligation to ensure safety, both physical and psychological, for their employees. In the United States, job stress is discounted, psychological safety is unknown, and employer accountability for nonphysical injuries is largely absent. This combination of factors makes appeals to health and safety to justify antibullying initiatives difficult.

Aligning Organizational Values and Practices

Appeals to an employer's morality could be made. Religious-based organizations, large health care systems, and universities should be open to challenges to honor their moral pronouncements regarding "respect for all individuals," including employees. Unfortunately, such principled espoused values are rarely enacted in the trenches where bullying occurs. Mission, vision, and value statements do not obligate unscrupulous employers to adhere to principled leadership.

WBI polled bullied targets in an online poll (Namie, 2012d) and asked what would be required for the majority of U.S. employers to take workplace bullying seriously. Forty-two percent of targets did not believe American employers will ever address bullying in their workplaces, either because it serves a purpose or they do not know how to stop it. Another 23 percent believed it will be stopped when employers learn how expensive bullying is (the business case rationale); 4 percent relied on recognition of bullying's immorality to convince employers. Nearly one-third (30%) of targets said employers will respond positively to bullying only when compelled by law to do so.

Assessing Legal Environment

Compliance with state or federal laws does explain the majority of pro-employee action by American employers. Research on bullying and mobbing in the workplace has been known about for 30 years. No significant voluntary U.S. employer action followed. The world's first antimobbing ordinance passed in 1994 in Sweden, with many other industrialized nations adopting laws or occupational health and safety provisions. Canadian provinces passed laws and OHS regulations. Still, American employers have not voluntarily taken action.

Lessons from nondiscrimination policies inform the route to widespread employer adoption: pass laws that trigger policies so that enforcement must follow if legal penalties are to be avoided. The absence of laws allows employers to ignore bullying and mobbing. To date, no law compelling action exists. Details about American efforts to enact much-needed legislation can be found in David Yamada's chapter (chapter 18) in this volume.

Mobilizing Union Support

Unions can provide the impetus for employer action. The strongest example of union-driven change comes from one of the unions for state workers in Minnesota, Minnesota Association of Professional Employees (MAPE). The union discovered that several of their members were suffering the ill effects of bullying. The first ones to report being harmed were clinical psychologists working in state facilities. (WBI started as the result of abuse in an HMO psychiatry clinic.) A business agent sensitive to those members' needs mobilized the union to provide emotional support. A task force formed. Leaders sought education in bullying and mobbing.

More important, MAPE sought to compel the state, as the employer, to collaborate and write an antibullying policy. It took the threat of legislation to convince the state to "voluntarily" cooperate with the union. A policy was written. With much hoopla and support from the governor's office, the policy was launched. Officially, the state adopted an antibullying position in 2015 for all state workers, not just MAPE members. In 2016, MAPE focused its effort on holding the state accountable for promised supervisory training in bullying and policy enforcement. The union-led initiative continues. A vigilant union can push employers to do what they should do voluntarily for the sake of self-interest, loss prevention, employee health and safety, and congruence with espoused values.

Other unions have encouraged their employers to learn about bullying and mobbing in a different way. Joint management-labor committees provide the forum. First, union members educate themselves about bullying. Then, they use regularly scheduled committee meetings to persuade management to take steps to prevent and correct bullying for all of the reasons stated above.

AMERICAN EMPLOYER ATTITUDES AND REACTIONS

WBI had the rare opportunity in 2013 to query 315 U.S. business leaders—owners, administrators, presidents, and vice presidents—about workplace bullying. We used the term *workplace bullying* and defined it parenthetically as abusive conduct, "status-blind harassment" that is currently legal. With respect to question one, in asking these corporate executives (CXOs) their opinion of workplace bullying, 68 percent characterized it as a serious problem, 17 percent had never heard of it, and 15 percent considered it irrelevant because bullying only affects children (Namie, 2013).

The second question we asked the CXOs was what their companies were doing about workplace bullying. Thirty-two percent of executives said nothing was being done because bullying did not occur in their workplaces, 23 percent relied on HR to handle bullying on a case-by-case basis, and 17.5 percent believed there was internal awareness raising being done. Sixteen percent thought their organizations had bullying-specific policies and procedures to address the problem systematically. A dubious response was that 6 percent claimed bullying was a top corporate priority (Namie, 2013).

An illuminating response was that 5 percent of executives claimed to have personally intervened in bullying cases (Namie, 2013). We believe this proportion of reports of bullying incidents rises to the executive team level. The C-suite dwellers (e.g., CEO, COO, CFO, CIO, or CNO) are the most important representatives of employers as institutions. They determine the workplace culture more than others. However, bullied targets most often experience HR as the employer's representative. But HR is not free to act without the guidance of, and approval from, executives. The low rate of executive familiarity with bullying reflects the efficiency of gatekeepers who prevent tales of bullying from becoming known beyond the HR level. It is a disservice to executives to be prevented from learning about the costs—fiscal and human—associated with bullying and mobbing.

Because independent consultants external to organizations are traditionally granted more access than internal staff, an important role for those consultants is to convince senior leadership to take workplace bullying seriously. Education from them is critical. Of course, large organizations have a cadre of internal consultants, often designated as organizational development (OD) specialists. When OD reports to HR, their access to the C-suite can be limited. However, some OD internal consultants do have the ear of executives, and they must convince senior leaders that they alone have the power to launch and guarantee the success of antibullying initiatives. As described above, this model of change and influence assumes that actors are rational. That is not always the case. Resistance to antibullying efforts ensues.

The *2014 WBI U.S. Workplace Bullying Survey* (Namie, 2014) provides another assessment of American employers' reactions to abusive conduct when it is not illegal discrimination. The respondents were adult Americans as part of a stratified random sample that enabled us to generalize the results of all adult Americans. The respondents were clear that employers fail to appropriately react. Denial ("it doesn't happen here," 25% of the sample) and discounting ("describes impact as not serious," 16%) were the most frequent descriptions of employer actions. Next came rationalization at 15 percent ("it's an innocent, routine way of doing business"). Other negative employer reactions to abusive conduct were defending abusive conduct ("when offenders are executives and managers," 11%) and encouraging it ("it is necessary for a competitive organization," 5%). All told, 72 percent of employers' reactions to abusive conduct were described by respondents as negative in nature. Three categories of positive reactions accounted for the other 28 percent of employers' reactions: 12 percent of respondents said employers eliminated abusive conduct ("creates and enforces policies and procedures"); 10 percent acknowledged it ("shows concern for affected workers"); and 6 percent condemned bullying and mobbing ("exercising zero tolerance"; Namie, 2014).

Bullied targets are part of the population of all adult Americans, but their immersion in the phenomenon gives them an unrivaled perspective of what employers are doing. According to a WBI online survey of bullied targets (Namie, 2012b), 30 percent of employers believe that bullying does not happen in their organizations. Note how closely this approximates the opinions of executives about their organizations. Only 12 percent of employers, according to targets, considered it management's responsibility to fix bullying. Sadly, one-quarter of employers (24%) conveyed the message that the targeted individuals themselves were responsible for reversing their plight.

INDIRECT ALTERNATIVES TO WORKPLACE BULLYING CONSULTING

A guiding principle of all consulting, not just for workplace bullying, is that solutions should match the identified problem. An example of a mismatch from the authors' prior consulting experience was an intervention in response to a workplace homicide-suicide by a state worker. The root problem was a cruel manager who had been shuttled to various offices across the state to "clean up" those offices on orders from senior administrators. The appropriate solution would have been to address administrators who treated the state agency as their experimental playground with total disregard for nonsupervisory workers and to have worked with the bullying manager on alternative processes until he either abandoned the cruelty or left the organization. Instead, the agency commissioned training for staff on "dealing with the hostile public client." This was the wrong solution for two reasons. First, it was the wrong target audience. Staff did not contribute to the deadly shooting event. Second, training is an effective solution only when there is deficiency in skills. There may have been a shortage of skills in this case, but it was managerial skill that was lacking.

Misnaming the problem leads to unsatisfactory solutions. In cases of workplace bullying in which several individuals are harmed and deserve relief from psychological violence, wasting time with a solution-problem mismatch precludes saving lives.

We lament that at the time this volume was written, what might be labeled as workplace bullying consulting by trainers, mediators, and consultants is a mislabeling of the problem for which solutions are being provided. Most consultants are delivering the wrong products and processes to adequately attack the root causes of workplace bullying and mobbing. They may be doing this for one or several reasons. Employer reticence or denial makes a direct intervention impossible. Consultants can only sell what client organizations are buying. Most consultants do not have the in-depth knowledge about the work environment factors that foster workplace bullying. So, they deliver what they know, mistakenly believing that bullying can be reduced by indirect approaches.

The simplest and least direct approach involves improving *communication* in the workplace. Of course, communication is important. A great deal of misunderstanding between bosses and subordinates is preventable with the clear and consistent expression of performance expectations. If communication were the only problem in bullying, it could be resolved by teaching supervisors to first identify what it is they need to accomplish. Then they can be taught how to express themselves clearly, with an emphasis that messages have to be consistent with regard to expectations.

Unfortunately, consistency is the antithesis of disparate treatment that characterizes bullying. The targeted workers are deliberately deprived of information. Most perpetrators are excellent communicators. They could do the training. The problem is not a paucity of communication skill, but rather its application in abusive ways that end up dominating individuals. Communication is not the key issue, but more specifically how to make communication about undiscussable issues safe for all employees. Driving out the realistic fear of reprisal for refusing to accept mistreatment that renders one subservient is a goal that communication training insufficiently addresses.

While workplace bullying consulting is a nascent field, *conflict resolution* enjoys a long history of employer acceptance. Conflict is perceived as natural and common within groups and between individuals. Intragroup conflict is addressed through team building and standard leadership training. Part of being a leader is cultivating loyal and engaged followers. Resolving interpersonal conflict, the appearance of which can look very much like dyadic bullying, is a specialty consulting industry with thousands of practitioners. Conflict resolution is the domain of trainers, mediators, arbitration specialists, and attorney-mediators.

There are proponents of mediation (Fox & Stallworth, 2004) who believe that the art of finding middle ground between two parties with intellectual differences is applicable to workplace bullying and mobbing. A working assumption is that reasonable people can hold divergent views. This is a version of the "personality differences" explanation for bullying. Mediation finds solutions by getting past personalities. In bullying cases, one party—the target—may be initially reasonable, but perpetrators seldom are reasonable, rational actors. Individuals willing to abuse their authority (when a boss) or to exploit a peer (when a coworker) do not consider themselves equal to their targets of mistreatment.

Most bullying experts do not approve of mediation as an appropriate or effective tool to deal with bullying. For example, in the definition of bullying for a recent study (Glambek, Skogstad, & Einarsen, 2015), the authors include the following: "It is not bullying when two persons of approximately equal 'strength' are in conflict" (p. 163). Thus, bullying, with its characteristic power differential between the actors, cannot be conflict. An additional reason to discount the conflict resolution toolkit for bullying and mobbing is that they are forms of violence, albeit nonphysical violence. Mediation is not used in domestic violence cases in which the abused spouse is dominated by the other. Neither should mediation be used for abused workers.

At WBI, we receive tales of employer-forced mediation or arbitration. Here's a first-person account of the impact of arbitration on one woman:

> I just finished forced arbitration against my employer for retaliation, harassment, and failure to accommodate. A ruling has not been made. But this system allows for further bullying. My employer's attorney

pulled police reports from over 10 years ago regarding past domestic violence that I had endured. I was forced to read line by line the report and stopped each line by the attorney to ask if it was true. I begged to stop as the bullies smirked while I cried. My attorney tried to stop it but the arbitrator allowed it. He said I had brought the suit against them so my life needs to be an open book. However, the bullies' lives were protected. My employer never once defended what happened to me, they just continued to attack me. The evidence showed that management and HR thought this was all a game. As I had begged my employer for help from the abuse, they forwarded my emails with comments like "for your reading pleasure," which was disgusting. I again was made to feel worthless. I attempted suicide and failed. My health has suffered, my family has suffered, and my financial future has suffered.

Another well-intentioned, but indirect, tack is to mistake bullying and mobbing for *diversity*. Diversity refers to an institutional recognition and valuing of differences across individuals and social groups. In its narrowest view, it pertains to differences by race, sex, disability, age, and other civil rights–based group definitions. Proponents broaden diversity to include differences in life experiences, personalities, and professional disciplines. Inherent in diversity approaches is that differences are positive and strengthen a culture, in the workplace or in society. However, differences also create tensions that can lead to conflict. Bullies and targets could be considered "diverse" with respect to differing attitudes toward violence. Perpetrators employ it, and targets abhor it because they are victimized by it. That difference is so great that it seems diversity hardly applies.

A very public illustration of diversity's misapplication to bullying happened in 2013. Jonathan Martin, a second-year professional football player, walked away from his lucrative NFL career weeks after the season had begun. He voluntarily sought treatment for clinical depression he attributed to an "abusive locker room culture." He bravely discussed bullying by other players as unacceptable. Walking away as he did had never happened before. The sport is a violent one. The stereotype that a "tough guy" with a physique like his—300 pounds and six foot two—should be able to resist and thwart bullying was reinforced by sports reporters, broadcasters, and fans.

One of Martin's perpetrators was publicly identified—Richie Incognito. Martin is African American, and Incognito is white. The public saw race as the cause. The association of team owners, the National Football League (NFL), acted quickly. First, they commissioned a prominent attorney to conduct an investigation. Second, they implemented a solution—mandatory diversity training for coaches and players—a one-hour session. The NFL was content to say that race was the root cause of Martin's mistreatment. Training delivered, and problem solved—or so they thought.

Martin walked away from his team, the Miami Dolphins, in October. The report was issued on February 14, 2014, after the season had concluded. The report contained information with which the authors of this chapter were familiar as the retained experts for Martin in the case. Incognito, the white perpetrator, always had two accomplices, both African American teammates. The problem for Martin was bullying, not racial discrimination or a diversity issue of intolerance of his race. The abuse he keenly felt transcended racial boundaries. It had nothing to do with diversity.

Another consultant mislabeling error when parties are eager to tackle bullying and mobbing is the desire to effect *culture change*. The goal is a long-term project. To stop bullying, there must be a coordinated effort to break the contingency link between abusive actions and positive reinforcement by persons or the institution, whether implicit or explicit. Behaviors that once brought promotions or indifference will now result in bothersome complaints, investigations, and negative consequences. Over time, the culture will change. Consultants who enter organizations proclaiming to change the culture engender resentment and resistance from workers who cling steadfastly to their traditions. We do not reject culture change as inappropriate as much as we question its timing. It is certainly not a quick solution.

We introduce our continuum of negative conduct that first appeared in our book, *The Bully-Free Workplace* (Namie & Namie, 2011). The continuum is a gradient connoting less impactful and less negative behaviors on the left side. The scale begins with minimally bothersome impoliteness. Bullying is nonphysical violence. Physical violence, battery, and homicide fall to the right of it on the continuum. Importantly, incivility and disrespect are placed to the left of bullying, indicating behaviors that are of lower-level impact (see figure 16.1).

Negative Conduct & Impact Continuum

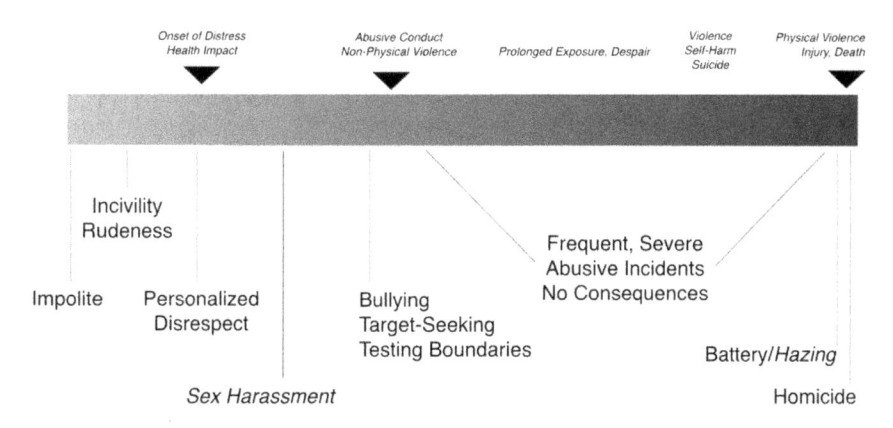

Figure 16.1

Incivility is one phenomenon used interchangeably with bullying and mobbing, as if they are synonyms for the same level of interpersonal exploitation. People behaving in an uncivil manner are rude, boorish, and nonnormative. They violate norms of respect and regard for others. They do not do things the "way we do things here." They are countercultural independent actors. Work groups attempt to bring uncivil workers into the fold informally at first. If resistance to accepting operational norms of conduct continues, attempts to make the person conform are made explicit. Continuing to reject norms leads groups to ostracize uncivil actors.

Incivility is an affront to the group and somewhat impersonal. Andersson and Pearson (1999) defined incivility as "low-intensity deviant behavior" (p. 457). Only 12 percent of workers surveyed considered looking for another job when faced with an uncivil workplace. Its impact on individuals is mild. Incivility authors do not use the terms *bullying* or *mobbing*, though they believe incivility could "spiral" into aggressive behaviors. Bullying is certainly an uncivil act and subsumes incivility, but incivility is not necessarily bullying.

Disrespect is more negative than incivility. It is personalized contempt for other persons. People who disrespect others believe they are superior, suggesting narcissistic tendencies. They disregard the opinions, qualifications, status, reputation, and experience of others. They believe that respect granted by them to others must be earned. To them, respect and dignity are not inherent rights of persons. Bullying is also disrespectful.

Disrespectful negative conduct toward an individual is harmful, primarily because it is aimed directly at someone. It triggers distress. The range of stress-related diseases that accompany the human stress response (think of the fight-or-flight response) becomes possible with disrespectful mistreatment. That is why we indicate the onset of harm above the gradient line in our model.

We pair incivility with disrespect as two subbullying phenomena that American employers will accept. Though both are negative, neither seems to scare away employers. Bullying is denied, discounted, or rationalized as described above. But policies proscribing uncivil or disrespectful conduct abound. It is common for employers to choose the positive valence. Policies encourage civil or respectful workplaces. Because incivility and disrespect are accepted and attempts to ameliorate bullying resisted, we consider the two benign labels as inappropriate substitutions for bullying and mobbing. If employers adopt such policies, they are stopping short of addressing the more serious problem of bullying.

On our continuum, we insert *sexual harassment* to the left of bullying, making sexual harassment less severe than bullying. We learned from the WBI *2007 U.S. Workplace Bullying Survey* (Namie, 2007) that 20 percent of bullying cases also had an illegal form of harassment present. In other words, targets could have complained to their employers about violations of nondiscrimination policies. It is a misnomer to say that bullying is not serious unless it rises to the level of illegal harassment. Findings from a meta-analysis of 112 studies suggest that health harm (anger and anxiety) from bullying is more damaging to affected individuals than harm from illegal sexual harassment (Hershcovis & Barling, 2010). The construct for this study was *workplace aggression*, defined as the combination of incivility, bullying, and interpersonal conflict. Workers aggressed against were also more likely to quit.

In a similar, but single-sample study, Rospenda, Richman, and Shannon (2009) found that *generalized workplace harassment* (GWH) approximated bullying with one exception. GWH included verbal aggression, disrespectful behavior, isolation or exclusion, threats, and physical aggression (the exception). GWH was more prevalent than sexual harassment (60% vs. 40% for men; 60% vs. 50% for women). Also, GWH negatively impacted the mental health of affected individuals more than sexual harassment. Based on these studies of relative harm and WBI anecdotal cases, we placed sexual harassment to the left of bullying on our continuum.

The process of bullying and mobbing begins with perpetrators testing boundaries of potential targets to find those unable to defend themselves. After the target is selected, two properties of the experience then determine the severity of harm inflicted on the target: the frequency of negative incidents and their duration. Mildly or moderately negative incidents cause harm if they are too frequently endured over too long a period of time. Harm derives from prolonged exposure. Leymann (1990) set the stage for the academic operational definition of mobbing and bullying by stipulating that two negative acts per week must be experienced for at least six continuous months. Later, Einarsen and Hoel (2001) developed the 22-item checklist of behaviors to be subjected, which requires both criteria of frequency and duration to score a person as having been bullied. The instrument is the Negative Acts Questionnaire (NAQ).

After sufficient exposure, and depending on individual coping strategies, the bullying becomes abusive. With unremitting exposure and no institutional resolution, the bullying and mobbing drives targets to despair. Slightly less than one-third of targets consider suicide (Namie, 2012c), and 16 percent actually devise a plan to take their lives. Suicide is violence turned inward. And a longitudinal study demonstrated the perseverance of bullying's destructive effect on targets; five years afterward, having experienced bullying doubled the risk of suicidal ideation (Nielsen, Nielsen, Notelaers, & Einarsen, 2015). Less than one-quarter of targets consider directing violence toward others at work (Namie, 2003).

The reader can see how incivility is far removed from suicidal ideation and severe stress-related health consequences associated with bullying. The small number of workers who consider changing jobs because of incivility pales in comparison to the 77 percent of bullied targets who lose their jobs from bullying in order to make it stop (Namie, 2012a).

In summary, the ability to eradicate bullying depends on the clarity of defining the problem and applying the correct interventions. Emphases on communication, conflict, diversity, incivility, or disrespect mislead both the consultant and client organization. Chances of success are greatly diminished using these approaches.

A REQUISITE POLICY

Consultants can agree, regardless of their academic and organizational experiences, that employers wishing to reduce or eliminate bullying and mobbing have to create a set of behavioral standards. Those standards act as the "line in the sand" across which employees must not cross. After the standards are communicated as expectations for employees, no one has the right to feign ignorance of the new rules.

To convey commitment to stop bullying, employers should create a policy that obligates them to protect employees from abusive conduct on the job. Of course, for some employers, the obligation is unappealing when neither state nor federal laws force or encourage them to do anything. Employers who voluntarily create workplace bullying policies are early adopters, the pioneers. One of the first decisions is whether to write a stand-alone bullying-specific policy or to meld it with existing policies. The two that could incorporate bullying and mobbing are the nondiscrimination and antiviolence policies.

All nondiscrimination policies describe categories of protected status group members as defined by state laws. State laws supplement the federal civil rights statutes. For instance, sexual orientation or marital status may be protected in a particular state, whereas federal law does not cover either. To be sure, discrimination is illegal. Employers minimize their exposure to liability by automatically launching investigations following complaints of discrimination or harassment. This happens even when the employee does not want the reprisal for filing a complaint. The process moves forward without the complainant's approval. No state currently has a legal standard against bullying that poses the risk of vicarious liability for employers. Therefore, employers may treat bullying differently than discrimination or harassment. They may state that they treat bullying as seriously as they do illegal misconduct, but they need not do so. Bullying complaints can be handled with more flexibility. By flexibility, we do not mean that complaints should be treated with indifference. Rather, innovative ways can be devised to protect individuals from retaliation by perpetrators for merely seeking help.

Confusion is inherent when combining nondiscrimination with bullying in a single policy. Bullying crosses intergroup boundaries that define protected classes of workers. Also, the mix of illegality and legality sends a mixed message to employees. It is perceived that bullying is not as serious as harassment because of its legality.

In 2014, California passed AB 2053, legislation that blended bullying (abusive conduct) with sexual harassment. All employers with 50 or more employees are required to biannually provide training for their supervisors on harassment and abusive conduct. No other mandate applies.

Violence prevention policies can be amended to include language specific to bullying and mobbing. It is a natural fit, given that bullying is a nonphysical form of workplace violence. Many current policies address verbal abuse and threatening behavior (without requiring specific utterances). To be thorough, employers should add ostracism and social exclusion, interference with work processes, and humiliation in private or public settings. The risk posed by merging bullying with violence policies is that employers typically include a "zero tolerance." In practice, few offenders are terminated after the first violation. Employees do not believe there is no tolerance for violence.

For bullying incidents, the consultant would guide employers to allow confirmed violators to change their workplace behavior and not repeat the misconduct. Bullying has historically been reinforced. It takes time for individuals and, thus, the organization to learn new ways to interact with one another. And people deserve the chance to demonstrate changed behavior. One of the fads from yesteryear was the "learning organization." The concept applies to bullying. Much relearning must be done. Zero tolerance has no place. Neither does an overindulgence by allowing five or more confirmed violations by a single perpetrator to occur without termination. In unionized workplaces operating with collective bargaining agreements, progressive disciplinary steps can allow for the retention of bullies, which sustains the harm they cause.

We prefer to collaboratively create a stand-alone policy with client organizations. Employers show a stronger commitment when bullying is not rolled into other policies. Do not use a boilerplate tear sheet. One nonspecific document does not fit all organizations.

Here are key features of ideal policies to adequately address bullying and mobbing:

- Designate a writing group that includes all ranks and disciplines in the organization. The added benefit of the group process is the in-depth discussions over values that emerge when the group invents corrective procedures. The task is too important to trust to HR acting alone.
- Include legal and any department that must approve policies before implementation. Have those individuals at the table so there is little to no postwriting review required.
- Prepare for the real-time writing task by having terms and language from other known policies.

- Choose what "IT" is: abusive conduct, psychological violence, or workplace bullying. Decide while considering the impact of the term on the future use and credibility of the policy. The label is less important than the details and enforcement procedures you create.
- Declare a level of organizational commitment—aspirational? a guarantee?
- Clearly define it. Abusive conduct is definable. Those who say it is impossible are defenders of the abuse.
- Provide organization-specific illustrations.
- Distinguish it from conduct described in other policies and cite those policies.
- State what it is not. For instance, it is not a credible use of the new policy for an employee unhappy with a performance evaluation to claim "bullying."
- Determine adverse consequences to the complainant required for formal complaint filing.
- Protect the integrity of the policy. What constitutes its abuse?
- Specify new managerial responsibilities for when bullying is seen or reported.
- Ensure that all employees at all levels are held accountable to the standards.
- Make retaliation a separable offense.
- Invent a response system to reports of bullying. What was the time line? Who is involved?
- Devise a system of informal solutions (no mediation) that is perhaps mandated before formal complaints can be filed.
- Engage union stewards and representatives in solution processes, if a union is present.
- Assign greater weight to repeat offenders. Have a tiered system of consequences.
- Choose a maximum number of confirmed violations for one person before termination.
- Design innovative remedies. Focus more on restorative justice (healing for individuals and the affected team; see chapter 12) than punishment.
- How will abused employees be made safe during investigations?
- Who and how many should investigate?
- How will uncooperative witnesses be incentivized to participate in investigations (not by mandating it in the policy)?
- Consider revisions to notifications about outcomes and remedies to increase employee trust in the adjudication system. What is the benefit and the cost of secrecy?
- Which individuals or group will be ambassadors of the policy and the larger antibullying initiative?

After the policy and procedures are crafted, all employees need to be educated. Topics include the rationale for, and purpose of, the policy, key features, protections for abused workers, and help available for all affected individuals (including policy violators). Separate supplemental education for supervisors and managers can identify and overcome skill deficiencies that may have led to the bullying. Also, supervisors and managers learn of their new responsibilities and are given tutorials (best coupled with mentoring) on how to recognize the early signs of bullying and how to intervene in internecine team bullying situations.

Employees will perceive the policy as credible and fair only if it is consistently enforced. There must be an end to case-by-case solutions. Though flexibility sounds positive, it is the route to favoritism. Perpetrators made powerful by protection from executive sponsors are rarely held accountable in traditional HR-run complaint systems. Frankly, HR staff lack the authority to enforce above their organizational rank.

In the new policy, everyone, regardless of rank or relationships, needs to be subject to scrutiny. The policy is not owned by HR, nor was it produced by HR. Senior-level administrators were part of the writing group. No one should be immune from adherence to the behavioral standards. If exceptions to the policy become habit, employees will learn about it, and the policy will be effectively undermined.

The authors are often asked to review newly written policies. Few are complete. There are always loopholes through which accused offenders may escape. It would be best to treat every policy as a draft subject to revision after some months of use. Policies that do a poor job of making bullied targets safe are typically biased in favor of protecting the organization. Pending revisions, institutions can exert leverage over offenders by using the same vague language. For example, there is an explicit or implied threat to the organization's "legitimate business interests" that is prohibited. This justifies the organization's investigation of claims of bullying. Perpetrators serve their own personal interest, often in opposition to the needs of the organization. A weak policy can be used to protect the organization from sabotage and secondarily make the bullied target whole again and safe.

Though a policy and its faithful enforcement are necessary for any antibullying consultation, they are not sufficient alone. Bullying is systemic in its origins and effects. Solutions need to be systemic also.

GOAL: A COMPREHENSIVE APPROACH TO WORKPLACE BULLYING SOLUTIONS

This section is a goal, a hypothetical or an ideal intervention. For all of the reasons described in this chapter that lead employers to prefer misdirected or partial solutions, the comprehensive solution is rare.

It is assumed that someone believes that the organization needs to address bullying and mobbing. With luck, other like-minded individuals meet regularly to plot and plan a campaign to introduce an intervention. During this preliminary stage, the internal champions and advocates need to educate themselves. The authors have written a book just for this purpose as a guide to obstacles ahead (Namie & Namie, 2011).

Here are the components of a comprehensive approach for what the authors call the WBI Blueprint. The sequence is important, not invariant, but critical. For example, training delivered before organizational readiness can undermine trust and credibility.

1. Prevalence assessment. This is the true starting point. Metrics replace worst-case fears about how common bullying is within the organization. Grant anonymity, but do drill down to unit levels to discover troubled areas.
2. Briefings for executives. As described in this chapter, their support is imperative.
3. Brief union officers. As with executives, complete cooperation is imperative. Assurances to not supersede bargaining agreement terms must be made.
4. Create policy and procedures. Details are found elsewhere in this chapter about the collaborative process. There will be both informal and formal complaint procedures.
5. Identify and screen a team of employee volunteers. These volunteers are willing to serve colleagues with clarification about bullying experiences, interpretations of the policy, referrals to mental health providers, information about other internal policies and laws, and education for all staff and management, and they serve as ambassadors for the antibullying initiative.
6. Train the expert peer team in all aspects of the workplace bullying phenomenon. WBI provides this training through their program: Workplace Bullying University.
7. Schedule the program rollout: managers first, then all staff. In large organizations, consider pilot rollout in a single division or department before system-wide dissemination.
8. Prepare an educational blitz. Use an intranet Web site for remote education. Tape online courses. Tape senior leaders' commitment to the program, pledging to enforce the policy.
9. Deliver standard, but needed, supervisory training modules before engaging them with antibullying training. Thereafter, integrate methods of nonabusive management practices with all management development programs.

10. Integrate behavioral standards from the policy with performance evaluation instruments. Now that abusive conduct is unacceptable, hold individuals at all levels accountable.
11. Revise hiring criteria based on recommendations from an expert team of peers, your organization's experts in bullying and mobbing. Stop hiring brilliant but cruel individuals. Find brilliant and respectful employees. Build bullying into orientation for new hires.
12. Now introduce the policy and bullying to the organization. Teach early recognition. Encourage coworker intervention. Make the workplace safe from retaliation.
13. In six months, reassess prevalence and trouble spots.
14. In one year, revisit the efficacy of the policy. Has enforcement been consistent and applied at all levels of the organization? Revise as necessary.

THE REALITY OF INCOMPLETE INITIATIVES

Earlier in this chapter, we described the problem of mislabeling the problem of bullying and mobbing that can lead to inappropriate programs that do not reverse the problem. Now we will review some of the appropriate, but incomplete, activities undertaken by consultants. They can move organizations forward in their quest to eliminate the problem.

First, organizations must choose whether to attack people or the system of reinforcement that sustains bullying. We have learned from our 19 years of specialized consulting in workplace bullying (and the 32 years of consulting in total) to ask more questions of clients than to dictate rigid programs or approaches. One of the first questions to clients seeking to reduce bullying and mobbing in their organizations is whether they want to focus on individual perpetrators or the toxic work environment that spawned the bullying.

The obsession with personality as the principal causal factor comes naturally to Americans. We have an individualistic culture. We cannot ignore celebrities, regardless of the source of their fame. So, we are prone to what social psychologists call the *fundamental attribution error* (Jones, 1979). External observers of events, such as bullying, tend to explain events as the sole responsibility of the actors observed. We cannot see past the personalities. Bullies are cruel, and targets are weak. This is rarely true, but it is the preferred, automatic perception.

From the targets' perspective, it is the work environment that is responsible for their misery. The perpetrators or team are part of that external world, as is the failure of the institution to respond as expected, to provide safety and requested relief. Observers—investigators, bullies, supporters of the bullies—fault internal dispositional factors of targets. Actors—targets themselves—rightly see the social system as responsible.

This divergence in attributional explanations for bullying helps the consultant see why employers, led by HR recommendations, historically rely on anger management education for accused bullies. The high failure rate for these costly interventions stems from the relative permanence of adult human personalities. People rarely change their life philosophies and belief structures honed over a lifetime. Hoping anger classes will convince bullies to change their interpersonal style is a fool's errand.

To paraphrase a former president's election slogan, it's the environment, stupid! It is managers and leaders who contract for consulting services. It is their perception of needs that dictates solutions. The management group is part of the harmful environment targets perceive so readily. The management group rarely tells consultants to change how they react to bullying, perpetrators, and targets. The responsibility to lead decision makers to insights about their role in the problem is the task of an ethical consultant. Of course, one has to be willing to offend a potential client and lose the prospects of a contract. But managers need convincing that personality-driven solutions to bullying will be expensive and fail. In the business, we call them "Band-aid" short-term fixes.

Another common error made by well-intentioned consultants is to "raise awareness" about bullying and mobbing in organizations that lack any system to address it. If the consultant is an articulate and inspirational trainer, the targets in the audience of employees will hear the validating message that the abusive conduct they face is not their fault. They will learn the statistical prevalence showing they are not alone in suffering. At the session's conclusion, targets will approach the managerial or HR hosts and question what their organization is doing to stop the bullying. To whom do targets complain? What will happen to those complaints? Have managers been told to banish the bullies? What does senior leadership think about the information shared?

As we outlined in the WBI Blueprint, sequencing is important. Policy and procedures should precede education to avoid the above questions. The concern is not simply that unanswerable questions will be asked, but that the organization appears feckless and unprepared. The ostensible generosity of management to start the discussion about bullying with staff backfires. It appears more cruel when services are implied but not delivered.

As always, it is the consultant's responsibility to not schedule such sessions in organizations before the organizations are ready for the messages. We have refused contracts over the years to avoid the quandary of "raising awareness." We advise other consultants to do the same.

A third type of incomplete initiative is to focus solely on managerial perpetrators. Employers who prefer the dispositional view of bullying and who believe that by fixing perpetrators the bullying problems will be solved may prefer this partial solution. Crawshaw (2007), author of the book *Taming the Abrasive Manager,* is a proponent of an approach that mainly focuses on working with managers. Essentially, this is a repackaging of the "difficult person" training approach to change management. However, abrasive managers are different from abusive managers. They are uncivil. They are rational and can be reasoned with. We agree that abrasive managers deserve coaching. The key point remains that abrasive managers and perpetrators of workplace abusiveness are not the same. Employers are not as threatened by accusations of abrasiveness as they are by perpetrators on the payroll who are abusing other employees.

Finally, kudos to our colleague Loraleigh Keashly (see chapter 2 and chapter 22) who applies her expertise as a social psychologist to mobilizing teams of coworkers to actively intervene in workplace bullying and mobbing incidents. Ever since pioneering research demonstrated the reluctance of witnesses to get involved in attacks on others, the bystander effect has explained the inactivity of coworkers in bullying situations. In fact, inactivity, the apparent act of doing nothing, provides perpetrators with tacit support and encouragement. Doing nothing is taking sides.

WBI research on the perceptions of bullied targets about what their witnessing coworkers do (Namie, 2008) supported the stereotype that coworkers hurt more than they help. In less than 1 percent of bullying cases, coworkers banded together with targets to confront the bully together and stop the bullying. Over one-third (35.5%) offered either specific advice or moral support to targets. Sixteen percent did nothing. Sadly, nearly half took actions against targets (45.6%), up to and including aggressing against the target on behalf of the bully. Any early intervention at the source of the bullying that reverses coworker hostility could preclude the need for employer policies.

FRAGILITY OF THE COMMITMENT TO CHANGE

The authors have watched and waited as internal champions of antibullying initiatives in organizations took months or years to win support for their pleas to take action. Most champions in American organizations are denied. This likely will not change until state laws force reluctant employers to pay attention. It is hard work to employ one or more of the arguments described in an earlier section to convince C-suite dwellers that most bullying is costly and preventable. Killing existing programs is quicker and easier. We have seen good programs die. We external consultants have been witnesses powerless to stop it.

An extreme illustration of failure is our engagement with a large government agency whose sole purpose was to support low-income families through the prevention of familial abuse. The client's mission was antiabuse. The marriage of an internal antiabuse program for staff with their mission seemed ideal. The new policy was written. A team of 30 internal experts were assembled for their training. Most members were mental health professionals experienced in the principles of abusive conduct and traumatization of victims. They readily translated the facets of adult abuse tactics to their lived experiences as employees. The team devised an elaborate system to provide emotional support to bullied peers as well as to educate them about how workplace bullying interfered with delivery of their critical services to families.

At the end of the team training, on day three, at the end of the day just prior to adjourning, the HR director stopped by. The team was eager to brief her on all they had accomplished and what lay ahead in the agency's bright future. When she heard the first few details, she exploded with rage. She screamed that they had no right to do all that they had done. Of course, we had facilitated that progress. We explained that the terms of the contract had been honored. The agency got what it signed up for. To the chagrin of everyone in the room, the HR director disbanded the group on the spot. In one emotional moment, she undid the hopes of the entire team. We have never seen such a swift ending to good work and good intentions to help abused workers.

Another example of disappearing an initiative comes from a university teaching hospital client. Prior to the beginning of our contract to deliver the full WBI Blueprint set of services, it had taken internal advocates three years to gain approval to "do something." The appointment of a new chief nursing officer broke resistance. We were invited in. We targeted one department as the pilot program site. They wrote a policy, with a commitment to disseminate system-wide after the pilot. A team of 35 experts were trained. Services for targeted colleagues were devised. New innovative remedies put healing ahead of punishment for offenders. Overall, the program was health-oriented. We spent several months on-site to oversee every step of implementation. They videotaped us delivering the first education sessions for nurses, technical staff, support staff, and physicians. We briefed all administrators.

In an unrelated activity in the same city, one of the authors was deposed as an expert witness for a lawsuit brought against a prominent cardiovascular surgeon. The surgeon did not work for or practice medicine at our client hospital system. He was questioned about any relationships with any health care providers in the region. The client was named. Within two weeks, all work ceased. Scheduled trips were canceled. The client broke our contract by halting the initiative. Representatives with whom we had grown close stipulated that they would deny that prior contracts existed or that the work (including videotaped sessions) ever occurred. For some reason, out of some misguided sense of loyalty to a surgeon who did not work for them, thousands of workers, hundreds of whom were abused, were denied the services we and the internal team had created for them. This was a most irrational decision, proving how irrational defending abuse can be.

Another demonstration of the fragility of antibullying initiatives is the death of programs that accompany executive transitions. It takes years to convince CEOs of the benefits from directly addressing bullying and mobbing. Once they are convinced, they can be effective advocates for the program. We have had two top executives sit on the policy-writing group and see the process from the beginning. They then assisted the launch of the initiatives' education phase by appearing in-person, when possible, or by video. They were truly champions. True culture change had begun as they began to purge offenders from the ranks of senior executives. However, at one of the client companies, all the good work was erased with the hiring of a new CEO. Though a cadre of executive team members was part of the antibullying program, they chose to not assert themselves to save the program. The new CEO, as king, felt entitled to make a unilateral decision. And decide he did. The program disappeared overnight.

We have two suggestions to make a successful antibullying initiative sustainable. First, the signature component of the WBI Blueprint system is the training of a team of internal experts. That team needs to have its own succession plan. They need to train future generations of involved team members. A generation should last no more than two or three years. Swift turnover protects members from burnout. It also brings in several new members quickly. The rotation makes it more likely that any single employee will be no more removed from the antibullying initiative than one or two friends. Over time, the message that abusive conduct is unacceptable is not a remote pronouncement. Instead, it becomes the lived experience of an increasing number of employees. Critical mass is attainable so that perpetrators and their allies become the shunned minority, with numbers dwindling to extinction. Then, short of a radical CEO reversing years of work, the workplace culture has a sufficient number of champions to sustain practices across changes in leadership.

We take a second route to sustainability when we implore client organizations to form the expert peer team. The team itself extends engagement beyond HR. Companies and agencies with which we have never worked frequently vest all power to deal with bullying and mobbing in the HR department. Those organizations see bullying as an HR-level concern. It is not. Only executive leadership sets the tone for workplace culture, not HR. Because bullying is so pervasive and many perpetrators outrank HR, we turn to leadership to deal with bullying. Only they can authorize the changes necessary to prevent and correct bullying.

Our deployment of the team of experts wrests control from HR. Representatives from HR may participate in policy writing, but not be its sole source.

HR can be on the expert team, but not be the majority (or chair, director, or administrator). HR has roles. They include record keeping, dealing with the tracking of formal complaints, and meting out justice after investigations.

We distribute power over the spirit and labor of the antibullying initiative to members of the expert team. The decisions we share as consultants with the expert team are intended to dilute the management support bias that HR brings to all endeavors. Antiabuse champions cannot be uncritical supporters of the group that provides the majority of perpetrators. Breaking, or weakening, the HR-management link may allow the expert team greater independence. With respect to sustainability, the greater the autonomy of the expert team, the longer the program may endure, despite changes in the C-suite.

EMERGENT UNION INTEREST

Unions are organizations, just like employers. They have an executive team (the E-Board), but it is elected by membership. They have middle managers and business agents. Union counterparts to first-line supervisors are stewards, with the exception that they are volunteers, with the principal job of assisting union members in disputes with nonunion members, typically managers. In some unions, members are also managers and supervisors.

Union officers often rise to the top thanks to the reputations they built as effective fighters for justice for members. It is noble work. It can toughen leaders to the point they either cannot or will not recognize that some members are not as rock hard as they. Tough union leaders can be as reluctant as stubborn corporate executives or government agency administrators to believe bullying and mobbing are real problems within their organizations.

The dwindling American unionization rate is the result of 40 years of relentless attacks on public sector unions by antiunion political factions. Those attacks push unions into survival mode. When crises are existential, asking to help members being bullied is not a top priority.

Another stumbling block for American unions was the mantra that when the bullies were union members, the union had to defend them. Member-on-member bullying paralyzes unions. We learned from the best union leaders familiar with bullying, Carol Fehner of AFGE (see chapter 10) and Greg Sorozan of NAGE/SEIU (see chapter 23), that the proper union role is to represent members. Stewards and representatives are required to ensure that employers adhere to contract provisions with respect to all members. Yes, bullies must be represented. Defending them is the job of attorneys. It is a false equivalence for unions to treat abusive and abused members equally. Each class of members needs help, but the assistance is very different. When target-members see the union supporting their abuser, they feel betrayed by the union.

When the abuser is a union member, the union has the opportunity to discover the hidden motives behind the mistreatment. As a friend, the designated union representative can dig into the person's past and present life stressors to be able to offer help to alleviate the strain. This is not possible when it is a supervisor nonmember. The abused target-member also needs help, but that is more obvious.

In the early years of the movement (begun in 1997), there was little interest in antibullying services for American unions for the reasons mentioned. The union of federal workers, AFGE, was the exception. However, Canadian unions were not resistant. They frequently sought our training services. Canadian unions mirrored the pioneering work of U.K. unions that assumed leadership of the antibullying movement with the passing of pioneer Andrea Adams in the mid-1990s.

Now with the U.S. movement in its 20th year, and employer interest in stopping workplace bullying and mobbing still rare, unions are awakening to the need to care for their abused target-members. In the early part of this chapter, we described the work of MAPE, the union of Minnesota state workers. Their commitment to a workplace bullying internal initiative was driven by the discovery that several of their members were suffering ill effects. One special business agent was the catalyst. She surrounded herself with supportive members on a task force. In turn, the task force identified more champions, called regional leads. The leads receive education and a compliance toolkit to ensure that the state, as the employer, honored the new policy that MAPE compelled them to write. When this chapter was written, the state was inconsistently applying the policy and refusing to educate the workforce. MAPE, on behalf of all state employees—members and nonmembers alike— is a relentless advocate for workers bullied and mobbed at work. They are a model of what union action can do when employers do not care.

WHEN COURTS ARE THE CLIENT

We end the chapter with a brief description of a much different type of consulting—expert witness services that educate state and federal courts about bullying and mobbing. At least three authors of various chapters in this volume have delivered these services.

There is no legal standard regarding bullying or mobbing in the United States. Therefore, the cases with which a bullying expert can be involved necessarily have an oblique relationship to bullying, at best. Of the nearly 40 cases for the authors, most have involved charges of discrimination, and intentional infliction of emotional distress (IIED; see chapter 18) often plays a part because of the adverse health consequences of bullying. Targets develop stress-related diseases. Licensed clinical psychologists (PhD), psychiatrists

(MD), and other licensed mental health practitioners can testify either as providers of treatment to target-plaintiffs or in a more general way describing those effects.

Rule 702 of the Federal Rules of Evidence, Article VII, states a witness is qualified as an expert by knowledge, skill, experience, training, or education. Experts may give an opinion if the specialized knowledge helps the court understand the evidence or to determine a fact in issue; and the testimony is based on sufficient facts or data; and the testimony is the product of reliable principles and methods; and the expert has reliably applied the principles and methods to the facts of the case.

One of the author's proudly testified at what was dubbed the "first bullying trial" in the United States, in Indiana state court in 2005. The relevant charge was emotional distress of the plaintiff, but the charge was dropped after testimony. The jury award for the plaintiff was based on an assault charge for which my testimony was irrelevant. Nevertheless, the defendant was successful in appellate court. The Indiana Supreme Court reversed the appeal and affirmed the trial court verdict in 2008. Testimony of the so-called workplace bullying expert Gary Namie figured prominently in arguments in both the appellate and Supreme Court. When the defendant's counsel challenged the existence of workplace bullying, Chief Justice Sullivan countered with the question, "Counsel, haven't we all been in third grade?" This is from the court's written decision:

> The phrase "workplace bullying," like other general terms used to characterize a person's behavior, is an entirely appropriate consideration in determining the issues before the jury. As evidenced by the trial court's questions to counsel during pre-trial proceedings, workplace bullying could "be considered a form of intentional infliction of emotional distress." (*Raess v. Doescher*, 2008, p. 10)

Bullied targets, in an infinitesimally small number of cases, become plaintiffs seeking redress against their employer in civil court. It is they who request help in explaining to courts (either juries or judges in bench trials) the sometimes baffling behavioral choices targets make when they are under assault from perpetrators. The unhelpful actions of coworkers are also counterintuitive and need to be understood.

In a recent case, the expert used his experience as a former professor of management to comment on best practices that the employer did not employ. With his expertise in bullying, he described to the jury the harm from the deprivation of the plaintiff's "psychological safety." The jurors awarded the target-plaintiff $1.1 million (Smith, 2016).

Defense attorneys also call for expert witness services. When organizations do the right thing and purge destructive perpetrators, they also require the services of the bullying expert. This expert testified at an on-campus committee hearing to remove a 22-year tenured professor. He was terminated. He sued the university, and the expert provided an opinion justifying the termination. The university prevailed in court.

In another case, a state department of corrections required help defending its termination of three officers. The officers had tormented a fellow officer who had transferred to their facility after 20 years working elsewhere. He was driven to take his life. The expert explained at a reinstatement hearing for the officers how this could happen to an adult. Only one worker returned to work.

For a large multinational corporation, the expert provided an opinion for the defense supporting the severing of a relationship with an entrepreneur. It was a complicated merger and acquisitions case replete with contractual issues. However, it was the destructive sabotaging behavior of the seller and his effect on others that warranted elaboration.

In the most unique situation, this expert was called upon to educate not a court, but the National Football League. A second-year player rather famously walked away from his team, alleging an abusive locker room. This expert provided a tutorial on how young strong males can experience abusive conduct and lack the ability to thwart the assaults from fellow players. The recipient of the tutorial was the high-profile attorney tasked with investigating the case and preparing a final report for the NFL. The report reflected an understanding that "even the largest, strongest and fleetest person may be driven to despair by bullying, taunting and constant insults" (Wells, 2014, p. 140).

CONCLUSION

In this chapter, we have looked at the role of consultants, discussed and critiqued different consulting approaches, offered a suggested template for those doing organizational consulting on bullying and mobbing behaviors, and shared some of our own experiences in doing this work. We described, in some detail, key consulting pitfalls to avoid; namely, problem-solution mismatch, poor sequencing of consulting activities, and focusing only on perpetrators instead of on the organization system-wide. Although it feels like we have been at this for a long time, as we suggested earlier, the world of consulting for bullying and mobbing is in its infancy. We imagine that future commentaries about it will incorporate progress made and insights gained. We hope that this chapter offers a good place from which to start.

REFERENCES

Andersson, L. M., & Pearson, C. M. (1999). Tit for tat? The spiraling effect of incivility in the workplace. *Academy of Management Review, 24*(3), 452–471.

Crawshaw, L. (2007). *Taming the abrasive manager: How to end unnecessary roughness in the workplace*. Hoboken, NJ: Jossey-Bass.

Duhigg, C. (2016, February 25). What Google learned from its quest to build the perfect team. *New York Times Magazine*. Retrieved from http://www.nytimes.com/2016/02/28/magazine/what-google-learned-from-its-quest-to-build-the-perfect-team.html

Edmondson, A. (1999). Psychological safety and learning behavior in work teams. *Administrative Review, 44*(2), 350–383.

Einarsen, S., & Hoel, H. (2001, May 16–19). *The negative acts questionnaire: Development, validation and revision of a measure of bullying at work*. Paper presented at the 10th European Congress on Work and Organisational Psychology, Prague, Czech Republic.

Fox, S., & Stallworth, L. E. (2004). Employee perceptions of internal conflict management and ADR processes in preventing and resolving incidents of workplace bullying: Ethical challenges for decision-makers in organizations. *Employee Rights and Employment Policy Journal of Chicago-Kent College of Law, 8*, 375–405.

Glambek, M., Skogstad, A., & Einarsen, S. (2015). Take it or leave: A five-year prospective study of workplace bullying and indicators of expulsion in working life. *Industrial Health, 53*, 160–170.

Hershcovis, M. S., & Barling, J. (2010). Comparing victim attributions and outcomes for workplace aggression and sexual harassment. *Journal of Applied Psychology, 95*, 874–888.

Jones, E. E. (1979). The rocky road from acts to dispositions. *American Psychologist, 34*(2), 107–117.

Leymann, H. (1990). Mobbing and psychological terrorization. *Violence and Victims, 5*(2), 119–126.

Morgan, S. (2010, November 7). The office-bully mogul. *Bloomberg Businessweek,4202*, 75–77.

Namie, G. M. (2003). *Report on abusive workplaces*. Retrieved from http://www.workplacebullying.org/multi/pdf/N-N-2003C.pdf

Namie, G. M. (2007). *WBI 2007 U.S. workplace bullying survey*. Retrieved from http://workplacebullying.org/multi/pdf/WBIsurvey2007.pdf

Namie, G. M. (2008). *How coworkers respond to workplace bullying*. Retrieved from http://www.workplacebullying.org/multi/pdf/N-N-2008A.pdf

Namie, G. M. (2012a). *Effectiveness of bullied target resolution strategies*. Retrieved from http://www.workplacebullying.org/multi/pdf/WBI-2012-StrategiesEff.pdf

Namie, G. M. (2012b). *Employers' attitudes toward responsibility for solving the workplace bullying problem*. Retrieved from http://www.workplacebullying.org/multi/pdf/WBI-2012-IP-E.pdf

Namie, G. M. (2012c). *Impact of workplace bullying on individuals' health*. Retrieved from http://www.workplacebullying.org/multi/pdf/WBI-2012-IP-D.pdf

Namie, G. M. (2012d). *U.S. employers stopping workplace bullying: When and why?* Retrieved from http://www.workplacebullying.org/multi/pdf/WBI-2012-IP-G.pdf

Namie, G. M. (2013). *Workplace bullying from the perspective of U.S. business leaders*. Retrieved from http://workplacebullying.org/multi/pdf/2013-WBI-Z-BL.pdf

Namie, G. M. (2014). *2014 WBI U.S. workplace bullying survey*. Retrieved from http://workplacebullying.org/multi/pdf/WBI-2014-US-Survey.pdf

Namie, G. M., & Namie, R. (2009). U.S. workplace bullying consulting: Some basic considerations and consultation interventions. *Consulting Psychology Journal, 61*(3), 22–219.

Namie, G. M., & Namie, R. (2011). *The bully-free workplace: Stop jerks, weasels and snakes from killing your organization*. Hoboken, NJ: John Wiley & Sons.

Nielsen, M. B., Nielsen, G. H., Notelaers, G., & Einarsen, S. (2015). Workplace bullying and suicidal ideation: A 3-wave longitudinal Norwegian study. *American Journal of Public Health, 105*(11), e23–e28.

Raess v. Doescher, 883 NE 2d 790 (Ind. 2008).

Rospenda, K. M., Richman, J. A., & Shannon, C. A. (2009). Prevalence and mental health correlates of harassment and discrimination in the workplace. *Journal of Interpersonal Violence, 24*(5), 819–843.

Saam, N. J. (2009). Interventions in workplace bullying: A multilevel approach. *European Journal of Work and Organizational Psychology, 19*(1), 51–75. doi:10.1080/13594320802651403

Smith, D. (2016, July 28). Former Folsom prison dental assistant awarded $1 million. *Sacramento Bee*. Retrieved from http://www.sacbee.com/news/local/crime/article92490217.html

Wells, T. V. (2014). *Report to the National Football League concerning issues of workplace conduct at the Miami Dolphins*. Retrieved from http://workplacebullying.org/multi/pdf/PaulWeissReport.pdf

17

The Role of the Ombuds in Addressing Workplace Bullying and Mobbing

Tony Belak

When a person is troubled or upset because of some workplace incident or decision, where should he or she turn for help, instruction, guidance, or answers? Perhaps a grievance officer, perhaps a human resource manager, sometimes a coworker, but most often there is no one in apparent authority who can render assistance or insight in an informal, meaningful, and nonaligned manner. An independent ombuds who is well integrated into an organization is positioned to identify conflict in these early stages and serve as an important resource to prevent seemingly minor conflict from becoming problematic or perilous. The cost to address or resolve difficult situations or assist people in distress is far less if done early, and an ombuds's engagement is less expensive than an executive's or administrator's. Leaders who do not proactively develop competence to deal with conflicts such as bullying while developing their own emotional intelligence and establishing a collaborative culture are damaging the organizations they represent. Due diligence requires that appropriate steps to improve organizational leadership and culture be taken to lead a company down the better business path.

Concerns about workplace bullying have grown in industrialized nations (Rayner, 1997). Workplace bullying can be classified in three general areas: (1) related precursors (e.g., power discrepancies between the parties, frustration, and disillusionment); (2) motivational circumstances supporting bullying behavior (e.g., an ethic of competition within the organization, potential rewards systems, and perceived beneficial outcomes); and (3) precipitating processes or triggering circumstances (e.g., layoffs, consolidation and restructuring, reassignment, workgroup reconfiguration; Salin, 2003). These areas are the purview of the organizational ombuds: the independent and neutral resource for those dealing with all forms of conflict within the organization. Accordingly, this chapter will examine potential involvement by ombuds in reported workplace bullying and mobbing situations.

HISTORICAL PERSPECTIVE ON THE OMBUDS

Ombudsman is a Swedish word meaning "agent" or "representative," specifically the words *om* meaning "about" and *bud* meaning "message." The usual translation is "representative"; it literally means "a person with a message about something" (Chaney & Hurst, 1980). This chapter will use the gender-neutral term *ombuds* to refer to a person who receives complaints and questions from individuals concerning the functioning of an entity, such as an organization or workplace, who works for the resolution of particular issues and who can make recommendations for the improvement of the general administration of the entity served. An ombuds's scope of duties and authority must be defined, but it is imperative that there be independence, impartiality, and confidentiality in the operation of the office.

The first ombuds, appointed by King Charles XII of Sweden in 1713, was responsible for curbing the power of agencies of the state by serving as a watchdog for government abuses (Stamatakos & Isachsen, 1970). The king's decision was based on an Ottoman tradition mentioned in the Qur'an (Coonrod, 2015). The role expanded in 1809 to include the investigation of citizens' complaints and grievances against the government. Although the Swedish version of an ombuds came from the king's desire to remedy mishandled governance, its purpose evolved to protecting individuals when it transferred to the United States.

During the 20th century in the United States, federal regulations followed social activism and publicity to raise awareness of the need for employee grievance procedures. In 1955, only 13 percent of workplaces had any grievance procedures, but by 1985, that had increased to 51 percent (Harrison, 2004). While most companies now have grievance and compliance programs, a 1997 survey by Cornell University and Pepperdine University School of Law found that just 10 percent of Fortune 1000 companies had an ombuds program (Bogoslaw, 2015). Employees who witness a serious workplace incident will inform someone if assured of confidentiality without fear of retaliation. Often, an employee does not know how to take a concern forward. An ombuds program is designed to be neutral and independent within an organization and reports to top leadership when required.

The ombuds became popular in the United States in the late 1960s, especially in public entities and governmental offices. It is now being recognized as an effective and efficient means of dealing with conflict in a broad range of workplace settings. The organizational ombuds has evolved from the classical ombudsman to an internal, neutral conflict resolver, often created by people who had never heard of the classical model. This role is perceived as a hallmark of an ethical and compassionate organization and an important component of an integrated conflict management system. An ombuds can be an effective presence prepared to address bullying behavior within the workplace.

THE DISTINCTIVE ROLE OF THE OMBUDS IN ORGANIZATIONAL CONFLICT RESOLUTION

An ombuds is not a substitute for a legal or personal representative and may be more instrumental and appropriate in the first stages of conflict. An ombuds can be the eyes, ears, and intellect of an enlightened organization that recognizes the value and importance of alert and proactive intervention with common and ordinary complaints. The importance of effective conflict resolution is to respond immediately to those hazy signals of negativity that frequently lead to serious conflict. The informal, confidential, and independent actions of the ombuds to address and deal with a complaint, assess its merit, and close the inquiry or investigation without formal action can be extremely beneficial to all involved. Small incidents that are ineffectively addressed may turn into major lawsuits or controversies of massive proportions. As such, this model of early-intervention conflict recognition and resolution can be seen as a form of risk management, with the added benefit of allowing people with a problem to work it out early and in a simple way before it can get out of control or become more difficult to manage.

The ombuds's involvement can be viewed as part psychologist, part anthropologist, part sociologist, and part coach in that the interconnectedness between the organizational and the individual perspective are not easy to delineate given the symbiotic relationship between organizations and individuals (O'Leary-Kelly, Griffin, & Glew, 1996). The organization requires the energy, creativity, time, and skills of the employees, who need monetary compensation, career pathways, and personal and professional development. People expect to be kept secure when at work, and governmental agencies monitor for occupational safety and health; it should be the same for emotional health (Jain and Sinha, 2005), and an ombuds can fulfill that role. Many employees yearn for an off-the-record discussion with a respectful professional who will listen and seek options and choices, formal or otherwise, to identify, address, and serve their needs. Ombuds do not represent the employer nor accept formal notice for their organizations, and people come to them without triggering an on-the-record process (Rowe, 2012). Independence and informality create reasons to trust the ombuds.

To be credible and effective, the ombuds office must be independent in its structure, function, and appearance. Independence means that the ombuds must be free from interference in the legitimate performance of duties. The office should conduct inquiries and investigations in an impartial manner, but the ombuds may become an advocate for change where the process demonstrates a need for it. An ombuds must not disclose and must not be required to disclose any information provided in confidence. Any records pertaining to a complaint, inquiry, or investigation must be confidential and not subject to disclosure outside the ombuds office. The ombuds should be able to develop, evaluate, and discuss options available to affected individuals and be capable of negotiating, facilitating, or mediating while conducting an inquiry. Finally, another important role is identifying complaint patterns and trends and making recommendations for the resolution of an individual complaint or a systemic problem to those persons who have the authority to act upon them (International Ombudsman Association, n.d.).

The ombuds must meet specific requirements to ensure ethical behavior, credibility, and effectiveness. These requirements are summarized in table 17.1.

Conflict is a natural phenomenon and should be expected when two or more people interact in any enterprise or endeavor. Because it occurs

Table 17.1 Ombuds Programs: Complement to Formal Channels

Roles and Responsibilities in Issue Management	Formal	Hotline	Ombuds
Reports to formal management channels	Yes	Yes	No
Partners with management on strategy	Yes	No	No
Sets and enforces policy	Yes	No	No
Performs formal investigation	Yes	No	No
Is a notice channel to the company	Yes	Yes	No
Keeps records	Yes	Yes	No
Provides official reporting on behalf of company	Yes	Yes	No
Provides anonymity	Limited	Yes	Yes
Provides unfiltered data to the board and senior executives	Yes	Yes	Yes
Acts as proactive change catalyst to prevent issues from recurring	Yes	No	Yes
Provides complete confidentiality; privilege supported by Federal Rule of Evidence 501 and implied contract	No	No	Yes
Allows employees to maintain control and determine resolution option (except when there is an imminent threat of serious harm)	No	No	Yes
Provides off-the-record guidance and coaching to get issue to most appropriate channel	No	No	Yes
Maintains official neutrality	No	No	Yes
Remains independent of company management structure and operates as an informal entity	No	No	Yes
Reports to the CEO and audit committee of the board	No	No	Yes

Note: Reprinted with permission from "Ethics, HR and the Importance of Ombuds Programs," by R. Williams and A. Redmond, 2005, Human Capital Strategies, 288, p. 5. Copyright (2005) by Human Resource Institute. Used by permission of the Institute for Corporate Productivity (i4cp).

naturally and cannot be completely avoided, an enlightened organization will focus on how best to deal with conflict rather than to pretend it does not exist. An ombuds in a workplace setting can be a valuable resource for conflict resolution. The ombuds is the lightning rod to not only attract people in conflict but also to seek out those individuals who appear involved in disputes or disagreements that negatively impact the workplace. One key is to interact early, before an interpersonal conflict spreads among other members of the group. Early stages of conflict often cannot be seen; rather, they are felt in the form of anxiety, stress, discomfort, suspicion, mistrust, low morale, disharmony, and an emotional malaise in the workplace. If left unresolved, this latent conflict can emerge as overt hostility, and the risk and cost to the organization is then amplified unless appropriate and decisive action is taken. Boorish or uncivil behavior in workplace relationships often precedes bullying when continued with an identified target.

THE OMBUDS AS A TRUST LEADER

Workplace bullying is toxic to organizations and traumatizes individuals (Einarsen & Mikkelsen, 2003; Hoel & Salin, 2003). It has received scholarly attention in recent years as more knowledge and information are compiled from research studies, brain science, and incident reports (Aquino, 2000; Einarsen, 1999; Hoel, Einarsen, & Cooper, 2003; Hoel & Salin, 2003; Mikkelsen & Einarsen, 2002; Skogstad, Matthiesen, & Einarsen, 2007). The destructive behaviors of workplace bullying and mobbing devastate people and disrupt workplaces (Moayed, Daraiseh, Shell, & Salem, 2006; Pearson, Andersson, & Wegner, 2001). There are many terms to explain this destructive workplace behavior, including *incivility* (Pearson, Andersson, & Porath, 2000); *bullying* (Einarsen, 1999; Namie & Namie, 2003); *mobbing* (Davenport, Schwartz, & Elliott, 2002); *workplace aggression* (Neuman & Baron, 1998); and *emotional abuse* (Lutgen-Sandvik, 2003). Whatever the name, the effects are very detrimental for both the organization and the individual.

If people do not have trust in the ombuds office, its operations and effectiveness are compromised because an ombuds should "enjoy a superlative moral authority engendered through her or his actions and reputation for integrity and fairness" (Coonrod, 2015, p. 379). Neutrality is essential for trust; without it, the ombuds office is likely to be perceived as part of management and as an advocate for the interests of the organization only. As many workplace bullying situations do not necessarily violate existing employment laws (unlike discrimination claims, which are formally investigated and addressed), the ombuds can have an instrumental role in their investigation. The ombuds can also affect a positive outcome by informal means in matters of concern, such as sexual harassment, that occur at levels not meeting legal definitions but that are nonetheless disruptive, inappropriate, and in need of correction.

In one case concerning an ombuds, a manager—who was aware of the function and role of an ombuds after attending a workshop—requested assistance with an issue involving two people on his team. The supervisor had noticed that this man and woman, who had previously had a good work relationship, were now expressing disdain for one another. Together, the pair came to visit the ombuds, following the supervisor's request. They explained that they had recently ended their romantic relationship, and the awkwardness and uncertainty of working together was causing stress, thus jeopardizing their ability to work together. The woman reported that their manager was not aware of their previous personal involvement. She complained that she felt harassed after the breakup. Both were respected and talented members of the team, and they wanted to continue to work together as well as to preserve their marriages.

The ombuds, who can function as a coach when people who are suffering request guidance and direction, listened to their story and asked what they each wanted to achieve from this visit. Shared interests were identified, and an agreement to a positive course of action was determined, even though previous attempts at civility had been unsuccessful. The parties were asked to again implement boundaries and limitations for the next two weeks and then confer together to decide which one would return first for a private session with the ombuds.

When the man returned alone to the second meeting with the ombuds, he expressed relief that the working relationship with his colleague had improved. Restrictions and disparaging treatment of his colleague had been discontinued, and he attributed the change to the first session with the ombuds. When the woman came to visit the ombuds later that week, she also expressed relief and gratitude for the improvement in the relationship with her colleague. The ombuds created the safe conditions under which the parties were free to express themselves in each other's presence, to fashion a self-determined course of action for their careers, and to preserve their individual dignity and self-respect. The unhealthy expressions of power they had expressed toward each other had been replaced with healthy power—a result of the informality, confidentiality, and guidance provided by the ombuds.

As trust leaders, ombuds must have professional conflict management skills and the emotional intelligence to be the change agents of the workplace and to act as neutrals and intermediaries when called on. To be able to harness the benefits of intervention by a knowledgeable, competent, and nonaligned person is invaluable. Due to the informal, neutral, confidential, and independent work of the ombuds, they typically do not engage in formal investigations, serve in any post that might compromise the neutrality of the office, receive legal notice to the organization, make binding decisions or mandate policies, or create or maintain records or reports for the organization. Formal training in mediation and other conflict resolution processes is vital for the ombuds role, and membership in the International Ombudsman Association is important to stay on the cutting edge of critical ombuds issues and to maintain skills.

Aristotle is credited with saying anybody can be angry, but to be angry with the right person, at the right time, in the right manner, and for the right reasons is not so easy. An ombuds can reduce the threat level and encourage realistic and practical approaches to sensible conflict management in a manner concordant with organizational culture, policies, and the interests of the disputing parties. These workers or clients are often referred to as "visitors" by the ombuds. Engagement of the ombuds should serve the needs of the entire organization, individually, collectively, and systemically.

ENHANCING WORKPLACE CULTURE

Organizations of all types are faced with the challenge of continuously improving efficiency to remain competitive. This means strict oversight and tight controls on those elements that affect an organization's cost structure. Traditionally, these efforts have focused on tangible costs that are easily identifiable and can be quantitatively measured. However, to continue down the path of increased efficiency, many organizations are focusing on costs that do not appear on the financial statements and that may not be easily analyzed with traditional metrics. Effective leaders in the workplace recognize that the workplace culture is a community of individuals who collectively are the organization and who individually are people with real human needs and concerns. Although an ombuds is not a therapist, the interaction with an ombuds can be therapeutic and allow the visitor the necessary behavioral transition to understand, accept, reject, or choose self-determination as a way to cope.

The value an organization places on its people is a measure of leadership's concern for a healthy and profitable workplace. In a more culturally complex and age-diverse workplace, managers must appreciate and better understand differences in communication and listening styles and develop the requisite emotional intelligence to be effective leaders. In the face of stressful interpersonal relationships, including the presence of bullying, individuals can and often do walk out the door. In 1999, the National Institute of Occupational Health and Safety reported that stressful working conditions led to higher levels of absenteeism and turnover with a lowering of motivation and morale.

Bullying and mobbing are among the most stressful experiences employees face in the workplace (Salin, 2003). Sometimes the best employees leave the organization and its culture, and the cost of replacing that talent is staggering compared with the cost of listening to their needs. To preserve and grow human capital that an employer has developed over time, an ombuds can foster teamwork and communication within the workplace community and thereby encourage social learning, a key skill in reducing bullying and mobbing (Sheehan, 1999). A skill set that includes active listening, productive communication, and building trusting relationships as a coach should be in every ombuds's capability.

BUILDING TRUST IN THE WORKPLACE

Employees' trust and commitment to their organizations are in decline (Glaude, 2012); yet, trust and commitment are essential for every organization's functioning and sustainability. Trust in the workplace is essential for durable, satisfying, and rewarding relationships. It is achieved through productive communication, understanding, and respect. Distrust breeds conflict, and conflict can consume time and energy, diverting management attention from more profitable activities and outcomes. Trust is one's assessment that another will not deliberately, accidentally, consciously, or unconsciously take unfair advantage (Belak, 2016). It is a person's hope and belief that the trustee will protect and preserve one's self-esteem, status, relationship, career, and even life. We must behave consistently over time to build trust and follow through on promises made. Trust is fragile and can disintegrate if not attended, just as a vintner must attend to his vines.

To achieve sufficient levels of trust, workplace expectations must be explained, followed by agreements related to the necessary steps to complete expectations, sanctions for not meeting expectations, and procedures to measure outcomes. Trust contains a strong emotional component, and parties should be able to share their expectations for one another, negotiate for expected behaviors, and openly acknowledge mutual distrust. Expectations are created with or without collaboration, and unilateral expectations, when broken, often bring the most harm.

A recent Gallup Poll confirmed that the most often cited reason employees leave their organization is because of their boss (Weber, 2015). Bad bosses contribute to a corrosive corporate culture through incivility, interpersonal mistreatment, psychological harassment, or abusive conduct via antisocial behavior and aggression. Nearly half of American workers would fire their boss if allowed, and 30 percent would refer their boss to a psychologist (Jayson, 2012). Corporate values that offer rewards for performance must include more than mere monetary exchange for time in place; recognition, communication, and trust must also be offered.

Simple training programs are not enough, and high commitment businesses must work hard to sustain their healthy cultures. Businesses should establish policies and encourage practices that reflect the values of compassion, authenticity in relationships, fairness, and trust. For example, bullying has been associated with high turnover, absenteeism, presenteeism, disengagement, and loss of productivity (Glaude, 2012). It is a drain on the efficiency and effectiveness of the organization, and employers should act proactively to establish practices and policies to prevent and appropriately address it.

Susan Duncan, dean of the Brandeis School of Law at the University of Louisville, believes the current legal framework for addressing workplace bullying is inadequate to alleviate the suffering it brings. Even in combination with any proposed healthy workplace law or within existing legal frameworks or regulatory response, solutions to workplace bullying should also include restorative justice principles and practices (Duncan, 2011). A multipronged approach should also include labor-management discussions on self-regulation for both management and labor, beyond statutes or regulations to include restorative practices.

Restorative practice is a term derived from criminal justice tenets that transfers focus from the actions of the antagonist to the effects of the harm caused by those actions. It looks to bring individuals or group representatives involved in seeking redress for harms done to discuss those harms and seek ways to make amends or repair relationships. Emphasis is not on punishment, but rather on providing opportunities for offenders to acknowledge and appreciate the negative impact their actions have had on targets or victims, to accept responsibility, and to offer means of restoring or amending ongoing interactions (Duncan, 2011). An organizational ombuds trained in mediation and restorative practices can serve as the catalyst to bring this type of remedy to workplace bullying when a policy, regulation, or statute requires some action.

A proposed statutory solution by David Yamada, a professor of law at Suffolk University Law School, is the Healthy Workplace Bill. If passed, the bill would make the practice of workplace abuse (including bullying and mobbing) illegal. The proposed legislation defines vicarious liability to the employer, damages, retaliation, and affirmative defenses and is receiving attention in state legislatures (Yamada, 2013). Yamada recognizes the challenges inherent in insisting that the workplace make proactive changes through fiat, but he believes a modest yet meaningful improvement to the status quo would be a starting point (Yamada, 2013).

Another starting point for improvement of workplace well-being is in understanding, as Rynes, Bartunek, Dutton, & Margolis (2012) point out, the interconnections between reason, emotions, and compassion. They state that there is a

> positive symbiotic relationship between emotions and reason, compassion and justice, and altruism and self-interest. There has been an emerging understanding by neuroscientists that emotions are not separate from reason and that emotions often enhance reasoning abilities rather than detract from them.... Social scientists have found we are born to interrelate and humans enjoy a dedicated neurobiological system that is responsive to social bonds and fosters other-interested feelings and behaviors... . Theoretical models that put care and concern for others at the center in order to explain behaviors, personal and professional development, and even organizational effectiveness have long been recognized in education and nursing, where relationships are fundamental to the work of the profession. Care and compassion are not separate from being professional or doing the work of the organization but are a natural and living representation of people's humanity in the workplace. (p. 507)

It is vitally important we have theories that reflect the accumulating evidence that other-centeredness and interconnectedness are central aspects of humanity and, therefore, also apply to the workplace.

CHALLENGES TO ESTABLISHING AN OFFICE OF THE OMBUDS

For those who understand and appreciate the impact and value an ombuds office can bring to an organization, establishing the position seems reasonable. But there are many challenges in educating leaders to the need for the continuing presence of an ombuds. A vast gap between what an ombuds contributes to the organization and what the organization values is common. Although the ombuds's contributions benefit the organization, both directly and indirectly, they are often characterized as something other than a value-added activity and, therefore, may not be appreciated (Schenck & Zinsser, 2014).

Another challenge to creating an ombuds presence is the response from authority figures such as middle managers or human resource professionals (Waxman, 2011), who are often among those most threatened. Bullying allegations or complaints are routinely referred to human resource departments, where policies regarding employee interactions are created, maintained, and enforced. Some researchers claim human resource departments and the ombuds office are both needed in an organization to provide a complete conflict management system (Williams & Redmond, 2005). However, if they compete or are threatened by each other, stakeholders may be dissuaded from accessing either one (Coonrod, 2015).

Leadership may feel some ambivalence toward an ombuds office, knowing that information that could put the organization at risk and given in confidence may not be shared. Nevertheless, if those who may be threatened know that the ombuds intends to utilize confidential information to create systemic change, it may be viewed as a service (Joyce, 2014). Ombuds should work on cooperative relationships with individuals or those who feel threatened or invalidated; it is only through open communication that their concerns can be understood and addressed (Tompkins-Byer, 2015).

When we believe others view us negatively or in a false light, we may struggle, as though trying to breathe in oxygen from a deprived atmosphere. The implications are significant, as the more we feel devalued the more energy and effort we expend in defending and restoring our value. The result is less energy to create that personal contribution. Empathetic communication—which the ombuds promotes during private meetings, along with mediations and training sessions—links people and performance while forming the basis for common action, generating power to leverage communication to targeted goals, and giving relationships their foundation to create rewarding and positive exchanges. When we express feelings about ourselves, others, the situation we currently face, and related topics, a new level of dialogue is opened. From there, we can exchange and share authentic relationship data that could strengthen bonds and build trust.

Because the ombuds office advocates for fairness and equity, it should complement but not compete with the functions of employee relations or human resources, although there is a difference in levels of formality and control asserted by the offices. Because human resources professionals must protect the interests of the organization, there are no guarantees of confidentiality, informality, or impartiality, as are expected from the ombuds. The multitude of options any member of the organization has to seek redress often begins with the ombuds office. Legal and compliance officers do not typically interface with the ombuds function, but, acting as a coach outside the corporate hierarchy, the ombuds may refer individuals to their services. This is attractive to employees who initially wish to vent informally before considering alternative actions. The ombuds should assist and not interfere with the operations of organizational departments (Isaac, 2014).

STRATEGIES FOR OMBUDS FOR ADDRESSING AND REDUCING WORKPLACE BULLYING

Rayner and Hoel (1997) derived five categories that characterize workplace bullying behaviors: threat to professional standing, threat to personal standing, isolation, overwork, and destabilizing the target. Threat to one's professional standing occurs when a coworker belittles or humiliates that person or includes public professional humiliation. Threat to one's personal standing includes behaviors by the bully, such as name-calling, insults, and otherwise devaluing the other. Isolation, which is another bullying behavior, refers to preventing access or withholding information. Overwork happens when a coworker applies undue pressure for deadlines or disrupts the flow of business repeatedly. And, finally, destabilization occurs when there is failure to give proper credit when earned, the use of meaningless tasks, or setting someone up to fail on purpose (Rayner & Hoel, 1997). These behaviors transpire at all levels in the workplace. They are also applied in multiple directions: from manager to employee, employee to employee, manager to manager, and employee to manager.

Bullying behavior, by definition, is repeated over time and, frequently, is totally unexpected by the target. Psychological violence such as bullying consists of repeated, unwelcome, unreciprocated, and imposed actions that often result in devastating effects for the victim. There is little distinction between mobbing (primarily viewed as collective harassment) and bullying (primarily seen as individual harassment); a conceptual assimilation of the two terms is acceptable. Workplace bullying falls under traditional considerations of health and safety, including dignity at work, human rights, and freedom from discrimination. This behavior is toxic to both organizations and individuals.

There are many reasons people believe workplace bullying occurs. Research indicates bullying negatively impacts the health of 64.8 percent of employees (targets, witnesses, and those not directly exposed) in American workplaces (Lutgen-Sandvik, Tracy, & Alberts, 2007), and it is roughly four times more prevalent than illegal harassment (Namie, 2007). As 15–17 percent of society suffers from personality disorders, and bullies have enduring patterns of dysfunctional behavior, one clinician has speculated that many of them have personality disorders (Eddy, n.d.). Eddy (n.d.) notes that the growth of workplace bullying appears to parallel the increase in personality disorders in modern society, and bullies cannot seem to stop themselves. This is aggravated by those organizations that tolerate them. With the societal trend toward increased self-centeredness and decreased empathy, can we expect to see the dysfunctional behavior of workplace bullying increase?

While reacting to reports of bullying behavior is vital, an effective organizational program will focus resources on active and passive strategies to prevent workplace bullying and to modify behaviors that might lead to bullying. Active prevention includes developing and disseminating policies, creating internal response structures, and early intervention by management when necessary. Passive prevention encompasses education and training, public awareness, and documentation, which can be accomplished through the ombuds's involvement.

Education and Training

Education and training of all workers is critical in the effort to eliminate or substantially reduce workplace bullying. It takes a concerted effort: management, unions, and professional and other representative bodies must take responsibility to provide training both in the workplace and as part of general vocational and professional training. Management training should include raising awareness, instruction on codes of practice, and recommending approaches to deal with allegations of workplace bullying. All members within an organization have a responsibility to raise awareness of both the issue of workplace bullying and its unacceptability in their workplace. Bystanders to bullying behavior must be informed of their responsibility to report incidents. The perception of a safe reporting system is vital to bystander engagement. Bullying can be misunderstood, and all training should clearly define what is and what is not considered workplace bullying. Bystanders have a responsibility to avoid enabling or supporting bullying behavior through their indifference or toleration—especially when remedies are available to assist the target and the bully (who is often unaware or feigns ignorance).

Training should also identify self-management of stress, anger, or frustration (emotional intelligence); a management approach that proactively promotes workplace health rather than one that reacts with judgment or punishment; an appreciation of diversity (cultural intelligence); effective early conflict management and relationship detoxification with emphasis on restoration; and the ability to act with compassion and wisdom regardless of circumstances (social intelligence).

Early Intervention and Conflict Resolution

Closure is difficult to achieve for many targets of workplace bullying, and there should be an emphasis on early resolution actions and timeliness. The further into the process the parties proceed, the more adversarial it may become; and while an adversarial approach might succeed in apportioning blame, it rarely succeeds in restoring a harmonious workplace. As such, a polarization of positions might divide the workplace and make it even more difficult for the target to return to productive work. Creative and inventive approaches are best implemented at the early stage, when victims of bullying may not yet be in a traumatized state and psychologically incapable of participating in the resolution process. It is very important that the ombuds's intervention be implemented in a timely yet efficient manner.

A case in point is an example of perceived bullying when two members of a 12-member work unit approached the ombuds with complaints that their female supervisor was a bully and was unduly harsh in her assessment of their work. When the ombuds asked whether others in the unit would be willing to come forward, three more corroborated the harsh treatment by their supervisor. This volume of information seemed compelling, and the ombuds asked to meet with the supervisor, who came to his office with her understanding and reasoning with respect to the situation. To the ombuds's surprise, what appeared to be a workplace bully situation may have been mobbing by the employees against their supervisor. Either way, the toxic environment had percolated into the beliefs of those who worked together.

The ombuds recommended a training session with all members of the unit, which resulted in better understanding of the nature of bullying behavior and of a manager with high work product and accountability standards. Subsequently, one person in the unit decided to transfer to another job, and the hostility within the particular workplace calmed. With minimal time and energy, the unhealthy situation was healed through early intervention.

Teaching Collaboration

An ombuds educates and trains employees in collaborative arts and advocacy skills for recognition and early intervention of conflict resolution. The preservation of workplace relationships, resolution of disputes, advocacy in conciliation and early intervention, and a focus on the interests of the parties (rather than their fixed positions)—particularly shared interests—are attainable through training, education, and coaching. To inspire changes in behavior and the corporate culture, leadership must model and exemplify healthy behaviors in their conduct and management style. These healthy management behaviors include productive human resource practices and policies and the philosophy of caring and compassion that reflects human values of love, responsibility, and authenticity in relationships built on fairness and trust.

Nevertheless, when interpersonal conflict becomes abusive and the target seeks assistance from the ombuds, the seriousness of the conflict is reflected in the stories of the suffering endured. In the case of workplace bullying, giving the abusive behavior a name can be an initial step to acceptance or understanding by the target, and reading and researching the topic can bring some solace. Knowing that many others have similar stories is not as comforting as actually making the bullying stop. The ombuds can also be helpful in coaching the target on how to respond to the bullying behaviors.

Approaching workplace aggressors to suggest that their actions and behaviors are inappropriate or disturbing brings with it the possibility of retaliation, but bullies may have little or no appreciation of the damage their actions are producing. The conundrum is that a bully's actions may be motivated by the best interest of the organization without regard for collateral damage to individuals, even though the bullying can bring about the opposite of the desired outcome. Targets often fear reprisal for alerting someone about the bully's actions. The bully may claim good purpose and reason, such as holding subordinates accountable or other managerial discretion. The neutrality of the ombuds can work very well when all parties recognize the opportunity to inform and educate through a facilitated conversation or some other conciliation process. If the organization has a policy addressing workplace bullying, it may allow the first accusation to be a teaching opportunity. Coaching through the ombuds may be effective in modifying behaviors, reestablishing relationships, and resolving the abusive behavior at the lowest level possible.

Responding to Destructive Conflict

Many everyday types of workplace conflict are constructive if the participants interpret and choose to deal with the conflict appropriately. Outcomes in workplace conflicts can be positive or negative. There are disputes that grow out of prejudice, ignorance, cultural traditions, or misplaced aggression, and these are disruptive as well as destructive. Conflict management training provides employees with tools to deal effectively with a broad range of conflict situations. Much like preventative medicine, raising awareness about conflict minimizes its harmful effects. Training becomes proactive and serves a preventative role by eliminating the discomfort of nonproductive communication or destructive conflict. Self-aware managers and workplace leaders are more likely to attend to issues early in the conflict cycle, thereby encouraging healthy relationships and productive communication. Appropriate communication and listening skills are essential to any preventative approach to dealing with conflict. Productive communication within the workplace can mean the difference between high performance and mediocrity.

Nevertheless, ombuds training alone will not produce a strong purpose and values-focused high commitment and high performance culture. A healthy corporate culture can be undermined by a few poor decisions or reactions by management or by the presence of an active bully. The ombuds should serve as the early warning system to alert others when matters or situations are leading in a destructive direction. Bullying spawns a spiral of abuse where targets become anxious and vulnerable to further harassment. One researcher suggests employers should crack down on bullies and assist targets to gain skills to cope with difficult situations (Williams, 2015). Education and information are powerful tools at the disposal of the ombuds to combat workplace bullying.

The ability to separate from the bullying and to competently ask for assistance goes to the heart of conflict resolution efforts. Learning about and using principled negotiation skills raise the probability of understanding and attending to expressed needs. Behavioral scientists have conducted research over the past several decades to learn how people can influence others' attitudes and actions. The way we communicate often has a direct influence on how we perceive and evaluate each other, and a vital element in productive communication is listening. We think we are better listeners than we are, and this shows when we listen to respond and not to understand. The Chinese character for the complex verb "to listen" is composed of the characters for the words eyes, ears, heart, and undivided attention. A primary skill for any ombuds is the ability to listen deeply.

EMERGING ADVANCED SKILLS FOR THE OMBUDS

The exercise of compassionate action can help the ombuds to more effectively serve those suffering from bullying. *Compassion* is a feeling of deep sympathy and sorrow for another who is stricken by misfortune, accompanied by a strong desire to alleviate the suffering. *Compassionate action* is taking personal responsibility for alleviating and preventing the suffering of others (Cowan, 2016).

The Integrative Conflict Management Model

A new and compassionate approach—the *integrative conflict management model* (ICM^2)—treats unhealthy conflict as a thought-borne pathogen, a destructive neurological transaction arising from an experience of power deprivation (Cowan, 2016). Built on a public health foundation, this new approach examines the nature of healthy, benign, and unhealthy power—ways to replace unhealthy expressions (demeaning others, taking a victim role, resorting to accusation, etc.) and replacing those with healthy expressions (value as part of the organization and workplace, belonging, respectful listening to concerns, etc.).

This emerging model of human dynamics informs the ombuds to better appreciate compassion and is not technique but a real transformation of self to better evaluate, educate, and relate to those in a bullying relationship. If bullying is the expression of unhealthy power, the ombuds may assist the bully to exchange it or swap for an infusion of healthy power and the requisite behaviors that reflect it.

The model portrays each individual as a person living in a unique construct of reality—a way of seeing themselves, their role within the organization, and their place in the world. This identity is formed by their experiences, beliefs, genetics, social circumstances, personal relationships, and environment. Everyone's construct is influenced by the economics, religion, media, education, peers, family, and other life elements to which they are exposed. By respecting and understanding every unique reality, the ombuds can better provide alternatives, choices, and guidance to assist in meeting the challenges that brought the person to the ombuds (Cowan, 2016).

There are a number of ICM^2 techniques that the ombuds can employ, including decreasing or eliminating the objectification of others and identifying key power deprivation issues. One of the most effective ways resides in how the ombuds responds; the ICM^2 includes a simple protocol that can be of value. This protocol is often referred to as the Five P's:

1. *Pause*—See if and how you (the ombuds) are affected by the conflict issue.
2. *Presentation*—Frame those involved as presenting with symptoms, rather than viewing them through a moral (right/wrong) lens. This is at the compassionate heart of the approach.
3. *Power issue*—Unhealthy conflict emerges from an experience of loss of power. Identify the power issue.
4. *Power swap*—Support replacing unhealthy conflict (unhealthy power) with healthy power by mirroring positive power that the visitor possesses but has discounted or failed to see.
5. *Power infusion*—Assist the visitor to create a *continuing* experience of power (by listening, caring, acknowledging, reframing, illustrating by example, etc.).

Effective application of the ICM^2 can increase the level of loyalty of those visiting the ombuds. Implementation of the model provides a powerful confirmation that the organization's leadership is committed to the well-being of its people and its people's productivity, creativity, and innovation. Power dynamics are a central concept to consider when analyzing issues of bullying and mobbing. In workplace bullying transactions, one party works to dominate another using a variety of strategies to get power and control.

If bullying emerges from a perceived need to get and maintain power, strategies to disempower the bullying party are counterproductive. Among the effective strategies for shifting power are the "power swap" and "mirroring"—responding to harmful behaviors with healthy manifestations of power. The challenge is to assist all parties to operate from wholesome, effective, and productive power positions, replacing unhealthy manifestations of power with healthy counterparts. This is where power swapping is most effective (Cowan, 2016).

Power swapping is a means to directly address the problem of unhealthy power. *Mirroring* is simply responding to displays of unhealthy power by replying using potent responses that embody healthy power. Bad versus good power struggles will test strength of conviction or offer morality-based solutions but not a change of behavior.

To successfully apply either of these approaches, an understanding of healthy and unhealthy power is necessary. For the purposes of this discussion, power in interpersonal transactions is expressed, rather than just felt. The distinction between the expression and the feeling of healthy or unhealthy power is important because the expression of power is a significant component of interpersonal relationships, where an unexpressed feeling is not. This is especially true in bullying transactions.

Bullying incorporates the application of unhealthy power. Historically, characteristics such as wrath, inflexibility, harshness, rigidity, and intimidation were acceptable elements of command and control forms of management, a style thought to be effective due to the belief that without these tactics employees would fail to adequately perform. Recent studies indicate bullies are motivated by ideals of entitlement, self-righteousness, integrity, and justification (Castle, 2014). Castle determined bullies act with intention and reason, consider themselves to be within their rights to employ these tactics, and are consciously aware and deliberate in the use of negative behaviors to stimulate performance. She found that perpetrators felt morally responsible for their behavior, but there was no indication they experienced feelings of guilt or remorse (except on rare occasions). Participants in her study reported that an apology was all that was needed to justify their behaviors and ease any guilt. Bullies seek validation through approval from their supervisor when the job at hand has been completed, as if it is justification for their behavior and actions.

Keeping the Focus on Healthy Power

A well-respected surgeon had directed a surgery department at a local hospital. When the hospital's surgery department closed for financial reasons, he sought out employment with the university group. Within six months of beginning work, he asked the university ombuds for a meeting to discuss his concerns. He felt targeted by his administrator and described the poor communication and interpersonal treatment within his workplace that was evident but ignored by others. The discomfort and unease he experienced caused him to leave following a series of conversations with the ombuds, whose offer to intervene was rejected as a wasted exercise by the administrator. This employee's pain was evident, and each time he met with the ombuds, he expressed disdain for the dysfunctional conflict climate he longed to leave.

One of the key tasks of the ombuds is to work with leaders to drop bullying approaches and to adopt an inclusive style that incorporates healthy power. By educating those engaged in bullying, swapping unhealthy power with healthy power, mirroring healthy behaviors, and demonstrating effective leadership, the ombuds can guide those in the workplace toward behaviors that produce positive, tangible, and measurable results. Working with employees in this way is preventative: it can reduce the number of bullying incidents that might occur in the future. The ombuds's function can work simultaneously on the individual level by assisting visitors with personal choices and on the systemic level through recognition of trends and patterns and offering recommendations. Of course, the when and the how must be considered for maximum impact. Castle's (2014) study found that while the bully is engaging in negative acts, there is often a moral undertone in the actions that might lead an ombuds to help redirect the behavior by drawing from the ethical thinking of such a perpetrator and applying restorative justice tactics (Curtin, 2016).

CONCLUSION

Organizational leaders set the tone for attitudes and perceptions by those they lead (Olson, Nelson, & Parayitam, 2006), and they have a powerful influence on the culture (Maxwell, 1993; Tepper, Duffy, Henle, & Schurer-Lambert, 2006; Van Fleet & Griffin, 2006). Leadership behavior is a primary factor in workplace bullying, and autocratic leadership styles contribute to the problem. An organization's culture develops over time, and those that tolerate these actions through promotions, accolades, sanitization, or denial encourage, support, or legitimize a bullying culture (Wilkin, 2010).

In one case, the ombuds office at a large public Midwestern university was established in response to the outcry of the faculty senate following several years of bullying by a dean. While the dean was being investigated for misappropriation of grant monies, allegations surfaced during interviews with staff and faculty, who stated the dean had humiliated professors in front of peers, retaliated when challenged, and took credit for others' work product. Although faculty had complained to the provost, their claims were dismissed, and they were labeled whiners who were resistant to change and functioning below standards. When the local newspaper reported the abusive treatment of the dean toward faculty, the provost and president issued apologies to people hurt by the dean and to those who lost trust in the university. Many faculty left the university because of the bullying and the administration's reluctance to listen to their pleas for help (Wilkin, 2010).

The faculty senate determined some protection against this occurring again was needed and established an ombuds office, hiring a highly qualified and experienced external candidate. Aware of the climate at the university and the prevailing mood of the leadership, including legal counsel, the ombuds worked to repair strained relations for several years and encouraged a workplace bullying policy be written. A subcommittee of two standing committees set about to write and propose a particular policy to address bullying, which was roundly rejected by the director of human resources, who claimed the university's existing policies covered such behavior. Ironically, that person was unceremoniously dismissed from employment following allegations of bullying. The ombuds's annual report to the faculty senate consistently spoke to the need for a comprehensive approach to bullying and a policy to enforce it. The ombuds was aware of units within the university where bullying was common, and people were leaving because of it, but he felt unsupported by the administration to intervene.

Currently, no industry standard exists to dictate what percentage of an organization should utilize ombuds services to make it a good investment. Each ombuds office must determine how much utilization is enough based on its context and has to be able to prove its worth and justify its existence to the leadership. Conversely, it is difficult for ombuds to demonstrate worth because benefits to visitors are protected by confidentiality and therefore not shared. This is the conundrum exemplified by paying insurance premiums or risking catastrophic loss. Ombudsry is finding the delicate balance between maintaining relationships and independence; between keeping records and protecting confidentiality; between neutrality and advocacy; between informality and an effort at systemic organizational change; between allowing people to continue their suffering or help them grow; and between compassionate action or selfish inaction (Tompkins-Byer, 2015). When leaders better understand these balances, they may appreciate what the ombuds does and what the capacity for the university can be.

Organizational policies undermined by unmanaged conflict are not fulfilling their purpose of guiding and directing. Managing conflict effectively can result in low-cost solutions that save time, resources, and relationships. These benefits also directly relate to increased productivity, satisfaction, and retention. Managers and employees alike can benefit from participating with the ombuds. Some of the benefits are listed here:

- Fosters equal opportunity in the workplace and treats people respectfully.
- Maximizes cost effectiveness and improves productivity.
- Is a very good method to address discrimination, harassment, and bullying complaints.
- Helps to diffuse hostile feelings and emotions that could lead to inappropriate solutions, such as theft or violence.
- Facilitates a direct contact and collaboration between managers and employees, something conducive to a more harmonious workplace.
- Allows managers and employees to have an active role in the resolution process.
- Is confidential and encourages dignity in the workplace.
- Moves parties from debate to dialogue for more authentic professional relationships.

Most conflict within and involving people revolves around unfulfilled needs, primarily the psychological needs for control, recognition, affection, and respect. These needs are natural and quite human in that we all crave them, but when unacceptable or problematic behavior has been rewarded in the past in fulfillment of these needs, difficult behavior motivates the individual. We should try not to reward difficult behavior or reinforce actions or inactions that manifest it. There is no magic pill, but there are specific ways of thinking and acting described in this chapter that can facilitate positive change in oneself and in others. It takes time and patience to transform negative behavior into acceptable behavior. It does not help to ignore problem behaviors or respond likewise or criticize rather than cure or just brand someone as a problem and be the psychiatrist to their craziness. An ombuds's presence and engagement can prevent unproductive and negative behavior that leads to bullying.

American workers across the spectrum should not be exposed to an unhealthy workplace, and there are laws to protect their safety, compensate for injury, and prevent discrimination within the workforce. It seems unnecessary to have a law against workplace bullying when the devastation it brings is self-evident. Theft in the workplace commonly involves a taking of property, time, or information that rightfully belongs to the employer. However, an expanded view might include the taking of creative energies or productivity from talented employees or the destruction of their engagement or intentional sabotage of their work product. Theft of employees' abilities and competencies by inadequate leadership has a direct negative causal impact on productivity and profits. If the culture of the workplace encourages or, at the least, does not address the basic emotional need of feelings of belonging, the theft of disengagement may fall upon the manager whose responsibility it is to provide guidance, feedback, and recognition. An enlightened workplace recognizes its people, communicates in a respectful fashion, and encourages trust. Bullied, stressed, overworked, or unhappy people are less likely to be creative or productive. An organizational ombuds, either internal or external, is necessary so long as our society fails to recognize the power of compassion.

REFERENCES

Aquino, K. (2000). Structural and individual determinants of workplace victimization: The effects of hierarchical status and conflict management styles. *Journal of Management, 26*(7), 171–193.

Belak, A. (2016, January–March). Should businesses have souls? *Corporate Disputes*. Retrieved from http://www.corporatedisputesmagazine.com

Bogoslaw, D. (2015, June 17). Ombuds programs: Creating a culture of trust rather than compliance. Retrieved from https://www.corporatesecretary.com

Castle, K. (2014). *The workplace bully: A grounded theory study exploring motivational influences of bullying behavior at work* (Unpublished doctoral dissertation). Sullivan University, Louisville, Kentucky.

Chaney, A. C., & Hurst, J. C. (1980). The applicability and benefits of a community mental health outreach model for campus ombudsman programs. *Journal of College Students Personnel, 21*(3), 215–222.

Coonrod, C. K. (2015). The role and function of the organizational ombudsperson. In R. R. Sims & W. I. Sauser (Eds.), *Legal and regulatory issues in human resources management* (pp. 375–402). Charlotte, NC: Information Age Publishing.

Cowan, A. (2016). *International Center for Compassionate Organizations*. Retrieved from http://www.compassionate.center

Curtin, J.-R., Jr. (2016). *An exploratory study of existing state anti-bullying statutes*. Electronic Theses and Dissertations. Retrieved from http://dx.doi.org/10.18297/etd/2459

Davenport, N., Schwartz, R. D., & Elliot, G. P. (2002). *Mobbing: Emotional abuse in the American workplace*. Ames, IA: Civil Society Publishing.

Duncan, S. (2011). Workplace bullying and the role restorative practices can play in preventing and addressing the problem. *Industrial Law Journal, 32*, 2331–2366.

Eddy, B. (n.d.). Bullies at work. Retrieved from http://www.mediate.com/articles/eddyb1.cfm

Einarsen, S. (1999). The nature and causes of bullying at work. *International Journal of Manpower, 20*(1/2), 16–27.

Einarsen, S., & Mikkelsen, E. (2003). Individual effects of exposure to bullying at work. In S. Einarsen, H. Hoel, D. Zapf, & C. Cooper (Eds.), *Bullying and emotional abuse in the workplace: International perspectives in research and practice* (pp. 127–142). New York: Taylor & Francis.

Glaude, P. (2012, November 23). Engagement at work. Retrieved from http://ezinearticles.com/?Bringing-Back--Engagement-at-Work&id=7393291

Harrison, T. R. (2004). What is success in ombuds processes? Evaluation of a University Ombudsman. *Conflict Resolution Quarterly, 21*(3), 313–335.

Hoel, H., Einarsen, S., & Cooper, C. L. (2003). Organizational effects of bullying. In S. Einarsen, H. Hoel, D. Zapf, & C. L. Cooper (Eds.), *Bullying and emotional abuse in the workplace: International perspectives in research and practice* (pp. 145–161). London: Taylor & Francis.

Hoel, H., & Salin, D. (2003). Organizational antecedents of workplace bullying. In S. Einarsen, H. Hoel, D. Zapf, & C. Cooper (Eds.), *Bullying and emotional abuse in the workplace: International perspectives in research and practice* (pp. 145–162). New York: Taylor & Francis.

International Ombudsman Association (n.d.). Retrieved from http://www.ombudsassociation.org

Isaac, K. D. (2014). The organizational ombudsman's quest for privileged communications. *Hofstra Labor & Employment Law Journal, 32*(1), 31–47.

Jain, A. K., & Sinha, A. K. (2005). General health in organizations: Relative relevance of emotional intelligence, trust, and organizational support. *International Journal of Stress Management, 12*(3), 257–273. http://dx.doi.org/10.1037/1072-5245.12.3.257

Jayson, S. (2012, August 5). Bad bosses can be bad for your health. *USA Today*. Retrieved from http://usatoday30.usatoday.com/news/health/story/2012-08-05/apa-mean-bosses/56813062/1

Joyce, C. M. (2014). Courage in ombuds work. *Journal of the International Ombudsman Association* 7(1), 13–22.

Lutgen-Sandvik, P. (2003). The communicative cycle of employee abuse: Generation and regeneration of workplace mistreatment. *Management Communication Quarterly, 16*(4), 471–501.

Lutgen-Sandvik, P., Tracy, S., & Alberts, J. (2007). Burned by bullying in the American workplace: Prevalence, perception, degree and impact. *Journal of Management Studies, 44*(6), 837–862.

Maxwell, J. C. (1993). *Developing the leader within you.* Nashville, TN: Thomas Nelson, Inc.

Mikkelsen, E. G., & Einarsen, S. (2002). Relationships between exposure to bullying at work and psychological and psychosomatic health complaints: The role of state negative affectivity and generalized self-efficacy. *Scandinavian Journal of Psychology, 43*(5), 397–405.

Moayed, F. A., Daraiseh, N., Shell, R., S. & Salem, S. (2006). Workplace bullying: A systemic review of risk factors and outcomes. *Theoretical Issues in Ergonomics Science, 7*(3), 311–327.

Namie, G. (2007, September). *U.S. workplace bullying survey.* Retrieved from http://workplacebullying.org/multi/pdf/WBIsurvey2007.pdf

Namie, G., & Namie, R. (2003). *The bully at work.* Naperville, IL: Sourcebooks.

Neuman, J. H., & Baron, R. A. (1998). Workplace violence and workplace aggression: Evidence concerning specific forms, potential causes, and preferred targets. *Journal of Management, 24,* 391–419.

O'Leary-Kelly, A., Griffin, R., & Glew, D. (1996). Organization-motivated aggression: A research framework. *Academy of Management Review, 21*(1), 225–253.

Olson, B. J., Nelson, D. L., & Parayitam, S. (2006). Managing aggression in organizations: What leaders must know? *Leadership & Organization Development Journal, 27,* 384–398.

Pearson, C. M., Andersson, L. M., & Porath, C. L. (2000). Assessing and attacking workplace incivility. *Organizational Dynamics, 29*(2), 123–137.

Pearson, C. M., Andersson, L. M., & Wegner, J. W. (2001). When workers flout convention: A study of workplace incivility. *Human Relations, 54*(11), 1387–1419.

Rayner, C. (1997). The incidence of workplace bullying. *Journal of Community & Applied Social Psychology, 7*(3), 199–208.

Rayner, C., & Hoel, H. (1997). A summary of literature relating to workplace bullying. *Journal of Community & Applied Social Psychology, 7*(3), 181–191.

Rowe, M. (2012). Informality the fourth standard of practice. *Journal of the International Ombudsman Association, 5*(1), 8–17.

Rynes, S. L., Bartunek, J. M., Dutton, J. E., & Margolis, J. D. (2012). Care and compassion through an organizational lens: Opening up new possibilities. *Academy of Management Review, 37*(4), 503–523.

Salin, D. (2003). Ways of explaining workplace bullying: A review of enabling, motivating and precipitating structures and processes in the work environment. *Human Relations, 56*(10), 1213–1232.

Schenck, A., & Zinsser, J. W. (2014). Prepared to be valuable: Positioning ombuds programs to assure their worth. *Journal of the International Ombudsman Association, 7*(1), 23–44.

Sheehan, M. (1999). Workplace bullying: Responding with some emotional intelligence. *International Journal of Manpower, 20*(1/2), 57–69.

Skogstad, A., Matthiesen, S., & Einarsen, S. (2007). Organizational changes: A precursor of bullying at work. *International Journal of Organizational Theory and Behavior, 10*(1), 58–94.

Stamatakos, L. C., & Isachsen, O. (1970). Towards Making the University Ombudsman a More Effective Force in Higher Education: A Comparative Study. *NASPA, 7*(4).

Tepper, B. J., Duffy, M. K., Henle, C. A., Schurer-Lambert, L. (2006). Procedural injustice, victim precipitation and abusive supervision. *Personnel Psychology, 59*, 101-123.

Tompkins-Byer, T. (2015). University ombuds offices: Their perspectives and impact on campus conflict (Unpublished master's thesis). Brandeis University, Waltham, Massachusetts.

Van Fleet, D. D., & Griffin, R. W. (2006). Dysfunctional Organization Culture: The Role of Leadership in Motivating Dysfunctional Work Behaviors. *Journal of Managerial Psychology, 21*, 698-708.

Waxman, J. A. (2011). The conflict competent organization: Assessing the perceived economic value of the corporate ombuds office. *Journal of the International Ombudsman Association, 4*(2), 60–73.

Weber, L. (2015, April 2). What do workers want from the boss? *Wall Street Journal*. Retrieved from http://blogs.wsj.com/atwork/2015/04/02/what-do-workers-want-from-the-boss

Wilkin, L. (2010). Workplace bullying in academe: A grounded theory study exploring how faculty cope with the experience of being bullied (Unpublished doctoral dissertation). Nova Southeastern University, Fort Lauderdale, Florida.

Williams, R. (2015, February 21). How workplace bullying destroys well-being and productivity. *Psychology Today* [blog]. Retrieved from https://www.psychologytoday.com/blog/wired-success/201502/how-workplace-bullying-destroys-well-being-and-productivity

Williams, R., & Redmond, A. (2005). Ethics, HR and the importance of ombuds programs. *Human Capital Strategies, 288*, 1–8.

Yamada, D. (2013). Emerging American legal responses to workplace bullying. *Temple Political & Civil Rights Law Review, 22*(2), 329–332.

PART V

The Legal Landscape in the United States for Workplace Bullying and Mobbing

18

The American Legal Landscape: Potential Redress and Liability for Workplace Bullying and Mobbing

David C. Yamada[*]

As other chapters in these volumes document, workplace bullying and mobbing are entering into the mainstream of discussions in fields such as employee relations, human resources, industrial and organizational psychology, and clinical psychology and counseling. Responses from the American legal system, by contrast, have emerged more slowly. In fact, until recently, the idea of American legislatures enacting laws concerning workplace bullying and mobbing had largely been discussed in speculative and aspirational terms. During the past five years, however, various state and local legislative bodies have enacted laws and ordinances related to bullying at work. In addition, significant advocacy efforts have been underway in many states on behalf of proposed workplace antibullying laws. A possibility once regarded somewhat dismissively is now becoming a reality.

This chapter offers an overview of the U.S. legal landscape in regard to workplace bullying and mobbing. It begins by taking a somewhat chronological perspective, starting with the importation of the terms *bullying* and *mobbing* into the American employment relations vocabulary, followed by early efforts to research and identify potential legal protections and liabilities relevant to this form of workplace mistreatment. It will then examine attempts to create direct legal protections against workplace bullying, centering on new and proposed "Healthy Workplace" legislation. It will also discuss existing legal protections and public-benefit programs that potentially apply to bullying and mobbing situations. Next, it will discuss the practical considerations emerging from these developments

---

[*] Work on this chapter was supported by a summer research stipend and sabbatical semester provided by Suffolk University Law School. Correspondence may be directed to: Professor David Yamada, Suffolk University Law School, 120 Tremont Street, Boston, MA 02108; dyamada@suffolk.edu.

for employee relations stakeholders, especially employers and labor organizations, as well as for the mental health community. Finally, it will consider some of the broader societal implications related to harnessing the American legal system to respond to workplace bullying and mobbing behaviors.

This chapter builds upon some 17 years of legal scholarship, legislative drafting, and public education work on the topic. As discussed below, I have been closely involved with efforts to research and create legal protections against workplace bullying and mobbing, including the drafting of model legislation known as the Healthy Workplace Bill, which has served as the main template for law reform efforts in the United States. I hope that the deep familiarity I bring to this topic will offset my lack of distant objectivity, at least in terms of contributing some contextual understanding to this examination. Readers who would like to explore this subject in greater detail are invited to review my ongoing body of law review scholarship (Yamada, 2000, 2004, 2010, 2013a, 2015).

EARLY RESEARCH FORAYS

The 1997 launch of the Campaign Against Workplace Bullying, a public education initiative led by Drs. Gary and Ruth Namie, is probably the signature event in introducing the term *workplace bullying* into the vocabulary of American employee relations. The Namies imported this term from Great Britain, where it had gained a foothold thanks to media coverage and public education initiatives. The Namies' first book, *BullyProof Yourself at Work* (Namie & Namie, 1999), furthered efforts to bring workplace bullying to the attention of an American audience. *Workplace mobbing* would enter the picture, too, marked by the publication of *Mobbing: Emotional Abuse in the American Workplace* (Davenport, Schwartz, & Elliott, 1999). However, during this time, neither workplace bullying nor workplace mobbing was popularly understood or used in the United States.

It was against this backdrop, and spurred by discussions with the Namies, that I began investigating potential legal protections for targets of severe workplace bullying. This work was shaped by a cluster of policy objectives that should inform potential legal interventions concerning bullying at work (Yamada, 2000), the three most important being prevention, self-help, and compensation:

- *Prevention:* Prevention of abusive behaviors benefits everyone. Workers enjoy better health and morale, and employers benefit from greater productivity. Accordingly, the law should provide liability-reducing legal incentives for employers who engage in preventive measures.
- *Self-help:* The law should protect employees who report abusive work behaviors and encourage employers to resolve potential bullying and mobbing situations earlier rather than later. Furthermore, all things

being equal, prompt, fair, and responsible in-house resolution is better than protracted litigation.
- *Compensation:* When bullying and mobbing do occur, targets should be compensated for the harm done to them. This should include, among other things, appropriate monetary damages and preservation or restoration of employment status.

My check into secondary sources indicated that workplace bullying was largely unexplored in American legal scholarship, and so I resolved to research and analyze this topic closely. I began my legal research with a hypothesis that the tort law claim of intentional infliction of emotional distress (IIED) would emerge as the primary legal protection against workplace bullying. I looked at hundreds of state court decisions on IIED claims brought against employers and coworkers for bullying-type behaviors. This analysis revealed that courts were frequently dismissing these claims before trial, usually holding that the bullying behaviors were not sufficiently severe and outrageous to meet the requirements of IIED, even when the complainants had experienced considerable psychological and physical impairment (Yamada, 2000).

After considering other potential legal protections, such as employment discrimination statutes, collective bargaining laws, and occupational safety and health laws, I concluded that many targets of severe workplace bullying were without sufficient legal protections (Yamada, 2000). I put these findings in a law review article that concluded with a proposal outlining the parameters for a new statute providing a civil claim for severe workplace bullying (Yamada, 2000).

THE HEALTHY WORKPLACE BILL

Building on the policy objectives and recommendations set out in my 2000 article, I drafted a prototypical workplace antibullying statute. The first version was completed in 2002, and it would soon become dubbed the "Healthy Workplace Bill" (HWB; Yamada, 2004). Since then, the template version of the HWB has undergone a number of changes and edits while retaining its original core structure. The following discussion summarizes and explains the main features of the current version of the bill, which is provided in full in the article "Emerging American Legal Responses to Workplace Bullying" (Yamada, 2013a).

Primary Cause of Action

The Healthy Workplace Bill defines its primary cause of action as follows: "It shall be an unlawful employment practice under this Chapter to subject an employee to an abusive work environment as defined by this Chapter"

(Yamada, 2013a, p. 352). Many definitions and provisions further shape and limit this cause of action. The critical definition is "abusive work environment," which "exists when an employer or one or more of its employees, acting with intent to cause pain or distress to an employee, subjects that employee to abusive conduct that causes physical harm, psychological harm, or both" (Yamada, 2013a, p. 351). "Abusive conduct" is defined as

> acts, omissions, or both, that a reasonable person would find abusive, based on the severity, nature, and frequency of the conduct. Abusive conduct may include, but is not limited to: repeated verbal abuse such as the use of derogatory remarks, insults, and epithets; verbal, non-verbal, or physical conduct of a threatening, intimidating, or humiliating nature; or the sabotage or undermining of an employee's work performance. It shall be considered an aggravating factor that the conduct exploited an employee's known psychological or physical illness or disability. A single act normally will not constitute abusive conduct, but an especially severe and egregious act may meet this standard. (Yamada, 2013a, p. 351)

The definition of abusive conduct is significantly influenced by the U.S. Supreme Court's definition of a hostile work environment for purposes of determining legally actionable sexual harassment under Title VII of the Civil Rights Act of 1964 (*Harris v. Forklift Systems, Inc.*, 1993). As explained below, this includes a totality of the circumstances approach that takes into account the frequency and severity of the conduct, viewed through the eyes of the "reasonable person."

Liability

A worker subjected to an abusive work environment may bring a civil claim, filed in state court, against an employer and individual coworkers. The HWB imposes strict liability on employers for actionable behavior by its employees. However, it also provides employers with an affirmative defense when

1. the employer exercised reasonable care to prevent and correct promptly any actionable behavior; and,
2. the complainant employee unreasonably failed to take advantage of appropriate preventive or corrective opportunities provided by the employer. (Yamada, 2013a, p. 352)

This defense, designed to provide a legal "carrot" incentive for employers to prevent and respond to abusive behaviors, is drawn directly from the U.S. Supreme Court's 1998 ruling concerning employer liability for harassment on the basis of protected class status under the Civil Rights Act of 1964

(*Burlington Industries v. Ellerth*, 1998). The "stick" is that the defense is not available when the abusive behavior culminates in an adverse employment decision, such as a demotion, suspension, or termination.

Damages

The Healthy Workplace Bill provides for standard forms of compensatory and injunctive relief, such as lost wages, medical expenses, and reinstatement, as well as for punitive damages and attorney's fees. These allowable damages largely mirror those commonly awarded in successful tort and employment discrimination claims, the two doctrinal areas of law that have most informed the HWB's drafting. In addition, the bill limits emotional distress and punitive damages imposed on an employer when bullying behaviors did not involve an adverse employment action, a provision designed to have the effect of encouraging employers to address potential bullying situations before they become acute.

Antiretaliation Protection

The Healthy Workplace Bill provides antiretaliation protection:

> It shall be an unlawful employment practice under this Chapter to retaliate in any manner against an employee because she has opposed any unlawful employment practice under this Chapter, or because she has made a charge, testified, assisted, or participated in any manner in an investigation or proceeding under this Chapter, including, but not limited to, internal complaints and proceedings, arbitration and mediation proceedings, and legal actions. (Yamada, 2013a, p. 352)

This is antiretaliation language is drawn from the Civil Rights Act of 1964 (2016) and other federal employment discrimination statutes. It is necessary to preserve the policy goals of the legislation, for if potential complainants and witnesses are not protected against retaliation, then the preventive and remedial objectives of the bill are severely compromised.

Additional Employer Defenses

The Healthy Workplace Bill provides three other affirmative defenses that are designed to protect employer prerogatives:

> It shall be an affirmative defense that:
> a. The complaint is based on an adverse employment decision reasonably made for poor performance, misconduct, or economic necessity; or

b. The complaint is based on a reasonable performance evaluation; or
c. The complaint is based on an employer's reasonable investigation about potentially illegal or unethical activity. (Yamada, 2013a, pp. 352–353)

HEALTHY WORKPLACE LEGISLATION, STATUTES, AND ORDINANCES

In 2003, the original version of the full Healthy Workplace Bill was formally introduced for the first time in an American legislature by a California Assembly member (Yamada, 2004). Since then, versions of the bill have been introduced in some 30 state legislatures, with most of this activity occurring during the past 10 years. Although the full version of the bill has not yet been enacted, in recent years, several states and municipalities have enacted workplace bullying legislation and ordinances that draw heavily upon the template language. The following sections provide a summary of major developments.

California

In 2014, the State of California enacted a limited workplace bullying provision as an amendment to the state's discrimination law (Cal. Govt. Code, 2014). California requires "(a)n employer having 50 or more employees" to "provide at least two hours of classroom or other effective interactive training and education regarding sexual harassment to all supervisory employees in California within six months of their assumption of a supervisory position" (Cal. Govt. Code, 2014, Subsect. a). Now, thanks to the 2014 amendment, covered employers must include "prevention of abusive conduct" in these training and education programs (Cal. Govt. Code, 2014, Subsect. b). "Abusive conduct" is defined as "conduct of an employer or employee in the workplace, with malice, that a reasonable person would find hostile, offensive, and unrelated to an employer's legitimate business interests" (Cal. Govt. Code, 2014, Subsect. g(2)). This definition is a verbatim adoption of language contained in an earlier version of the Healthy Workplace Bill.

The California amendment constitutes the first enacted workplace bullying legislation to cover both public and private employers. However, it does not create an independent legal claim for abusive conduct. Accordingly, the existing provisions of the state's discrimination law that create legal claims are inapplicable to bullying situations not implicating protected class status.

Tennessee

In 2014, Tennessee enacted a law directing a state commission to develop a model workplace antibullying policy for potential adoption by state, county, and local governmental entities (Healthy Workplace Act, Tenn. Code, 2014):

(a) No later than March 1, 2015, the Tennessee advisory commission on intergovernmental relations (TACIR) shall create a model policy for employers to prevent abusive conduct in the workplace. The model policy shall be developed in consultation with the department of human resources and interested municipal and county organizations including, but not limited to, the Tennessee municipal league, the Tennessee county services association, the municipal technical advisory service (MTAS), and the county technical assistance service (CTAS).
(b) The model policy created pursuant to subsection (a) shall:
   (1) Assist employers in recognizing and responding to abusive conduct in the workplace; and
   (2) Prevent retaliation against any employee who has reported abusive conduct in the workplace.
(c) Each employer may adopt the policy created pursuant to subsection (a) as a policy to address abusive conduct in the workplace. (Tenn. Code, 2014, Subsect. 503)

The statute's definition of "abusive conduct" adopts elements of the Healthy Workplace Bill's definition, but the new law does not create a legal cause of action for bullied workers. Rather, adoption of the state's model policy or one that comports with its essential features will insulate a public entity from liability (Tenn. Code, 2014):

> If an employer adopts the model policy . . . or adopts a policy that conforms to the requirements set out in [the statute], then the employer shall be immune from suit for any employee's abusive conduct that results in negligent or intentional infliction of mental anguish. Nothing in this section shall be construed to limit the personal liability of an employee for any abusive conduct in the workplace. (Tenn. Code, 2014, Subsect. 504)

The immunity provision potentially transforms the Tennessee statute into an employer safeguard measure rather than an employee protection law. Under the statutory language, adoption of the model policy (or one like it) is sufficient to insulate a covered employer for liability for bullying-type behaviors. There is no obligation under the law for an employer to actually follow and enforce its own policy.

Utah

In 2015, Utah enacted a law requiring state executive agencies to train its supervisors and employees about how to prevent abusive conduct (Utah State

Personnel Management Act, 2015). The new law requires biennial training covering the definition of "abusive conduct" (drawn heavily from the Healthy Workplace Bill); its ramifications, "resources available to employees who are subject to abusive conduct"; and the employer's grievance process (Utah State Personnel Management Act, 2015, Subsect. 3(b)). In addition, professional development training must cover ethical conduct and "organizational leadership practices based in principles of integrity" (Utah State Personnel Management Act, 2015, Subsect. 4(a)).

The law expressly does not create a private legal claim for bullying-related conduct. However, in recognizing the presence of a grievance process, it anticipates complaints grounded in allegations of abusive conduct. This gives the Utah law slightly stronger teeth than the California amendment, which requires only training and education.

Fulton County, Georgia

In 2012, the commissioners of Fulton County, Georgia, adopted a workplace antibullying policy that covers county employees (Fulton County, 2012):

> Employees will treat all other employees with dignity and respect. Management will provide a working environment as safe as possible by having preventative measures in place and by dealing immediately with threatening or potentially violent situations. No employee will engage in threatening, violent, intimidating or other abusive conduct or behaviors. (Fulton County, 2012, p. 3)

To a degree unusual for a workplace policy, Fulton County places direct obligations on its employees to implement its provisions:

> All County employees and officials covered by this policy and procedure shall immediately remove themselves from any threat as soon as possible. Employees shall immediately report any threats, physical or verbal, and/or any abusive, disruptive or intimidating behavior of any individual to their immediate supervisor or Appointing Authority. Employees shall cooperate with any subsequent investigation of their complaints. No attempt to engage or antagonize a person threatening violence shall be made. (Fulton County, 2012, pp. 3–4)

The Fulton County policy uses the Healthy Workplace Bill's definition of abusive conduct. Under the policy, suspension and termination are possible sanctions for those who engage in prohibited behaviors. It does not, however, provide compensation to those who are mistreated in ways that violate the policy.

Support for and Opposition to Healthy Workplace Legislation

Public support for workplace bullying legislation appears to be strong. For example, in a scientific 2014 national public opinion survey on workplace bullying sponsored by the Workplace Bullying Institute and conducted by Zogby Analytics, 63 percent of respondents "strongly" supported and 30 percent of respondents "somewhat" supported the enactment of workplace bullying legislation (Namie, 2014). Respondents to this question were those who reported on the survey that they were "aware" of workplace bullying (Namie, 2014).

Central organizing support for the Healthy Workplace Bill has come from grassroots Healthy Workplace Advocates groups operating in many states (Yamada, 2013a). Labor unions (especially those representing public sector workers) and other worker advocacy groups have provided significant support as well. Among these supporters, social media outlets have proven useful for sharing information and planning activities.

Opposition to workplace bullying legislation has typically come from the employer and corporate side, raising concerns about unwanted litigation and the challenges of distinguishing between bullying and the ordinary strains of workplace interactions (Yamada, 2013a). Occasionally, the criticism takes on a deeper, philosophical tone. In a 2007 article, two management-side employment lawyers claimed that enacting legal protections against workplace bullying will undermine high performance expectations for workers and healthy competition (Van Dyck & Mullen, 2007). They posited that "tension created by competition" fuels productivity at work, and that antibullying laws "would not only inhibit productivity and employers' freedom to hire and fire at-will employees but moreover, it would chill critical workplace communication" (Van Dyck & Mullen, 2007, p. 3).

The future of Healthy Workplace legislation likely will continue to be shaped by these constituencies. Although opponents to workplace bullying legislation are strong and powerful, public support for legal protections appears to be significant. The recent adoption of workplace bullying laws and ordinances in several states, however limited in coverage and scope, does indicate that receptivity to antibullying legislation has crossed from mere deliberation into actual enactment.

ADDITIONAL POTENTIAL LEGAL PROTECTIONS, LIABILITY RISKS, AND EMPLOYEE BENEFIT PROVISIONS

Apart from legislative drafting, advocacy, and deliberations discussed above, there exists a body of employment and labor law that may, in some instances, be applicable to workplace bullying and mobbing situations (Yamada, 2000;

Yamada, 2004; Yamada, 2010, Yamada, 2013a). While the scope of this chapter precludes an in-depth examination of all potential legal issues, the following summary and discussion covers the basics. I refer readers to my published law review articles for more details.

Tort Law Claims

Tort law creates civil liability exposure for injuries to person and property. As noted above, my initial forays into researching potential legal protections for targets of workplace bullying began with the hypothesis that the tort claim of intentional infliction of emotional distress would serve as an effective legal claim. I proceeded to research state court decisions where workers had used IIED to sue employers and coworkers for severe bullying-type behaviors. After conducting a qualitative analysis of hundreds of IIED cases, I made the following overall conclusion (Yamada, 2000):

> An analysis of case law reveals that typical workplace bullying, especially conduct unrelated to sexual harassment or other forms of status-based discrimination, seldom results in liability for IIED. This is because the courts have tended to find workplace bullying cases lack two of the required elements for IIED liability—either that the complained-of conduct was not severe or outrageous, or that the employee did not suffer severe emotional distress. (Yamada, 2000, p. 494)

In fact, many workplace-related IIED claims did not even survive pretrial dismissal motions. A prime exemplar was a 1996 Arkansas Supreme Court decision, *Hollomon v. Keadle* (1996), which involved a female employee, Hollomon, who worked for a male physician, Keadle, for two years before she voluntarily left the job. Hollomon claimed that during this period of employment, "Keadle repeatedly cursed her and referred to her with offensive terms, such as 'white nigger,' 'slut,' 'whore,' and 'the ignorance of Glenwood, Arkansas'" (*Hollomon v. Keadle*, 1996, p. 413). Keadle frequently used profanity in front of his employees and patients and often remarked that women working outside of the home were "whores and prostitutes" (*Hollomon v. Keadle*, 1996, p. 413). According to Hollomon, Keadle "told her that he had connections with the mob" and mentioned "that he carried a gun," allegedly to "intimidate her and to suggest that he would have her killed if she quit or caused trouble" (*Hollomon v. Keadle*, 1996, p. 413). Hollomon claimed that, as a result of this conduct, she suffered from "stomach problems, loss of sleep, loss of self-esteem, anxiety attacks, and embarrassment" (*Hollomon v. Keadle*, 1996, p. 413). On these allegations, the Arkansas Supreme Court affirmed the trial court's pretrial dismissal of Hollomon's claim, reasoning that Keadle's conduct was not sufficiently outrageous to meet the legal requirements of IIED (*Hollomon v. Keadle*, 1996, p. 413).

A second major impediment to using IIED claims in response to bullying and mobbing behaviors is that, in some states, workers' compensation laws prohibit tort claims brought directly against an employer (Yamada, 2000). These statutory bars are grounded in the policy rationale that workers' compensation is designed as the exclusive remedy for work-related injuries.

Since the publication of my 2000 article, I have continued to monitor IIED claims brought for bullying-type behaviors. Unfortunately, for severely bullied workers, the general state of this body of law has not markedly changed.

Of course, tort law may also come into play in the less frequent instances when bullying behaviors include physically aggressive or violent behavior, thus raising claims such as battery for harmful or offensive touching. For example, a 1993 Ohio Court of Appeals decision, *Snyder v. Turk*, involved a surgeon, Turk, who was performing a gallbladder operation (*Snyder v. Turk*, 1993). The nurse plaintiff, Snyder, was allegedly making mistakes and complicating a difficult procedure. Turk became so angered that when Snyder handed him the supposedly wrong instrument, he grabbed her shoulder, pulled her face down toward the surgical opening, and said, "Can't you see where I'm working? I'm working in a hole. I need long instruments" (*Snyder v. Turk*, 1993, p. 1055). After the trial court held against the nurse plaintiff on all counts, the court of appeals reinstated the claim for battery, finding a jury could have found the physical contact to be offensive physical contact.

Employment Discrimination Law

Bullying and mobbing motivated by a target's membership in a legally protected class established by employment discrimination laws may offer legal relief for some individuals. At the federal level, three major statutes come into play. Title VII of the Civil Rights Act of 1964 establishes race, color, religion, national origin, and sex as protected classes (Civil Rights Act of 1964, 2016). The Age Discrimination in Employment Act covers individuals age 40 or over (Age Discrimination in Employment Act of 1967, 2016). And the Americans with Disabilities Act covers employees on the basis of recognized disabilities (Americans with Disabilities Act of 1990, 2016). Most states also have their own discrimination statutes, including some that add sexual orientation as a protected class.

For bullying and mobbing behaviors, the most likely type of discrimination claim is harassment on the basis of a legally protected class, most commonly in the form of a hostile work environment. The legal standard for determining what constitutes a "hostile work environment" was set out by the U.S. Supreme Court in an aforementioned decision, *Harris v. Forklift Systems,*

Inc. (1993), a sexual harassment claim. The court adopted a two-part test to determine whether a hostile work environment is present under the Civil Rights Act. First, the harassing behavior must be objectively hostile, that is, it must create "an environment that a reasonable person would find hostile or abusive" (*Harris v. Forklift Systems, Inc.*, 1993, p. 21). In assessing whether an objectively hostile work environment exists, the facts are examined in their totality. The frequency and severity of the discriminatory conduct; whether the conduct was "physically threatening or humiliating, or a mere offensive utterance"; and whether the conduct "unreasonably interfere[d] with an employee's work performance" are among the factors to be weighed (*Harris v. Forklift Systems, Inc.*, 1993, p. 23). Second, the victim must "subjectively perceive the environment to be abusive" to satisfy the requirement that the conduct "actually altered the conditions of the victim's employment" (*Harris v. Forklift Systems, Inc.*, 1993, pp. 21–22).

The *Harris* test remains good law. It has been applied to harassment claims for all protected classes established under employment discrimination laws. Furthermore, as noted above, the objective totality of the circumstances part of the test has significantly informed the drafting of the Healthy Workplace Bill.

In addition, the Americans with Disabilities Act may provide bullying and mobbing targets with potential relief if they can demonstrate a qualifying disability that entitles them to a reasonable accommodation. Under such scenarios, separation or transfer away from the aggressor may qualify. Workplace harassment that triggers a disability or aggravates an existing disability may also implicate ADA rights, although legal questions of causation can prove challenging.

Antiretaliation and Whistle-Blower Provisions

If individuals are bullied or mobbed in retaliation for making complaints about alleged illegalities or unethical behavior committed by their employer or coworkers, then the antiretaliation provisions of specific statutes or whistleblower laws may offer legal protection (Yamada, 2000). Most protective employment statutes, such as discrimination, wage and hour, and workplace safety and health laws, include antiretaliation provisions. Whistle-blower laws may be more general in nature or apply to specific areas, such as environmental standards or securities fraud.

Collective Bargaining Laws

Federal and state collective bargaining laws potentially create contractual protections and obligations concerning bullying behaviors. For example, if a course of bullying or mobbing culminates in a dismissal, then the just cause termination provisions of a collective bargaining agreement may make it a viable grievance. Furthermore, as discussed below and in chapter 23, labor unions can introduce concerns about bullying behaviors in contract negotiations.

In addition, the National Labor Relations Act grants most nonsupervisory and nonmanagerial employees the right to engage in concerted activity for "mutual aid or protection" (National Labor Relations Act of 1935, 2016). Although this provision is most frequently invoked in union organizing and advocacy contexts, it applies to all workers covered under the statute, regardless of whether they are union members. The provision may protect rank-and-file workers who join together to raise concerns about workplace bullying from employer retaliation. However, the requirement of concerted activity means that a worker raising concerns about bullying or mobbing behaviors as a "lone wolf" is not protected under the statute.

Employee Handbooks

In states where employee handbooks have potential contractual effect, those containing provisions that cover bullying, mobbing, and generic harassment may create legal obligations for an employer. For example, a policy stating that workplace bullying will not be tolerated and providing a procedure for lodging a complaint about bullying behaviors may be contractually enforceable. An employer's failure to enforce and follow that policy could offer potential relief to a targeted worker.

Occupational Safety and Health Laws

As discussed in chapter 19 and analyzed by Harthill (2011), other nations have harnessed their occupational safety and health laws to cover workplace bullying behaviors. This is not the case in the United States. The federal Occupational Safety and Health Act (OSHA), the primary workplace safety law covering private sector employees, mandates that every covered employer "shall furnish to each of [its] employees employment and a place of employment which are from recognized hazards that are causing or are likely to cause death or serious physical harm to [its] employees (Occupational Safety and Health Act of 1970, 2016). Despite a plausible need for intervention by occupational health and safety agencies in workplace bullying and mobbing situations (Harthill, 2011), the overwhelming focus of these agencies remains on purely physical workplace hazards. It is unclear at this juncture whether there will be any movement on this in the near future.

Public Benefit Programs

Targets of workplace bullying and mobbing may be able to access a variety of public benefit programs to provide them with leave time and income replacement. These benefit programs vary in terms of eligibility standards and are hardly generous in terms of monetary benefits and coverage. Also, to date, they have not been sufficiently researched in terms of specific applications to bullying and mobbing targets. Nonetheless, here are four potential options for bullied workers: workers' compensation, family and medical leave, unemployment benefits, and Social Security disability benefits.

Workers' compensation

State workers' compensation programs "provide cash benefits, medical care, and rehabilitation services" to workers who have suffered injuries that "arise out of employment" and in "the course of employment" (Burton, 2011, p. 1). Workers' compensation is a no-fault system designed to replace tort lawsuits for workplace accidents. Its original and continuing focus has been on physical injuries and impairments, which places claims for injuries suffered by nonphysical bullying behaviors in a legal gray area.

Workers' compensation authority John Burton has noted that "mental-mental" claims, that is, "those that involve both a mental cause and a mental consequence," are the most problematic cases for workers' compensation, especially given strong trends toward limiting claims for psychological stress (Burton, 2011, p. 2). He has further reported that "over a dozen states . . . never compensate 'mental-mental' cases," instead requiring "some physical component to the injury" (Burton, 2011, p. 3). There is a significant need for more comprehensive research on claimant success rates for obtaining workers' compensation for workplace bullying and mobbing.

Family and medical leave

The federal Family and Medical Leave Act (FMLA) of 1993 entitles eligible employees to up to 12 weeks of unpaid leave during a 12-month period in several circumstances, including "a serious health condition that makes the employee unable to perform the functions of the position of such employee" (Family and Medical Leave Act of 1993, 2016). Presumably someone suffering from an abusive work environment could present health conditions sufficient to meet this eligibility standard.

Of course, the FMLA is hardly a panacea to the many individuals who cannot easily afford to leave paid employment for an extended period of time. Although some employers and a few states have adopted some form of paid family leave, most workers are left with FMLA benefits when employer-provided paid sick days and vacation time are used up, if they are offered at all. However, if removal from a toxic workplace can help a targeted worker assess his or her options and stabilize his or her health, then FMLA benefits at least open the door to that possibility.

Unemployment benefits

For bullied workers who lose or leave their jobs, unemployment insurance benefits may provide some income replacement. However, most states hold that workers who voluntarily resign without good cause are presumptively ineligible to receive unemployment benefits. This frequently leaves targets of workplace bullying in a bind when it comes to qualifying for unemployment benefits, for all too often, leaving a job is the best way to escape further abuse.

Here, too, there is a significant need for research, in this case examining unemployment eligibility for targets of bullying and mobbing across the states. However, to illustrate relevant developments in one state, New York potentially allows those who leave their jobs due to toxic work environments to retain eligibility (Yamada, 2013b). Recent decisions by the state's Unemployment Insurance Appeal Board have held that being subjected to workplace behaviors that "exceed the bounds of propriety" may constitute good cause to voluntarily leave a job and thus preserve a claimant's eligibility (Yamada, 2013b). Here is an excerpt of a New York administrative law judge's 2013 ruling for a claimant, building on those decisions:

> I credit the claimant's credible sworn testimony that his supervisor's repeated criticism and scolding of him in a raised voice made him feel bullied and harassed, especially in the presence of other employees. I further credit the claimant's credible sworn testimony that the supervisor's actions including pointing and reprimanding him, consisted of the word "stupid," and other language which embarrassed the claimant and that the claimant believed he was being ridiculed by the supervisor. . . . I conclude that the claimant had good cause within the meaning of the unemployment insurance Law to quit when he did. (Yamada, 2013b)

Social Security disability

At times, targets of workplace bullying and mobbing may develop conditions so serious that they cannot return to work for an extended period of time. In these circumstances, they may be eligible to receive federal Social Security disability benefits (Social Security Disability Benefits, 2015). To qualify for federal disability benefits, claimants must be able to establish that they cannot work due to a medical condition "expected to last at least one year or result in death" (Social Security Disability Benefits, 2015, p. 4). Those who are experiencing conditions frequently associated with bullying and mobbing, such as post-traumatic stress disorder and severe clinical depression, may qualify.

IMPLICATIONS FOR EMPLOYEE RELATIONS STAKEHOLDERS AND MENTAL HEALTH PROVIDERS

Even in the current absence of direct, statutorily imposed lines of liability for workplace bullying and mobbing in the United States, employee relations stakeholders and mental health providers may find themselves addressing the legal ramifications of these behaviors.

Lawyers for Employees

The current paucity of workplace bullying laws calls upon plaintiffs' employment lawyers to assess whether existing legal protections may provide potential relief to individuals alleging such mistreatment. This leads to consideration of whether workplace bullying and mobbing events can be "shoehorned" into existing laws. It should come as no surprise that targets are often told by lawyers that their legal options are limited, especially if their situations do not implicate protected class status covered by employment discrimination laws. However, as the foregoing discussion indicates, viable legal and benefits options may exist.

The impacts of bullying and mobbing behaviors on career and employment prospects, psychological and physical health, and overall well-being are such that helping a client get time away from an abusive work setting or cope with a resulting job loss may be a very desirable goal, regardless of whether prospects for legal relief look promising. Thus, in addition to considering litigation options, lawyers can help clients sort out and apply for potential benefits that may provide leave time and income replacement. Chief among these options are family and medical leave, workers' compensation, unemployment insurance, and disability payment, which have been previously discussed.

Labor Unions

Unions can play, and some are playing, at least four roles where workplace bullying and mobbing behaviors cross with potential legal protections (Yamada, 2009b). First, in collective bargaining, they can propose provisions designed to protect union members against abusive supervision. Second, even in the absence of specific provisions against abusive supervision, they can raise general substantive and procedural contract rights on behalf of bullied or mobbed union members who have been subjected to discipline or termination.

Third, they can train union shop stewards to identify and resolve bullying situations, including those between union members. Fourth, and finally, unions can actively support the passage of antibullying legislation such as the Healthy Workplace Bill. (Further commentary about how labor unions can respond to bullying and mobbing may be found in chapter 23).

Employers and Their Lawyers

Although many instances of generic workplace bullying and mobbing fall between the cracks of current employment protections, employers may face liability when such behaviors overlap with existing wrongful discharge claims and employment discrimination laws. Also, the organizational costs of bullying and mobbing behaviors (such as lower productivity and higher employee turnover) may cause wiser employers to consider proactive preventive and responsive measures. These are among the questions that lawyers for employers may want to discuss with clients and their human resources personnel:

- Even without a direct line of legal liability for workplace bullying and mobbing behaviors, what existing legal protections are implicated by these behaviors in the client's legal jurisdiction(s) of business and operations?
- Should the employer adopt a policy on workplace bullying for its employee handbook, keeping in mind that following such policy may be deemed a contractual obligation?
- Should the employer have a protocol for handling complaints about workplace bullying, keeping in mind that it will be expected to follow any such protocol?
- Should the employer include workplace bullying in its in-house employee training programs?

The client counseling role of an employer's lawyer comes into play here. An attorney who understands the organizational costs of bullying and mobbing behaviors may want to engage the client in a conversation about the potential benefits of addressing these behaviors more affirmatively. This includes, however, acknowledging the trade-offs and potential liability exposure created by adopting policies, procedures, and training programs that are not necessarily required by law.

Mental Health Providers

As chapters 5 and 13 examine in detail, targets of workplace bullying may experience clinical depression, post-traumatic stress disorder, and other conditions. Mental health providers obviously play the primary role in providing therapy, counseling, and treatment to patients in this context. In addition, they may be involved in providing diagnoses and insights associated with legal and benefits matters, such as

- Helping clients to understand the potential stressors of engaging in employment litigation and referring them to legal assistance and relevant enforcement agencies when appropriate;
- Providing diagnoses that potentially inform eligibility for family and medical leave, workers' compensation, disability benefits, and unemployment benefits; and,
- Providing expert support and testimony in employment litigation.

In these settings, mental health providers are not asked nor expected to make legal conclusions or to engage in legal analyses. However, those who possess a basic familiarity with how mental health conditions and diagnoses intersect with relevant eligibility standards and legal frameworks will be more effective in assisting their clients.

LARGER PERSPECTIVES

This chapter has provided an overview of the current American legal state of the art concerning workplace bullying and mobbing. Some 15 years ago, the prospects of American legislatures seriously considering and adopting workplace bullying laws were quite slim. After all, workplace bullying and workplace mobbing were just starting to enter into the vocabulary of American employee relations. Today, as U.S. employee relations stakeholders increasingly recognize the harmful impact of these behaviors, the intervening roles of law and public policy are becoming more pronounced. Gradually, at least, it appears that the law is catching up to our understanding of the human and organizational damage wrought by abusive work environments.

Beyond some of the early legislative successes, other indicators suggest that the American legal infrastructure is becoming more hospitable to legal interventions for workplace bullying and mobbing:

> During the last decade, workplace bullying has gained the attention of the legal profession. Workplace bullying has been the topic of major articles in bar association journals, legal newspapers, and legal newsletters. . . . It has been a featured topic at national programs sponsored by legal

groups such as the American Bar Association, Association of American Law Schools, National Employment Lawyers Association, and International Academy of Law and Mental Health. . . . The American legal academy has been slower to recognize workplace bullying as a topic of scholarship and teaching than its counterparts in fields such as organizational psychology, organizational behavior, and labor relations, but that is changing. . . . More recently, articles discussing and critiquing the Healthy Workplace Bill and related developments have appeared in the legal literature. (Yamada, 2013a, pp. 347–348)

Diversity and Dignity: Competing or Complementary Frameworks?

Nevertheless, as chapter 19 illustrates, many other nations have enacted laws and regulations to protect workers against bullying and mobbing on the job. One may accurately claim that the United States is now significantly behind the curve in this regard. To understand this state of affairs, one must grasp that in the United States, "protected class status remains the dominant paradigm of how we frame legal issues of worker harassment and mistreatment" (Yamada, 2004, p. 507).

Perhaps this makes sense in view of recent history, in that America played a lead role in diversifying its workforce, especially in terms of race and sex. Because these difficult societal transitions have been far from seamless, the law has intervened when discrimination and harassment entered the picture. Nations with more homogeneous demographics and patriarchal attitudes toward employment managed to sidestep these conflicts and the accompanying need for legal protections, at least until later.

It follows, in any event, that America's approach to addressing psychological abuse at work has been grounded in a diversity framework, whereas other nations have looked at these behaviors through a more status-blind dignity lens. A question remains as to whether the United States can embrace the latter while preserving the former. America's affinity for identity-based legal interventions suggests difficulty in achieving this kind of paradigmatic coexistence, but plenty of bullied and mobbed workers who have found themselves without legal recourse would urge us to make it work.

Therapeutic Jurisprudence

A dignity-informed approach for American employment law would do well to embrace therapeutic jurisprudence, a school of legal philosophy and practice that examines the therapeutic and antitherapeutic properties of our laws and legal systems and favors psychologically healthy legal outcomes (Yamada, 2009a). From the standpoint of protecting workers from significant, health-harming dignity violations and supporting individual well-being, a therapeutic jurisprudence perspective on workplace bullying and mobbing easily favors legal interventions to fill the current gaps in our laws and regulations as well as a stronger safety net of employee benefits to help targeted workers cope with and, when appropriate, transition out of abusive work situations.

Taking these concepts of dignity and therapeutic jurisprudence into account, it could be fairly argued that efforts to enact Healthy Workplace legislation reflect a broader attempt to advance the underlying values of American employment law in two significant ways. First, our laws should protect everyone from disabling abuse on the job. Second, our laws should embrace psychologically healthy workplaces as a worthy public policy goal. Higher levels of employee morale, organizational productivity, and public health will surely follow.

REFERENCES

Age Discrimination in Employment Act of 1967, 29 U.S.C. §§ 621–634 (2016).
Americans with Disabilities Act of 1990, 42 U.S.C. § 12101 (2016).
Burlington Industries, Inc. v. Ellerth, 524 U.S. 742 (U.S. 1998).
Burton, J. F. (2011, January 8). *Workers' compensation benefits for workplace stress*. Paper presented at the Annual Meeting of the Labor and Employment Relations Association, Denver, Colorado.
Cal. Gov't Code § 12950.1 (2014).
Civil Rights Act of 1964, Title VII, 42 U.S.C. § 2000e et seq. (2016).
Davenport, N., Schwartz., R. D., & Elliott, G. P. (1999). *Mobbing: Emotional abuse in the American workplace*. Ames, IA: Civil Society Publishing.
Family and Medical Leave Act of 1993, 29 U.S.C. §§ 2601–2654 (2016).
Fulton County. (2012). *Resolution to establish a Fulton County policy prohibiting bullying in the workplace*. Retrieved from http://mm1.co.fulton.ga.us/cache/00010/272/2012-0998.pdf
Harris v. Forklift Systems, Inc., 510 U.S. 17 (U.S. 1993).
Harthill, S. (2011). Workplace bullying as an occupational safety and health matter: A comparative analysis. *Hastings International & Comparative Law Review*, 34(2) 253–302.
Healthy Workplace Act, Tenn. Code, § 50-1-501 et seq. (2014).
Hollomon v. Keadle, 931 S.W.2d 413 (Ark. 1996).
Namie, G. (2014). *2014 WBI U.S. workplace bullying survey*. Retrieved from http://workplacebullying.org/multi/pdf/WBI-2014-US-Survey.pdf
Namie, G., & Namie, R. (1999). *Bullyproof yourself at work*. Benicia, CA: DoubleDoc Press.
National Labor Relations Act of 1935, 29 U.S.C. §§ 151–169 (2016).
Occupational Safety and Health Act of 1970, 29 U.S.C. §§ 651 et seq. (2016).
Snyder v. Turk, 627 N.E.2d 1053 (Ohio App. 2 Dist. 1993).
Social Security Disability Benefits. (2015). Retrieved from https://www.ssa.gov/pubs/EN-05-10029.pdf

Utah State Personnel Management Act, Abusive Conduct, Utah Code 67-19-44 (2015).
Van Dyck, T. P., & Mullen, P. M. (2007). Picking the wrong fight: Legislation that needs bullying. *Mealey's Litigation Report, 3*(11), 1–4.
Yamada, D. C. (2000). The phenomenon of "workplace bullying" and the need for status-blind hostile work environment protection. *Georgetown Law Journal, 88*(3), 475–536.
Yamada, D. C. (2004). Crafting a legislative response to workplace bullying. *Employee Rights and Employment Policy Journal, 8*(2), 475–521.
Yamada, D. C. (2009a). Human dignity and American employment law. *University of Richmond Law Review, 43*(2), 523–570.
Yamada, D. C. (2009b, November 17). The role of unions and collective bargaining in combating workplace bullying [Blog post]. Retrieved from https://newworkplace.wordpress.com/2009/11/17/the-role-of-unions-and-collective-bargaining-in-combating-workplace-bullying
Yamada, D. C. (2010). Workplace bullying and American employment law: A ten-year progress report and assessment. *Comparative Labor Law & Policy Journal, 32*(1), 251–284.
Yamada, D. C. (2013a). Emerging American legal responses to workplace bullying. *Temple Political & Civil Rights Law Review, 22*(2), 329–354.
Yamada, D. C. (2013b, August 13). Workplace bullying targets winning unemployment benefits appeals in New York State [Blog post]. Retrieved from https://newworkplace.wordpress.com/2013/08/13/workplace-bullying-targets-winning-unemployment-benefits-appeals-in-new-york-state
Yamada, D. C. (2015). Workplace bullying and the law: U.S. legislative developments 2013–15. *Employee Rights and Employment Policy Journal, 19*(1), 49–60.

19

Comparing and Contrasting Workplace Bullying and Mobbing Laws in Other Countries with the American Legal Landscape

Ellen Pinkos Cobb

In terms of legal protections and liability, workplace bullying and mobbing have entered into the law of the workplace. As chapter 18 indicates, in the United States, this process is still in its infancy. However, in other nations, employment laws that expressly cover bullying and mobbing behaviors—sometimes using different terminology—have firmly entered that landscape.

Accordingly, this chapter will compare and contrast workplace bullying and mobbing laws in Europe and a number of European countries, Australia and Australian States, Canada and Canadian Provinces, and Japan with the United States' legal landscape. Legal provisions will be examined to inform employment lawyers, labor relations personnel, and human resources professionals how other parts of the world approach and manage abusive workplace conduct. The relevance of these laws for multinational employers and the varying cultural contexts of regions and countries in regard to the awareness and treatment of workplace bullying and mobbing will also be discussed.

INTERNATIONAL OVERVIEW OF WORKPLACE BULLYING AND THE LAW

A variety of terms are used around the world for workplace bullying and mobbing. The term *workplace bullying* is commonly used in Anglo-Saxon jurisdictions, including the United Kingdom and Australia. French-speaking jurisdictions tend to use either the term *harcèlement moral* ("moral harassment"), as in Belgium and France, or the term *harcèlement psychologique* ("psychological harassment"), as in Quebec. The term *mobbing* is used in

Scandinavia and Germany, while Japan refers to workplace bullying as *power harassment*. No single definition of bullying has been agreed on internationally (Milczarek, 2010). Some countries use the term *harassment* to address abusive workplace behavior that is based on a protected class (status-based harassment). Others define harassment without the mention of protected grounds (status-blind harassment). Only status-blind harassment provisions will be discussed in this chapter.

Generally speaking, occupational health and safety laws protect workers from risks that pose a physical threat to their health and safety in the workplace. In many regions, countries, states, and territories around the world, there is a developing realization that psychosocial risks at the workplace can also pose a threat to workers' health and safety. In response, laws have been enacted requiring an employer to provide a safe work environment for employees, with a duty to prevent both physical and psychological risks. Along these lines, workplace bullying is often addressed in occupational health and safety legislation as arising out of this concept that an employer's duty of care encompasses protecting against abusive work environments. The requirement to ensure persons in the workplace are both psychologically and physically safe has been interpreted to require a workplace free from bullying and mobbing, as will be discussed below.

EUROPEAN REGION AT THE FOREFRONT

Europe has played a lead role in the enactment of legal and policy measures responding to bullying and mobbing. The Charter of Fundamental Rights of the European Union (2000), Article 31(1), states, "Every worker has the right to working conditions which respect his or her health, safety and dignity" (p. 15). Although there is no European-wide law addressing and prohibiting workplace bullying and mobbing, this concept of bullying and mobbing as a violation of a worker's dignity has influenced a broad interpretation of European workplace legislation and the creation of nonlegislative instruments. Moreover, European countries were the first to enact laws to measure, regulate, prevent, and punish workplace bullying and mobbing.

In Europe, bullying at work is frequently considered to fall implicitly within the scope of the primary directive on health and safety at work, EU Occupational Health and Safety Directive 89/391/EEC, also known as the Framework Directive, dating back to 1989 (European Agency for Safety and Health at Work, n.d.; European Foundation for the Improvement of Living and Working Conditions (Eurofound), 2010). Under the Framework Directive, employers "have a duty to ensure the safety and health of workers in every aspect related to the work" (Council Directive 89/391/EEC of 12 June 1989, n.d.) on the basis of prescribed general principles of prevention. The

European Agency for Safety and Health at Work (EU-OSHA), the European Union's information agency for occupational safety and health, has interpreted this language to mean that European employers are legally required to assess occupational safety and health risks in the workplace, including psychosocial risks (EU-OSHA, 2014). Psychosocial risks include bullying and mobbing.

In the United States, however, occupational health and safety laws only address matters related to physical safety. Although harassment in the workplace based on protected characteristics is addressed through federal and state antidiscrimination laws, there typically is little protection for abusive conduct in the workplace when it is not based on a protected trait. Employee relations, human resources, and health and safety professionals involved with multinational companies should be aware of these distinctions.

Global companies should also be aware of the strength and prominence of the European social partners. The European social partners represent the two sides of industry: employers and employees. In this role, they consult with the European Commission, support negotiation of collective bargaining agreements, and sit with the European Economic and Social Committee alongside other organizations representing civil society. In the words of Leka and Jain (2014), the social partners "play a vital role in the European decision-making process in the field of safety and health at work, as they have to be consulted at various stages" (p. 238). There is not a comparable organization with such strength and recognition in the United States.

The social partners state, "Employers are legally obliged through the EU Framework Directive on health and safety at work to protect their workers regarding all elements of occupational health and safety. This is a general obligation, which also covers harassment and violence at work to the extent that they have an impact on workers' health and safety" (European Social Partners, 2011, p. 26).

Social partners may negotiate Framework Agreements that have contractual force on signatories and their members. In 2007, the social partners signed the Framework Agreement on Harassment and Violence at Work (Commission of the European Communities, 2007; European Social Partners, 2007). The aim of this agreement is to build awareness of workplace violence and harassment among employee relations stakeholders and to provide them with tangible guidance for preventing and managing these behaviors: "The text commits the members of the signatory parties to combat all unacceptable behavior that can lead to harassment and violence at the workplace" (European Social Partners, 2007, para. 1). The agreement "condemns all forms of harassment and violence and confirms the duty of the employer to protect workers against them. Companies in Europe are requested to adopt a policy of zero tolerance of such behavior and to specify procedures to deal with cases of harassment and violence where they occur" (Commission of the European Communities, 2007, para. 4).

In the words of Cobb (2012, p. 18), "Employers are required to publish a statement that: [(1)] Makes it clear that violence and harassment in the workplace will not be accepted; [(2)] specifies procedures to be followed where cases arise; and [(3)] ensures procedures are underpinned by a short checklist of simple principles included in the social partners agreement" (Commission of the European Communities, 2007).

According to Cobb (2012, p. 17), the "Agreement does not address bullying by name [but] defines harassment and violence as unacceptable behavior by one or more individuals that can take many different forms," stating "harassment occurs when someone is repeatedly and deliberately abused, threatened and/or humiliated in circumstances relating to work" (European Social Partners, 2007, p. 3). As outlined in Sweeney et al. (2009)., harassment

> may be carried out by one or more manager[s], worker[s], service user[s], or member[s] of the public with the purpose or effect of violating a manager's or worker's dignity, affecting his/her health, and/or creating a hostile work environment.
> The . . . Agreement recognizes that harassment and violence can:
> - Be physical, psychological, and/or sexual;
> - Be one off incidents or more systematic patterns of behaviour;
> - Be amongst colleagues, between superiors and subordinates or by third parties such as clients, customers, patients, pupils, etc.;
> - Range from minor cases of disrespect to more serious acts, including criminal offences, which require the intervention of public authorities. (Sweeney et al., 2009, p. 6)

Subsequently, 16 countries have implemented the agreement through national cross-industry social partner agreements, while in other countries, laws implement the agreement. For example, the Danish Working Environment Act is the legal means by which the Framework Agreement has been implemented in Denmark (European Social Partners, 2011).

WORKPLACE BULLYING AND MOBBING LAWS IN INDIVIDUAL EUROPEAN COUNTRIES

Individual European countries have introduced workplace bullying and mobbing legislation or incorporated provisions addressing it into existing occupational health and safety laws. In addition, or alternatively, government agencies have issued guidance on workplace bullying. While not legally binding, the guidance offers instructive information. Through these regulations and publications, employers and employees become aware of the existence of workplace bullying and mobbing, what behavior constitutes it, the prohibition against it, as well as measures to address and prevent it. France and Sweden were among the first nations to enact workplace bullying and mobbing laws, with Norway, Denmark, Belgium, and the Netherlands following suit. This reflects, in particular, a Northern European recognition that the psychological risks inherent in the workplace must be prevented and protected, just as physical ones have been for years.

The Swedish Work Environment Authority, in issuing new provisions on the organizational and social work environment in March 2016, noted, "Our mental and social work environment is just as important as the physical." (Swedish Work Environment Authority, 2015). This statement is fitting and consistent, as Sweden became the first country to combat workplace bullying through legislation in the early 1990s.

Some European nations, including those in Scandinavia, have "coordinated, established policies on preventing and tackling violence and harassment" (Eurofound, 2015a, p. 91). Public awareness, coverage in legislation, and involvement of the social partners are all contributing factors toward the effectiveness of these policies. By contrast, in other nations, health and safety laws, employment laws, and criminal laws may lack these types of specified directives for preventing and responding to harassment and violence at work.

RELEVANT PROVISIONS OF INDIVIDUAL EUROPEAN COUNTRIES' LAWS

Overall, Europe has played a lead role in adopting legal and policy measures that cover workplace mobbing and bullying. In addition to the aforementioned EU policy initiatives, many individual European nations have enacted laws and regulations or extended existing legal protections that address these behaviors. The following discussion reviews a representative sampling of these developments.

Nations Adopting a Workplace Health and Safety Regulatory Approach

In Sweden, workplace bullying falls under the Ordinance of the Swedish National Board of Occupational Safety and Health, adopted September 21, 1993, designed to guard against victimization in the workplace through a series of provisions. *Victimization*, according to this ordinance, is "recurrent reprehensible or distinctly negative actions which are directed against individual employees in an offensive manner and can result in those employees being placed outside the workplace community" (Swedish National Board of Occupational Safety and Health, 1993, p. 3). Victimization includes "adult bullying, mental violence, social rejection, and harassment" (Swedish National Board of Occupational Safety and Health, 1993, p. 7). The Ordinance requires employers to prevent victimization of workers by appropriately managing the workplace and to instruct employees not to engage in victimization. The employer's duties include catching the early warning signs of workplace victimization and enacting swift countermeasures against it as well as providing support for victimized employees (Swedish National Board of Occupational Safety and Health, 1993).

Denmark has also proclaimed that the physical and psychological work environment are equivalent, amending its Working Environment Act in 2013 to clarify that the law covers both the physical and psychological working environment (Arbeidstilsynet, 2016).

Laws on workplace bullying often include requirements for the employer concerning the organization of work. Norway's Working Environment Act, No. 62/2005, amended by the Act of 14 December 2012, No. 80, and most recently on July 1, 2015 (Arbeidstilsynet, 2016), addresses bullying in organizations as follows, per the Norwegian Labour Inspection Authority (2009):

> Efforts to combat bullying are to be part of the systematic health, safety and environment work in the undertaking. It is important to develop routines that provide a basis for an inclusive working environment and that foster a corporate culture that discourages bullying. This work must be carried out on three levels:
> - Prevention, in order to reduce the likelihood of the problem arising;
> - Handling, in order to stop any bullying that occurs; and
> - Follow-up, in order to learn from the situation and implement corrective measures so as to prevent recurrence. (Norwegian Labour Inspection Authority, 2009, p. 3)

Requirements for the psychosocial work environment in the act include the following:

- Managing work to safeguard workers' integrity and dignity,
- Ensuring that employees are not exposed to harassment or other improper conduct, and
- Protecting workers from threats, violence, and other forms of mistreatment (Arbeidstilsynet, 2016).

The act covers all aspects of employment, including training, working conditions, and termination (Arbeidstilsynet, 2016).

In Belgium, the law requires the employer to conduct a risk analysis, inform and train workers, and appoint a prevention adviser and confidential counselor, a person trusted by management and the workforce. According to Eurofound (2015a),

> new legislation came into force in Belgium in September 2014 that placed harassment in the more general framework of psychosocial risks and stated that employers [must recognize harassment] like any other risk to employees' health. The legislative framework introduces a counselor for psychosocial risks, mandates compulsory training for confidential counselors, and extends the definition of "moral harassment." Workers reporting any abusive attack benefit from shorter response times by the prevention counselor, who has to carry out an inspection unless the employer takes suitable measures, offers better protection against retaliation, and sets the right to compensation. (p. 40)

Slovenia requires that the employer "adopt measures to prevent, eliminate, and manage cases of violence, mobbing, harassment and other forms of psychosocial risks at the workplace which can pose a threat to workers' health" (Health and Safety at Work Act, 2011, Art. 24). The aforementioned act imposed a fine between €2,000 and €40,000 on employers who do not "adopt measures to prevent, eliminate and manage cases of violence, mobbing, harassment and other forms of psychosocial risks at the workplace that can pose a threat to workers' health" (Health and Safety at Work Act, 2011, Art. 76). Additionally, a 2013 amendment to the Employment Relationships Act prohibits bullying at work (Ministry of Labour, Family, Social Affairs, and Equal Opportunities, 2002).

The aforementioned laws reveal that a number of European countries have enacted similar provisions for management of bullying and mobbing in the workplace. The underpinning of these laws is that health and safety encompasses psychological risks as well as physical risks. Accordingly, an employer's obligation is to conduct work in a manner such that a risk of bullying and mobbing is minimized. Measures to ensure this obligation include defining bullying and mobbing and making it clear that such behavior is not acceptable in the workplace. Requirements concerning the organization of work or a risk analysis may be specified, with the employer assessing psychological risks and implementing measures to prevent them or reduce their occurrence.

Further supportive preventive measures include a written antibullying policy, posting and distribution of the policy, and training. The appointment of a confidential counselor or a similar type person for an employee to speak with, as Belgium has implemented, may also be a component of ensuring protection against bullying. A complaint filing and investigation process that respects principles of confidentiality, impartiality, and fair treatment are an essential part of the process, as is protection from retaliation. Appropriate measures to be taken against a perpetrator, and follow-up, including implementation of corrective measures, are often included.

France: Health and Safety and Criminal Law Address Bullying

France's Social Modernization law of 2002 authorized criminal and civil liability as punishment for moral harassment in the Criminal Code (Criminal Code of the French Republic, 2016) and Labor Code (Code du Travail, 2016). The Labour Code (in French, *Code du travail*) imposes an obligation on employers to prevent moral harassment (*harcèlement moral*). Bullying and other behaviors that result in the violation of individuals' dignity in the workplace are all included under the designation of "moral harassment," which is defined in the code as a prohibition: "No employee shall suffer repeated acts of moral harassment that are aimed at, or may result in, a degradation of his or her working condition and are likely to harm his/her individual rights and dignity, or affect his/her health or career" (Cobb, 2015, p. 79).

Employers must take "all necessary measures to prevent bullying in the workplace" (Code du Travail, 2016, Art. L. 1152-4). The code specifies that "formal obligations include (1) establishing internal policies prohibiting bullying in the workplace; and (2) displaying in the workplace a copy of article 222-33-2 of the Criminal Code concerning the criminal offense of bullying, with the criminal sanctions attached thereto" (Code du Travail, 2016, Art. L.1152-4).

French criminal law also prohibits bullying: "Harassing another person by repeated conduct which is designed to or which leads to a deterioration of his conditions of work liable to harm his rights and his dignity, to damage his physical or mental health or compromise his career prospects is punished by a year's imprisonment and a fine of 15,000 EUR" (Criminal Code of the French Republic, 2016, Art. 222-33-2).

French Supreme Court (Court of Cassation) rulings have recognized "that moral harassment can occur even without malicious intent on the part of the perpetrator and considered that certain management methods constituted moral harassment when they consisted of repeated actions against an employee" (Numhauser-Henning & Laulom, 2011). A 2012 ruling by the Criminal Chamber of the French Supreme Court found that an employee may be convicted of harassment even in cases where the perpetrator is the subordinate of the victim. Here, an employee had harassed his superior for years by portraying the victim as professionally incompetent and spreading false rumors, which had led the victim to eventually commit suicide (Court of Cassation, Criminal Division, 2011).

In July 2016, the Paris public prosecutor recommended that France Telecom's former executive and other key figures be put on trial for moral harassment for a wave of suicides at the multinational telecommunications corporation in 2008 and 2009. The prosecutor's investigation found that managers had been trained to demoralize their teams in order to encourage employees to leave, with work inspectors reinforcing the "brutality" of such management methods, which had an adverse effect on employees' physical and mental well-being, and management failed to take into account the "alarms and warnings" over the impact of its actions and the "psychological risks" to staff. The next step is for an examining judge to decide whether or not to order a trial. (BBC News, 2016).

Ireland: Code of Practice as Guidance and Evidence in Court

The employer in Ireland must also take reasonable steps to prevent bullying in the workplace. Ireland's Health and Safety Authority states,

> Bullying is a workplace issue and a human relations issue. Therefore it comes under the authority of various agencies and is on the agenda of many interested parties. It is a health and safety issue in so far as bullying has been identified as hazardous or dangerous as it can lead to both safety problems and health problems. It is also an IR issue, a HR issue, often a legal issue and a personal and public health issue. So many agencies and interested parties are stakeholders in this difficult area. (Health and Safety Authority, 2016, para. 4)

Ireland approaches the management of bullying through guidance set forth in a comprehensive, though not legally binding, Code of Practice. The Irish Health and Safety Authority Code of Practice for Employers and Employees on the Prevention and Resolution of Bullying at Work states,

> Provides practical guidance for employers on identifying and preventing bullying at work arising from their duties under section 8 (2) (b) of the 2005 Act as regards "managing and conducting work activities in such a way as to prevent, so far as is reasonably practicable, any improper conduct or behaviour likely to put the safety, health and welfare at work of his or her employees at risk". It also applies to employees in relation to their duties under section 13 (1) (e) of the 2005 Act to "not engage in improper conduct or behaviour that is likely to endanger his or her own safety, health and welfare at work or that of any other person". (Health and Safety Authority, 2007, p. 2)

The Code of Practice instructs parties on developing and communicating antibullying policies, staff training, naming of a contact person for complaints about bullying at work, informal and formal processes for resolving bullying at work, investigation, action, appeals, and closure.

Though the Codes of Practices are not laws, but only guidance, a court may refer to a Code of Practice as evidence in a bullying case. Irish courts have used the definition of bullying and other provisions from the Code of Practice as guidance in determining whether bullying has occurred (Health and Safety Authority, 2007).

More of Europe and the United Kingdom

Not all European countries have enacted laws expressly prohibiting workplace bullying and mobbing. Germany does not have a specific workplace bullying law. However, the German Federal Ministry of Labor and Social Affairs states, "Employers are obliged to protect their employees' right of privacy and health. They must therefore prevent mobbing, act against employees who mob others and take all possible measures to prevent mobbing in their companies" (Federal Ministry of Labour and Social Affairs, 2011, para. 4).

The laws of the United Kingdom do not directly prohibit workplace bullying that is unrelated to a protected characteristic, with the U.K. government stating, "Bullying and harassment is behaviour that makes someone feel intimidated or offended. Harassment is unlawful under the Equality Act 2010. . . . Bullying itself isn't against the law, but harassment is" (GOV.UK, 2016, para. 1–4). However, claims may be brought under the following laws:

- The Health and Safety at Work etc. Act of 1974 (Legislation.gov.uk, 2015) imposes a statutory duty on "every employer to ensure, so far as is reasonably practicable, the health, safety and welfare at work of all his employees";
- The Equality Act 2010 prohibits harassment on the basis of protected categories (Equality Act 2010, Chapter 10, 2016); and,
- The Protection from Harassment Act (1997) creates a statutory tort for interpersonal harassment.

The Protection from Harassment Act has infrequently been applied in an employment context. However, in 2005, an employer was held civilly vicariously liable for harassment committed by an employee in the course of employment (*Majrowski v. Guy's and St. Thomas's NHS Trust*, 2005).

Australia: Antibullying Orders

In Australia, workplace bullying is covered by national antibullying laws as well as state and territory laws and health and safety bodies. The Fair Work

Ombudsman (n.d.) states, "Bullying happens when someone in the workplace repeatedly behaves unreasonably towards another person or group of people and causes a risk to health and safety in the workplace. This behavior doesn't have to be related to the person or group's characteristics and adverse action does not have to have happened" (para. 12).

Australia's federal government passed the Fair Work Amendment Bill, effective January 1, 2014, giving the Fair Work Commission the power to handle antibullying complaints. Any worker who "reasonably believes he/she is, or has been, the victim of workplace bullying will be able to apply to the Commission to have an investigation conducted into the matter and have their grievances heard" (Fair Work Amendment Act, 2013, Part 6-4B).

A worker is bullied at work as follows:
While the worker is at work in a constitutionally covered business: an individual; or a group of individuals; repeatedly behaves unreasonably towards the worker, or a group of workers of which the worker is a member; and that behaviour creates a risk to health and safety. It does not include "reasonable management practices" related to performance management or disciplinary action. (Fair Work Amendment Act, 2013, Part 6-4B)

For particular behaviors to be considered actionable bullying, they must be repeated, unreasonable, and pose a risk to workplace safety and health. Procedurally, the act empowers the commission to engage in investigations, hold conferences and hearings, and issue remedial orders

Australia has also enacted protections at the state level. For example, in the state of Victoria, workplace antibullying legislation came about largely in response to a bullying-related suicide. In September 2006, a 19-year-old woman named Brodie Panlock committed suicide after being subjected to a horrific course of bullying at her workplace. This tragedy served as the major impetus behind "Brodie's Law," which makes serious workplace bullying a criminal offense punishable by up to 10 years in prison. Brodie's Law "extend[ed] the application of the stalking provisions in the Crimes Act 1958 to include behavior" typical of serious workplace bullying (Department of Justice and Regulation, 2015, para. 3). The law applies to all serious bullying, regardless of form—physical, psychological, verbal, and cyberbullying are all covered—and is directed at employees engaged in bullying rather than employers (Crimes Amendment (Bullying) Act 2011, No. 20 of 2011, n.d.; Department of Justice and Regulation, 2015). In Victoria, the Fair Work Commission's jurisdiction is parallel to and operates separately from its Occupational Health and Safety Act and workers' compensation laws.

Canada: Protection from Psychological Harassment, Province by Province

There is much the United States can learn from its neighbor to the north on measures to address and prevent workplace bullying, as a number of Canadian jurisdictions have specific legislation on workplace bullying and psychological harassment or include bullying under a definition of workplace violence. According to Cobb (2015, p. 14), "Quebec was the first North American governmental entity to pass anti-bullying legislation, defining psychological harassment" and requiring employers to "take reasonable action to prevent [it] and, whenever they become aware of such behavior, . . . put a stop to it" (Act Respecting Labour Standards, 2016, § 81.19).

Provinces, including Ontario, Manitoba, and Saskatchewan, have subsequently enacted laws to protect workers from psychological harassment. Further, in jurisdictions "where there is no legislation which specifically addressed bullying, the general duty clause establishes the duty of employers to protect employees from risks at work. These risks can include harm from both physical and mental health aspects" (Canadian Centre for Occupational Health and Safety, 2014, para. 6). Here, the general duty clause refers to an employer's general duties under Occupational Health and Safety Laws.

Under Canadian Federal Occupational Health and Safety Regulations, workplace violence is defined as "any action, conduct, threat, or gesture of a person towards an employee in their workplace that can reasonably be expected to cause harm, injury, or illness to that employee" (Canada Occupational Health and Safety Regulations, 2016, §20.2). Covered employers must generate workplace prevention policies, which should be posted in accessible locations.

Canadian provinces have also enacted antiharassment laws and regulations. For example, Ontario's Occupational Health and Safety Act (OHSA; Ontario Ministry of Labour, 2016) further protects employees from psychological harassment. An employer is "required to (a) prepare policies with respect to workplace harassment, (b) develop and maintain programs to implement their policies, and (c) provide information and instruction to workers on the contents of policies and programs" (Lee & Lovell, 2014, p. 36). In addition, amendments to the Ontario statute require every employer, "in consultation with the committee or a health and safety representative, if any, [to] develop and maintain a written program to implement the policy with respect to workplace harassment" (Occupational Health and Safety Act, 2016, Clause 32.0.6), as well as to conduct appropriate investigations concerning reported workplace harassment and inform the relevant parties of any findings and corrective action.

Manitoba's Workplace Safety and Health Act and Regulations, effective in 2011, introduced "requirements to protect workers from psychological harassment in the workplace, such as intimidation, bullying and humiliation" (Cobb, 2012, p.15). An employer must develop and implement a written policy to prevent harassment in the workplace and ensure that workers comply with it (Manitoba Workplace Safety and Health Act and Regulations, 2014). As with Ontario, the harassment prevention policy must be developed in consultation with the committee at the workplace; the representative at the workplace; or when there is no committee or representative, the workers at the workplace (Manitoba Workplace Safety and Health Act and Regulations, 2014).

British Columbia's WorkSafe BC approved three workplace bullying and harassment policies, effective November 2013. The policies arise from the provisions of the Workers Compensation Act requiring "an employer to take all reasonable steps in the circumstances to ensure the health and safety of its workers . . . [and] to inform, instruct, train, and supervise workers to ensure their safety and that of other workers" (WorkSafeBC, 2013, Item D3-115-2, Note 2). The policies clarify the obligations of employers, workers, and supervisors by defining bullying and harassment and setting forth steps that "WorkSafeBC considers to be reasonable for an employer to take to address the hazards of workplace bullying and harassment" (WorkSafeBC, 2013, Item D3-115-2, Note 2).

Japan: Workplace Bullying Tied to Stress and Overwork

In Japan, workplace bullying is referred to as *power harassment*; this term refers to any behavior toward a person in the same workplace that, taking advantage of one's superior position and going beyond the appropriate scope of duties, inflicts physical or psychological pain on that person or negatively impacts the working environment. There is not a requirement that the behavior be intentional.

Japan's Ministry of Health, Labour, and Welfare released the first definition of power harassment through issuance of a report titled the "Working Group Roundtable Regarding Workplace Bullying and Harassment," published on January 30, 2012. The report defines six categories of power harassment:

- Committing acts of physical abuse or assault, such as punching, kicking, and throwing items;
- Committing mental or psychological attacks, including intimidation, defamation, and slander;
- Isolation or ostracism;
- Forcing an employee to perform clearly unnecessary tasks;
- Not assigning an employee any work, or assigning menial tasks that require far less ability or experience than the employee has; and
- Invasion of privacy. (Ministry of Health, Labour, and Welfare, 2012)

The report recommends that a company have a clear message from top management about eliminating power harassment from the workplace, including internal agreement as to which actions constitute power harassment; that it determine company rules on the subject and announce the company's policy to all employees; and that it provide internal and external consultation areas and conduct training to prevent reoccurrence of incidents of which it has become aware (Ministry of Health, Labour, and Welfare, 2012).

Although power harassment is not a cause of action in itself, an employee who has been power harassed may potentially bring a civil claim against the employer for failing in its duties to supervise and create a safe working environment. Under Japan's November 2014 law, Promoting Measures to Prevent Death from *Karoushi* (death due to overwork), two types of *karoushi* are identified: related health problems causing death and stress-related suicide (Cobb, 2015). In November 2014, Tokyo's District Court awarded JPY 58 million ($472,164) to the aggrieved family members of a 24-year-old shop manager of a fast-food chain who committed suicide. The court found that the employee had committed suicide as a result of overwork and power harassment by his supervisor (Kinder, 2014).

An amendment to Japan's Industrial Safety and Health Act, effective December 2015, requires an employer regularly employing 50 or more workers to offer an annual stress check to employees, with the results to be kept confidential (Ministry of Health, Labour, and Welfare, 2015). This measure demonstrates a realization of stress as a measure of a harmful working environment. As the Tokyo District Court decision above recognized in its ruling, bullying causes stress.

CULTURAL INFLUENCES

International laws on workplace bullying and their applications must be considered in a cultural context, as the experience of abusive behaviors at work often differs depending on cultural norms. Consideration of various economic climates is also important.

Cultural norms and stereotypes inform perceptions of what constitutes workplace harassment and can both mitigate and aggravate harassment. What is perceived as bullying in one culture may not be construed as bullying in a different culture. Various cultural expectations play into what is appropriate behavior. Perceptions and interpretations vary from region to region.

According to Eurofound (2015a), "Awareness of the causes and consequences of harassment at work varies greatly among [European countries]. Awareness is generally low in southern and eastern European countries and tends to increase in Scandinavian countries, the Netherlands, and the UK" (p. 52). Procedures designed to deal with workplace bullying and harassment are "most common in companies in the Scandinavian countries and Belgium, and less observed in the southern and eastern countries, as well as in some continental countries, such as Austria and Germany" (Eurofound, 2015b, p. 47).

The Eurofound report titled "Violence and Harassment in European Workplaces," a survey of 28 EU nations and Norway, sorted the countries into groups based on prevalence rates of applicable behaviors, workplace procedures and policies, and overall public awareness (Eurofound, 2015b). The report found distinct regional differences between the Northern European countries and the Southern and Eastern European countries.

Scandinavian and Northern European countries have the most awareness and laws, leading the way in regard to the societies and public authorities in these countries acknowledging workplace bullying as a serious issue. Accordingly, policies aimed at counteracting workplace bullying have been enacted by stakeholders in these countries, including governments, businesses, and social partners, and there is a higher level of awareness and reporting by workers. In contrast, most Eastern European countries demonstrated very little awareness of the issue, despite higher prevalence rates than in Europe as a whole. In the Czech Republic, Estonia, Latvia, and Lithuania, awareness levels were low, and employers were slow in development policies and procedures.

According to the Eurofound report, "In general, a high share of workers in Scandinavian countries report experiencing violence and harassment, followed by other countries in Northern and Central Europe. Overall, violence and harassment is less reported in southern countries" (2015b, p. 57). The results of this report indicate the importance of giving a name and an avenue for reporting and regulating workplace bullying. Identification leads to awareness, an essential starting point for countries, organizations, and workers.

In another study, Professor Nikos Bozionelos and 19 international scholars examined the extent to which white collar workers will tolerate office bullies, ultimately finding that national cultures make a difference (Bozionelos, 2013). In nations with high *performance orientation* cultures "that value accomplishments, a sense of urgency and explicit communication," such as the United States, England, and Australia, bullying was found to be more acceptable. The study found that in these cultures, there is an extremely low *power distance*, which leads to a large and strong degree of suffering as workers' experience bullying as unfair and unnatural. In contrast, a high rate of acceptance of bullying was found in Singapore, Hong Kong, and Taiwan, where there is the cultural characteristic of high performance orientation combined with a link to strong power distance. The study determined this combination made workplace bullying more acceptable in Confucian Asian countries. The power distance feature results in a high acceptance of the actions of those in power.

The study found that Latin American cultures are less accepting of bullying in the workplace. Bozionelos speculated that some of these countries place greater value on humane working conditions than on economic performance. However, few Latin American countries have enacted workplace bullying laws.

LESSONS FOR THE UNITED STATES AND MULTINATIONAL EMPLOYERS

Much may be learned by the United States, and should be, from the international legal landscape, as the workplace becomes increasingly globalized and more areas of the world regulate bullying and mobbing in the workplace. A key starting point should be the realization that many countries regard health and safety in the workplace as encompassing both physical and psychological risks to workers' health and safety. Denmark's law expressly states this premise, and much of the EU and Canada have enacted legislation for the workplace with this as an underpinning.

The United States lags much of the world in realizing that bullying and mobbing signify a risk to the health and safety of employees and need to be managed in the work environment. Based on the legislation and guidance discussed in this chapter, indicating the growing global realization of addressing psychological risks such as bullying and mobbing, the United States' lack of regulation is a particularly glaring omission from the legal landscape.

Further, multinational corporations must navigate the legal landscape of bullying and mobbing laws in some of the countries in which they conduct business. In an increasingly globalized workplace, a comprehension of international laws regulating bullying and mobbing is a necessity for these companies and their employee relations and human resource professionals. Additionally, liability for workplace bullying may and has been imposed by courts, civilly and criminally, through fines and imprisonment. This requires multinational employers to be aware of varying legal strictures to engage in employee education and training, prevention, and response concerning bullying and mobbing behaviors. In some countries, these obligations may differ between individual states and provinces.

Not so long ago, voices within the United States argued sexual harassment was too difficult to regulate. But regulation and laws would follow, and the workplace has become better for it. Companies and government agencies in the United States would do well to keep this in mind and to learn from what many other countries have come to know and provide for through their laws and policies: that acknowledging and regulating bullying is part of creating today's safe and healthy workplace.

REFERENCES

Act Respecting Labour Standards, Chapter N-1.1, § 81.19 (2016). Retrieved from http://legisquebec.gouv.qc.ca/en/showdoc/cs/N-1.1

Arbeidstilsynet. (2016). *Act relating to working environment, working hours and employment protection, etc. (Working Environment Act)*. Retrieved from http://www.arbeidstilsynet.no/binfil/download2.php?tid=92156

Arbejdstilstynet. (2016). *Working environment act*. Retrieved from http://engelsk.arbejdstilsynet.dk/en/regulations/acts/working-environment-act/arbejdsmiljoeloven1

BBC News. (2016, July 7). France Telecom suicides: Prosecutor calls for bullying trial. Retrieved from http://www.bbc.com/news/world-europe-36733572

Bozionelos, N. (2013). White collar bullying: Country cultures make their mark on workplace bullying. *International HR Advisor, 55*, 10–11.

Canada Occupational Health and Safety Regulations, SOR/86-304 (2016). Retrieved from http://laws.justice.gc.ca/PDF/SOR-86-304.pdf

Canadian Centre for Occupational Health and Safety. (2014). *Bullying in the workplace*. Retrieved from https://www.ccohs.ca/oshanswers/psychosocial/bullying.html

Charter of Fundamental Rights of the European Union, 2000/C 364/01 (2000). Retrieved from http://www.europarl.europa.eu/charter/pdf/text_en.pdf

Cobb, E. P. (2012). Workplace bullying: A global health and safety issue. In International Labor and Employment Relations Association (Ed.), *Proceedings of the 16th ILERA World Congress*. Retrieved from http://ilera2012.wharton.upenn.edu

Cobb, E. P. (2015). *Workplace bullying, violence, harassment, discrimination and stress*. Printed by CreateSpace Publishing Platform.

Code du Travail. (2016). Retrieved from https://www.legifrance.gouv.fr/affichCode.do?cidTexte=LEGITEXT000006072050&dateTexte=20160415

Commission of the European Communities. (2007). *Communication from the Commission to the Council and the European Parliament transmitting the European framework agreement on harassment and violence at work*. Retrieved from http://www.europarl.europa.eu/hearings/20071121/femm/framework_agreement_en.pdf

Council Directive 89/391/EEC of 12 June 1989 (n.d.).

Court of Cassation, Criminal Division. (2011, December 6). Appeal No. 10-82266. *Criminal Bulletin 2011, 249*. Translation retrieved from https://translate.googleusercontent.com/translate_c?depth=1&hl=en&prev=search&rurl=translate.google.com&sl=fr&u=https://www.legifrance.gouv.fr/affichJuriJudi.do%3FoldAction%3DrechJuriJudi%26idTexte%3DJURITEXT000025119012%26fastReqId%3D25775373%26fastPos%3D1&usg=ALkJrhhNcm06oa14grQBNGD0Umer7cARkg

Crimes Amendment (Bullying) Act 2011, No. 20 of 2011. (n.d.). Retrieved from http://www.austlii.edu.au/au/legis/vic/num_act/caa201120o2011302

Criminal Code of the French Republic. (2016). Retrieved from http://www.legislationline.org/documents/section/criminal-codes/country/30

Department of Justice and Regulation. (2015). Bullying—Brodie's Law. Retrieved from http://www.justice.vic.gov.au/home/safer+communities/crime+prevention/bullying+-+brodies+law

Equality Act 2010, Chapter 10 (2016). Retrieved from http://www.legislation.gov.uk/ukpga/2010/15/contents

European Agency for Safety and Health at Work (EU-OSHA). (n.d.). Directive 89/391/EEC—OSH "Framework Directive" of 1989. Retrieved from https://osha.europa.eu/en/legislation/directives/the-osh-framework-directive/1

European Agency for Safety and Health at Work (EU-OSHA). (2014). *2014–2015 campaign: Healthy workplaces manage stress*. Retrieved from https://osha.europa.eu/en/healthy-workplaces-campaigns/healthy-workplaces-manage-stress

European Foundation for the Improvement of Living and Working Conditions (Eurofound). (2010). *Foundation findings: Physical and psychological violence at the workplace*. Retrieved from http://www.eurofound.europa.eu/sites/default/files/ef_files/pubdocs/2010/54/en/1/EF1054EN.pdf

European Foundation for the Improvement of Living and Working Conditions (Eurofound). (2015a). *Violence and harassment in European workplaces: Extent, impacts and policies*. Retrieved from http://www.eurofound.europa.eu/observatories/eurwork/comparative-information/violence-and-harassment-in-european-workplaces-extent-impacts-and-policies

European Foundation for the Improvement of Living and Working Conditions (Eurofound). (2015b). *Violence and harassment in European workplaces: Causes, impacts and policies*. Retrieved from http://www.eurofound.europa.eu/sites/default/files/ef_comparative_analytical_report/field_ef_documents/ef1473en.pdf

European Social Partners. (2007). *Framework agreement on harassment and violence at work*. Retrieved from https://drive.google.com/file/d/0B9RTV08-rjErYURTckhMZzFETEk/view

European Social Partners. (2011). *Implementation of the European autonomous framework agreement on harassment and violence at work*. Retrieved from https://www.etuc.org/IMG/pdf/BROCHURE_harassment7_2_.pdf

Fair Work Amendment Act, No. 73 (2013). Retrieved from https://www.legislation.gov.au/Details/C2013A00073

Fair Work Commission. (2016). *What is the process?* Retrieved from https://www.fwc.gov.au/disputes-at-work/anti-bullying/what-is-the-process

Fair Work Ombudsman. (n.d.). Bullying & harassment. Retrieved from https://www.fairwork.gov.au/employee-entitlements/bullying-and-harassment

Federal Ministry of Labour and Social Affairs. (2011). *Bullying at work*. http://www.bmas.de/EN/Our-Topics/Labour-Law/bullying-at-work.html

GOV.UK. (2016). Workplace bullying and harassment. Retrieved from https://www.gov.uk/workplace-bullying-and-harassment

Health and Safety at Work Act. (2011). *Official Gazette of the Republic of Slovenia*, 43, 5649. Retrieved from http://www.ilo.org/wcmsp5/groups/public/---ed_protect/---protrav/---ilo_aids/documents/legaldocument/wcms_175696.pdf

Health and Safety Authority. (2007). *Code of Practice for employers and employees on the prevention and resolution of bullying at work*. Retrieved from http://www.hsa.ie/eng/Publications_and_Forms/Publications/Occupational_Health/Code_of_Practice_for_Employers_and_Employees_on_the_Prevention_and_Resolution_of_Bullying_at_Work.html

Health and Safety Authority. (2016). *Bullying at work*. Retrieved from http://www.hsa.ie/eng/Topics/Bullying_at_Work

Kinder, T. (2014, November 5). Japanese restaurant manager commits suicide after doing 190 hours overtime in a month. *International Business Times*. Retrieved from http://www.ibtimes.co.uk/japanese-restaurant-chain-must-pay-320000-damages-after-manager-commits-suicide-1473346

Lee, R. T., & Lovell, B. L. (2014). Workplace bullying: A Canadian perspective. In R. Csiernik (Ed.), *Workplace wellness: Issues and responses* (pp. 33–50). Toronto, Canada: Canadian Scholars' Press.

Legislation.gov.uk. (2015). Health and Safety at Work etc. Act 1974, Chapter 37 Retrieved from http://www.legislation.gov.uk/ukpga/1974/37

Leka, S., & Jain, A. (2014). Policy approaches to occupational and organizational health. In G. F. Bauer & O. Hämmig (Eds.), *Bridging occupational, organizational, and public health: A transdisciplinary approach* (pp. 231–249). New York: Springer.

Majrowski v. Guy's and St. Thomas's NHS Trust, EWCA Civ. 251 (2005).

Manitoba Workplace Safety and Health Act and Regulations. (2014). Retrieved from https://www.gov.mb.ca/labour/safety/pdf/2014_whs_act_regs.pdf

Milczarek, J. (2010). *European risk observatory report: Workplace violence and harassment: A European picture*. Retrieved from https://osha.europa.eu/en/tools-and-publications/publications/reports/violence-harassment-TERO09010ENC

Ministry of Health, Labour and Welfare. (2012). *Syokuba no ijime iyagarase-mondai ni kansuru entakukaigi working group houkoku* [Roundtable Working Group report on workplace bullying, harassment problem]. Retrieved from http://www.mhlw.go.jp/stf/shingi/2r98520000021hkd.html

Ministry of Health, Labour, and Welfare. (2015). *Sutoresu chekku tou no syokuba ni okeru mentaru herusu taisaku kajyuu-roudou taisaku tou* [Stress checks and other overwork prevention and mental health measures for the workplace]. Retrieved from 2015 http://www.mhlw.go.jp/bunya/roudoukijun/anzeneisei12

Ministry of Labour, Family, Social Affairs, and Equal Opportunities. (2002). *Employment Relationships Act*. Retrieved from http://www.mddsz.gov.si/en/legislation/veljavni_predpisi/zdr_1

Norwegian Labour Inspection Authority. (2009). *The bully-free workplace: Working together to stop bullying at the workplace*. http://www.arbeidstilsynet.no/binfil/download2.php?tid=97306

Numhauser-Henning, A., & Laulom, S. (2011). *Harassment related to sex and sexual harassment law in 33 European countries*. Retrieved from http://ec.europa.eu/justice/gender-equality/files/your_rights/final_harassement_en.pdf

Occupational Health and Safety Act, R.S.O. 1990, c. O.1 (2016). Retrieved from https://www.ontario.ca/laws/statute/90o01?_ga=1.211205525.1498100697.1462979171

Ontario Ministry of Labour. (2016). *Workplace violence*. Retrieved from https://www.labour.gov.on.ca/english/hs/pubs/wpvh/violence.php

Protection from Harassment Act. (1997). Retrieved from http://www.legislation.gov.uk/ukpga/1997/40/contents

Swedish National Board of Occupational Safety and Health. (1993). *Victimization at work* (Ordinance AFS 1993:17). Retrieved from https://www.av.se/globalassets/filer/publikationer/foreskrifter/engelska/victimization-at-work-provisions-1993-17.pdf

Swedish Work Environment Authority. (2015). *Mental ill health, stress, threats and violence*. https://www.av.se/en/health-and-safety/mental-ill-health-stress-threats-and-violence

Sweeney, E., Lambert, R., Fleetwood, I., Young, A., Hackitt, J., & Barber, B. (2009). *Preventing workplace harassment and violence: A joint guidance implementing a European social partner agreement.* Retrieved from http://www.hse.gov.uk/violence/preventing-workplace-harassment.pdf

WorkSafeBC. (2013). *BOD decision: 2013/03/20-03: Employer duties: Workplace bullying and harassment.* Retrieved from https://www.worksafebc.com/en/resources/law-policy/board-of-directors-decisions/bod-2013-03-20-occupational-health-and-safety-workplace-bullying-and-harassment-policies?lang=en

PART VI

Workplace Bullying and Mobbing within Specific Employment Sectors

20

Workplace Bullying and Mobbing in the Health Care Sector

Susan Johnson

> *One of the risks of being a nurse is that you can be exposed to deadly diseases and deadly co-workers.*—Nursing unit manager for 15 years

The health care sector, both internationally and in the United States, has been identified as an occupational sector with a high prevalence of workplace bullying and mobbing (Asfaw, Chang, & Ray, 2013; Zapf, Escartin, Einarsen, Hoel, & Vartia, 2011). Workplace bullying in this sector is concerning, as the negative consequences of bullying affect not just the targets of bullying but society as a whole. There is evidence that workplace bullying in clinical settings takes energy away from patient care (Purpora, 2012; Rosenstein & O'Daniel, 2008; Vogelpohl, Rice, Edwards, & Bork, 2013) and can lead to miscommunication and medical errors (Shannon, 2015; Wright & Khatri, 2015). As medical errors are thought to be the third major cause of death in the United States (Makary & Daniel, 2016), workplace bullying in the health sector can be thought of as a public health issue.

Workplace bullying also negatively impacts health care organizations' bottom line. As workplace bullying is associated with poor health outcomes among those who experience bullying (Nielsen & Einarsen, 2012), it is not surprising that it is also associated with increased sick leave use among both targets and witnesses of bullying (Asfaw et al., 2013; Nielsen, Indregard, & Øverland, 2016). Costs associated with sick leave use include loss of productivity and paying for a replacement worker. In health care, covering the shift of a worker who is on sick leave is particularly expensive because these shifts are covered either by coworkers who are working overtime or agency staff whose hourly rate is higher than regular staff.

Additional costs associated with workplace bullying are related to the turnover of employees. Workers who are being bullied often find the only way to end the bullying is to leave the organization (Lutgen-Sandvik, 2006). Nurses who have experienced workplace bullying are more likely to look for another job or to think about leaving the profession (Johnson & Rea, 2009; Simons, 2008). Given ongoing and recurrent shortages of nurses, nurse turnover can be particularly costly to health care organizations who need to hire costly temporary staff as they struggle to fill vacancies (Johnson, Butler, Harootunian, Wilson, & Linan, 2016).

While the effects of workplace bullying in the health sector may ripple out into society as a whole, the individuals who are targets of, and witnesses to, this behavior are the ones who incur the most harm. As workplace bullying has been associated with a multitude of poor health outcomes (Nielsen & Einarsen, 2012), it is first and foremost an occupational health hazard.

This chapter will provide an overview of the current research on workplace bullying in medicine, nursing, and allied health professions in the United States. We will begin this discussion with an exploration of the various terms that researchers have used to describe workplace bullying and an examination of what is known about the prevalence of workplace bullying in the health care sector. The root causes of the workplace bullying, especially those that may explain the high prevalence rate of workplace bullying in this sector, will then be explored. With these root causes in mind, current practices to deal with workplace bullying will be critically examined. Where current practices fall short, alternative solutions will be suggested. To date, most of the research that has been done on workplace bullying in the U.S. health sector is based on samples of nurses who work in hospitals. Therefore, the discussion in this chapter will primarily be about workplace bullying among nurses.

LABELS USED TO DESCRIBE BULLYING-TYPE BEHAVIORS

Within the general academic literature, there has been a proliferation of different terms used to describe the phenomenon of workplace bullying (Crawshaw, 2009; Keashly & Jagatic, 2011, see also chapter 1), and the health care literature is no different (Johnson, Boutain, Tsai, & de Castro, 2015a; Stanley, 2010; Vessey, Demarco, & DiFazio, 2010). Within the health care literature, the most common terms that are used interchangeably with *workplace bullying* are *lateral* or *horizontal violence* and *disruptive behavior* (Longo, 2010). The term *mobbing* is used less often to describe abusive workplace behavior in nursing in the United States.

The terms *lateral, horizontal,* or *vertical violence* are primarily used within the nursing literature, and some authors use these terms interchangeably with *workplace bullying* within the same article (e.g., Ceravolo, Schwartz, Foltz-Ramos, & Castner, 2012; Purpora, 2012; Sellers, Millenbach, Kovach, & Yingling, 2009; Stanley, Martin, Michel, Welton, & Nemeth, 2007; Waschgler,

Ruiz-Hernández, Llor-Esteban, & Jiménez-Barbero, 2013). Lateral violence and horizontal violence are used to describe bullying among coworkers, and vertical violence is used to describe bullying by supervisors toward those with less hierarchical status (Waschgler et al., 2013). A representative definition of lateral violence is "injurious behavior aimed by one worker toward another who is of equal status within a hierarchy that seeks to control the person by disregarding and diminishing his or her value as a human being" (Purpora, Blegen, & Stotts, 2012, p. 306). Examples of behaviors that are classified as lateral violence are "making faces or raising eyebrows in response to a colleague, making rude or demeaning comment[s], acting in ways that undermine the ability to help others, sabotaging another by withholding information, group infighting, scapegoating, passive aggressive communication, gossiping and failure to respect privacy or breaking confidences" (Roberts, 2015, p. 36).

Because these behaviors are all included in most definitions of workplace bullying, it is generally acknowledged that lateral and horizontal violence are essentially the same concept as workplace bullying (Vessey et al., 2010). What differentiates the concept of lateral violence from workplace bullying is that the former originated from the belief that nurses are an oppressed group who, instead of confronting those with power in the organization, turn their anger and aggression toward their peers (Purpora & Blegen, 2012; Roberts, 1983). The concept of workplace bullying was first used in Europe in research that included all occupational sectors and is not characterized by a unified theoretical explanation (Einarsen, Hoel, Zapf, & Cooper, 2011). Nursing researchers base their choice of terminology on their theoretical understandings of the concept or to align their research with a wider body of literature (Purpora & Blegen, 2012; Simons, 2008; Vessey et al., 2010).

Another label for bullying-type behaviors that is used in the nursing and medical literature is *disruptive behaviors*. This term is often used without a formal definition (e.g., Rosenstein & O'Daniel, 2005; Small, Porterfield, & Gordon, 2015), but where it is defined, it too shares many similarities with the concept of workplace bullying. Longo (2010) describes disruptive behavior as follows:

> Overt and covert actions that are displayed by any healthcare worker and that threaten the performance of the healthcare team. . . . [Disruptive behavior] includes emotional-verbal abuse[;] . . . threatening or abusive language; making demeaning or degrading comments; humiliating someone in front of others, including staff and patients; rolling eyes in disgust; sending nasty emails; refusing to mentor; refusing to help others; ignoring attempts at conversations; throwing items; physically assaulting team members; and intimidating others. (p. 2)

Notably, the definition of disruptive behavior includes the idea that these behaviors "threaten the performance of the healthcare team" (Longo, 2010, p. 2), and, by extension, they have the potential to negatively impact patient safety. Although workplace bullying may have the same effect (Wright & Khatri, 2015), not all workplace bullying will necessarily disrupt patient care. Furthermore, workplace bullying is by definition repeated and prolonged behavior directed toward one or more coworkers, whereas disruptive behaviors can be occasional and may not have a specific target. Nevertheless, the terms *disruptive behaviors* and *workplace bullying* are often used interchangeably (Johnson et al., 2015a; Longo, 2010).

There are several unfortunate consequences of the proliferation of different terms for similar behaviors. Within organizations, the use of different labels can mean that policies cannot be located or are not seen as applicable to a given situation (Johnson, Boutain, Tsai, & de Castro, 2015b). One study reported that managers who were familiar with the concept of *workplace bullying* were not familiar with the term *disruptive behavior* (Johnson et al., 2015b). As a result, they were unaware of the existence of a policy within their organization that was labeled "Management of Disruptive Behavior" but also addressed workplace bullying.

Lack of uniform terminology also inhibits targets' and witnesses' ability to communicate their experiences with managers and human resource personnel (Lutgen-Sandvik & Tracy, 2012). Research indicates that instead of focusing on getting the behaviors to stop and repairing the damage caused by the behaviors, unit managers and human resource directors often spend time trying to decide how to label bullying-type behaviors and whether their label fits with terminology found within organizational policies (Cowan, 2012; Johnson, Boutain, Tsai, Beaton, & de Castro, 2015). Finally, lack of common language can hinder research efforts because researchers who use one term for these behaviors may not be aware of similar research that has been done by others who use a different term.

PREVALENCE RATES: CURRENT ESTIMATES AND METHODOLOGICAL ISSUES

Due to methodological issues in the current research, reports of the prevalence of workplace bullying among the health care sector in the United States can best be described as estimates, and comparisons across studies can be difficult. Current issues with the research include inconsistencies in the way workplace bullying is defined and measured, use of localized or nonrandom samples, and the small sample size of many studies. Use of a common measurement tool, such as the Negative Acts Questionnaire (NAQ; Einarsen, Hoel, & Notelaers, 2009), and a common measurement window (such as bullying in the past six months) would resolve some of the definitional and measurement issues.

The second issue is less easily resolved. Researchers who are studying workplace bullying have tended to utilize local samples because this is their accessible population. Health care providers are certified at a statewide level; therefore, national databases of health care workers do not exist. To access participants, researchers have obtained mailing lists from professional organizations (e.g., Johnson & Rea, 2009; Varekojis et al., 2014) or from state certification boards (e.g., Purpora et al., 2012; Simons, 2008). However, taken as a whole, the research is identifying consistent trends in the data. Therefore, despite the limitations of individual studies, reports of the prevalence of workplace bullying in this sector should not be dismissed.

In one of the only nationwide studies of a random sample of workers in the United States, Alterman, Luckhaupt, Dahlhamer, Ward, and Calvert (2013) reported that 8.5 percent of health professionals and 11.1 percent of health care support workers said they had experienced some form of bullying, harassing, or threatening behaviors in the previous 12 months. By comparison, the same study reported that 7.8 percent of the general population of workers said they had been bullied or harassed (N.B.: this figure includes workers in the health care industry; Alterman et al., 2013). This data does suggest that health care workers are more at risk for experiencing workplace bullying than the general population of workers. However, because of the way the question on the survey was phrased (i.e., "DURING THE PAST 12 MONTHS [sic] were you threatened, bullied, or harassed by anyone while you were on the job?"; Alterman et al., 2013, p. 662), this data also may reflect exposure to negative behaviors from the general public and exposure to behavior that is conceptually slightly different from workplace bullying.

When broken down by profession, most of the research on the prevalence of workplace bullying in health care has been among nurses (e.g., Berry, Gillespie, Gates, & Schafer, 2012; Johnson & Rea, 2009; Purpora et al., 2012; Simons, 2008; Small et al., 2015; Stanley et al., 2007; Vessey, DeMarco, Gaffney, & Budin, 2009). The prevalence rates reported by these studies range from 21 percent to 70 percent. Comparison across these studies is difficult due to use of different sampling methods, different terms or definitions, and different measurement tools. However, if one only compares studies with similar sampling methods that used the same instrument to measure workplace bullying (the NAQ) and that defined bullying as experiencing one or more negative acts on a weekly basis, it would appear that the prevalence of workplace bullying among nurses is in the 21–31 percent range (Johnson & Rea, 2009; Purpora et al., 2012; Simons, 2008). While the received wisdom in nursing is that "nurses eat their young" and that newer nurses are more likely to be bullied than experienced nurses (Egues & Leinung, 2013), research findings have not supported this belief. Studies have found no difference in workplace bullying rates among new nurses when compared with more experienced nurses (Chipps, Stelmaschuk, Albert, & Bernhard, 2013; Johnson & Rea, 2009; Simons, 2008).

There is scant research on the prevalence of workplace bullying in the allied health professions. Johnson and Trad (2014) reported that, based on a survey of radiation therapists ($N = 308$) across the United States, 71 percent of respondents were bullied at some time in their career, 68 percent said bullying was present in their current workplace, and 94 percent said they had witnessed workplace bullying. Only 1 percent of respondents said their organizations did not tolerate workplace bullying, and only 10 percent said it was not accepted as normal behavior by employees (Johnson & Trad, 2014).

A study of respiratory therapy managers and supervisors in Ohio ($N = 750$) reported that 25 percent of respondents had been bullied (Varekojis et al., 2014). In this study, respondents who worked in a teaching hospital and had less than 15 years of experience were more likely to report they were targets of workplace bullying (Varekojis et al., 2014). A study of perioperative nurses, surgical techs, and unlicensed perioperative personnel ($N = 167$) reported that 34 percent of the sample had experienced workplace bullying and 59 percent had witnessed it (Chipps et al., 2013). Clearly, more research into the prevalence and correlates of workplace bullying among allied health care workers is needed, particularly among those professions that do not appear to have been studied to date (e.g., occupational and physical therapists, emergency medical technicians, and lab technicians).

Research on workplace bullying in the medical profession is also limited, and most of the research has explored the experiences of residents, interns, and fellows, a population that occupies a middle ground between being a student and being an employee (Kesselheim & Austad, 2011). This status places them at the bottom of the medical hierarchy and makes them particularly vulnerable to workplace bullying (Chadaga, Villines, & Krikorian, 2015). Chadaga et al. (2015) reported that 48 percent of surveyed residents and fellows said they had been bullied in the past 12 months. Mullan, Shapiro, and McMahon (2013) reported that 54 percent of interns reported experiencing disruptive behaviors at least once a month, while only 15 percent of faculty reported experiencing similar levels of disruptive behaviors.

Another study, which asked family physicians whether they had "ever been bullied at work" (Rouse, Gallagher-Garza, Gebhard, Harrison, & Wallace, 2016, p. 3), reported that 28.9 percent of respondents answered affirmatively. At first glance, the prevalence rates of bullying and disruptive behavior reported in these studies are higher than those reported for nurses and allied health workers, but that is probably because the researchers defined and measured the concepts differently. For example, Mullan et al. (2013) reported the prevalence of behaviors that occurred monthly, Chagada et al. (2015) did not specify how often participants had been bullied, and Rouse et al. (2016) measured lifetime experiences of workplace bullying. All three of these measurement methods would yield higher prevalence rates than those reported by studies with stricter parameters for defining workplace bullying.

Interns, residents, and fellows have reported that nurses were the most frequent perpetrators of bullying and disruptive behaviors (Chadaga et al., 2015; Mullan et al., 2013). In contrast, physicians reported that other physicians were the most common perpetrators of disruptive behaviors (Mullan et al., 2013). However, 15 percent of physicians indicated they had been bullied by nursing staff (Mullan et al., 2013). Female (Chadaga et al., 2015; Rouse et al., 2016) and nonwhite (Chadaga et al., 2015) physicians, interns, residents, and fellows are more likely to indicate they have been bullied. In the study by Rouse et al. (2016), which also asked respondents whether they had "ever displayed bullying behaviors toward someone at work" (p. 2), male respondents were more likely than female respondents to report having perpetrated bullying behaviors.

While the data is limited, it indicates that all members of the health care profession may be exposed to workplace bullying, and at rates that are higher than the general sector of U.S. workers. Future studies, especially those that are conducted within a specific organization, should include all professionals and, where possible, should report findings by profession. In addition, larger studies that utilize random sampling methods are needed. In the meantime, the lack of robust data should not deter organizations and regulatory agencies from tackling workplace bullying.

FACTORS WHICH CONTRIBUTE TO WORKPLACE BULLYING IN HEALTHCARE

While a casual observer of workplace bullying might conclude that it is a localized issue between one or more perpetrators and one or more targets, research actually suggests that workplace bullying is a systemic issue that is the result of cultural norms and organizational structures and practices (Fevre, Lewis, Robinson, & Jones, 2013; Neuman & Baron, 2011; Salin & Hoel, 2011). In this section, some of the systemic and organizational antecedents for workplace bullying in the health care sector will be explored. This examination will set the stage for a critical evaluation of current efforts to address workplace bullying in the health care sector, which will be the focus of the next section.

Organizational Structures and Workplace Bullying

The hierarchical nature of health care appears to be one of the primary organizational antecedents of workplace bullying in the health care sector (Hutchinson, Wilkes, Jackson, & Vickers, 2010; Purpora & Blegen, 2012; Wright & Khatri, 2015). Hierarchy, by definition, creates power differentials between different classes of employees. Power, be it formal or informal, is an element that can allow bullying to occur, and which can make it difficult for targets to bring about an end to the bullying (Einarsen et al., 2011; Saunders, Huynh, & Goodman-Delahunty, 2007). Managers and supervisors (e.g., charge nurses and attending physicians) all wield this type of power, and several studies have indicated that members of these groups are more likely to be identified as the perpetrators of bullying (Chadaga et al., 2015; Johnson & Trad, 2014; Johnson & Rea, 2009).

Physicians have traditionally been viewed as the profession that is at the top of the health care hierarchy. However, the current trend is to view medicine, nursing, and allied health professions as collaborative practices, each of which bring a different, but equally important, perspective and skill set to patient care (Siedlecki & Hixson, 2015). As a possible reflection of these changing dynamics, several studies have reported that physician-on-nurse bullying occurs less frequently than nurse-on-nurse bullying (Berry et al., 2012; Johnson & Rea, 2009). However, Vogelpohl et al. (2013) reported that new nurses reported similar rates of being bullied by physicians (59.8%) as by their peers (63.9%). As Berry et al. (2012) also utilized a sample of new nurses, and both studies were done in similar regions of the United States and used the same measurement tool (the NAQ), one cannot merely attribute the differences in their findings to their research methods. The differences in findings between these studies may be a product of the organizations in which the respondents worked and the presence or absence of a nurses' union. Hospital nursing unit managers have indicated that physician-on-nurse bullying can be easier to deal with than bullying between staff nurses, in part because the presence of a nurses' union complicates disciplinary actions when nurses of equal rank are involved (Johnson, 2013). This is clearly an area of research where more studies are needed.

The power differential between the perpetrator and the target may also be based on informal or nonstructural power differences—such as differences in social power in the workplace (i.e., how much social capital each of the involved parties possesses), differences in knowledge about how to get resources, and differences in understanding the unwritten rules of the workplace (Zapf & Einarsen, 2011). This type of power differential would most likely manifest between employees on the same organizational level and may explain some of the bullying of newer nurses by more experienced nurses.

Informal power differences may also explain some of the bullying that occurs between nurses and medical interns and residents. Nurses, who have longer tenure within an institution and more clinical experience, have more informal power than interns and residents (Schlitzkus, Vogt, Sullivan, & Schenarts, 2014).

Working Conditions and Workplace Bullying

Working conditions and organizational practices within organizations also seem to be major risk factors for workplace bullying (Fevre et al., 2013; Hodson, Roscigno, & Lopez, 2006). Based on a national survey of a representative sample of working adults in the United Kingdom, Fevre et al. (2013) concluded that employees who work in organizations where they do not feel valued as individuals, where they feel they have to compromise their principles, and where violence is present are at the greatest risk of experiencing workplace bullying. There is evidence that all three of these conditions may be found in health care organizations in the United States.

Violence is a major occupational hazard for health care workers. According to the Occupational Safety and Health Administration (OSHA, 2015), "Workers in hospitals, nursing homes, and other healthcare settings face significant risks of workplace violence.... Violence is a more common source of injury in healthcare than in other industries" (p. 1). When health care providers experience violence on the job, these experiences may contribute to an overall feeling that the organization cannot keep them safe and that it does not value them as individuals. The failure to provide a safe environment can be seen as a breach in the social contract between organizations and workers. The violation of this social contract has been hypothesized to create an environment in which workplace bullying thrives (Parzefall & Salin, 2010). Additionally, health care providers are expected to respond to violence with equanimity, a process that involves emotional labor (the state in which internal emotions are incongruent with expressed or external emotions; Smith & Cowie, 2010). This emotional labor may manifest as incivility toward, and eventually bullying of, coworkers (Branch, Ramsay, & Barker, 2013).

Violence, caring for traumatic injuries, critically ill and dying patients, and dealing with worried patients and families are all chronic and acute stressors that health care professionals deal with on a regular basis. Neurological research has demonstrated that acute stressors, such as might be experienced by health care providers who are trying to resuscitate a dying person, cause a shift from cognitive (rational) to affective (emotional) thinking processes (Oei et al., 2011; Sandi, 2013). This shift can result in reduced social inhibitions, which may be expressed as incivility and bullying (Bowen,

Privitera, & Bowie, 2011). Chronic stress can lead to increased aggression, which will also increase the likelihood that workplace bullying will occur (Bartholomew, 2014; Neuman & Baron, 2011).

Fevre et al. (2013) also reported that workplace bullying was more likely to be found in organizations where employees said they did not feel valued as individuals. In one survey, the majority of nurses reported that they did not feel their organization valued them as individuals, and this lack of respect manifested in lower wages and diminished ability to bargain for better working conditions (McHugh, Kutney-Lee, Cimiotti, Sloane, & Aiken, 2011). Lack of respect for health care providers as individuals is also exemplified by trends within many health care organizations to adopt management techniques (e.g., Taylorism and the Toyota Lean process) that were originally developed to manage interchangeable factory workers (Hartzband & Groopman, 2016).

In the Fevre et al. (2013) study, organizations with high rates of bullying also had more employees who said they had to compromise their values to continue to work within the organization. Nurses have stated that they have to compromise their values of patient safety and quality of care because of high patient-to-nurse ratios that exist in most organizations (Aiken, Clarke, Sloane, Sochalski, & Silber, 2002). Physicians have also expressed the need to compromise their principles as they reconcile the competing interests of practicing medicine as they were taught while negotiating the reimbursement limitations imposed on them by hospitals and insurance companies (O'Hare & Kudrle, 2007; Whitlock & Stark, 2014).

Fatigue is another factor that can contribute to workplace bullying. Health care providers who work nonday shifts, who work overtime, or who work shifts longer than eight hours experience chronic fatigue (Chen, Davis, Daraiseh, Pan, & Davis, 2014; Lockley et al., 2007). In many parts of the health sector, the work can be fast-paced, with little opportunity for workers to consistently take adequate rest and meal breaks (Rogers, 2008). Shift work, mandatory overtime, and the challenges of balancing work and family issues are all additional factors that contribute to chronic fatigue among nurses (Chen et al., 2014; Rogers, 2008). Physicians, especially residents and interns, are also prone to fatigue. Most physicians work more than 40 hours per week, and while on call, they may experience interrupted sleep (Eddy, 2005; Lockley et al., 2007). Fatigue can cause increase irritability, anger, or aggression (Kamphuis, Meerlo, Koolhaas, & Lancel, 2012), which can be expressed as incivility and bullying (Meier & Gross, 2015).

Finally, employees who work in organizations that are undergoing change are especially vulnerable to workplace bullying (Agervold, 2009; Hutchinson, Vickers, Jackson, & Wilkes, 2005). This may be because managerial focus is on the change, rather than employee behavior, or that during the time when change is occurring managers are not consistently and fairly enforcing standards (Hodson et al., 2006). Employees may also use bullying tactics during change processes as a way of marginalizing or ousting other employees or to consolidate their own organizational power (Hutchinson et al., 2005). In recent years, change in organizational structures and practices seems to be a constant occurrence in health care organizations (Hader, 2013). To minimize the chaos and potential increase in workplace bullying during times of reorganization or change in practice, organizational leaders should consciously manage the process while attending to the emotional needs of employees (Braungardt & Fought, 2008).

Educational Systems and Workplace Bullying

Workplace bullying, like any professional behavior, can be thought of as a learned behavior. Students and new nurses report that instructors and clinical preceptors often use bullying behaviors, instead of constructive criticism, when pointing out deficiencies in their performance (Altmiller, 2012; Del Prato, 2013). Students also report that bullying is used to weed out those whom instructors do not think will be good nurses, or who do not fit the traditional image of a nurse, and it can be used to intimidate minority and nontraditional nursing students (Del Prato, 2013; Moceri, 2010). The practice of weeding out nurses has been traced to Florence Nightingale, one of the founders of modern nursing practice, and is a self-perpetuating practice (Lim & Bernstein, 2014). Nursing students who are targets of, or witnesses to, bullying by staff nurses and professors report they begin to emulate these behaviors themselves to survive (Farrell, 2001; Randle, 2003; Stevenson, Randle, & Grayling, 2006), and nurses who learn that bullying is an acceptable method of professional socialization often adopt this behavior when orienting new nurses in clinical settings. This behavior is so pervasive that the phrase "nurses eat their young" was coined to describe it (Lim & Bernstein, 2014).

While new nurses are targets of workplace bullying, older and more experienced nurses also experience workplace bullying (Johnson & Rea, 2009; Longo, 2013). There is evidence that some of this bullying is perpetrated toward nurses who are viewed as less clinically competent (Johnson, 2013; Lindy & Schaefer, 2010). When this type of workplace bullying occurs, it may also be a legacy of an educational system that demonstrated that the easiest way of correcting mistakes is by using bullying-type behaviors rather than constructive feedback.

The medical profession has also used bullying behaviors to socialize and teach medical students, residents, and interns (Fnais et al., 2014; Mavis, Sousa, Lipscomb, & Rappley, 2014). Public humiliation of students by professors, of residents by interns, and of interns by attending physicians is the form of mistreatment most frequently reported by medical students, residents, and interns (Chadaga et al., 2015; Mavis et al., 2014). This hierarchical humiliation often occurs in the context of what the medical profession calls "pimping" (McCarthy & McEvoy, 2015; Reifler, 2015). Pimping is described as a method of teaching based on the Socratic method of questioning, where the instructor asks a student a series of questions, often in rapid succession. The alleged goal of this instructional method is to teach medical students and residents to think quickly and "on their feet," and some endorse the use of pimping as a legitimate educational tool (Detsky, 2009). However, students have reported feeling humiliated by this practice because it is used as an expression of power to reinforce hierarchical differences, and it can be used to silence genuine questions regarding practice (McCarthy & McEvoy, 2015; Reifler, 2015). Regardless of intent, the negative consequences of this behavior are that physicians learn early in their program that bullying-type behaviors are an acceptable way of teaching, and there is anecdotal evidence that pimping as a form of instruction may also be used by physicians in interactions with patients (Whetzel, 2015).

CURRENT RESPONSES TO WORKPLACE BULLYING

In this section, the current responses to workplace bullying by regulatory agencies, professional organizations, educational programs, and health care organizations will be examined. Where data is available, evidence of the effectiveness of these efforts will be presented. Additionally, suggestions for improving current practice will be offered.

Regulatory Agencies

Currently, there are no regulations on the national level that require organizations to address workplace bullying. The Occupational Safety and Health Administration (OSHA), the entity responsible for regulating the health and safety of employees on a national level, briefly acknowledges that workplace bullying is a form of violence, but it does not offer guidance to organizations on this topic. The publication *Preventing Workplace Violence: A Road Map for Healthcare Facilities* (OSHA, 2015) contains the following advice for health care organizations:

> St. John's leaders have recognized that a nonviolent workplace also requires action against bullying. Because bullying sometimes stems from clinical hierarchies—for example, a physician behaving dismissively toward a nurse—it is particularly important to engage physicians when designing and implementing anti-bullying policies. At St. John,

this engagement starts at the top, where the head of the medical staff has stated unequivocally that bullying will not be tolerated. St. John's electronic incident reporting system allows staff to report bullying and to route this report around their supervisor if he or she is the perpetrator. Nurses have become confident enough to report occasional bullying events by physicians, thanks to a "no fear" environment. (OSHA, 2015, pp. 9–10)

This passage suggests that workplace bullying is mainly perpetuated by physicians and supervisors and that all organizations need to do to address the issue is to draft antibullying policies and create reporting mechanisms.

As has been discussed previously in this chapter, evidence suggests that physicians are not major perpetrators of bullying toward nurses. Furthermore, current research indicates that to address workplace bullying, organizations need to adopt a comprehensive approach that addresses the workplace culture and environment (Vartia & Leka, 2011).

While the reasons that OSHA has not comprehensively addressed workplace bullying are complex, and beyond the scope of this chapter, analyses of some of their earlier documents on violence in the health care sector suggest that OSHA has historically viewed workplace bullying as a patient safety issue, rather than an occupational safety issue (Johnson et al., 2015a). The General Duty Clause, Section 5(a)1, of the Occupational Safety and Health Act of 1970 (the directive under which OSHA was granted authority to regulate workplaces) says that employers are required to provide workplaces that are "free from recognizable hazards that are causing or likely to cause death or serious harm to employees." Some authors have suggested that OSHA can use this clause to regulate workplace bullying (Harthill, 2010). However, as OSHA currently frames workplace bullying as a patient safety issue, it is unlikely that they will issue stronger directives regarding workplace bullying in the near future.

Guidelines for health care organizations also come from the Joint Commission, an independent nonprofit organization that provides accreditation for health care organizations. While voluntary, Joint Commission accreditation is tied to Medicare, Medicaid, and other insurance reimbursement. The Joint Commission is primarily concerned with patient safety; however, under their Environment of Care Standard, they do require health care organizations to monitor, report, and investigate occupational illnesses and injury (Joint Commission, 2016). The Joint Commission (2008, 2016) has several documents that address disruptive behavior, which they describe as follows:

> Overt actions such as verbal outbursts and physical threats, as well as passive activities such as refusing to perform assigned tasks or quietly exhibiting uncooperative attitudes during routine activities. Intimidating and

disruptive behaviors are often manifested by health care professionals in positions of power. Such behaviors include reluctance or refusal to answer questions, return phone calls or pages; condescending language or voice intonation; and impatience with questions. Overt and passive behaviors undermine team effectiveness and can compromise the safety of patients. All intimidating and disruptive behaviors are unprofessional and should not be tolerated. (Joint Commission, 2008, p. 1).

While the Joint Commission does not use the term "workplace bullying" in any of their documents, their description of disruptive behavior closely matches most definitions of workplace bullying, and these documents are commonly viewed as directives that require health care organizations to address workplace bullying (Castronovo, Pullizzi, & Evans, 2016; Johnson et al., 2015a; Johnston, Phanhtharath, & Jackson, 2009).

In the *Sentinel Event Alert, Issue 40: Behaviors That Undermine a Culture of Safety* (Joint Commission, 2008), the Joint Commission outlines a list of actions that organizations can take to address disruptive behaviors. This list includes education on appropriate behaviors, conflict resolution training, creation of policies and procedures that address violations of behavioral standards, and the establishment of a surveillance system to monitor the progress of these initiatives. However, like OSHA, the Joint Commission's discussion of disruptive behaviors primarily focuses on how these behaviors affect patient safety (Johnson et al., 2015a). The only passage that acknowledges the effect these behaviors can have on coworkers is the following: "Conduct all interventions within the context of an organizational commitment to the health and well-being of all staff, with adequate resources to support individuals whose behavior is caused or influenced by physical or mental health pathologies" (Joint Commission, 2008, p. 2). While this passage pays lip service to the needs of targets and witnesses of bullying, it primarily calls on organizations to consider the needs of perpetrators.

Health Care Organizations

There is no nationwide data on the number of health care organizations that have initiatives to deal with workplace bullying, but the Joint Commission's (2016) report indicates that disruptive behavior continues to be a problem that health care organizations have not effectively addressed. In response to the Joint Commission's directives, some health care organizations have adopted policies that address disruptive behavior and workplace bullying (Johnson et al., 2015a; Sellers, Millenbach, Ward, & Scribani, 2012). When backed by top-level leadership and continual education and enforcement, policies and codes of conduct may be effective tools to change organizational culture (Capitulo, 2009). However, evidence suggests that in many organizations, these policies are not consistently enforced and that members of the organizations, including managers, may be unaware of their existence (Johnson et al., 2015b; Sellers et al., 2012).

Some of the other strategies that have been utilized by organizations, or tested by researchers within an organizational setting, include educating employees about workplace bullying, giving classes on effective communication, and training employees to respond to incidents of bullying, incivility, and aggression (e.g., Ceravolo et al., 2012; Chipps & McRury, 2012; Keller, Budin, & Allie, 2016; Stagg, Sheridan, Jones, & Speroni, 2011). While research on the effectiveness of educational interventions has been limited by small sample sizes, the lack of a control group, and the lack of long-term assessment, the evidence suggests that education alone does not address the issue of workplace bullying.

In one study, Chipps and McRury (2012) reported that four months after attending an education program, which included creating a common vision for effective communication and the development of a zero-tolerance policy on workplace bullying, nurses' ($N = 16$) scores on the NAQ actually increased. The authors attributed this increase to a greater awareness of workplace bullying. This program was based in two nursing units in one organization and was not accompanied by systemic changes. Another study, which tested a team-building exercise on four nursing units, reported that lateral violence only decreased in the unit where the manager was committed to sustaining change (Barrett, Korber, Padula, & Piatek, 2009). A third program, which consisted of a 60- to 90-minute workshop designed to teach nurses ($N = 4,000$) about lateral violence and to train them to use assertive communication techniques, reported a decrease in nurse turnover and an increase in reported self-esteem, but little change in reports of verbal abuse after three years of ongoing workshops (Ceravolo et al., 2012). Ceravolo et al. (2012) caution that improvements in retention might not have been due to the workshops, as this was also a time when the U.S. economy was contracting and jobs for nurses were not readily available.

By far the most widely discussed educational intervention in the nursing literature involves a method called *cognitive rehearsal*. In this educational program, nurses are trained to respond to specific incidents of bullying using prerehearsed responses, which may be written on cue cards that the nurses carry with them (Griffin, 2004; Griffin & Clark, 2014; Stagg & Sheridan, 2010; Stagg et al., 2011; Stagg, Sheridan, Jones, & Speroni, 2013). The seminal study that tested this intervention reported that cognitive rehearsal helped new nurses ($N = 26$) confront lateral violence and that as a result of this confrontation, the lateral violence ended (Griffin, 2004). However, the author also noted that four nurses stated that despite responding to incidents of lateral violence as they had been taught, they felt they were "walking on eggshells" (Griffin, 2004, p. 262); were afraid to ask questions; and had to be transferred to another unit within the department. It is possible that the nurses who were able to use cognitive rehearsal to end what was described as lateral violence were merely experiencing conflict or incivility, whereas the nurses who had to be transferred experienced actual workplace bullying.

A recent study that was designed to replicate Griffin's (2004) study reported that after attending an educational program that included cognitive rehearsal ($N = 15$), only one nurse felt comfortable confronting workplace bullying (Stagg et al., 2013). However, there may be some benefit to this training, as seven of the attendees said they were more aware of when their own behaviors could be construed as bullying, and they had made an effort to change their behavior as a result of the workshop (Stagg et al., 2013).

A few studies have detailed systemic efforts to address workplace bullying. These studies are also limited in that they did not provide robust assessments of their effectiveness and lack a control group. Hickson, Pichert, Webb, and Gabbe (2007) described a comprehensive program to address disruptive behavior and unprofessional behaviors at Vanderbilt University School of Medicine; however, they did not include data on the effectiveness of the program. Keller et al. (2016) discussed a comprehensive initiative that included periodic evaluations of the extent of bullying in the organization, education on conflict resolution, empowering bystanders to intervene, instituting a mechanism for reporting bullying, and holding managers accountable for addressing reports of bullying. Data on the effect of this program on the prevalence of workplace bullying was not presented; however, Keller et al. (2016) stated that, based on surveys, the organization is continuing its commitment to the program and is making efforts to improve it. While these initiatives were both organization-wide, they did not include efforts to change any of the working conditions that may give rise to workplace bullying and can therefore best be classified as individual-level initiatives.

Professional Organizations and Educational Institutions

Professional health care organizations have also begun to address the topic of workplace bullying and related behaviors. Within nursing, national professional organizations (e.g., American Nurses Association, National League for Nursing) and state professional organizations (e.g., Washington State Nurses Association, New York State Nurses Association, South Carolina Nurses Association) have issued position statements and educational tools on the topic of workplace bullying and disruptive behavior. The American Medical Association also offers resources that address physician disruptive behavior and medical student mistreatment.

Schools of nursing and medicine have traditionally included education about professional behavior and interprofessional collaboration in the curriculum. In many institutions, this education now explicitly includes discussions of workplace bullying and related concepts (Reifler, 2015; Vogelpohl et al., 2013). Formal residency programs, which support and train new nurses in the clinical setting, are also addressing workplace bullying in an effort to end the practice of "nurses eating their young" (Vogelpohl et al., 2013). Despite these efforts, only 22 percent of new nurses reported learning about workplace bullying in school, and only 36 percent reported learning about it in new employee orientation (Vogelpohl et al., 2013).

GOING FORWARD: MOVING FROM INDIVIDUAL LEVEL TO SYSTEMIC INITIATIVES

Despite the research on workplace bullying that indicates that, for the most part, workplace bullying is a behavior that is shaped by the environment in which workers find themselves, rather than the result of individual attributes of the target and the perpetrator (Neuman & Baron, 2011; Salin & Hoel, 2011; Zapf & Einarsen, 2011), current interventions within the health care sector predominantly focus on the individual rather than the system. While it is laudatory that this sector is addressing workplace bullying, if any real progress is to be made in reducing the prevalence of the phenomenon, systemic changes will need to occur. It is beyond the scope of this chapter to discuss these changes at length; however, they need to include addressing the violence inflicted on health care workers by clients and visitors, creating fair and equitable work practices, and treating all employees as individuals who are worthy of respect. At the same time, organizations need to establish comprehensive programs that specifically address workplace bullying. These programs should include recurring training about workplace bullying, policies and procedures for dealing with incidents of bullying and caring for targets and witnesses, and periodic evaluation of the effectiveness of these interventions.

CONCLUSION

Health care is one of the occupational sectors in the United States with the highest prevalence of workplace bullying, but it is also leading the way in addressing the issue. Health care organizations, regulatory bodies, educational institutions, professional associations, and academic researchers have begun to address the phenomenon of workplace bullying. To date, most of the effort has been focused on workplace bullying experienced by nurses. Future research and organizational interventions need to include physicians and allied health professions. Finally, comprehensive approaches that address both individual and systemic issues need to be deployed and tested.

REFERENCES

Agervold, M. (2009). The significance of organizational factors for the incidence of bullying. *Scandinavian Journal of Psychology, 50*(3), 267–276.

Aiken, L. H., Clarke, S. P., Sloane, D. M., Sochalski, J., & Silber, J. H. (2002). Hospital nurse staffing and patient mortality, nurse burnout, and job dissatisfaction. *Journal of the American Medical Association, 288*(16), 1987–1993.

Alterman, T., Luckhaupt, S. E., Dahlhamer, J. M., Ward, B. W., & Calvert, G. M. (2013). Job insecurity, work-family imbalance, and hostile work environment: Prevalence data from the 2010 National Health Interview survey. *American Journal of Industrial Medicine, 56*(6), 660–669.

Altmiller, G. (2012). Student perceptions of incivility in nursing education: Implications for educators. *Nursing Education Perspectives, 33*(1), 15–20.

Asfaw, A. G., Chang, C. C., & Ray, T. K. (2013). Workplace mistreatment and sickness absenteeism from work: Results from the 2010 National Health Interview survey. *American Journal of Industrial Medicine, 57*(2), 202–213.

Barrett, A., Korber, S., Padula, C., & Piatek, C. (2009). Lessons learned from a lateral violence and team-building intervention. *Nursing Administration Quarterly, 33*(4), 342–351.

Bartholomew, K. (2014). *Ending nurse-to-nurse hostility: Why nurses eat their young and each other* (2nd ed.). Danvers, MA: HCPro.

Berry, P. A., Gillespie, G. L., Gates, D., & Schafer, J. (2012). Novice nurse productivity following workplace bullying. *Journal of Nursing Scholarship, 44*(1), 80–87.

Bowen, B., Privitera, M. R., & Bowie, V. (2011). Reducing workplace violence by creating healthy workplace environments. *Journal of Aggression, Conflict and Peace Research, 3*(4), 185–198.

Branch, S., Ramsay, S., & Barker, M. (2013). Workplace bullying, mobbing and general harassment: A review. *International Journal of Management Reviews, 15*, 280–299.

Braungardt, T., & Fought, S. G. (2008). Leading change during an inpatient critical care unit expansion. *Journal of Nursing Administration, 38*(11), 461–467.

Capitulo, K. L. (2009). Addressing disruptive behavior by implementing a code of professionalism to transform hospital culture. *Nurse Leader, 7*(2), 38–43.

Castronovo, M. A., Pullizzi, A., & Evans, S. (2016). Nurse bullying: A review and a proposed solution. *Nursing Outlook, 64*, 208–214.

Ceravolo, D. J., Schwartz, D. G., Foltz-Ramos, K. M., & Castner, J. (2012). Strengthening communication to overcome lateral violence. *Journal of Nursing Management, 20*(5), 599–606.

Chadaga, A. R., Villines, D., & Krikorian, A. (2015). Bullying in the American graduate medical education system: A national cross-sectional survey. *PLOS ONE, 11*(3), e0150246. doi:10.1371/journal.pone.0150246

Chen, J., Davis, K. G., Daraiseh, N., Pan, W., & Davis, L. S. (2014). Fatigue and recovery in 12-hour dayshift hospital nurses. *Journal of Nursing Management, 22*, 593–603.

Chipps, E. M., & McRury, M. M. (2012). The development of an educational intervention to address workplace bullying: A pilot study. *Journal for Nurses in Staff Development, 28*(3), 94–98.

Chipps, E. M., Stelmaschuk, S., Albert, N. M., & Bernhard, L. (2013). Workplace bullying in the OR: Results of a descriptive study. *Association of Perioperative Registered Nurses Journal, 98*(5), 479–493.

Cowan, R. L. (2012). It's complicated: Defining workplace bullying from the human resource professional's perspective. *Management Communication Quarterly, 26*(3), 377–403.

Crawshaw, L. (2009). Workplace bullying? Mobbing? Harassment?: Distraction by a thousand definitions. *Consulting Psychology Journal: Practice and Research, 61*(3), 263–267.

Del Prato, D. (2013). Students' voices: The lived experience of faculty incivility as a barrier to professional formation in associate degree nursing education. *Nurse Education Today, 33*(3), 286–290.

Detsky, A. S. (2009). The art of pimping. *Journal of American Medical Association, 301*(13), 1379–1381.

Eddy, R. (2005). Sleep deprivation among physicians. *British Columbia Medical Journal, 47*(4), 176–180.

Egues, A. L., & Leinung, E. Z. (2013). The bully within and without: Strategies to address horizontal violence in nursing. *Nursing Forum, 48*(3), 185–190.

Einarsen, S., Hoel, H., & Notelaers, G. (2009). Measuring exposure to bullying and harassment at work: Validity, factor structure and psychometric properties of the Negative Acts Questionnaire–Revised. *Work and Stress, 23*(1), 24–44.

Einarsen, S., Hoel, H., Zapf, D., & Cooper, C. L. (2011). The concept of bullying and harassment at work: The European tradition. In S. Einarsen, H. Hoel, D. Zapf, & C. L. Cooper (Eds.), *Bullying and harassment in the workplace: Developments in theory, research, and practice* (2nd ed., pp. 3–39). New York: CRC Press.

Farrell, G. A. (2001). From tall poppies to squashed weeds: Why don't nurses pull together more? *Journal of Advanced Nursing, 35*(1), 26–33.

Fevre, R., Lewis, D., Robinson, A., & Jones, T. (2013). *Trouble at work.* New York: Bloomsbury.

Fnais, N., Soobiah, C., Chen, M. H., Lillie, E., Perrier, L., Tashkhandi, M. . . . Tricco, A. C. (2014). Harassment and discrimination in medical training: A systematic review and meta-analysis. *Academic Medicine: Journal of the Association of American Medical Colleges, 89*(5), 817.

Griffin, M. (2004). Teaching cognitive rehearsal as a shield for lateral violence: An intervention for newly licensed nurses. *Journal of Continuing Education in Nursing, 35*(6), 257–263.

Griffin, M., & Clark, C. M. (2014). Revisiting cognitive rehearsal as an intervention against incivility and later violence in nursing: 10 years later. *Journal of Continuing Education in Nursing, 45*(12), 535–542.

Hader, R. (2013). The only constant is change. *Nursing Management*, 44(5), 6.

Harthill, S. (2010). The need for a revitalized regulatory scheme to address workplace bullying in the United States: Harnessing the federal Occupational Safety and Health Act. *University of Cincinnati Law Review*, 78(4), 1250–1306.

Hartzband, P., & Groopman, J. (2016). Medical Taylorism. *New England Journal of Medicine*, 374(2), 106–108.

Hickson, G. B., Pichert, J. W., Webb, L. E., & Gabbe, S. G. (2007). A complementary approach to promoting professionalism: Identifying, measuring, and addressing unprofessional behaviors. *Academic Medicine*, 82(11), 1040–1048.

Hodson, R., Roscigno, V., & Lopez, S. (2006). Chaos and the abuse of power. *Work and Occupations*, 33(4), 382–416.

Hutchinson, M., Vickers, M. H., Jackson, D., & Wilkes, L. (2005). "I'm gonna do what I wanna do": Organizational change as a legitimized vehicle for bullies. *Health Care Management Review*, 30(4), 331–336.

Hutchinson, M., Wilkes, L., Jackson, D., & Vickers, M. (2010). Integrating individual, work group and organizational factors: Testing a multidimensional model of bullying in the nursing workplace. *Journal of Nursing Management*, 18(2), 173–181.

Johnson, J., & Trad, M. (2014). Bullying behavior among radiation therapists and its effects on personal health. *Radiation Therapist*, 23(1), 11–20.

Johnson, S. L. (2013). *An exploration of discourses of workplace bullying of organizations, regulatory agencies and hospital nursing unit managers* (Doctoral dissertation). Retrieved from ResearchWorks Archive. (Accession No. 23598)

Johnson, S. L., Boutain, D. M., Tsai, J. H.-C., Beaton, R., & de Castro, A. B. (2015). An exploration of managers' discourses of workplace bullying. *Nursing Forum*, 50(4), 265–273.

Johnson, S. L., Boutain, D. M., Tsai, J. H.-C., & de Castro, A. B. (2015a). An investigation of organizational and regulatory discourses of workplace bullying. *Workplace Health & Safety*, 63(10), 452–461.

Johnson, S. L., Boutain, D. M., Tsai, J. H.-C., & de Castro, A. B. (2015b). Managerial and organizational discourses of workplace bullying. *Journal of Nursing Administration*, 45(9), 457–461.

Johnson, S. L., & Rea, R. E. (2009). Workplace bullying: Concerns for nurse leaders. *Journal of Nursing Administration*, 39(2), 84–90.

Johnson, W. G., Butler, R., Harootunian, G., Wilson, B., & Linan, M. (2016). Registered nurses: The curious case of a persistent shortage. *Journal of Nursing Scholarship*, 48(4), 387–396.

Johnston, M., Phanhtharath, P., & Jackson, B. S. (2009). The bullying aspect of workplace violence in nursing. *Critical Care Nursing Quarterly*, 32(4), 287–295.

The Joint Commission. (2008, July 9). *Behaviors that undermine a culture of safety*. Retrieved from https://www.jointcommission.org/sentinel_event_alert_issue_40 _behaviors_that_undermine_a_culture_of_safety

The Joint Commission. (2016). Patient safety systems. *Comprehensive Accreditation Manual for Hospitals*. Retrieved from https://www.jointcommission.org/assets/1/18 /PSC_for_Web.pdf

Kamphuis, J., Meerlo, P., Koolhaas, J. M., & Lancel, M. (2012). Poor sleep as a potential causal factor in aggression and violence. *Sleep Medicine*, 13(4), 327–334.

Keashly, L., & Jagatic, K. (2011). North American perspectives on hostile behaviors and bullying at work. In S. Einarsen, H. Hoel, D. Zapf, & C. L. Cooper (Ed.), *Bullying and harassment in the workplace: Developments in theory, research, and practice* (2nd ed., pp. 41–71). New York: CRC Press.

Keller, R., Budin, W. C., & Allie, T. (2016). A task force to address bullying. *American Journal of Nursing, 116*(2), 52–58.

Kesselheim, A. S., & Austad, K. E. (2011). Residents: Workers or students in the eyes of the law? *New England Journal of Medicine, 364*(8), 697–699.

Lim, F. A., & Bernstein, I. (2014). Civility and workplace bullying: Resonance of Nightingale's persona and current best practices. *Nursing Forum, 49*(2), 124–129.

Lindy, C., & Schaefer, F. (2010). Negative workplace behaviours: An ethical dilemma for nurse managers. *Journal of Nursing Management, 18*(3), 285–292.

Lockley, S. W., Barger, L. K., Ayas, N. T., Rothschild, J. M., Czeisler, C. A., & Landrigan, C. P. (2007). Effects of health care provider work hours and sleep deprivation on safety and performance. *Journal of Quality and Patient Safety, 33*(11 Suppl), 7–18.

Longo, J. (2010). Combating disruptive behaviors: Strategies to promote a healthy work environment. *Online Journal of Issues in Nursing, 15*(1). doi:10.3912/OJIN.Vol15No01Man05

Longo, J. (2013). Bullying and the older nurse. *Journal of Nursing Management, 21*(7), 950–955.

Lutgen-Sandvik, P. (2006). Take this job and . . . : Quitting and other forms of resistance to workplace bullying. *Communication Monographs, 73*(4), 406–433.

Lutgen-Sandvik, P., & Tracy, S. J. (2012). Answering five key questions about workplace bullying. *Management Communication Quarterly, 26*(1), 3–47.

Makary, M. A., & Daniel, M. (2016). Medical error—the third leading cause of death in the US. *British Medical Journal, 353*, i2139. doi:http://dx.doi.org/10.1136/bmj.i2139

Mavis, B., Sousa, A., Lipscomb, W., & Rappley, M. D. (2014). Learning about medical student mistreatment from responses to the medical school graduation questionnaire. *Academic Medicine, 89*(5), 705–711.

McCarthy, C. P., & McEvoy, J. W. (2015). Pimping in medical education: Lacking evidence and under threat. *Journal of American Medical Association, 314*(22), 2347–2348.

McHugh, M. D., Kutney-Lee, A., Cimiotti, J. P., Sloane, D. M., & Aiken, L. H. (2011). Nurses' widespread job dissatisfaction, burnout and frustration with health benefits signal problems for patient care. *Health Affairs, 30*(2), 202–210.

Meier, L. L., & Gross, S. (2015). Episodes of incivility between subordinates and supervisors: Examining the role of self-control and time with an interaction-record diary study. *Journal of Organizational Behavior, 36*(8), 1096–1113.

Moceri, J. T. (2010). Being cabezona: Success strategies of Hispanic nursing students. *International Journal of Nursing Education Scholarship, 7*(1). doi:10.2202/1548-923X.2036

Mullan, C. P., Shapiro, J., & McMahon, G. T. (2013). Interns' experiences of disruptive behavior in an academic medical center. *Journal of Graduate Medical Education, 5*(1), 25–30.

Neuman, J. H., & Baron, R. A. (2011). Social antecedents of bullying: A social interactionist perspective. In S. Einarsen, H. Hoel, D. Zapf, & C. L. Cooper (Eds.),

Bullying and harassment in the workplace: Developments in theory, research, and practice (2nd ed., pp. 201–225). New York: CRC Press.

Nielsen, M. B., & Einarsen, S. (2012). Outcomes of exposure to workplace bullying: A meta-analytic review. *Work and Stress, 26*(4), 309–332.

Nielsen, M. B., Indregard, A.-M. R., & Øverland, S. (2016). Workplace bullying and sickness absence: a systematic review and meta-analysis of the research literature. *Scandinavian Journal of Work, Environment & Health, 42*(5), 359–370.

Occupational Safety and Health Administration (OSHA). (2015). Preventing workplace violence: A roadmap for healthcare facilities. Retrieved from https://www.osha.gov/Publications/OSHA3827.pdf

Oei, N. Y. L., Veer, I. M., Wolf, O. T., Spinhoven, P., Rombouts, S. A. R. B., & Elzinga, B. M. (2011). Stress shifts brain activation towards ventral affective areas during emotional distraction. *Social Cognitive and Affective Neuroscience, 7*(4), 403–412.

O'Hare, D., & Kudrle, V. (2007). Increasing physician engagement: Using norms of physician culture to improve relationships with medical staff. *Physician Executive, 33*(3), 38–45.

Parzefall, M.-R., & Salin, D. (2010). Perceptions of and reactions to workplace bullying: A social exchange perspective. *Human Relations, 63*(6), 761–780.

Purpora, C. (2012, May). *Horizontal violence and its relationship to quality of care*. Paper presented at the National Conference for Workplace Violence Prevention & Management in Healthcare Settings, Cincinnati, Ohio.

Purpora, C., & Blegen, M. A. (2012). Horizontal violence and the quality and safety of patient care: A conceptual model. *Nursing Research and Practice, 2012*. doi:10.1155/2012/306948

Purpora, C., Blegen, M. A., & Stotts, N. A. (2012). Horizontal violence among hospital staff nurses related to oppressed self or oppressed group. *Journal of Professional Nursing, 28*(5), 306–314.

Randle, J. (2003). Bullying in the nursing profession. *Journal of Advanced Nursing, 43*(4), 395–401.

Reifler, D. R. (2015). The pedagogy of pimping: Educational rigor or mistreatment? *Journal of the American Medical Association, 314*(22), 2355–2356.

Roberts, S. J. (1983). Oppressed group behavior: Implications for nursing. *Advances in Nursing Science, 5*(4), 21–30.

Roberts, S. J. (2015). Lateral violence in nursing: A review of the past three decades. *Nursing Science Quarterly, 28*(1), 36–41.

Rogers, A. E. (2008). The effects of fatigue and sleepiness on nurse performance and patient safety. In R. G. Hughes (Ed.), *Patient Safety and quality: An evidence-based handbook for nurses*. Rockville: MD: Agency for Healthcare Research and Quality.

Rosenstein, A. H., & O'Daniel, M. (2005). Disruptive behavior and clinical outcomes: Perceptions of nurses and physicians. *American Journal of Nursing, 105*(1), 54–64.

Rosenstein, A. H., & O'Daniel, M. (2008). A survey of the impact of disruptive behaviors and communication defects on patient safety. *Joint Commission Journal on Quality and Patient Safety, 34*(8), 464–471.

Rouse, L. P., Gallagher-Garza, S., Gebhard, R. E., Harrison, S. L., & Wallace, L. S. (2016). Workplace bullying among family physicians: A gender focused study. *Journal of Women's Health, 25*(9), 882–888. doi:10.1089/jwh.2015.5577

Salin, D., & Hoel, H. (2011). Organizational causes of workplace bullying. In S. Einarsen, H. Hoel, D. Zapf, & C. L. Cooper (Ed.), *Bullying and harassment in the workplace: Developments in theory, research, and practice* (2nd ed., pp. 227–243). New York: CRC Press.

Sandi, C. (2013). Stress and cognition. *Cognitive Science, 4*(3), 245–261.

Saunders, P., Huynh, A., & Goodman-Delahunty, J. (2007). Defining workplace bullying behaviour professional lay definitions of workplace bullying. *International Journal of Law and Psychiatry, 30*(4–5), 340–354.

Schlitzkus, L. L., Vogt, K. N., Sullivan, M. E., & Schenarts, K. D. (2014). Workplace bullying of general surgery residents by nurses. *Journal of Surgical Education, 71*(6), e149–e154.

Sellers, K., Millenbach, L., Kovach, N., & Yingling, J. K. (2009). The prevalence of horizontal violence in New York State registered nurses. *Journal of the New York State Nurses Association, 40*(2), 20–25.

Sellers, K., Millenbach, L., Ward, K., & Scribani, M. (2012). Horizontal violence among hospital staff RNs and the quality and safety of patient care. *Journal of Nursing Administration, 42*(10), 483–487.

Shannon, S. E. (2015). Ebola, team communication, and shame: But shame on whom? *American Journal of Bioethics, 15*(4), 20–25.

Siedlecki, S., & Hixson, E. (2015). Relationships between nurses and physicians matter. *Online Journal of Issues in Nursing, 20*(3). doi:10.3912/OJIN.Vol20No03PPT03

Simons, S. (2008). Workplace bullying experienced by Massachusetts registered nurses and the relationship to intention to leave the organization. *Advances in Nursing Science, 31*(2), e48–e59.

Small, C. R., Porterfield, S., & Gordon, G. (2015). Disruptive behavior within the workplace. *Applied Nursing Research, 28*(2), 67–71.

Smith, P., & Cowie, H. (2010). Perspectives on emotional labour and bullying: Reviewing the role of emotions in nursing and healthcare. *International Journal of Work Organisation and Emotion, 3*(3), 227–236.

Stagg, S. J., & Sheridan, D. (2010). Effectiveness of bullying and violence prevention programs. *Journal of the American Association of Occupational Health Nurses, 58*(10), 419–424.

Stagg, S. J., Sheridan, D., Jones, R. A., & Speroni, K. G. (2011). Evaluation of a workplace bullying cognitive rehearsal program in a hospital setting. *Journal of Continuing Education in Nursing, 42*(9), 395–401.

Stagg, S. J., Sheridan, D., Jones, R. A., & Speroni, K. G. (2013). Workplace bullying: The effectiveness of a workplace program. *Workplace Health and Safety, 61*(8), 333–338.

Stanley, K. M. (2010). Why so many names for bad behavior? *South Carolina Nurse, 17*(1), 2.

Stanley, K. M., Martin, M., Michel, Y., Welton, J., & Nemeth, L. (2007). Examining lateral violence in the nursing workforce. *Issues in Mental Health Nursing, 28*(11), 1247–1265.

Stevenson, K., Randle, J., & Grayling, I. (2006). Inter-group conflict in health care: UK students' experiences of bullying and the need for organisational solutions. *Online Journal of Issues in Nursing, 11*(2). doi:10.3912/OJIN.Vol11No02Man05

Varekojis, S. M., Chen, E., Kaiser, K., Monks, E., Washington, T., & Wolpert, T. (2014). Workplace bullying among respiratory therapy managers and supervisors in Ohio. *Respiratory Care*, 59(10), OF32.

Vartia, M., & Leka, S. (2011). Interventions for the prevention and management of bullying at work. In S. Einarsen, H. Hoel, D. Zapf, & C. L. Cooper (Eds.), *Bullying and harassment in the workplace: Developments in theory, research, and practice* (2nd ed., pp. 359–379). New York: CRC Press.

Vessey, J. A., Demarco, R., & DiFazio, R. (2010). Bullying, harassment, and horizontal violence in the nursing workforce: The state of the science. *Annual Review of Nursing Research*, 28(1), 133–157.

Vessey, J. A., DeMarco, R. F., Gaffney, D. A., & Budin, W. C. (2009). Bullying of staff registered nurses in the workplace: A preliminary study for developing personal and organizational strategies for the transformation of hostile to healthy workplace environments. *Journal of Professional Nursing*, 25(5), 299–306.

Vogelpohl, D. A., Rice, S. K., Edwards, M. E., & Bork, C. E. (2013). New graduate nurses' perception of the workplace: Have they experienced bullying? *Journal of Professional Nursing*, 29(6), 414–422.

Waschgler, K., Ruiz-Hernández, J. A., Llor-Esteban, B., & Jiménez-Barbero, J. A. (2013). Vertical and lateral workplace bullying in nursing: Development of the Hospital Aggressive Behaviour Scale. *Journal of Interpersonal Violence*, 28(12), 2389–2412.

Whetzel, A. (2015, May 29). Pimped. *Pulse: Voices from the Heart of Medicine*. Retrieved from http://pulsemagazine.org/index.php/archive/stories/491-pimped

Whitlock, D. J., & Stark, R. (2014). Understanding physician engagement and how to increase it. *Physician Leadership Journal*, 1(1), 8–12.

Wright, W., & Khatri, N. (2015). Bullying among nursing staff: Relationship with psychological/behavioral responses of nurses and medical errors. *Health Care Management Review*, 40(2), 139–147.

Zapf, D., & Einarsen, S. (2011). Individual antecedents of bullying: Victims and perpetrators. In S. Einarsen, H. Hoel, D. Zapf, & C. L. Cooper (Eds.), *Bullying and harassment in the workplace: Developments in theory, research, and practice* (2nd ed., pp. 177–200). New York: CRC Press.

Zapf, D., Escartin, J., Einarsen, S., Hoel, H., & Vartia, M. (2011). Empirical findings on the prevalence and risk groups of bullying in the workplace. In S. Einarsen, H. Hoel, D. Zapf, & C. L. Cooper (Eds.), *Bullying and harassment in the workplace: Developments in theory, research, and practice* (2nd ed., pp. 75–106). New York: CRC Press.

21

Workplace Bullying and Mobbing in K–12 Settings: School Principal Mistreatment and Abuse of Teachers

Jo Blase and Joseph Blase

His abuse made me physically sick. It made me emotionally unable to handle my daughter and my husband in a sane and stable way. I couldn't leave it at school. It affected my self-concept, because, after 28 years of teaching, somebody was discrediting me. Physically, it tore me apart. I lost weight, got sick, spent my days and nights crying. I didn't have time for my family.... Every time I am with my husband, I am complaining about school. My husband is to the point where he really wants to slug the guy. He is really upset. He doesn't even like to come in the building. The abuse has affected every aspect of my life. (Blase & Blase, 2003a, p. 135)

It was a very depressing, stifling atmosphere. We were all paranoid, insecure, with low self-esteem. I felt mainly anxiety with occasional panic attacks. Can you imagine all of us eating lunch in silence? It was the same group of people who were laughing their heads off, joking and talking, the year before. My integrity and professionalism were under attack and that threatened me. I always felt I would lose my job. I was always afraid. I always felt a lot of distrust. (Blase & Blase, 2003a, p. 119)

THE PERVASIVENESS OF WORKPLACE MISTREATMENT AND ABUSE

Two decades ago, Hornstein et al. (1995) constructed a model of supervisory *abusive disrespect*, drawing on theories such as symbolic interaction and organizational justice and the related psychology and stress literature. In essence, Hornstein et al. (1995) argued that one's self-worth and security are affected by the respect or disrespect conveyed by others, which, in turn, affects one's mental and physical well-being. From his longitudinal study of 1,000 participants over eight years, Hornstein (1996) concluded that over 90 percent of American workers have been abused by their superiors during their careers, and 20 percent of employees report to abusive bosses on any given day. Other scholars who have specifically focused on administrative mistreatment and abuse in the workplace include Ashforth (1994; *petty tyranny*); Tepper (2000; *abusive supervision*); and Blase, Blase, and Du (2008; *administrative mistreatment and abuse*). Throughout this chapter, the term *mistreatment and abuse* is used, except when particular researchers have used the term *bullying*.

Since Hornstein's (1996) study was published, empirical work on workplace mistreatment and abuse in general has consistently demonstrated its significance as a worldwide problem. In the United States, for example, Keashly and Jagatic (2000; $N = 700$) found that 27 percent of American workers were subjected to mistreatment and abuse in the workplace. Cortina, Magley, Williams, and Langhout (2001) reported that 71 percent of study participants experienced workplace bullying during the previous five years. Lutgen-Sandvik, Tracy, and Alberts (2007) found that 46.8 percent of American workers were bullied (e.g., in business administration, health and social services, education, and professional and scientific fields; $N = 403$). A national survey of 1,000 adult Americans conducted by the Workplace Bullying Institute (WBI; http://www.workplacebullying.org) in collaboration with Zogby International (WBI & Zogby International, 2014) found that 27 percent of the respondents experienced abusive behavior at work.

Mistreatment and Abuse by Administrators

Empirical work on abuse by administrators has confirmed the following:

1. Mistreatment and abuse is defined as "pervasive;" that is, a patterned or persistent use of harmful behavior, such as unwarranted reprimands, unfair evaluations, and termination. Further, mistreatment and abuse occurs often or very often and results in personal (e.g., psychological, physical) and professional harm (e.g., Blase & Blase, 2002, 2003a, 2003b; Blase et al., 2008; Einarsen, Hoel, Zapf, & Cooper, 2003; Fox & Stallworth, 2010; Rayner & Keashly, 2005).
2. Abuse of power and the potential for abuse of power by administrators is well established in the social sciences (e.g., Adams & Balfour, 1998; Baumeister, 1996; Kets de Vries, 1989; Kipnis, 1972; Lee-Chai & Bargh, 2001).
3. Administrators (vs. coworkers) are the most frequent workplace abusers (e.g., Australian Council of Trade Unions, 2001; Björkvist,

Österman, & Hjelt-Bäck, 1994; Canada Safety Council, 2006; Einarsen & Skogstad, 1996; Hoel & Cooper, 2000; Hornstein, 1996; Keashly, Trott, & MacLean, 1994; Namie & Namie, 2000; Northwestern National Life Insurance Company, 1993; WBI & Zogby International, 2014). For instance, the Employment Law Alliance's (2007) poll found that 44 percent of American workers reported having abusive administrators.
4. Mistreatment and abuse is frequently linked to administrative cultures that directly or indirectly permit or reward abuse by administrators (e.g., Ashforth, 1994; Blase & Blase, 2002, 2003a, 2003b; Grubb, Roberts, Grosch, & Brightwell, 2004; Jennifer, Cowie, & Ananiadou, 2003; Leymann, 1990).
5. Rates of abuse in the United States by administrators exceed those reported for European countries. This is possibly due to power inequalities that render subordinates unable to adequately defend themselves. In fact, in "high power distance" countries such as the United States, superiors are rarely challenged (Hofstede, 1980; Keashly, 2002). In other words, subordinates in the United States accept that power is distributed unequally (i.e., principals have significant formal and informal power over teachers, and teachers tend to comply and seldom challenge principals). This unequal distribution of power and acceptance of it is characteristic of U.S. culture in general. In contrast, Australia is a "low power distance" country, where superiors and subordinates often consult and share problem-solving work.
6. Little scholarly attention has been given to the dark side of organizational life in either the general management literature (Ashforth, 1994; Yukl, 2001) or the educational administration literature (Blase & Blase, 2002, 2003a, 2003b, 2010; Hodgkinson, 1991; Kimbrough, 1985; Starratt, 1991). In fact, "something approaching a 'scholarly taboo' may explain the neglect of workplace bullying" (Coleman, 2004, p. 310).

School Principal Mistreatment and Abuse of Teachers

Several large-scale, cross-occupational studies in Norway (Matthiesen, Raknes, & Rokkum, 1989); Sweden (Leymann, 1990); Ireland (Irish Taskforce on the Prevention of Workplace Bullying, 2001); Great Britain (Hoel & Cooper, 2000); and Australia (Queensland Government Workplace Bullying Taskforce, 2002) suggest that teaching in primary and secondary schools (i.e., kindergarten through 12th grade, typically for children aged 5–18) is one of the highest risk occupations for administrator mistreatment and abuse. Further, prominent Web sites devoted to workplace mistreatment and abuse have reported that teachers are among the largest group of abused workers (www.bullybusters.org) and the largest group of inquirers (www.bullyonline

.org). Over a decade ago, the National Association for Prevention of Teacher Abuse created a Web site (www.endteacherabuse.org) to address the problem of teacher mistreatment and abuse in the United States.

Despite such provocative findings and developments, only a handful of published studies produced in the United States, South Africa, and Australia address school principal mistreatment and abuse of teachers. Two studies focused on principal mistreatment and abuse of teachers in the United States, one study described principal mistreatment and abuse of teachers in South Africa, one study examined all-personnel mistreatment and abuse of other adults in one U.S. school district, one study investigated all-personnel mistreatment and abuse of other adults in all Australian schools, and two studies addressed all-personnel mistreatment and abuse of other adults in one U.S. state.

As described below, studies in education demonstrate that school principal mistreatment and abuse of teachers is consistent with the findings of numerous studies of abuse by administrators nationally and internationally and across occupations and organizations in describing a range of similar abusive behaviors and significant negative psychological, physical, professional, and personal-life effects (e.g., Lutgen-Sandvik et al., 2007; Samnani & Singh, 2012; WBI & Zogby International, 2014).

School principal mistreatment and abuse of teachers in the United States

Reviews of extant streams of research on teacher stress (Adams, 1988; Barnette, 1990; Black, 2003; Blase, 1984; Diehl, 1993; Dunham, 1984; Dworkin, Haney, Dworkin, & Telschow, 1990; Guglielmi & Tatrow, 1998) and on the micropolitics of schools (Ball, 1987; Blase, 1990, 1991a, 1991b; Blase & Anderson, 1995) provided early but limited findings about school principal mistreatment and abuse of teachers and its harmful effects on teachers, teaching, and learning. Therefore, Blase and Blase (2002, 2003a, 2003b) conducted the first study of principals' mistreatment and abuse of public school teachers in the United States. They used an intensive and qualitative grounded theory research method (e.g., Glaser, 1978; Glaser & Strauss, 1967) to study 50 U.S. teachers who were victims of long-term (six months to nine years), repeated mistreatment and abuse by principals throughout the United States. It should be mentioned that study participants were exceptionally successful teachers with histories of outstanding professional evaluations and achievements.

Study participants described (a) the types of behavior that teachers defined as mistreatment and abuse by principals and (b) its harmful effects. All teachers who participated in this study had been subjected to multiple principal mistreatment and abusive behaviors over extended periods of time. Blase and Blase's (2002, 2003a, 2003b) model of principal mistreatment and abuse consists of three levels of aggression (Level 1—indirect, moderate aggression; Level 2—direct, escalating aggression; and Level 3—direct, severe aggression; see table 21.1).

Blase and Blase (2002, 2003a, 2003b) also found that mistreatment and abuse by principals had serious, long-term devastating effects on teachers, including significant initial and chronic psychological and emotional harm, physical and physiological harm, and damage to the quality of teaching and student learning as well as leaving one's job and harm to one's personal and family life (see table 21.2).

Table 21.1 Principal Mistreatment and Abuse Behaviors toward Teachers

Level 1 Principal Mistreatment and Abuse Behaviors (indirect, moderately aggressive)
Discounting teachers' thoughts, needs, feelings
    Ignoring
    Personal insensitivity
    Stonewalling
Isolating and abandoning teachers
    Controlling teacher-teacher interaction
    Failing to support teachers in difficult interactions with students and parents
Withholding resources and denying approval, opportunities, and credit
    Withholding resources and denying approval
    Obstructing opportunities for professional development
    Withholding or taking credit
Favoring "select" teachers
Offensive personal conduct

Level 2 Principal Mistreatment and Abuse Behaviors (direct, escalating aggression)
Spying
Sabotaging
Stealing
Destroying teacher instructional aids
Making unreasonable demands
    Nitpicking
    Overloading
Criticism: The ubiquitous form of level 2 mistreatment and abuse
    Private criticism
        Stigmatizing and pejorative labeling
        Intentionally vague criticism
        Gossiping
        Unfounded third-party criticism
        Soliciting others
    Public criticism
        Location: Front office, faculty meetings, classroom, intercom, lunchroom, hallway, parking lot

(Continued)

Table 21.1 *Continued*

Level 3 Principal Mistreatment and Abuse Behaviors (direct, severely aggressive)

Lying
Explosive behavior
Threats
Unwarranted reprimands
Unfair evaluations
Mistreating students
Forcing teachers out of their jobs (reassign, transfer unilaterally, terminate)
Preventing teachers from leaving or advancing
Sexual harassment
Racism

Blase, J., & Blase, J. (2002). The dark side of leadership: Teacher perspectives of principal mistreatment. *Education Administration Quarterly*, 38(5), 686. Copyright © 2002. Reprinted with permission of SAGE Publications, Inc.

Table 21.2 Effects of Principal Mistreatment and Abuse of Teachers

Initial psychological and emotional harm
    Shock and disorientation
    Humiliation
    Loneliness
    Injured self-confidence and self-esteem
    Feeling corrupted and guilty
Chronic (long-term) psychological and emotional harm
    Fear and anxiety
    Anger
    Depression
        Feeling isolated
        Feeling trapped
        Feeling unmotivated
Physical and physiological problems
    Chronic sleep disorders (e.g., insomnia, nightmares, obsessive thinking)
    Chronic fatigue
    Stomachaches, nausea, vomiting, weight gain or loss
    Neck or back pain
    Headaches, migraines
    Lowered immunity
    Heart problems
    Other
Damaged schools
    Damaged relationships
    Damaged classrooms
    Impaired decision making

(Continued)

Table 21.2 (*Continued*)

Leaving one's job
Effects on a teacher's personal and family life
        Inability to compartmentalize mistreatment and abuse experiences
        Conflict with family, dysfunctional communication
        Distance from family

Blase, J., & Blase, J. (2002). The dark side of leadership: Teacher perspectives of principal mistreatment. *Education Administration Quarterly, 38*(5), 701. Copyright © 2002. Reprinted with permission of SAGE Publications, Inc.

In addition,

- Mistreated and abused teachers felt intentionally threatened, vulnerable, and unjustifiably wronged. Indeed, the chronic fear and anger experienced by abused teachers are primary, toxic, even primitive human emotions (Izard & Youngstrom, 1996; Tomkins, 1962).
- Social support by colleagues was often offset by other colleagues' fear of being mistreated and abused themselves. Consequently, mistreated and abused teachers frequently experienced isolation and alienation at work.
- Family members were seldom able to provide adequate support to mistreated and abused teachers because of persistent crying or conflictive, negative behavior by victimized teachers. This exacerbated teachers' experience of isolation and alienation.

Blase and Blase (2002, 2003a, 2003b) also identified gender differences of abusive principals:

- Male principals tended to use explosive verbal (e.g., yelling) and nonverbal behaviors (e.g., pounding their fists on tables) more than female principals.
- Male principals engaged in sexual harassment.
- Male principals engaged in offensive personal conduct (e.g., repulsive personal habits, having affairs with teacher-colleagues).

Gender differences were also apparent among teachers who were the victims of mistreatment and abuse:

- Female teachers experienced severe self-doubt and self-blame early in their mistreatment and abuse experience more than males.
- Females reported crying frequently during their mistreatment and abuse experience and, in fact, often cried during the interviews conducted for the study, in effect reexperiencing the trauma of their experiences.

In a second study, Blase et al. (2008) used an online, quantitative survey to investigate school principal mistreatment and abuse of 172 public school teachers throughout the United States. This study confirmed and extended findings produced by the first study with respect to principal mistreatment and abusive behaviors and their effects. Teachers' coping strategies were also directly examined. Statistical tests determined demographic differences in frequencies of various mistreatment and abusive behaviors, most frequently reported effects of mistreatment and abuse, and the use of coping strategies (see Blase et al., 2008, for details). Differences were also evident for the total intensity of the mistreatment and abuse experience: female teachers, teachers with union contracts, and divorced teachers experienced higher total intensity of harm from mistreatment and abuse.

The 10 most harmful (i.e., using quantitative measures of intensity) principal mistreatment and abusive behaviors were reported as follows: (1) tried to intimidate me (66% of the participants); (2) failed to recognize or praise me for work-related achievements (64%); (3) failed to support me in difficult interactions with students or parents (64%); (4) gave me unwarranted reprimands (62%); (5) made unreasonable demands on me (62%); (6) favored other teachers (62%); (7) lied to me or about me (58%); (8) nitpicked about time or micromanaged me (58%); (9) used pejorative terms to label me and my behavior (58%); and (10) unjustly criticized me (58%). Twenty-one additional principal mistreatment and abusive behaviors were rated at least moderately harmful by over 40 percent of the study participants.

Eighty percent of teachers who participated in the study indicated that principal mistreatment and abuse substantially damaged or undermined their classroom instruction; specifically, one-third of these teachers reported such effects as decreased motivation, creativity, innovativeness, and risk taking. Teachers indicated that principals forced them to use authoritarian, rigid, dated, and ineffective instructional methods. Teachers also discussed feeling significant stress, paranoia, insecurity, fear, dread, and self-doubt about teaching. Relationships with students also suffered significantly; teachers reported being less caring, patient, and tolerant toward students.

Blase et al. (2008) also noted that principal mistreatment and abuse persisted for at least three years for 73 percent of teachers and for more than three years for 27 percent of teachers. During and after their mistreatment and abusive experiences, 51 percent of teachers required medical or psychological treatment for physical and psychological harm caused by principal mistreatment and abuse. Fully 77 percent of mistreated and abused teachers indicated a desire to leave their teaching jobs, and nearly half wanted to leave the teaching profession altogether. Blase et al. (2008) also found that mistreated and abused teachers were typically unable to directly confront abusive principals; rather, they employed passive and palliative coping strategies to cope with mistreatment and abuse, such as avoiding, talking, enduring, rationalizing, reading, listening to music, watching television, and receiving support from others.

Finally, teachers described factors that contributed to their mistreatment and abuse, including school-level politics (61%; e.g., expressing disagreement with the principal, advocating on behalf of students, and being a threat because of their superior skills and knowledge or popularity) and factors that included the teacher's age (35%); gender (24%); race (14%); religion (13%); union or association affiliation (13%); political beliefs (12%); health, illness, or disability (11%); ethnicity (10%); and sexual orientation (3%).

Principal mistreatment and abuse of teachers in South Africa

De Wet (2010) conducted a small interview-based study of 10 exceptional and dedicated public school teachers (i.e., male and female, primary and secondary, urban and rural) in South Africa. The study focused on reasons for and effects of principal bullying. Major reasons for bullying included problematic grievance procedures, lack of communication between teachers and the trade union, and poor principal leadership (e.g., authoritarian leadership style; incompetence; lack of passion for teaching; and personal characteristics such as envy, destructive narcissism, hypocrisy, and evil (i.e., dishonesty, manipulation, lack of empathy and compassion, lack of remorse, and enjoyment of the fear and pain one inflicts)). De Wet (2010) described harmful effects on teachers' personal lives (e.g., psychological distress, depression, preoccupation, sadness, and shame) and professional lives (e.g., apathy, mediocrity, lack of enthusiasm, self-doubt, passivity, sense of isolation, damaged collegiality, and interest in leaving teaching).

All-personnel mistreatment and abuse of teachers in one U.S. school district

Fox and Stallworth (2010) investigated public school teachers' responses to violence, bullying, and other work stressors. The study was grounded in transactional stress theory, which emphasizes the moderating role of control and support. Bullies were administrators or principals, coworkers, parents, and students. This study included 779 teachers (all union members) working in a U.S. urban school district who had completed a workplace bullying checklist of scales for satisfaction (Cammann, Fichman, Jenkins, & Klesh, 1979); physical symptoms (Spector & Jex, 1998); burnout (Halbesleben & Demerouti, 2005); job-related emotions (Van Katwyk, Fox, Spector, & Kelloway, 2000); and bullying (Fox & Stallworth, 2005). The checklist used six conceptual domains: threatening or intimidating behavior (nonverbal and verbal acts and threats of physical violence); demeaning behavior (e.g., insults and put-downs); isolation (e.g., the silent treatment, exclusion from work meetings, and failing to return phone calls and e-mails); work sabotage (e.g., attacking or failing to support teachers' plans to others and intentionally destroying, stealing, or sabotaging teachers' work materials); harm to reputation (e.g., spreading rumors and taking credit for teachers' work); and abusive supervision (e.g., threatening job loss or demotion, excessively harsh criticism of job performance, applying rules and punishments inconsistently, and making unreasonable work demands).

Fox and Stallworth (2010) found that 45.6 percent of teachers were repeatedly bullied by their principals. Compared to teachers who were not bullied, abused teachers reported more negative emotions, burnout, physical symptoms, and lower job attachment and satisfaction. Specifically, bullying included 18 effects (e.g., anxiety, depression, headaches, insomnia, fatigue, and upset stomach) and job-related emotions (e.g., feeling isolated, anxious, unmotivated, and furious as well as intending to quit).

Interestingly, Fox and Stallworth (2010) reported that social support by fellow teachers failed to mitigate harmful effects of bullying; to the contrary, social support had a reverse buffering effect (i.e., greater social support yielded greater stress from bullying), a finding consistent with Powell, Powell, and Petrosko's (2015) research but inconsistent with findings discussed by Wiley (2000). The authors speculate that the reverse buffering effect may be related to victims' reluctance to involve colleagues or to allow colleagues to witness their mistreatment and abuse and the inappropriateness of the colleagues' support, colleagues' tendency to minimize bullying experiences, and the exacerbating effects of complaining.

All-personnel mistreatment and abuse of others in all Australian schools

The Riley, Duncan, and Edwards (2012) study was the first national online survey of school personnel bullying in all Australian schools, including public, Catholic, and independent schools. The researchers conducted a meta-analysis of several studies of 2,500 employees' experiences of bullying, which identified risk factors, behaviors, and effects by position within school bureaucracies. They examined three types of bullying: top-down bullying (e.g., principal to support staff); horizontal and peer bullying (e.g., teacher to teacher); and bottom-up bullying (e.g., parent to teacher).

Riley et al. (2012) reported that all reference groups engaged in bullying at schools; however, principals were most frequently identified as bullies. This is consistent with Fox and Stallworth (2010) and J. Powell (2012). Workplace conditions determined one's risk of being bullied (i.e., who controls time and tasks, uncertainties about work, and exposure to job-related changes) as well as one's work role (i.e., all personnel, including executives, principals, teacher-colleagues, students, parents, and support staff were identified as both bullies and victims of bullying).

Bullying behaviors included personal confrontation (e.g., threats to personal and professional status) and professional destabilization (e.g., isolation, overwork, changing work conditions, assignment of meaningless tasks, and withholding information and recognition). Major effects of bullying included psychological illnesses, psychosomatic illnesses, cardiovascular disease, chronic diseases, stress, absenteeism, and lower job satisfaction. These effects are consistent with those reported by Blase and Blase (2002, 2003a, 2003b); Blase et al. (2008); De Wet (2010); and Fox and Stallworth (2010). Major contributors to bullying were poor lines of communication, unclear roles and responsibilities, and lack of clarity about objectives—all administrative responsibilities.

All-personnel mistreatment and abuse of others related to school culture in one U.S. state

J. Powell (2012) examined workplace incivility and bullying and school culture or climate for 380 public school educators, including administrators or principals and teachers, in 52 public elementary, middle, and high schools in Kentucky. Research participants completed the Workplace Incivility Scale, the Workplace Bullying Checklist, and the School Culture Triage Survey. School culture or climate referred to situational factors, environmental factors, work conditions, and the quality of the work environment. J. Powell (2012) reported that administrators or principals, and coworkers initiated incivility and bullying 48 percent and 38 percent of the time, respectively. He also found that workplace incivility and bullying were inversely related to school culture; in fact, school culture ratings predicted incivility and bullying among educators. In addition, J. Powell (2012) reported that marital status predicted total incivility scores, age predicted incivility among coworkers, and gender predicted frequency of bullying (i.e., males reported being bullied more frequently than females).

All-personnel mistreatment and abuse of others related to school (student) achievement in one U.S. state

A. Powell (2012) examined workplace incivility, bullying, and culture related to student achievement. Her study consisted of 228 teachers from 28 public elementary, middle, and high schools in Kentucky, a selected subset of participants from J. Powell's (2012) study. Participants completed the Workplace Incivility Scale, the Workplace Bullying Checklist, and the School Culture Triage Survey. Culture was defined as the prevailing beliefs, attitudes, and behaviors in a school; positive school culture consisted of traditions that reflect a family or community with agreement on overall goals.

A. Powell (2012), like J. Powell (2012), found that individual perceptions of school culture predicted workplace incivility and bullying; that is, higher culture ratings were related to lower incivility and bullying ratings. A. Powell (2012) also found that student achievement was a significant predictor of workplace bullying only when the alpha was increased to 0.06; she noted that this may have occurred because achievement was obscured by climate (e.g., a higher climate rating intervenes in the prediction of lower achievement with more bullying and higher achievement with less bullying). In essence, A. Powell (2012) suggested that schools low in climate or student achievement may produce bullying. Relevant research in education has also concluded that school climate is predictive of student achievement (e.g., Clifford, Menon, Gangi, Condon, & Hornung, 2012).

Multilevel analysis of climate as a predictor of incivility and bullying

Based on earlier research (J. Powell, 2012, and A. Powell, 2012), Powell et al. (2015) produced a multilevel (individual and school-level) analysis of school climate (defined by a subset of variables from the School Culture Triage instrument) as a predictor of incivility and bullying among public school employees. They found that school climate (including mutual support among teachers) had an inverse relationship with stress experienced from bullying, a finding consistent with Fox and Stallworth (2010). Gender and years of experience (a correlate of age) were not predictors of bullying.

PRINCIPAL MISTREATMENT AND ABUSE STUDIES RELATED TO STUDIES OF OTHER ORGANIZATIONS AND OCCUPATIONS

Taken together, studies of principal mistreatment and abuse in education are generally consistent with research on abusive administration or supervision across organizations (e.g., Ashforth, 1997; Tepper, 2000) and occupations (e.g., Lutgen-Sandvik et al., 2007; WBI & Zogby International, 2014). For example,

- Researchers' definitions of mistreatment and abuse in education (despite variation in terminology) were consistent with those used in studies across occupations and organizations and codified in the Healthy Workplace Bill (Yamada, 2013), the leading legislative effort in the United States to address workplace abuse.
- Principals' abusive behaviors and adverse effects on teachers' personal and professional lives (e.g., psychological, physical, medical) and on school culture and school climate were consistent with studies across occupations and organizations (e.g., Baron & Neuman, 1996; Björkvist et al., 1994; Hoel & Cooper, 2000; Irish Taskforce on the Prevention of Workplace Bullying, 2001; Keashly & Jagatic, 2000; Price-Spratlen, 1995; Queensland Government Workplace Bullying Taskforce, 2002;

WBI & Zogby International, 2014; Westhues, 2004). Behaviors such as failure to praise or recognize, ignoring or snubbing, and nitpicking or micromanaging appear in the top 10 most frequently used mistreatment and abusive behaviors in education (e.g., Blase et al., 2008) and other organizations and occupations (e.g., Glomb, 2002; Salin, 2001).

- A host of factors contributed to principals' mistreatment and abuse of teachers, including authoritarian or autocratic leadership, anger disorder, self-aggrandizement, vindictiveness, sexism, politics, gender, race, religion, union affiliation, and political beliefs (Blase & Blase, 2002, 2003a, 2003b; Blase et al., 2008). Problematic grievance procedures, poor communication between teachers and unions, destructive narcissism, hypocrisy, and evil dispositions also contributed to principal mistreatment and abuse of teachers (De Wet, 2010). Workplace conditions, work roles, lack of clarity about objectives, and climate predicted one's risk of being bullied (Powell et al., 2015; Riley et al., 2012). A synthesis of the causes of teacher stress from being bullied included poor lines of communication, unclear roles and responsibilities, and lack of clarity about objectives (Riley et al., 2012; Wiley, 2000). Findings described above are consistent with studies conducted outside of education; for example, Samnani & Singh (2012) found that organizational culture and climate are antecedents to workplace mistreatment and abuse.

- Abusive principals typically relied on active and direct verbal or nonverbal behaviors (Blase & Blase, 2003a), a finding consistent with some studies of other occupations (e.g., Keashly, 1998) and inconsistent with other studies that report an emphasis on the use of indirect and passive verbal and nonverbal behaviors (e.g., Neuman & Baron, 1997). To reiterate, this may be due in part to the significant power imbalance (Hofstede, 1980; Keashly, 2002; Salin, 2003) between principals and teachers and the inflexibility of educational bureaucracies or because victims are likely to have their mistreatment and abuse experiences minimized and labeled by others as minor personality conflicts or their own fault (Ferris, 2004). Mistreated educators also required longer terms of counseling than victims working in other types of organizations.

Apart from mistreatment and abuse studies in other organizations and occupations, research on mistreatment and abuse in education, specifically between principals and teachers, has demonstrated the following:

- Principals accounted for much of the mistreatment and abuse that occurred among adults in education. Fox and Stallworth (2010) and J. Powell (2012) reported that principals were responsible for 45.6 percent and 48 percent of all bullying, respectively. Meta-analyses of

several studies by Riley et al. (2012) indicated that principals were most frequently identified as bullies in schools.
- Mistreated and abused teachers tended to employ passive forms of coping with principal mistreatment and abuse and had few avenues of personal support. Specifically, Blase et al. (2008) described the limited efficacy of teachers' coping strategies. Further, Blase and Blase (2002, 2003a, 2003b) noted that teacher-colleagues frequently withheld social support from mistreated and abused teachers for fear of retribution from principals. Fox and Stallworth (2010) reported that social support had a reverse buffering effect on the stress and job attachment of bullied teachers. Powell et al. (2015) found that school climate, including mutual support, led to greater stress from bullying. As a result, social isolation and alienation frequently compounded a teacher's mistreatment and abuse.
- In educational studies, relationships between gender and age (i.e., more years of experience) and mistreatment and abuse are unclear; however, some studies—inside and outside of education—have shown that females and males were equally subjected to workplace mistreatment and abuse (e.g., Einarsen & Skogstad, 1996; Powell et al., 2015). Other studies have found that the incidence and intensity of mistreatment and abuse tends to be higher for females (e.g., Björkvist et al., 1994; Blase et al., 2008; Price-Spratlen, 1995; Salin, 2001, 2003; Samnani & Singh, 2012). In educational studies, female teachers experienced severe self-doubt and self-blame and cried more than males, and female teachers, teachers with union contracts, and divorced teachers experienced higher total intensity of harm (total intensity of harm was the degree of severity of harm as perceived by the victim; it was determined by pooling each participant's rankings of the severity of harm experienced—five levels, from not harmful to very highly harmful—for each of 38 principal mistreatment behaviors) from mistreatment and abuse (Blase & Blase, 2002; Blase et al., 2008). Older teachers (Blase et al., 2008) and older workers outside of education were more likely to be targets of mistreatment and abuse (Einarsen & Skogstad, 1996; Samnani & Singh, 2012). However, Powell at al. (2015) reported that age did not predict bullying in education. It should be mentioned that discrimination violates educators' codified commitment to gender equity and age nondiscrimination (Council of Chief State School Officers, 2008).
- The significant power imbalance between principals and teachers may exacerbate perpetrator-victim interactions (e.g., Blase & Blase, 2004b; Lamertz & Aquino, 2004.) In effect, the nature of educational bureaucracies (i.e., schools are typically rule-bound) and the legal authority of principals give them substantial power over teachers, a condition

that may increase the probability of abuse (Kipnis, 1972). In fact, Salin (2003) argued that bullying is enabled by certain organizational processes and structures, including "a perceived power imbalance between the possible victim(s) and perpetrators, low perceived costs for the perpetrator, and dissatisfaction and frustration in the work environment" (p. 1219).

Overall, the study of mistreatment and abuse inside and outside of education relies on similar definitions of abusive behaviors and describes similar harmful effects. However, in education, school principal abusive behavior tends to be more active and direct as compared to those used by administrators in other occupations. Also, teachers use passive coping mechanisms in response to principal mistreatment and abuse as compared to employees in other occupations. The demographics of teacher-victims as related to principals' mistreatment and abuse are mixed.

A note about research on mobbing among adults in education

To be sure, much research has been done on student-on-student bullying in education, and many school districts have implemented antibullying policies for students based on this research (Orpinas & Horne, 2006). However, research on mobbing of teachers (i.e., harassment of a teacher by other teachers or coworkers designed to secure their removal; Duffy & Sperry, 2007) is limited. Riley et al. (2012), for example, reported that although bullying exists between and among all personnel (with principals most frequently bullies and teachers most frequently targets), research on mobbing of victimized teachers by other teachers as well as other adults (e.g., parents, staff) is notably lacking. Not surprisingly, policies prohibiting mistreatment and abuse of adults—which include by definition the phenomenon of mobbing—are nearly nonexistent in education in the United States.

COMPARISON OF FINDINGS PRODUCED BY THE U.S. WORKPLACE BULLYING SURVEY WITH FINDINGS OF RESEARCH ON MISTREATMENT AND ABUSE IN U.S. EDUCATION

Gary Namie, a social psychologist and expert on workplace bullying, directs the Workplace Bullying Institute (WBI; see http://www.workplacebullying.org), the only educational and research organization that focuses on bullying in the U.S. workplace. Namie and Zogby Analytics collaborated to create and administer the Workplace Bullying Survey (WBS), the largest ($N = 1000$) scientific survey of bullying in the U.S. workplace to date (WBI & Zogby International, 2014). This survey used the definition of workplace bullying codified in the Healthy Workplace Bill (HWB; Yamada, 2013).

The following is a comparison of research findings produced by the Workplace Bullying Survey (WBI & Zogby International, 2014) with findings in education in the United States (i.e., Blase & Blase, 2002, 2003a, 2003b; Blase et al., 2008; Fox & Stallworth, 2010; A. Powell, 2012; J. Powell, 2012; Powell et al., 2015). (Note: Survey data were not disaggregated by occupation.) WBS researchers found that 56 percent of perpetrators were likely to be administrators who held higher rank than the victims. The WBS also demonstrated that bullies typically abused others with impunity; in fact, employers typically condoned bullying or did nothing in response (38%); to wit, for every four targets of bullying, one perpetrator was punished or received negative consequences. This is consistent with research on mistreatment and abuse in education in the United States. Moreover, 61 percent of victims who participated in the survey lost their jobs; they voluntarily quit or they were terminated. However, in education, mistreatment and abuse victims were persistently threatened with probation or dismissal, but they were seldom terminated. Even when teacher-victims wanted to leave their jobs, they were typically less likely to do so because of financial pressures (Blase & Blase, 2003a; Blase et al., 2008).

According to WBS findings, targets and perpetrators of bullying frequently exhibited work-related skill deficiencies or personality flaws; for example, targets were described as compassionate, kind, cooperative, and agreeable as well as aggressive and abusive. Similarly, in education studies of mistreatment and abuse, principals' leadership and personality deficiencies were underscored; however, mistreated and abused teachers were consistently among the best and most effective professionals (Blase & Blase, 2003a; Blase et al., 2008).

Furthermore, findings produced by the Workplace Bullying Survey and education studies revealed that workplace conditions contributed to the likelihood of being bullied or mistreated and abused, and both survey victims and mistreated and abused teachers were ostracized by coworkers. Finally, unlike abused individuals in general, mistreated and abused teachers tended to use passive coping strategies.

Implications

Despite the significant stream of national and international research on workplace mistreatment and abuse and its incredibly damaging effects on employees across organizations and occupations, little has been accomplished at any level of the educational establishment to ameliorate the specific problem of principal mistreatment and abuse of public school teachers. Therefore, we suggest the following measures.

Local, state, and national efforts

Teachers and principals should work together at the local, state, and national levels to vigorously confront the mistreatment and abuse problem. For example, educators should

- Learn to identify and analyze abusive administrative behavior and its effects on teachers, teaching, and student learning; relationships with colleagues; school culture and climate; and teachers' personal lives.
- Develop effective teacher coping skills (e.g., how to establish boundaries and solicit help) and avenues to address administrative mistreatment and abuse (e.g., make formal complaints).
- Provide effective support to abused teachers (e.g., listening, empathizing, suggesting possible approaches, such as positively confronting the bully, filing a grievance, talking with a union representative, soliciting support from family and friends, and consulting a therapist).
- Propose and actively participate in relevant professional development programs at the school and district levels. Such programs teach educators about legal precedents, ethical standards, school context factors, and research related to mistreatment and abuse.
- Promote awareness of administrative mistreatment and abuse through professional associations for educators and education researchers (e.g., AERA, ASCD, ATE, NASSP, NAESP, NCPEA, UCEA).
- Actively encourage and lobby educational stakeholders who play educational policy and advocacy roles. This includes teachers, principals, central office administrators, parents, students, alumni, school board members, community members, academics, legislators, and union representatives. In the latter case, union representatives can educate teachers about their rights, mistreatment and abuse, bargaining efforts for antiharassment and antibullying policies, and endorsement of related legislation. For example, the Massachusetts Teachers Association and the Boston Teachers Union have endorsed the Healthy Workplace Bill (see below), thus encouraging related legislation (see http://www.mahealthyworkplace.com/bill/endorsement.html).
- Advocate for the development and implementation of effective, status-blind antiharassment and antibullying policies and related procedures in all school districts.

With some exceptions (e.g., the U.S. Equal Employment Opportunity Commission, U.S. Occupational Safety and Health Administration, and the De Pere, Wisconsin, and Springfield, Massachusetts, school districts), few U.S. public employers have policies prohibiting general mistreatment and abuse.

However, even the aforementioned existing policies are based on protected status (e.g., sex, age, religion, race) and afford no protection to employees based on mistreatment and abuse (i.e., bullying, harassment) alone.

Thus, every school district must develop a status-blind antiharassment and antibullying policy in which workplace bullying of adult employees is specifically defined and prohibited. Sioux City Community Schools in Iowa is one U.S. school district that has a status-blind antibullying policy that protects employees, although it is silent on procedural matters. In addition, in 2008, the Florida legislature passed the Jeffrey Johnston Stand Up for All Students Act, a law requiring all schools to adopt policies prohibiting bullying and harassment of any student or *employee* of a public K–12 institution; these policies must include a definition and description of bullying and harassment, training, procedures, consequences, and a statement of immunity from retaliation for reporting bullying and harassment. In fact, all 50 states now have either a school antibullying law or policy. A number of systems have written their policies to include all school employees as well as the students. As such, the Sioux City Community Schools and the state of Florida schools are helping to lead the way among public school districts in having concrete, status-blind workplace antibullying policies. Such policies are designed to ensure a work environment free of harassment and abuse of authority; they also require employees to treat each other with respect and dignity regardless of rank. Nevertheless, unless teachers and administrators have an adequate understanding of such policies, they may be ineffective.

Active support of the Healthy Workplace Bill

Riley et al. (2012) noted that the only way to eliminate bullying in schools is to enact *legislation*. As noted, in the United States, only complaints about mistreatment and abuse that are based in allegations related to a victim's protected status (e.g., sex, age, religion, race) have access to legal protection (Yamada, 2013). Professor David Yamada has concluded that existing statutory and common law are woefully inadequate legal responses to workplace mistreatment and abuse. Although the federal government has not passed comprehensive workplace bullying legislation, Yamada's Healthy Workplace Bill (HWB) has emerged as the template legislative proposal to create antibullying laws in the United States.

The HWB provides a legal claim for damages to severely bullied workers and creates liability-reducing incentives for employers to proactively address bullying behaviors (Yamada, 2013). It defines an abusive work environment as, "when an employer or one or more of its employees, acting with intent to cause pain or distress to an employee, subjects that employee to abusive conduct that causes physical harm, psychological harm, or both" (Yamada,

2013, p. 351). The HWB has been introduced in over 30 state legislatures and has recently gained traction as several states and municipalities have enacted workplace bullying laws drawing upon the bill's language. (These developments are explained in chapter 18, as well as in Yamada, 2013, 2015, and www.healthyworkplacebill.org.)

Academic programs in education

In general, academic programs in administrator and teacher education must respond to an overwhelming range of programmatic issues, and they tend to emphasize the positive aspects of school life. Consequently, prospective (and practicing) administrators and teachers are not prepared to develop a deeply reflective approach to school leadership or teaching. This is unfortunate, as social learning theory and theories of self-regulation indicate that people often derive their most profound learning from a reflective understanding of social and linguistic experiences (Bandura, 1973; Tharp & Gallimore, 1988). It follows that such an understanding is necessary for confronting the mistreatment and abuse problem in schools. Thus, academic programs should help educators to

- Develop professional reflection skills designed to understand interpersonal, group, and organizational interactions and experiences.
- Identify administrators' abusive behaviors and the effects of such behavior.
- Develop effective strategies to inform, confront, coach, or discipline abusive administrators.
- Identify and address contextual factors that contribute to the problem of abuse (e.g., abusive administrative cultures, conflicting and excessive role expectations, lack of effective antimistreatment policies and procedures).
- Promote awareness of administrative mistreatment and abuse through professional associations for educators (e.g., principals, teachers, personnel directors, and human resource specialists) and education researchers, as noted above.
- Enact transformational and instructional leadership approaches for all educational leaders as discussed in the best contemporaneous studies of school improvement (e.g., administrator and teacher professional development, student academic performance) and the latest Professional Standards for Educational Leaders (National Policy Board for Educational Administration, 2015). Such leadership approaches emphasize professional norms, ethics, clarity of vision, openness, communication, shared values, trust and team building, use of data to enhance teaching and learning, a range of development opportunities, and problem-solving

skills (e.g., Blase, Blase, & Phillips, 2010; Day, Gu, & Sammons, 2016; Hallinger, 2011).
- Support the development of status-blind district-level mistreatment and abuse policies.
- Support the Healthy Workplace Bill legislation.

All educators share an important mission, core values, and support for students. Now they must unite to codify district-level policies and state and federal legislation to ensure that all teachers subject to the vagaries of mistreatment and abuse have opportunities for legal redress.

CONCLUSION

During the past 25 years, a considerable amount of research has been published nationally and internationally on the serious problem of workplace mistreatment and bullying. However, to date, there are only a handful of published studies focused on the problem of school principal mistreatment and abuse of public school teachers (see Blase & Blase, 2002, 2003a, 2003b, and Blase et al., 2008, for discussions of needed research on this topic). In addition, preservice and in-service administrator and teacher preparation and training seldom deal with this important problem, school districts in the United States have not developed antimistreatment and abuse policies for adult employees, and there are no laws providing viable opportunities to address mistreatment and abuse incidents.

This state of affairs is particularly disturbing with regard to teaching not only because victimized teachers incur substantial personal and professional harm as a result of mistreatment and abuse but also because quality teaching is critically important for student achievement and school improvement. This means addressing and replacing destructive approaches to school leadership (through policy, law, and professional growth) with constructive approaches. In other words, it is absolutely essential that school administrators follow the best empirical research in education, which demands that they become transformational, instructional leaders who create collaborative, open, trusting, respectful, honest, and supportive relationships with teachers (Blase & Blase, 2004a; Blase et al., 2010; Day et al., 2016; DuFour & Marzano, 2011; Hattie, 2012; NPBEA, 2015).

In his foreword to *Breaking the Silence: Overcoming the Problem of Principal Mistreatment of Teachers* (Blase & Blase, 2003a), AASA American Superintendent of the Year, Don Saul, wrote,

> Leaders who attempt to work with teachers and principals to promote systemic change . . . realize district efforts to create a positive atmosphere and common purpose leading to improved student achievement and

well-being are hindered by behaviors which create a loss of trust among school professionals. Funding difficulties, curricular narrowing, high-stakes testing of debatable utility, special interest advocacy, and other factors already conspire to evoke a feeling of powerlessness and frustration among staff. When these elements are combined with a teacher's perception that "I will probably never truly trust an administrator again," it's hard to imagine how the organizational *gestalt* essential for reform and improvement can be generated and sustained in a district or school.

The challenges implicit in [Blase and Blase's] findings reflect issues affecting the gamut of school performance and the success of related initiatives to guide and improve teaching and learning: abuse and denigration of staff members is seldom dealt with easily or without creative, dedicated effort and courage. The . . . findings . . . must not be brushed aside as a natural outcome of human interaction in the form of so-called personality conflicts or as grousing from poorly performing staff members. On the contrary, the complexity and depth of change required to ensure consistent progress in education demands that the problem of mistreatment of teachers be taken very seriously and that appropriate preventative and corrective action serve as one of the keystones of growth and productivity in district and school cultures. (p. ix)

REFERENCES

Adams, B. P. (1988). *Leader behavior of principals and its effect on teacher burnout* (Unpublished doctoral dissertation). University of Wisconsin–Madison, Madison, Wisconsin.

Adams, G. B., & Balfour, D. L. (1998). *Unmasking administrative evil.* Thousand Oaks, CA: Sage.

Ashforth, B. (1994). Petty tyranny in organizations. *Human Relations, 47*(7), 755–778.

Ashforth, B. E. (1997). Petty tyranny in organizations: A preliminary examination of antecedents and consequences. *Canadian Journal of Administrative Sciences, 14*(2), 126–140.

Australian Council of Trade Unions. (2001). *The workplace is no place for bullying.* Retrieved from http://www.actu.asn.au

Ball, S. J. (1987). *The micropolitics of the school: Towards a theory of school organization.* London, England: Methuen.

Bandura, A. (1973). *Aggression: A social learning analysis.* Englewood Cliffs, NJ: Prentice Hall.

Barnette, J. E. (1990). *The relationship between leadership styles of school principals and teacher stress as perceived by teachers* (Unpublished doctoral dissertation). West Virginia University, Morgantown, West Virginia.

Baron, R. A., & Neuman, J. H. (1996). Workplace violence and workplace aggression: Evidence of their relative frequency and potential causes. *Aggressive Behavior, 22*(3), 161–173.

Baumeister, R. F. (1996). *Evil: Inside human cruelty and violence*. New York: W. H. Freeman.

Björkvist, K., Österman, K., & Hjelt-Bäck, M. (1994). Aggression among university employees. *Aggressive Behavior*, 20(3), 173–184.

Black, S. (2003). Stressed out in the classroom. *American School Board Journal*, 190(10), 36–38.

Blase, J. (1984). School principals and teacher stress: A qualitative analysis. *National Forum for Educational Administration and Supervision*, 1(32), 35–43.

Blase, J. (1990). Some negative effects of principals' control-oriented and protective political behavior: The teachers' perspective. *American Educational Research Journal*, 27(4), 727–753.

Blase, J. (1991a). The micropolitical orientation of teachers toward closed school principals. *Education and Urban Society*, 23(4), 356–378.

Blase, J. (Ed.). (1991b). *The politics of life in schools: Power, conflict, and cooperation*. Newbury Park, CA: Sage.

Blase, J., & Anderson, G. (1995). *The micropolitics of leadership: From control to empowerment*. London, England: Cassell Teachers College Press.

Blase, J., & Blase, J. (2002). The dark side of leadership: Teacher perspectives of principal mistreatment. *Education Administration Quarterly*, 38(5), 671–727.

Blase, J., & Blase, J. (2003a). *Breaking the silence: Overcoming the problem of principal mistreatment of teachers*. Thousand Oaks, CA: Corwin.

Blase, J., & Blase, J. (2003b). The phenomenology of principal mistreatment: Teachers' perspectives. *Journal of Educational Administration*, 41(4), 367–422.

Blase, J., & Blase, J. (2004a). *Handbook of instructional leadership: How successful principals promote teaching and learning* (2nd ed.). Thousand Oaks, CA: Corwin Press.

Blase, J., & Blase, J. (2004b). School principal mistreatment of teachers: Teachers' perspectives on emotional abuse. *Journal of Emotional Abuse*, 4(3/4), 151–175.

Blase, J., & Blase, J. (2010). Leader mistreatment of teachers. In E. Baker, P. Peterson, & B. McGaw (Eds.), *The international encyclopedia of education* (3rd ed., pp. 790–796). Oxford, England: Elsevier.

Blase, J., Blase, J., & Du, F. (2008). The mistreated teacher: A national study. *Journal of Educational Administration*, 46(3), 263–301.

Blase, J., Blase, J., & Phillips, D. (2010). *Handbook of school improvement: How high-performing principals create high-performing schools*. Thousand Oaks, CA: Corwin Press.

Cammann, C., Fichman, M., Jenkins, D., & Klesh, J. (1979). *The Michigan Organizational Assessment Questionnaire*. Unpublished manuscript, University of Michigan, Ann Arbor, Michigan.

Canada Safety Council. (2006). *Bullying in the workplace*. Retrieved from http://www.safety-council.org/info/OSH/bullies.html

Clifford, M., Menon, R., Gangi, T., Condon, C., & Hornung, K. (2012). *Measuring school climate for gauging principal performance: A review of the validity and reliability of publicly accessible measures*. Washington, D.C.: American Institutes for Research.

Coleman, B. (2004). Pragmatism's insult: The growing interdisciplinary challenge to American harassment & jurisprudence. *Employee Rights and Employment Policy Journal*, 8(2), 239–214.

Cortina, L. M., Magley, V. J., Williams, J. H., & Langhout, R. D. (2001). Incivility in the workplace: Incidence and impact. *Journal of Occupational Health Psychology*, 6(1), 64–80.

Council of Chief State School Officers. (2008). *Educational leadership policy standards: ISLLC 2008*. Washington, D.C.: Author.

Day, C., Gu, Q., & Sammons, P. (2016). The impact of leadership on student outcomes: How successful school leaders use transformational and instructional strategies to make a difference. *Educational Administration Quarterly*, 52(2), 221–258.

De Wet, C. (2010). The reasons for and the impact of principal-on-teacher bullying on the victims' private and professional lives. *Teaching and Teacher Education*, 26(7), 1450–1459.

Diehl, D. B. (1993). *The relationship between teachers' coping resources, feelings of stress, and perceptions of the power tactics employed by the administrators* (Unpublished doctoral dissertation). Georgia State University, Atlanta, Georgia.

Duffy, M., & Sperry, L. (2007). Workplace mobbing: Individual and family health consequences. *The Family Journal: Counseling and Therapy for Couples and Families*, 15(4), 398–404.

DuFour, R., & Marzano, R. J. (2011). *Leaders of learning: How district, school, and classroom leaders improve student achievement*. Bloomington, IN: Solution Tree Press.

Dunham, J. (1984). *Stress in teaching*. London, England: Croom Helm.

Dworkin, A. G., Haney, C. A., Dworkin, R. J., & Telschow, R. L. (1990). Stress and illness behavior among urban public school teachers. *Educational Administration Quarterly*, 26(1), 60–72.

Einarsen, S., Hoel, H., Zapf, D., & Cooper, C. (2003). The concept of bullying at work: The European tradition. In S. Einarsen, H. Hoel, D. Zapf, & C. Cooper (Eds.), *Bullying and emotional abuse in the workplace: International perspectives in research and practice* (pp. 3–30). London, England: Taylor & Francis.

Einarsen, S., & Skogstad, A. (1996). Bullying at work: Epidemiological findings in public and private organizations. *European Journal of Work and Organizational Psychology*, 5(2), 185–201.

Employment Law Alliance. (2007, April 9). Battle scars: Readers pour out tales of abusive bosses. *Boston Business Journal*. Retrieved from http://www.bizjournals.com/boston/stories/2007/04/09/story16.html

Ferris, P. (2004). A preliminary typology of organizational response to allegations of workplace bullying: See no evil, hear no evil, speak no evil. *British Journal of Guidance and Counseling*, 32(3), 389–395.

Fox, S., & Stallworth, L. E. (2005). Racial/ethnic bullying: Exploring links between bullying and racism in the U.S. workplace. *Journal of Vocational Behavior*, 66(3), 438–456.

Fox, S., & Stallworth. L. E. (2010). The battered apple: An application of stressor-emotion-control/support theory to teachers' experience of violence and bullying. *Human Relations*, 63(7), 927–954.

Glaser, B. G. (1978). *Theoretical sensitivity: Advances in the methodology of grounded theory*. Mill Valley, CA: Sociology Press.

Glaser, B. G., & Strauss, A. L. (1967). *The discovery of grounded theory: Strategies for qualitative research*. Chicago, IL: Aldine.

Glomb, T. M. (2002). Workplace anger and aggression: Informing conceptual models with data from specific encounters. *Journal of Occupational Health Psychology, 7*(1), 20–36.

Grubb, P. W., Roberts, R. K., Grosch, J. W., & Brightwell, W. S. (2004). Workplace bullying: What organizations are saying. *Employee Rights and Employment Policy Journal, 8*(2), 407–422.

Guglielmi, R. S., & Tatrow, K. (1998). Occupational stress, burnout, and health in teachers: A methodological and theoretical analysis. *Review of Educational Research, 68*(1), 61–99.

Halbesleben, J. R. B., & Demerouti, E. (2005). The construct validity of an alternative measure of burnout: Investigating the English translation of the Oldenburg Burnout Inventory. *Work & Stress, 19*(3), 208–220.

Hallinger, P. (2011). Leadership for learning: Lessons from 40 years of empirical research. *Journal of Educational Administration, 49*(2), 125–142.

Hattie, J. (2012). *Visible learning for teachers: Maximizing impact on learning.* New York: Routledge.

Hodgkinson, C. (1991). *Educational leadership: The moral art.* Albany, NY: State University of New York Press.

Hoel, H., & Cooper C. L. (2000, November). *Destructive conflict and bullying at work* (Unpublished report). University of Manchester Institute of Science and Technology, Manchester, England.

Hofstede, G. (1980). *Culture's consequences: International differences in work-related values.* Newbury Park, CA: Sage.

Hornstein, H. A. (1996). *Brutal bosses and their prey.* New York: Riverhead Books.

Hornstein, H. A., Michela, J. L., Van Eron, A. M., Cohen, L. W., Heckelman, W. L., Sachse-Skidd, M., & Spencer, J. L. (1995). *Disrespectful supervisory behavior: Effects on some aspects of subordinates' mental health* (Unpublished manuscript). Teachers College, Columbia University, New York, New York.

Irish Taskforce on the Prevention of Workplace Bullying. (2001). *Dignity at work: The challenge of workplace bullying.* Report of the Task Force on the Prevention of Workplace Bullying. Dublin, Ireland: The Stationery Office.

Izard, C. E., & Youngstrom, E. A. (1996). The activation and regulation of fear and anxiety. In R. A. Dienstbier & D. A. Hope (Eds.), *Perspectives on anxiety, panic, and fear* (pp. 1–59). Lincoln: University of Nebraska Press.

Jennifer, D., Cowie, H., & Ananiadou, K. (2003). Perceptions and experience of workplace bullying in five different working populations. *Aggressive Behavior, 29*(6), 489–496.

Keashly, L. (1998). Emotional abuse in the workplace: Conceptual and empirical issues. *Journal of Emotional Abuse, 1*(1), 85–117.

Keashly, L. (2002). *Interpersonal and systemic aspects of emotional abuse at work.* Retrieved from http://www.worktrauma.org/foundation/research/Loraleigh.html

Keashly, L., & Jagatic, K. (2000). *The nature, extent, and impact of emotional abuse in the workplace: Results of a statewide survey.* Paper presented at the annual conference of the Academy of Management, Toronto, Canada.

Keashly, L., Trott, V., & MacLean, L. M. (1994). Abusive behavior in the workplace: A preliminary investigation. *Violence and Victims, 9*(4), 341–357.

Kets de Vries, M. F. R. (1989). *Prisoners of leadership.* New York: Wiley.

Kimbrough, R. B. (1985). *Ethics: A course of study for educational leaders.* Arlington, VA: American Association of School Administrators.

Kipnis, D. (1972). Does power corrupt? *Journal of Personality and Social Psychology, 24*(1), 33–41.

Lamertz, K., & Aquino, K. (2004). Social power, social status and perceptual similarity of workplace victimization: A social network analysis of stratification. *Human Relations, 57*(7), 795–822.

Lee-Chai, A. Y., & Bargh, J. A. (2001). *The use and abuse of power: Multiple perspectives on the causes of corruption.* Philadelphia, PA: Psychology Press.

Leymann, H. (1990). Mobbing and psychological terror at workplaces. *Violence and Victims, 5*(2), 119–126.

Lutgen-Sandvik, P., Tracy, S. J., & Alberts, J. K. (2007). Burned by bullying in the American workplace: Prevalence, perception, degree, and impact. *Journal of Management Studies, 44,* 837–862.

Matthiesen, S. B., Raknes, B. I. & Rokkum, O. (1989). Mobbing på arbeidsplassen [Bullying in the workplace]. *Tidsskrift for Norsk Psykologforening, 26*(11), 761–774.

Namie, G., & Namie, R. (2000). *The bully at work: What you can do to stop the hurt and reclaim your dignity on the job.* Naperville, IL: Sourcebooks.

National Policy Board for Educational Administration (NPBEA). (2015). *Professional Standards for Educational Leaders 2015.* Reston, VA: Author.

Neuman, J. H., & Baron, R. A. (1997). Aggression in the workplace. In R. Giacalone & J. Greenberg (Eds.), *Anti-social behavior in organizations* (pp. 37–57). Thousand Oaks, CA: Sage.

Northwestern National Life Insurance Company. (1993). *Fear and violence in the workplace.* Minneapolis, MN: Author.

Orpinas, P., & Horne, A. M. (2006). *Bullying prevention: Creating a positive school climate and developing social competence.* Washington, D.C.: American Psychological Association.

Powell, A. (2012). *The effects of workplace incivility, workplace bullying, and school culture on student achievement* (Unpublished doctoral dissertation). University of Louisville, Louisville, Kentucky.

Powell, J. (2012). *Workplace incivility in public education* (Unpublished doctoral dissertation). University of Louisville, Louisville, Kentucky.

Powell, J. E., Powell, A. L., & Petrosko, J. M. (2015). School climate as a predictor of incivility and bullying among public school employees: A multilevel analysis. *Journal of School Violence, 14*(2), 217–244.

Price-Spratlen, L. (1995). Interpersonal conflict which includes mistreatment in a university workplace. *Violence and Victims, 10*(4), 285–297.

Queensland Government Workplace Bullying Taskforce. (2002). *Report of the Queensland Government Workplace Bullying Taskforce.* Brisbane, Australia: Queensland Government Department of Industrial Relations.

Rayner, C., & Keashly, L. L. (2005). Bullying at work: A perspective from Britain and North America. In S. Fox & P.E. Spector (Eds.), *Counterproductive work behavior: Investigations of actors and targets* (pp. 271–296). Washington, D.C.: APA Press.

Riley, D., Duncan, J., & Edwards, J. (2012). *Bullying of staff in schools*. Camberwell, Victoria, Australia: ACER Press.

Salin, D. (2001). Prevalence and forms of bullying among business professionals: A comparison of two different strategies for measuring bullying. *European Journal of Work and Organizational Psychology, 10*(4), 425–441.

Salin, D. (2003). Ways of explaining workplace bullying: A review of enabling, motivating, and precipitating structures and processes in the work environment. *Human Relations, 56*(10), 1213–1232.

Samnani, A-K., & Singh, P. (2012). 20 years of workplace bullying research: A review of the antecedents and consequences of bullying in the workplace. *Aggression and Violent Behavior, 17*(6), 581–589.

Spector, P. E., & Jex, S. M. (1998). Development of four self-report measures of job stressors and strain: Interpersonal conflict at work scale, organizational constraints scale, quantitative workload inventory, and physical symptoms inventory. *Journal of Occupational Health Psychology, 3*(4), 356–367.

Starratt, R. J. (1991). Building an ethical school: A theory for practice in educational leadership. *Educational Administration Quarterly, 27*(2), 185–202.

Tepper, B. J. (2000). Consequences of abusive supervision. *Academy of Management Journal, 43*(2), 178–190.

Tharp, R. G., & Gallimore, R. (1988). *Rousing minds to life*. New York: Cambridge University Press.

Tomkins, S. S. (1962). *Affect, imagery, consciousness: The negative effects*. New York: Springer.

Van Katwyk, P. T., Fox, S., Spector, P. E., & Kelloway, E. K. (2000). Using the Job-related Affective Well-being Scale (JAWS) to investigate affective responses to work stressors. *Journal of Occupational Health Psychology, 5*(2), 219–230.

Westhues, K. W. (2004). *Workplace mobbing in academe: Reports from twenty universities*. Lampeter, Wales: Edwin Mellen Press.

Wiley, C. (2000). A synthesis of research on the causes, effects, and reduction strategies of teacher stress. *Journal of Instructional Psychology, 27*(2), 80–87.

Workplace Bullying Institute (WBI) & Zogby International. (2014). *2014 U.S. Workplace Bullying Survey*. Retrieved from http://www.workplacebullying.org

Yamada, D. C. (2013). Emerging American legal responses to workplace bullying. *Temple Political & Civil Rights Law Review, 22*(2), 329–354.

Yamada, D. C. (2015). Slowly but surely, workplace bullying laws are becoming a reality in the U.S. Retrieved from https://newworkplace.wordpress.com/2015/05/15/slowly-but-surely-workplace-bullying-laws-are-becoming-a-reality-in-the-U-S

Yukl, G. A. (2001). *Leadership in organizations* (5th ed.). Upper Saddle River, NJ: Prentice Hall.

22

Workplace Bullying and Mobbing in U.S. Higher Education

Loraleigh Keashly and Joel H. Neuman

As evidenced in the preceding chapters, researchers have learned a great deal about the nature, prevalence, causes, and consequences of workplace bullying and mobbing over the past four decades. This work has led (and continues to lead) to the development and implementation of interventions designed to prevent the occurrence and escalation of interpersonal aggression and ameliorate its impact on individuals and organizations. Interestingly, over this significant time span, academic researchers (ourselves included) had paid little attention to the occurrence of bullying and mobbing in our own "backyard." While diligently exploring aggression by "other people" in "other settings" and publishing our findings in academic journals, we failed to explore these issues in our own academic work settings. In recent years, we have begun to address this shortcoming through systematic research and the publication of our findings in traditional academic venues.

At the same time, academic trade journals have increasingly focused stories on these issues. For example, articles have appeared in *The Chronicle of Higher Education* (Fogg, 2008; Gravois, 2006); *Inside Higher Education* (Flaherty, 2014); and *Academe* (Wajngurt, 2014), a publication of the American Association of University Professors (AAUP). In a blog post for *Academe*, Petry (2011) identified harassment by colleagues and bullying by administrators as among the top 10 workplace issues for faculty. In addition, there are special issues of academic journals (Misawa & Rowland, 2015; Petrina & Ross, 2014); recent books (Hollis, 2012; Twale & De Luca, 2008); and numerous blogs (e.g., http://bulliedacademics.blogspot.com, http://www.mobbingportal.com, http://www.historiann.com, and Hiatt, 2008). These sources provide evidence of increasing attention being paid to academic bullying and mobbing and provide opportunities for detailed discussion and analysis of what has been described as a "bully culture" in academe.

Extending on the work cited above, as well as building on our own work (Keashly & Neuman, 2010, 2013) and that of our colleagues, the focus of this chapter is on workplace bullying and mobbing in institutions of higher education. We believe that this focus is important for the following reasons. First, if the study of psychology has taught us anything, it is that human behavior is multimotivated or overdetermined. Specifically, human actions are motivated and shaped by social, situational, environmental, and personal factors (Maslow, 1954; Pinder, 2008). Put simply, *context* strongly impacts and shapes behavior and the way specific behaviors are motivated, perceived, interpreted, understood, and acted upon (e.g., Johns, 2006). Considering that relatively little attention has been paid to the higher education context, we believe that such work will add to our growing knowledge base on workplace bullying and mobbing and help us test hypotheses derived from extant theory, developed across a number of workplace domains.

Second, workplace bullying and mobbing (manifestations of human aggression) are fundamentally relational in nature, and different types of relationships tend to facilitate or inhibit interpersonal aggression. As we will demonstrate, academic environments are unique in many ways, and some of these distinctive aspects may contribute to workplace bullying and mobbing as well as the mechanism by which behaviors are perceived and acted upon.

In the following section, we will address important definitional, conceptual, and methodological issues associated with our focus of attention. Our overall intent is to cover the landscape of what is known about bullying and mobbing in the academy, highlight known gaps in our knowledge, and discuss what is needed to fill those gaps. We conclude with a discussion about what we have learned about effective interventions.

DEFINITIONAL, CONCEPTUAL, AND METHODOLOGICAL ISSUES

In this section, we will briefly restate some definitional and conceptual issues that have been discussed in earlier chapters and highlight some methodological issues that impede our ability to capture accurate prevalence data.

Definition of Workplace Bullying and Mobbing

A common observation in the literature on workplace bullying and workplace mobbing is the lack of a single consensus definition (Einarsen, Hoel, & Notelaers, 2009). This is further complicated by a proliferation of constructs that are, from our perspective, often used interchangeably in the literature on workplace bullying and mobbing, such as *generalized workplace harassment*

(Brodsky, 1976; Richman et al., 1999); *emotional abuse* (Keashly & Harvey, 2005); *social undermining* (Duffy, Ganster, & Pagon, 2002); and *incivility* (Andersson & Pearson, 1999). Though each of these other constructs covers important and related phenomena, their overlapping usage in the research literature is often misleading. For a thorough discussion of construct issues, we refer the reader to several excellent reviews (Einarsen, Hoel, Zapf, & Cooper, 2011; Hershcovis, 2011; Keashly, 1998).

What is distinctive about *workplace bullying*, as compared with other forms of workplace mistreatment, is the persistent and enduring nature of the experience—statistically characterized as occurring at least weekly for six months or longer in duration (Leymann, 1996). Additionally, bullying involves power imbalance (either real or imagined) between actors (bullies) and targets. *Mobbing* is a form of bullying characterized by the involvement of more than one actor, with the particular quality of "ganging up" on others (Davenport, Schwartz, & Elliott, 1999). Thus, workplace bullying and mobbing are more accurately captured as ongoing, dynamic relational phenomena rather than as discrete events (Aquino & Lamertz, 2004; Keashly & Jagatic, 2003). In our research with academics, and thus for this chapter, we utilize Einarsen's (1999) definition: "All those repeated actions and practices that are directed to one or more workers, which are unwanted by the victim, which may be done deliberately or unconsciously, but that cause humiliation, offense, and distress, and that may interfere with job performance and/or creates an unpleasant working environment" (p. 17).

While this provides a good operational definition of bullying, it seems somewhat sterile, as it was not designed to capture the intensity and depth of impact and despair that are part and parcel of the experience. To provide a flavor of how this is depicted, we share the following three examples of descriptions employed in the literature:

> Bullying is a profound attack on one's viability as a social and professional being in the context of work. (Zabrodska, Linnell, Laws, & Davies, 2011, p. 709)
>
> Mobbing can be understood as the stressor to beat all stressors. It is an impassioned, collective campaign by co-workers to exclude, punish, and humiliate a targeted worker. (Westhues, 2002, p. 32)
>
> Academic mobbing is a non-violent, sophisticated, "ganging up" behaviour adopted by academicians to "wear and tear" a colleague down emotionally through unjustified accusation, humiliation, general harassment and emotional abuse. These are directed at the target under a veil of lies and justifications so that they are "hidden" to others and difficult to prove. (Khoo, 2010, p. 61)

Conceptual and Methodological Issues

The central questions to ask when exploring instances of workplace bullying and mobbing are, who is being *targeted* and who is doing the *targeting*? Just as we would expect differences in the nature and consequences of bullying by (or toward) superiors, peers, subordinates, and customers and clients in non-academic work settings, academic work settings primarily consist of students, staff, faculty, and administrators. While all members of an institution may be involved in bullying as targets, bullies, or bystanders, faculty members are uniquely situated among these groups because of their centrality in fulfilling the primary mission of the institution, as relates to conducting the curricular and research missions of colleges and universities. As such, the health and well-being of faculty at large has profound implications for the character and success of the institutions. For this reason, initial research (and the current chapter) tends to focus on the experiences of faculty with bullying and mobbing as targets, actors, and observers.

Quantitative vs. qualitative measures

The research on bullying and mobbing falls into two types: (1) quantitatively focused surveys, often cross-sectional in nature, and (2) qualitative research, which includes ethnographies, interviews, case studies, and personal accounts, capturing the "lived experience" of targets, responders, and, to a more limited extent, actors. The cross-sectional survey research permits a discernment of the nature and prevalence of bullying and mobbing within and across work units in a particular organization (in which the same research methods and tools are employed). This can prove useful in identifying problem areas within an organization, work unit, or demographic group (e.g., department, faculty, staff, administration, junior or senior faculty, gender, etc.). Qualitative research allows an in-depth look into the dynamics of the experience and the intersectionality of a number of antecedents in the conditioning or shaping of experiences from the perspective of the target(s). This research provides the thick description and meaning behind the numbers, which is critically important in both designing and evaluating intervention programs.

In table 22.1, we summarize key findings from survey studies (published, dissertations, and theses). As with all research, the nature and interpretation of these findings are conditioned by the methodologies employed. Prevalence and incident rates associated with all forms of bullying and mobbing are influenced by the way dependent measures are operationalized and the time frame over which they are measured. With respect to the operational issues, there are two primary methods of measuring workplace bullying behavior: (1) the self-labeling approach and (2) behavioral checklists. The self-labeling

Table 22.1 Studies of Bullying and Mobbing in Academic Settings

Study	Sample	Method	Time Frame	Rates	Actors
Price-Spratlen, 1995 (USA)	Employees at one university; N = 805; **208 faculty**; 92 professional staff; 506 classified staff (51% response rate)	Mail questionnaire – single item re mistreatment	Prior 18 months	Experienced (yes/no) 23% overall; **11% faculty**; 38% professional staff; 25% classified staff 26% female; 19% male Witnessed 27%; **19% faculty**; 27% professional staff; 31% classified staff	Overall Superior 49% Peer 30% Subordinate 9% Other 12% **Faculty:** Superior 52% Peer 36% Subordinate 4% Other 8% including students
Richman et al., 1999 (USA)	Employees at one university; N = 2,492; 765 faculty; 295 service; 557 clerical; 875 student workers (51.6% response rate)	Mail questionnaire – behavioral checklist	Prior 12 months	Experienced (at least one behavior more than once) 55% overall; **50% faculty**; 57% service; 63% clerical, 53% student workers Overall: 56% female; 54% male; **faculty 68% female; 52% male**	Not asked
Keashly & Neuman, 2008 (USA)	Employees at one university; N = 1,185 (34.3% response rate)	Online questionnaire – respond to definition + behavioral checklist	Prior 12 months	Experienced 32% self-label overall; **39% faculty**; 43% staff; 53% directors and dept. chairs; 9% student workers.	Superior 43% (**20% faculty**) Peer 42.2% (**63% faculty**) Subordinate 4% Customer/student 2% 1 actor 43% 2 actors 30%

(Continued)

Table 22.1 Continued

Study	Sample	Method	Time Frame	Rates	Actors
				Researcher defined (≥ 1 event at least weekly) 23% overall.	≥ 3 actors 27% Superior 44% Peer 40% Subordinate 6% Customer/student 2%
				33% women; 27% men	
				Witnessed 41%	
McKay et al., 2008 (Canada)	Teaching staff and librarians at one university; N = 100 (12% response rate)	Online questionnaire – define bullying in own words + behavioral checklist	Prior 5 years	Experienced 52% self-label (32% "seriously")	*Superior 34% Peers 61% Students 32%
Fox, 2009 (USA)	Faculty; convenience sample N = 228	Online questionnaire – behavioral checklist	Prior 5 years	Experienced 36% pervasive/ frequent bullying	Superior 22% Peer 24%
				Females > Males	
Neuman, 2009 (USA)	Faculty at one university; N = 241 (55% response rate)	Online questionnaire – respond to definition + behavioral checklist	Prior 12 months	Experienced 26% (self-label)	Superior 24% Colleague 66% – Senior colleague 37% – Equal status 21% – Junior colleague 8%
				Witnessed 50.5%	1 actor 43% 2 actor 21% ≥ 3 actors 36%
					Superior 28% Colleague 71% – Senior colleague 49% – Equal status 15% – Junior colleague 7%

Hollis, 2012	175 colleges and universities—all employee groups; $N = 401$ (15.5% response rate)	Respond to definition	Prior 18 months	Experienced 31% self-label Females > Males African American > White LGTBQ > straight Witness 32%	Not asked.
Dellifraine et al., 2014	National sample health administration faculty $N = 134$ (53% response rate)	Online questionnaire – define bullying in own words + behavioral checklist	Prior 5 years	Experienced 64% self-label (55% "seriously") Witness in career 78%	Dean 18% Full professor 43% Associate professor 25% Assistant professor 12% 1 actor 66% 2 actors 20% ≥ 3 actors 14%
Williams & Ruiz, 2012	Employees at one institution; $N =$ (28% response rate)	Respond to definition	Prior 2 years	Experienced 28% Females > Males Witness 48%	*Supervisor 38% Coworker 32% Faculty 23%
Landes, 2013	Employees at one institution; $N = 304$ (8.2% response rate)	Respond to definition	Prior 2 years	Experienced 38% Females > Males Witness 50%	*Supervisor 37% Someone of higher rank 31% Coworker 33% Faculty 30%
Raineri et al., 2011	Business and economics faculty, multiple institutions; $N = 60$ (2.7% response rate)	Online questionnaire – behavioral checklist; respond whether "observed" each behavior by faculty, by administrator	Prior 6 months	Witness (at least one behavior occurring at least monthly) 48% for faculty actor; 30% administrator actor	Senior faculty 52% Junior faculty 8% Administration 36% Staff 4%

(Continued)

Table 22.1 Continued

Study	Sample	Method	Time Frame	Rates	Actors
Mourssi-Alfash, 2014	Employees at one institution; N = 786; **163 faculty** (16% response rate)	Online questionnaire – respond to definition + behavioral checklist	Prior 6 months	Experienced 38% self-label; 82% at least one behavior in six months	Not asked
Beckmann et al., 2013	Nursing faculty in three NE states; N = 473 (42% response rate)	Online questionnaire – behavioral checklist	Prior 6 months	Experienced 36% (at least one behavior)	Administration 20% Senior faculty 60% Junior faculty 11%
Cassidy et al., 2014	Faculty at one institution; N = 121	Online questionnaire – definition of cyberbullying	Prior 12 months	Experienced cyberbullying 17% Female > Male People of color > Whites	Students 12% Colleague 9%
Lampman, 2012	Faculty at 100 institutions; N = 524 (66% response rate)	Online questionnaire – behavioral checklist re student behaviors	Prior 12 months	Experienced 91% at least one behavior; 10%–15% several behaviors Females > Males re degree of upset	Students as actors
Lampman et al., 2009	Faculty at one institution; N = 399 (61% response rate)	Mail questionnaire – behavioral checklist re student behaviors	Prior 12 months	Experienced 98% at least one behavior Females > Males re degree of upset	Students as actors
Taylor, 2012	Faculty at one institution; N = 1,060 (43% response rate)	Online questionnaire – respond to definition + behavioral checklist	Prior 6 months	Experienced 12% (self-label) Female > Male LGBT > Heterosexual Witness 22%	Not asked

Peters, 2014. *More than one actor could be identified.
N.B.: Percentages are rounded to closest number.

method involves providing respondents with a definition of workplace bullying and asking whether they have personally experienced this within a specified period of time (e.g., the preceding day, week, month, six months, year, etc.). For those indicating they believe they have been bullied, they are often asked to describe the situation: who were the actors, how long did it go on, and what was the impact on them. Using this method, mobbing is identified when more than one actor is involved.

The behavioral checklist method provides the respondent with a list of behaviors that researchers believe fit within the domain of bullying and mobbing. Respondents respond within a specific time frame, typically using Likert scales of increasing frequency defined in terms of never, rarely, monthly, weekly, and daily (Einarsen et al., 2009; Neuman & Keashly, 2004). In some measures, these items are endorsed with respect to specific actors (Keashly & Neuman, 2008; Neuman, 2009) to discern downward or hierarchical bullying, horizontal or peer bullying, and subordinate or contrapower bullying (Lampman, Phelps, Bancroft, & Beneke, 2009).

In the case of faculty as victims, these types of actors are equivalent to a chair, dean, or administrator and more senior faculty, faculty of equal rank, and students, respectively. People are identified as bullied based on the researchers' application of criteria. For example, some studies define a respondent as bullied if they have had at least one behavior in the specified time frame (e.g., Beckmann, Cannella, & Wantland, 2013; Lampman, 2012; Lampman et al., 2009; Mourssi-Alfash, 2014), while others look at the number of behaviors occurring at least weekly and then create categories or degrees of bullying (Keashly & Neuman, 2008; Lampman, 2012; Lampman et al., 2009; Neuman, 2009). Obviously, these different methods of measurement yield somewhat different findings. To complicate matters further, bullying and mobbing are considered to be an escalatory process (Matthiesen, Aasen, Holst, Wie, & Einarsen, 2003), and so even single behavior experiences provide important signals of potential problems.

The preceding section was meant to sensitize readers to some of the enormous challenges confronted by researchers trying to establish the nature, prevalence, and consequences of bullying and mobbing. It is also meant to suggest caution in interpreting the data we present in this chapter—as well as data from other sources that one may consider. As might be suspected, the self-labeling and behavioral checklist methods provide different estimates of prevalence, with more people being identified as "bullied" from checklists than from self-labeling approaches (Salin, 2001). This may be due to a reluctance on the part of individuals to view themselves as victims or this may be a reflection of different aspects of bullying, that is, exposure to bullying behaviors and the experience of victimization, respectively.

THE PREVALENCE, NATURE, AND EXPERIENCE OF ACADEMIC BULLYING AND MOBBING

Consistent with our discussion in the preceding section, the prevalence rates associated with self-labeling range from 12 percent (Taylor, 2012) to as high as 64 percent (Dellifraine, McClelland, Erwin, & Wang, 2014), with several in the 25–36 percent range. Digging into these rates, there is evidence of multiple experiences with being bullied (Dellifraine et al., 2014; McKay, Arnold, Fratzl, & Thomas, 2008; Williams & Ruiz, 2012), with upward of one-third to one-half of those self-identifying as being bullied reporting 4 or more experiences. Rates based on behavioral checklists suggest that, by far, the majority of respondents (82%–98% range) have been exposed, particularly when the minimal definition of at least one behavior during the time frame is used. When the element of several behaviors within the time frame is utilized, the rates range from 10 percent to 36 percent. For comparison, a recent survey of a representative sample of the U.S. working population reported 7 percent of respondents self-identified as being bullied in the prior 12 months (Namie, Christensen, & Philips, 2014). Thus, rates in academic environments are higher on average.

The prevalence of mobbing in these studies is particularly notable. Defining mobbing as two or more actors, one-third to one-half of faculty respondents are affected (Dellifraine et al., 2014; Keashly & Neuman, 2008; Neuman, 2009). In our 2008 study of university employees (Keashly & Neuman, 2008), faculty were twice as likely as staff to report multiple actors, and staff were 1.5 times more likely to report a single actor. Thus, the experience of faculty is often one characterized by a number of actors (and perhaps targets).

Variability within each of these methods appears to be tied to the nature of the sample and the context it reflects. Specifically, rates vary across different institutions. For example, controlling for the same measure and time frame, Keashly and Neuman (2008) report a rate of 39 percent for faculty, while Neuman (2009) reports a rate of 26 percent. Using the University of Massachusetts Amherst survey, Williams and Ruiz (2012) report a rate of 28 percent, and the rate reported by Landes (2013) is 38 percent. Using the Negative Acts Questionnaire–Revised (NAQ-R) global item, Taylor (2012) reports a rate of 12 percent of faculty and Mourssi-Alfash (2014) reports 21 percent of the faculty experienced bullying. Further, discipline-specific studies (health administration faculty, Dellifraine et al., 2014; nursing faculty, Beckmann et al., 2013) show differences in rates may also be influenced by disciplinary context (64% vs. 36%, respectively). Taylor (2012) reports higher rates of bullying in the college of arts and humanities than in other colleges on campus. These sample differences echo our earlier discussion about the importance of considering the context within which these experiences occur.

What is clear in examining these studies is that bullying and mobbing often occur in the presence, and with the knowledge, of other faculty. Rates of witnessing ranged from 32 percent to 78 percent, with most in the 40–50 percent range. Witnessing is important for a number of reasons. First, it is an indicator of the overall climate of the unit. Second, witnesses to bullying and mobbing show similar negative effects as targets, spreading the impact net more broadly (Hansen et al., 2006; Vartia, 2001). Third, witnesses are rarely uninvolved, and that involvement can be constructive (e.g., intervening, defusing the situation, bringing in help) or destructive (e.g., instigating the encounter, joining in, remaining silent; Namie & Lutgen-Sandvik, 2010). The challenge will be to leverage these others to engage productively in managing and addressing these situations early on. We will discuss strategies for building faculty bystander efficacy in the section on approaches for addressing bullying and mobbing,

Relationship between Actors and Targets

The relationship between actors and targets appears to vary by an individual's location within the institutional structure. Peer-to-peer bullying (colleague-to-colleague) appears to characterize the majority of faculty experiences more so than instances of bullying by administrators (e.g., Beckmann et al., 2013; Dellifraine et al., 2014; Keashly & Neuman, 2008; McKay et al., 2008; Neuman, 2009; Williams & Ruiz, 2012). Hierarchy is still involved in peer-to-peer bullying, as evidenced by the higher rates of actors being senior faculty versus those of lower or junior rank. Contrapower (student) bullying also shows up in studies focused on faculty experience (Cassidy, Faucher, & Jackson, 2014; Lampman, 2012; Lampman et al., 2009; McKay et al., 2008). Thus, faculty "get it from all sides," most notably from their colleagues. Staff appear to have a different experience. In our own research, staff was more likely to report a higher up as an actor and faculty more likely to report colleagues (53% vs. 63%, respectively; Keashly & Neuman, 2013). Thus, an individual's location within the institutional structure as defined by occupational group and hierarchal or professional status may leave targets vulnerable to abuse from particular actors or agents.

The issue of who the actor is vis-à-vis the target is not simply demographic. Evidence from other workplace contexts indicates that this relationship affects both the expression and experience of bullying (Hershcovis & Reich, 2013; Lamertz & Aquino, 2004; Neuman & Keashly, 2010). The key relational feature is the power difference and what it permits an actor to do and whether or how a target and others may be able (or willing) to respond. This power can be defined organizationally (e.g., tenured faculty to untenured faculty, dean to faculty) or in terms of social bases of power as captured by in-group membership, such as gender, race or ethnicity, sexual orientation, and class. The survey studies reviewed here provide evidence that women, African Americans, and LGTBQ faculty are at greater risk for bullying and mobbing. The selective use of bullying and mobbing broadly based on identity group membership in society is troubling, and it is particularly troubling to find this in academe. Thus, we want to take the time to dig into this here.

Social identity group membership

Academe generally, and the professoriate in particular, are often described as white, male, upper middle class, and heteronormative, a far from diverse group (Lee & Leonard, 2001). To the extent this is true, any faculty member who "deviates" from that becomes "noticeable" (Dentith, Wright, & Coryell, 2015), at risk for being viewed as counternormative, and, thus, a threat to the status quo (Berdahl, 2007), even if he or she has not engaged in actual provocative behavior. By virtue of this positionality (Misawa, 2015), these faculty are in a power-down position vis-à-vis other faculty and, thus, have less resources at their disposal to defend themselves. Even one's status as a tenured and full professor does not counter the impact of these identity-related differences (Johnson-Bailey, 2015). Ethnographic and interview studies detailing the experiences of women faculty (e.g., Dentith et al., 2015; Lester, 2009; Sedivy-Benton, Strohschen, Cavazos, & Boden-McGill, 2015); faculty of color (e.g., Frazier, 2011; Johnson-Bailey, 2015); and LGBTQ faculty (e.g., Misawa, 2015) are remarkably and sadly similar in their experiences of being targeted and bullied. All report behaviors that silence (e.g., being excluded from decision making, not being asked for input despite relevant expertise, continually being interrupted); question their legitimacy (e.g., diminishing the rigor and value of their work and strength of their scholarly record); and seek to undermine their competency and credibility in the eyes of others (e.g., actively searching for issues and problems, soliciting student comments regarding problems).

By highlighting the "otherness" of the faculty member and subsequent devaluing of this quality, these behaviors effectively "recontextualize targeted victims' ambient circumstances to suggest their inadequacy" (Kennison, Dzurec, Cary, & Dzurec, 2015, p. 28), making them vulnerable to "efforts" to get them to conform or leave (Westhues, 2006). Another common experience is that when faculty resist these "attacks," or insist that their perspectives and experiences be heard, they are framed as "difficult" and "uncollegial" (Johnson-Bailey, 2015; Westhues, 2002). Thus, the "problem" is the "target," and bullying and mobbing are framed as justified responses to provocation. These studies and experiences highlight that bullying and mobbing may reflect identity-related biases.

Being a high performer and critic as a risk factor

A theme in the personal accounts, interviews, and ethnographies is that the faculty members, regardless of identity group membership or professional status, were "successful" as academics in terms of their scholarship, teaching, and service. Being a "high performer," whose accomplishments and achievements challenge and threaten their colleagues (i.e., "rate busting") has been proposed as a difference that can make a faculty member "noticeable" and vulnerable (e.g., Kotleras, 2007; Friedenberg, 2008; Kim & Glomb, 2014; Westhues, 2006). Friedenberg's (2008) profile of the "classic" academic mobbing victim depicts a faculty member who is notable for his or her success. Junior faculty may be particularly vulnerable here. On the one hand, given the increasing requirements for gaining tenure, junior faculty will be among the high performers and, thus, should anticipate institutional support and protection as their work helps the university achieve its mission. However, the lack of job security on the tenure track, and the reliance on tenured faculty support to achieve tenure, restricts their abilities to defend themselves, particularly when the actors are senior tenured faculty. However, as Westhues's (2004) extensive research of academic mobbing cases reveals, many victims are senior tenured faculty who are also high performers.

Being high performers, though, could also be a predictor for becoming a bully—by using their status and power to fend off attempts to manage their behavior. Williams, Campbell, and Denton's (2013) study of department chairs' efforts to manage *high-performing instigators* (HPI), who engage in unprofessional and destructive behavior, is a vivid depiction of how faculty as actors can mobilize their status and frame their actions to resist any attempts to moderate or manage their behaviors. This perception of ineffective administrative action may lay the groundwork for other faculty to take action against the HPI, resulting in a mobbing situation. Indeed, Westhues (2006) has suggested that mobbing is often seen as the only way to get rid of a "troublesome" tenured faculty member; Zapf and Warth (1997) have referred to this as "personnel work by other means" (as cited in Salin, 2003).

Being vocal and persistent in one's criticism is another vulnerability factor for faculty (Friedenberg, 2008; Westhues, 2006; Nelson & Lambert, 2001). Based on his extensive analysis of hundreds of mobbing cases, Westhues (2006) observes that these targets were often not "innocent" in that they engaged in behavior that would be considered provocative and were often highly critical of established practices or "ways of doing things" and the people associated with them. Like being a high performer, being persistently critical is particularly interesting as a vulnerability because such behavior could be framed as appropriate within the principles of academic freedom, and an actor may use this to resist any attempts to moderate his or her behavior (see

Nelson & Lambert, 2001). While there is not disagreement in the literature or in academe that these are difficult and challenging interactions to have, the concern is that mobbing as a response is out of proportion to the "offense." As Friedenberg (2008) notes, "the contrast between the routine annoyances that targets of mobbing are seen as visiting upon their colleagues and superiors and the extremity of the latter's response is one of the enduring psychological puzzles in mobbing" (p. 11).

These differences as vulnerabilities highlight the importance of the nature and structure of academe in providing frames and accounts for what is considered acceptable and unacceptable faculty conduct and, thus, responses to them. We will discuss this in the section on the culture and structure of academe.

Duration and Process of Exposure

The experience of being bullied or mobbed is enduring. For example, McKay et al. (2008) report that 21 percent of faculty who self-identified as being bullied indicated it had lasted more than five years. In our own research with two institutions (Keashly & Neuman, 2008; Neuman, 2009), almost half of faculty report bullying that has lasted more than three years. Duration is a concern not only for the accumulation and intensification of negative effects but also for the possibility of pulling others into the experience, with faculty ganging up or choosing sides, creating spirals or cascades of hostility throughout a unit (Andersson & Pearson, 1999). This may also be an artifact of being tenured, as these are long-standing relationships, and the longer the relationship, the more opportunity for conflict (Neuman & Keashly, 2010) and for aggression (Jawahar, 2002). Indeed, tenure may actually make some faculty vulnerable to bullying and mobbing (Taylor, 2012; Westhues, 2006). Thus, being tenured could be considered a risk factor for both bullying and being bullied. We will return to the issue of tenure in our discussion of the context of academe.

What is clear from both the survey and qualitative studies is that bullying and mobbing involve a number of different behaviors. From the survey studies, the most frequently identified behaviors are work-related as opposed to person-related (Taylor, 2012), yet the impact is very much felt as a personal attack. Specific categories of behavior included threats to professional status (e.g., gossip and malicious rumors, belittling remarks, demeaning comments about research or teaching, harsh public critique); isolation and exclusion (e.g., ignoring or dismissing contributions, excluding from work-related activities, not seeking input); flaunting status (reminders of rank, condescending tones); and physical intimidation or aggression (e.g., threatening gestures, temper tantrums; hostile eye contact). The use of technology and electronic communication, which knows no time or work or life boundaries and permits anonymity, is showing up as a powerful means to target others in the form of cyberbullying, (e.g., Cassidy et al., 2014).

What the survey studies as snapshots do not reveal are the dynamics of the process. Qualitative research (e.g., Buitenhuis, 2015; Goldberg, Beitz, Wieland, & Levine, 2013; Johnson, 2014) reveals escalatory patterns of intimidation and silencing, questioning of legitimacy of scholarship and person, abuse of power, implied threats to tenure and promotion, and magnification of a mistake to become a fatal flaw. These behaviors, particularly taken together, communicate devaluation and diminution of the target (Johnson-Bailey, 2015; Young, Anderson, & Stewart, 2015). The depiction of the process across these different settings and with different faculty is strikingly similar, demonstrating a progressive and increasingly hostile process, which, over time, moves from informal mechanisms of engagement and management to more formal processes of review and evaluation (Lester, 2009). For a detailed description of this process, we refer to Westhues (1998), as his model of mobbing, based on his experience and hundreds of case studies, captures the experiences depicted in the qualitative literature reviewed here. This process is remarkably similar to what is described in other workplaces. Although specific behaviors and tactics may vary based on the context and the resources and mechanisms available, the overall dynamics and progression of being bullied or mobbed are universal, as are its outcomes (e.g., Einarsen et al., 2011; Leymann, 1996).

In sum, bullying and mobbing are familiar and unfortunately frequent experiences for faculty and others in the academy. It also appears that working in an academic environment, particularly as a faculty member, has a greater risk for experience with and prolonged exposure to bullying and mobbing than many other working environments. Faculty who are noticeable in some way are at particular risk of being targeted.

Most of the examples of bullying and mobbing presented in this section occurred within institutions of higher education, but even the casual reader will probably recognize that these examples could have be drawn from nonacademic organizations as well. In the section that follows, we focus more explicitly on contextual variables that are fairly unique to the academy.

UNDERSTANDING THE CONTEXT

We now provide specific detail on two important aspects of context (both social and structural) as they relate to the instigation and perception of bullying and mobbing in higher education.

The Culture of Academe

According to Robert J. Sternberg, a psychology professor at Cornell University and the former president of the University of Wyoming, "When you choose a career in academe, you need to be prepared not only for *rough-and-tumble politics*, but also for the *verbal abuse* that goes with it" (italics added, Sternberg, 2015, p. A26). In normative terms, this quote suggests that faculty should expect to deal with verbal abuse from an assortment of sources and the dark side of organizational politics. While there are many people who would disagree with that assessment, it does capture the distinctive discursive environment of the university workplace, the unique place that faculty occupy in this environment, and what this suggests about what is considered "appropriate" faculty conduct.

In traditional organizational settings, leadership—often in the form of a single individual or leadership team—assumes the responsibility for building the culture and climate of the organization. This "dominant coalition" defines expected role-related behaviors (norms) of organizational members and sets expectations for appropriate conduct (Bennett, Aquino, Reed, & Thau, 2005). In the case of academe, faculty members do not occupy those traditional leadership roles, but they are leaders in the sense that they occupy a central role in developing and executing the research and education missions of the university. Their leadership is recognized in university structure through shared governance, which, in its ideal form, includes the faculty as full partners with administrators and boards of trustees and governors.

Thus, major institutional decisions involve faculty members in meaningful and substantive ways, with respect to their voice, expertise, and associated resources. In this structure, faculty members are expected to engage with their administrative colleagues in vibrant discussion and problem-solving, which is needed when addressing institutional planning and its inherent challenges. This position privileges, and indeed requires, faculty to engage in vigorous debate and critique of administrative decisions. While employee groups in other organizational settings, including the university, may engage in critique, they do so at a greater risk than faculty. By virtue of academic freedom, faculty are "officially" afforded protection from institutional retaliation for being involved in crafting, countering, and challenging the discourse and decision making of the institution. Tenure provides additional protection from certain forms of institutional retaliation, but this does not mean that the faculty is immune from bullying or mobbing, as the research we have presented indicates.

More broadly, the culture of academe is one of debate, critique, and argumentation. Thus, faculty will, and indeed are expected to, engage in dissent, disagreement, argumentation, and refutation; these are necessary for the development and refinement of ideas and truths (Nelson & Lambert,

2001; Tannen, 2002). In essence, we are an argument culture, with all of its fire and thrill resulting in "a professional obligation to enter into disputes with . . . colleagues" (Heiser, 2003, p. 3). Further, failing to do so is framed as hugely problematic. As Friedenberg (2008) notes, "the greatest problem in the (academic) workplace is actually the lack of workers willing to swim against the current, question, challenge, change and argue" (p. 26). Taken together, shared governance, academic freedom, tenure, and the culture of debate and critique scaffold or frame the faculty role and, thus, what is considered appropriate and, indeed, expected faculty conduct. While disputation and argumentation are defining features of the broader academic culture, we recognize that the tolerance for and support of such engagement may vary considerably from institution to institution, depending on the institutional mission and environmental pressures. We will return to this in our discussion of structural influences in academe.

These conduct expectations are reflected in the positions of the American Association of University Professors (AAUP) in the United States and the Canadian Association of University Teachers (CAUT) in Canada. Both have written extensively on the management of faculty conduct, often in response to calls for increased civility and the invocation of collegiality. For example, the AAUP (1999) has argued that collegiality, often interpreted as working constructively (and positively, whatever that means) with others, and its discursive partner, civility, should not be the fourth criterion for tenure and promotion. The concern is that collegiality and civility may be used to silence or remove those whose approach is challenging to current doctrine within the discipline, status quo in the department, and, more broadly, contrary to the views of administration. Both organizations do affirm that faculty are expected to respect their colleagues and their ideas and opinions and to work to ensure all voices are heard, that is, ensuring each other's academic freedom. However, they argue that management of faculty conduct is best handled through the community of peers via suasion (vs. coercion) and collaboration (vs. regulation) (Campbell, 2014).

One challenge is that these rules of engagement are somewhat different from what other institutional members may be expected to follow. For example, staff roles have been characterized as supportive and involving cooperation and collaboration, which requires different norms for interacting, such as seeking common ground to facilitate the job getting done (Christy, 2010; Fratzl & McKay, 2013). Thus, if and when faculty take these conduct expectations into their interactions with other institutional members, on other than "academic" issues, it is not surprising that people within and outside the institution may find engagement with faculty "disconcerting and unpleasant" ("is everything an argument?"), affecting their subsequent interactions with, and experiences of, faculty. Recognizing these expectation differences and the resultant challenges, Christy (2010) produced a guide for higher education staff and managers on how to work effectively with faculty.

This discussion of expectations is important because people's assessment of what is problematic or unfair is based on their sense of norm violation (Skarlicki & Kulik, 2004). Thus, what a faculty member may view as appropriate and reasonable conduct, others may perceive as unjust, inappropriate, and harmful. As we discussed earlier, being defined as different is frequently framed as a "norm violation." Perceptions of norm violations are often met with challenge and, sometimes, aggression (Neuman, 2004; Salin, 2003).

Normative differences also have interesting implications for the accounts that faculty can make to justify or excuse behavior that may be perceived as a norm violation by others. In their analysis of three cases of "ivory tower bullying," Nelson and Lambert (2001) illustrate how faculty accused of bullying drew on academic rhetoric to frame their behavior in terms of the higher principles of academic freedom and "speaking truth to power," thus making their behavior seem normal and, in some cases, noble. This framing also (re) positioned the "others" as the ones who were bullying and mobbing, that is, the other is violating the norms. This points out a unique feature of faculty vis-à-vis other workers. Faculty are verbally adept and skilled in the art of framing and narrative construction. Indeed, faculty bullying and mobbing accounts have been characterized as "framing contests" in which parties on each side discursively position themselves as the innocent victim(s) of unwarranted and unprovoked attack by the other(s) (Friedenberg, Schneider, & Westhues, 2009; Nelson & Lambert, 2001), thus creating a justification for past, current, and future actions. For observers and others asked to manage the situation, this is a very confusing because everyone is accusing everyone else of bad behavior, making attributions for responsibility difficult. As a result, these third parties often feel at a loss of what to do. Whoever has made the more compelling case will likely gain the support of others, expanding the situation and subsequent disruption further.

The Structure of Academe

Workplace bullying and mobbing have been described as systemic in nature, stimulated and supported (and ultimately can be challenged) by features of the organizational structure and environment. This is true in academe. Drawing on Salin's (2003) discussion of enabling, motivating, and precipitating organizational practices and policies, Twale and De Luca (2008) examined how the academic institution and its surrounding environment can "set the stage" for and promote bullying and mobbing. We will briefly describe these features here, while pointing to Twale and De Luca's (2008) work for more detailed discussion.

- Enabling features affect whether bullying and mobbing are even possible.
  - Rigid hierarchy, low perceived costs or risks; lack of enforceable policies; qualities of work environment, such as perceived injustice and role state stressors; negative conflict climate.
- Motivating features frame bullying and mobbing as a "rational response" to those viewed as threats or burdens.
  - Internally competitive environment; perceived norm violation.
- Precipitating features trigger bullying and mobbing, assuming enabling and motivating features are in place.
  - Organizational change in the form of budget cuts, restructuring, changing or unstable leadership.

The current higher education environment and academic institutions have a number of these features. In terms of enabling factors, despite the egalitarian philosophy inherent in the notion of academic freedom, there is a hierarchy of rank among faculty and associated privilege (Barsky, 2002). Tenure protection contributes to the perception of little risk in engaging in behaviors and also reduced mobility out of difficult situations. Subjective performance processes such as tenure, promotion, and merit lay the groundwork for the undue influence, for example, "lack of collegiality" as a reason for denial. The increased emphasis on scholarly and creative productivity and shifting funding priorities privileges certain faculty over others and challenges faculty with different career trajectories. Increased faculty job responsibilities and associated time demands threaten career progress (Berryman-Fink, 1998).

Thus, faculty can feel diminished and threatened by others' accomplishments. Shrinking budgets facilitate interdepartmental competition. Changes in leadership in terms of orientation (corporatization, neoliberalism; Zabrodska et al., 2011) and increasing influence of administration and boards in the management of the institution pose threats to faculty voice and shared governance. In such scarce resource and competitive environments, faculty status is threatened. In such a context, bullying and mobbing may become a strategy for maintaining or gaining power and influence. Bullying and mobbing may also be viewed as a survival strategy, as faculty attempt to position themselves as productive and central to institutional missions and, thus, entitled to increasingly scarce resources and protection from job loss.

APPROACHES FOR ADDRESSING ACADEMIC BULLYING AND MOBBING

Our discussion of the context of faculty bullying and mobbing has focused on the nature of academe as shaped by academic freedom, shared governance, and, to some extent, tenure—as well as the current higher education environment and university structure and practices. We have discussed how this context shapes the conduct that occurs and how it can be framed and perceived. We have also argued that the current higher education environment creates a context in which bullying and mobbing can be framed as a rational means for power and, in some cases, survival. Just as these aspects shape the nature and impact of bullying and mobbing, these aspects need to be considered in the focus and development of actions, which address these situations. We are impressed by the variety of efforts and tools that have been developed to address bullying and mobbing in the academy. Due to space, we will discuss three that recognize the multicausal nature of these issues and illustrate the range of possibilities.

Policies and Procedures

Policies and their associated procedures are codifications of desired conduct and practices, as reflected in a university's mission, vision, and values specifically, and academe more broadly. Policies provide the framework for solving problematic situations and managing risk (Meacham & Gaff, 2006). A frequent concern noted in the literature is that many of the situations described occurred in a context that lacked or had ineffective policies (Westhues, 2007). This resulted in situations in which responses to issues of bullying and mobbing were either nonexistent or inconsistently applied, often strongly dependent on the relationship of administrators to the parties involved (Friedenberg et al., 2009). In recent years, there has been great interest in the development of policies regarding civility and respect at universities (Keashly & Wajngurt, 2016). This interest has been accompanied by deep and necessary concern for protected speech and academic freedom. The Foundation for Individual Rights in Education (FIRE) and the American Association of University Professors (AAUP) provide thoughtful and passionate critiques of the structure and content of policies focused on influencing conduct and speech. The National Labor Relations Board (NLRB) has also weighed in on policies in other workplaces that seek to restrict certain expressions of speech and conduct as they pertain to concerted activity (Kaiser, 2014). Clearly, there are many rights, voices, and interests that need to be considered in the development of such policies. Given shared governance, policies affecting academic members require the central involvement of faculty in discerning the nature of the issues, and the policies and practices to address them. The nature of faculty involvement in policy development has implications for whether the policy will be grounded in a deep understanding of academic freedom and, thus, accepted and implemented appropriately and effectively. We encourage those who are interested in pursuing such policies to read Ken Westhues's (2007) article on the process of policy development. A good example of a policy that reflects these considerations is the University of South Carolina policy on workplace bullying (University of South Carolina (USC), 2014).

The impetus for the policy came from faculty who, over a number of years, had expressed concern about problematic behaviors and confrontations among faculty and the need to establish standards of conduct (Jim Augustine, University Ombudsman, personal communication, October 28, 2013). The Faculty Welfare Committee of the Faculty Senate developed the policy, consulting with faculty and administrators in the process. The policy was approved by the Faculty Senate in late 2013 and became university policy in February 2014. While a detailed discussion of this policy is beyond the scope of this chapter, we would like to highlight several features that we believe reflect the deep consideration of the needs and rights of faculty as well as the institution.

First, the policy was positioned as an expression of the Carolinian Creed, which is a statement of the ideals for conduct for the community of scholars. Bullying was positioned as antithetical to these ideals. Second, recognizing that distinguishing bullying from conflict and other forms of challenging engagement that one would expect in academe was critical, they crafted a definition of bullying that required a "high standard for misconduct," specifically that it had to be severe and pervasive behavior. Workplace bullying is repeated, unwelcome *severe and pervasive behavior* that intentionally threatens, intimidates, humiliates, or isolates the targeted individual or undermines his or her reputation or job performance (USC, p. 1).

Third, the policy provides for informal and formal processes for resolution, recognizing that a range of concerns may be brought forward, some of which may be resolved informally. Fourth, peer review is enshrined as a core process in the formal complaint process. Given our discussion of the unique normative expectations for faculty conduct, it is important that fellow faculty be involved in this discernment. Peer review manifests in two ways: (1) the role of faculty civility advocate and (2) an investigative committee of tenured faculty. The faculty civility advocate (FCA) is a tenured faculty member appointed by the provost in consultation with the chair of the Faculty Senate.

The FCA is the first step in the formal complaint process. This individual is trained in recognition and investigation of workplace bullying and strategies for resolving conflicts. They serve as an independent party in resolving complaints. They are empowered to work with parties and relevant administrators to resolve valid complaints. If complaints are not resolved at this level or if the complaints are repeated or egregious, they move further in the process, which is the Office of Provost. It is at this point that the second peer review process comes into play. The provost will appoint an ad hoc investigative committee of five tenured members of the faculty (full professors) and the tenured librarians. Three members are to come from the Faculty Committee on Professional Conduct (a committee of the Faculty Senate). The purpose of the investigative committee is to determine whether bullying has occurred as defined by policy and to suggest remedies. The committee report is then sent to the provost, who directs final action. Thus, this policy is notable as one developed by and for faculty and reflective of faculty needs and rights.

The Power of Community Involvement

The next two initiatives are grounded in the idea of the power and responsibility of institutional members as a community for the manifestation of the climate and culture of the institution through their actions.

Facilitating conversations: Toxic Friday

The development and implementation of the USC policy illustrates the importance of engaging faculty and other institutional members in many, many conversations about what the issues are and how best to address them. A very interesting approach for establishing these conversations is illustrated by an initiative called "Toxic Friday," which was developed by the Center for Advancing Faculty Excellence at the University of Alaska Anchorage (Roderick, 2016). This book and its accompanying video were developed to be a resource for faculty, administrators, and other academic leaders to raise awareness of, and facilitate conversations about, problematic and toxic behaviors that occur in academic departments with an eye to jointly developing strategies that would lead to substantive climate and cultural change in the way faculty and others engaged one another, particularly in conflict.

For several years, the UAA Difficult Dialogues Initiative has focused on helping faculty learn to introduce and manage difficult dialogues in their classrooms. Throughout these discussions, Roderick and her colleagues at the center were often asked for advice on how to address difficult situations with colleagues. In its first incarnation, Toxic Friday was an interactive theater presentation depicting a variety of toxic faculty behaviors. The screenplay was based on interviews with faculty across campus about difficult situations they had encountered and found themselves at a loss as to how to respond. This presentation and subsequent facilitated discussion provided the opportunity for the audience to engage in conversation with the actors and with each other regarding what they had seen, what was problematic and why, and what opportunities were there to "change the scene."

Based on this success, Roderick and her colleagues have recorded the play and developed the book as a resource for the academic community writ large.

What is particularly appealing about this initiative is that it embraces faculty experiences and harnesses their desire to be more constructively engaged in addressing these issues. As Roderick (2016) notes, "faculty-driven problems are best addressed by faculty-driven solutions" (p. 1).

Building peer efficacy through bystander training

This next initiative focuses on the fact that bullying and mobbing often occurs in the presence or with the knowledge of others, that is, other faculty. As we know from the research on academic mobbing, other faculty can become drawn in as the dynamics progress (Westhues, 2006). Others may remain uninvolved, sometimes because they are uncertain what to do and whether it will make a positive difference (Keashly & Neuman, 2013). Thus, another focus of action is leveraging colleague influence to address extant bullying and mobbing situations by developing faculty skills and confidence in intervention to help faculty become active and constructive bystanders.

Bystander training has been utilized on university campuses, most often focused on students engaging their peers around high-risk behavior such as drinking and sexual violence (e.g., Banyard, Plante, & Moynihan, 2004) and responding to prejudiced and discriminatory behavior (e.g., Ashburn-Nardo, Morris, & Goodwin, 2008) These trainings are grounded in the five-step bystander decision-making model developed by Latané and Darley (1970). That is, a bystander must (1) notice a behavior; (2) assess whether it is problematic and thus requires action; (3) discern whether it is their responsibility to take action; (4) choose action(s); and (5) implement those actions.

We were inspired by this work and its success in leveraging peer pressure in constructive ways. This "power of peers" was made visible to us in our 2008 study (Keashly & Neuman, 2008), when we found that many witnesses actually tried multiple actions to ameliorate hostile situations, indicating that peers were in fact willing to help. Thus, we believe that there is tremendous opportunity to constructively address bullying and mobbing by engaging faculty in deliberate constructive peer influence, or suasion (AAUP, 1999). As a result, I (Loraleigh) have developed bystander training for faculty. Briefly, the research on the nature and effects of faculty bullying and mobbing is shared with participants. This helps highlight when behaviors become problematic (Notice) and when harm is likely, and thus action is needed (Assess). This is a critical part of the workshop because, as we have indicated earlier, many behaviors can be framed as part of the cut and thrust of academic debate and, thus, "normal" faculty behavior.

Discussion among participants about when a behavior or interaction moves from being challenging to destructive surfaces the discussion of normative expectations and the principle of academic freedom. This leads into the discussion of colleagues' responsibility for taking action. In this segment, we focus on building the case for faculty ability; peer responses as communications of norms of conduct; the costs of not responding for themselves (guilt, strained relationships with targets, toxic work environments); and, most importantly, their responsibility as a peer in a self-managing professional community to respond (Responsibility).

Assuming accepted responsibility, the focus is then on identifying goals for action (e.g., disrupting situation, preventing damage, enforcing professional norms, changing the environment; Massachusetts Institute of Technology, 2004; White & Malkowski, 2014) and the consideration of possible actions ranging from low involvement to high involvement and from immediate to later action (Bowes-Sperry & O'Leary-Kelly, 2005) to achieve those goals (Choose action). It is in this section that discussion of mobbing is raised. Real-life scenarios are utilized for applying and practicing these steps (Taking action). To date, these trainings have been piloted at four institutions and are continuing to evolve. Preliminary responses indicate that faculty participants find the training useful and feel more confident that they can take an action that will influence the course of problematic interactions in more constructive directions.

CONCLUSION

In this chapter, we have attempted to provide the best current research and thinking related to workplace bullying and mobbing in institutions of higher education. We have highlighted the importance of considering the context in which all forms of human behavior occur and discussed many contextual factors that are unique to the academy. These factors include, but are not limited to, the unique role of faculty, the culture of academe, and the structural features and pressures of universities, and higher education in particular.

Throughout our presentation, we have included a substantial number of references to current and seminal peer-reviewed empirical and conceptual literature and citations for trade publications and Web-based material. Should the muse strike, readers will have ample opportunity to satisfy their desires for more detail than we have room for in this chapter.

We have also provided our own context for interpreting and assessing statistical data related to the nature, prevalence, and consequences of bullying and mobbing—not just in higher education but across the range of workplaces in which these behaviors occur. Specifically, we highlighted the challenges of capturing accurate data given the variety of measures and methodologies that have been, and continue to be, employed in this stream of research. Many of us pursuing research in this field have been calling for consensus definitions and valid measures for the past 20 years. While some progress has been made, more has to be done before we can feel confident in the statistical conclusions that we draw about bullying and mobbing across organizational settings. Having said this, we do believe that the evidence clearly demonstrates that aggressive behaviors generally and bullying and mobbing in particular are unfortunate and damaging aspects of our daily experience in academe in need of effective action.

We concluded our chapter by providing exemplars of policies, practices, and intervention techniques. These are meant to serve as examples rather than as prescriptive. Over the past 20 years, we have engaged in a number of research and consulting activities, and we are confident of one thing. One size does not fit all. Effective interventions are not administered; rather, they are designed, executed, and assessed by the very people they are meant to help. But being mindful of the types of behaviors subsumed under the headings of bullying and mobbing and understanding the underlying acts that motivate or inhibit such behavior are critically important. To that end, we believe that the present volumes, and hopefully our own contribution, will provide some guidance in thinking about, and dealing with, these pernicious phenomena.

REFERENCES

American Association of University Professors (AAUP). (1999). On collegiality as a criterion for faculty evaluation. Retrieved from https://www.aaup.org/AAUP/pubsres/policydocs/contents/collegiality.htm#b2

Andersson, L. M., & Pearson, C. (1999). Tit-for-tat? The spiraling effect of incivility in the workplace. *Academy of Management Review, 24*(3), 452–471.

Aquino, K., & Lamertz, K. (2004). Relational model of workplace victimization: Social roles and patterns of victimization in dyadic relationships. *Journal of Applied Psychology, 89*(6), 1023–1034.

Ashburn-Nardo, L., Morris, K. A., & Goodwin, S. A. (2008). The confronting prejudiced responses (CPR) model: Applying CPR in organizations. *Academy of Management Learning & Education, 7*(3), 332–342.

Banyard, V. L., Plante, E. G., & Moynihan, M. M. (2004). Bystander education: Bringing a broader community perspective to sexual violence prevention. *Journal of Community Psychology, 32*(1), 61–79.

Barsky, A. E. (2002). Structural sources of conflict in a university context. *Conflict Resolution Quarterly, 20*(2), 161–176.

Beckmann, C. A., Cannella, B. L., & Wantland, D. (2013). Faculty perception of bullying in schools of nursing. *Journal of Professional Nursing, 29*(5), 287–294.

Bennett, R. J., Aquino, K., Reed, A., II, & Thau, S. (2005). The normative nature of employee deviance and the impact of moral identity. In S. Fox & P. E. Spector (Eds.), *Counterproductive work behavior: Investigations of actors and targets* (pp. 107–125). Washington, D.C.: American Psychological Association.

Berdahl, J. L. (2007). Harassment based on sex: Protecting social status in the context of gender hierarchy. *Academy of Management Review, 32*(2), 641–658.

Berryman-Fink, C. (1998). Can we agree to disagree? Faculty-faculty conflict. In S. A. Holton (Ed.), *Mending the cracks in the ivory tower: Strategies for conflict management in higher education* (pp. 141–163). Bolton, MA: Anker Publishing Company.

Bowes-Sperry, L., & O'Leary-Kelly, A. M. (2005). To act or not to act: The dilemma faced by sexual harassment observers. *Academy of Management Review, 30*(2), 288–306.

Brodsky, C. M. (1976). *The harassed worker.* Lexington, MA: Lexington Books.

Buitenhuis, E. B. (2015). Bullying in the context of politics, pedagogy and power (Unpublished doctoral dissertation). University of Calgary, Calgary, Alberta, Canada.

Campbell, J. (2014). Giving and taking offence: Civility, respect, and academic freedom. In J. L. Turk (Ed.), *Academic freedom in conflict: The struggle over free speech rights in the university* (pp. 287–304). Toronto, Ontario, Canada: James Lorimer & Company.

Cassidy, W., Faucher, C., & Jackson, M. (2014). The dark side of the ivory tower: Cyberbullying of university faculty and teaching personnel. *Alberta Journal of Educational Research, 60*(2), 279–299.

Christy, S. C. (2010). *Working effectively with faculty: Guidebook for higher education staff and managers.* Berkeley, CA: University Resources Press.

Davenport, N., Schwartz, R. D., & Elliott, G. P. (1999). *Mobbing: Emotional abuse in the American workplace.* Ames, IA: Civil Society.

Dellifraine, J. L., McClelland, L. E., Erwin, C. O., & Wang, Z. (2014). Bullying in academia: Results of a survey of health administration faculty. *Journal of Health Administration Education, 31*(2), 147–163.

Dentith, A. M., Wright, R. R., & Coryell, J. (2015). Those mean girls and their friends: Bullying and mob rule in the academy. *Adult Learning, 26*(1), 28–34.

Duffy, M. K., Ganster, D. C., & Pagon, M. (2002). Social undermining in the workplace. *Academy of Management Journal, 45*(2), 331–351.

Einarsen, S. (1999). The nature and causes of bullying at work. *International Journal of Manpower, 20*(1/2), 16–27.

Einarsen, S., Hoel, H., & Notelaers, G. (2009). Measuring exposure to bullying and harassment at work: Validity, factor structure and psychometric properties of the Negative Acts Questionnaire–Revised. *Work & Stress, 23*(1), 24–44.

Einarsen, S., Hoel, H., Zapf, D., & Cooper, C. L. (2011). The concept of bullying and harassment at work: The European tradition. In S. Einarsen, H. Hoel, D. Zapf, & C. L. Cooper (Eds.), *Bullying and harassment in the workplace: Developments in theory, research, and practice* (2nd ed., pp. 3–39). London, England: CRC Press.

Flaherty, C. (2014, December 2). Bully-free zone. Retrieved from https://www.insidehighered.com/news/2014/12/02/u-wisconsin-madison-faculty-approves-anti-bullying-policy

Fogg, P. (2008, September 19). Academic bullies: The Web provides new outlets for combating workplace aggression. *Chronicle of Higher Education, 55*(3), B10–B13.

Fratzl, J., & McKay, R. (2013). Professional staff in academia: Academic culture and the role of aggression. In J. Lester (Ed.), *Workplace bullying in higher education* (pp. 41–59). New York: Taylor & Francis.

Frazier, K. N. (2011). Academic bullying: A barrier to tenure and promotion for African-American faculty. *Florida Journal of Educational Administration & Policy*, 5(1), 1–13.

Friedenberg, J. E. (2008). The anatomy of an academic mobbing. In K. Westhues (Ed.), *The anatomy of an academic mobbing: Two cases* (pp. 1–36). Lewiston, NY: Mellen Press.

Friedenberg, J. E., Schneider, M. A., & Westhues, K. (2009, June). *Mobbing as a factor in faculty work life*. Paper presented at the International Conference on Globalization, Shared Governance, and Academic Freedom, Washington, D.C.

Goldberg, E., Beitz, J., Wieland, D., & Levine, C. (2013). Social bullying in nursing academia. *Nurse Educator*, 38(5), 1–7.

Gravois, J. (2006, April 14). Mob rule. *Chronicle of Higher Education*, 52(32), A10–A12.

Hansen, Å. M., Hogh, A., Persson, R., Karlson, B., Garde, A. H., & Ørbæk, P. (2006). Bullying at work, health outcomes, and physiological stress response. *Journal of Psychosomatic Research*, 60(1), 63–72.

Heiser, G. M. (2003). Because the stakes are so small: Collegiality, polemic, and professionalism in academic employment decisions. *University of Kansas Law Review*, 52, 385.

Hershcovis, M. S. (2011). "Incivility, social undermining, bullying . . . oh my!": A call to reconcile constructs within workplace aggression research. *Journal of Organizational Behavior*, 32(3), 499–519.

Hershcovis, M. S., & Reich, T. C. (2013). Integrating workplace aggression research: Relational, contextual, and method considerations. *Journal of Organizational Behavior*, 34(S1), 526–542.

Hiatt, G. (2008, February 19). Mean and nasty academics [Blog post]. Retrieved from http://academicladder.com/mean-and-nasty-academics

Hollis, L. P. (2012). *Bully in the ivory tower: How aggression and incivility erode American higher education.* n.p.: Author.

Jawahar, I. M. (2002). A model of organizational justice and workplace aggression. *Journal of Management*, 28(6), 811–834.

Johns, G. (2006). The essential impact of context on organizational behavior. *Academy of Management Review*, 31(2), 386–408.

Johnson, P. (2014). Bullying in academia up close and personal: My story. *Workplace: A Journal for Academic Labor*, 24, 33–41.

Johnson-Bailey, J. (2015). Academic incivility and bullying as gendered and racialized phenomena. *Adult Learning*, 26(1), 42–47.

Kaiser, A. V. (2014). The death of courtesy and civility under the National Labor Relations Act. *Employment Law Commentary*, 26(8), 1–5.

Keashly, L. (1998). Emotional abuse in the workplace: Conceptual and empirical issues. *Journal of Emotional Abuse*, 1, 85–117.

Keashly, L., & Harvey, S. (2005). Emotional abuse in the workplace. In S. Fox & P. E. Spector (Eds.), *Counterproductive work behavior: Investigations of actors and targets* (pp. 201–236). Washington, D.C.: American Psychological Association.

Keashly, L., & Jagatic, K. (2003). By any other name: American perspectives on workplace bullying. In S. Einarsen, H. Hoel, D. Zapf, & C. L. Cooper (Eds.),

Bullying and emotional abuse in the workplace: International perspectives on research and practice (pp. 31–61). London, England: Taylor Francis.

Keashly, L., & Neuman, J. H. (2008). *Final report: Workplace behavior (bullying) project survey*. Minnesota State University–Mankato. Retrieved from https://www.mnsu.edu/csw/workplacebullying/workplace_bullying_final_report.pdf

Keashly, L., & Neuman, J. H. (2010). Faculty experiences with bullying in higher education: Causes, consequences, and management. *Administrative Theory and Praxis, 32*(1), 48–70.

Keashly, L., & Neuman, J. H. (2013). Bullying in higher education: What current research, theorizing, and practice tell us. In J. Lester (Ed.), *Workplace bullying in higher education* (pp. 1–22). New York: Routledge.

Keashly, L., & Wajngurt, C. (2016). Faculty bullying in higher education. *Psychology and Education: An Interdisciplinary Journal, 53*(1/2), 79–90.

Kennison, M., Dzurec, L. C., Cary, A., & Dzurec, D. (2015). Seeking the "Magis": A pathway to enhancing civility in higher education. *Jesuit Higher Education: A Journal, 4*(1), 27–35.

Khoo, S. B. (2010). Academic mobbing: Hidden health hazard at workplace. *Malaysian Family Physician, 5*(2), 61–67.

Kim, E., & Glomb, T. M. (2014). Victimization of high performers: The roles of envy and work group identification. *Journal of Applied Psychology, 99*(4), 619–634.

Kotleras, R. (2007). The workplace mobbing of highly gifted adults: An unremarked barbarism. *Advanced Development, 11*, 130.

Lamertz, K., & Aquino, K. (2004). Social power, social status and perceptual similarity of workplace victimization: A social network analysis of stratification. *Human Relations, 57*(7), 795–822.

Lampman, C. (2012). Women faculty at risk: US professors report on their experiences with student incivility, bullying, aggression, and sexual attention. *NASPA Journal about Women in Higher Education, 5*(2), 184–208.

Lampman, C., Phelps, A., Bancroft, S., & Beneke, M. (2009). Contrapower harassment in academia: A survey of faculty experience with student incivility, bullying, and sexual attention. *Sex Roles, 60*(5–6), 331–346.

Landes, C. (2013). *Workplace bullying at James Madison University* (Unpublished master's thesis). James Madison University, Harrisonburg, VA.

Latané, B., & Darley, J. M. (1970). *The unresponsive bystander: Why doesn't he help?* New York: Appleton-Century Crofts.

Lee, L. J., & Leonard, C. A. (2001). Violence in predominantly white institutions of higher education: Tenure and victim blaming. *Journal of Human Behavior in the Social Environment, 4*(2–3), 167–186.

Lester, J. (2009). Not your child's playground: Workplace bullying among community college faculty. *Community College Journal of Research and Practice, 33*(5), 444–464.

Leymann, H. (1996). The content and development of mobbing at work. *European Journal of Work and Organizational Psychology, 5*(2), 165–184.

Maslow, A. H. (1954). *Motivation and personality*. New York: Harper and Row.

Massachusetts Institute of Technology. (2004). Active bystander program and mediation @MIT. Retrieved from http://web.mit.edu/bystanders

Matthiesen, S. B., Aasen, E., Holst, G., Wie, K., & Einarsen, S. (2003). The escalation of conflict: A case study of bullying at work. *International Journal of Management and Decision Making, 4*(1), 96–112.

McKay, R., Arnold, D. H., Fratzl, J., & Thomas, R. (2008). Workplace bullying in academia: A Canadian study. *Employee Responsibilities and Rights Journal, 20*(2), 77–100.

Meacham, J., & Gaff, J. G. (2006). Learning goals in mission statements: Implications for educational leadership. *Liberal Education, 92*(1), 6–13.

Misawa, M. (2015). Cuts and bruises caused by arrows, sticks, and stones in academia: Theorizing three types of racist and homophobic bullying in adult and higher education. *Adult Learning, 26*(1), 6–13.

Misawa, M., & Rowland, M. L. (Eds.). (2015). Academic bullying and incivility in adult, higher, continuing, and professional education [Special issue]. *Adult Learning, 26*(1).

Mourssi-Alfash, M. F. (2014). *Workplace bullying and its influence on the perception of organizational justice and organizational citizenship behavior among faculty and staff in the public higher education in the Minnesota System* (Unpublished doctoral dissertation). Capella University, Minneapolis, Minnesota.

Namie, G., Christensen, D., & Phillips, D. (2014). *2014 WBI U.S. Workplace Bullying Survey*. Workplace Bullying Institute. Retrieved from http://workplacebullying.org/multi/pdf/WBI-2014-US-Survey.pdf

Namie, G., & Lutgen-Sandvik, P. (2010). Active and passive accomplices: The communal character of workplace bullying. *International Journal of Communication, 4*, 343–373.

Nelson, E. D., & Lambert, R. D. (2001). Sticks, stones and semantics: The ivory tower bully's vocabulary of motives. *Qualitative Sociology, 24*(1), 83–106.

Neuman, J. H. (2004). Injustice, stress, and aggression in organizations. In R. W. Griffin & A. M. O'Leary-Kelly (Eds.), *The dark side of organizational behavior* (pp. 62–102). San Francisco, CA: Jossey-Bass.

Neuman, J. H. (2009). Workplace behavior project survey. Unpublished raw data.

Neuman, J. H., & Keashly, L. (2004, April). Development of the Workplace Aggression Research Questionnaire (WAR-Q): Preliminary data from the Workplace Stress and Aggression Project. In R. J. Bennett & C. D. Crossley (Chairs), *Theoretical advancements in the study of anti-social behavior at work*. Symposium conducted at the meeting of the Society for Industrial and Organizational Psychology, Chicago, Illinois.

Neuman, J. H., & Keashly, L. (2010). Means, motive, opportunity and aggressive workplace behavior. In J. Greenberg (Ed.), *Insidious workplace behavior* (pp. 31–76). New York: Psychology Press.

Petrina, S., & Ross, E. W. (Eds.). (2014). Academic bullying & mobbing [Special issue]. *Workplace: A Journal for Academic Labor, 24*. Retrieved from http://ices.library.ubc.ca/index.php/workplace/issue/view/182392

Petry, G. (2011). Top ten workplace issues for faculty members and higher education professionals. Retrieved from https://www.aaup.org/article/top-ten-workplace-issues-faculty-members-and-higher-education-professionals#.V2IKsTV8lm4

Pinder, C. C. (2008). *Work motivation in organizational behavior* (2nd ed.). New York: Psychology Press.

Roderick, E. (Ed.). (2016). *Toxic Friday: Resources for addressing faculty bullying in higher education.* Anchorage: University of Alaska Anchorage.

Richman, J. A., Rospenda, K. M., Nawyn, S. J., Flaherty, J. A., Fendrich, M., Drum, M. L., & Johnson, T. P. (1999). Sexual harassment and generalized workplace abuse among university employees: Prevalence and mental health correlates. *American Journal of Public Health, 89*(3), 358–363.

Salin, D. (2001). Prevalence and forms of bullying among business professionals: A comparison of two different strategies for measuring bullying. *European Journal of Work and Organizational Psychology, 10*(4), 425–441.

Salin, D. (2003). Ways of explaining workplace bullying: A review of enabling, motivating and precipitating structures and processes in the work environment. *Human relations, 56*(10), 1213–1232.

Sedivy-Benton, A., Strohschen, G., Cavazos, N., & Boden-McGill, C. (2015). Good ol'boys, mean girls, and tyrants: A phenomenological study of the lived experiences and survival strategies of bullied women adult educators. *Adult Learning, 26*(1), 35–41.

Skarlicki, D. P., & Kulik, C. T. (2004). Third-party reactions to employee (mis)treatment: A justice perspective. *Research in Organizational Behavior, 26,* 183–229.

Sternberg, R. J. (2015, July 24). Coping with verbal abuse. *Chronicle of Higher Education, 61*(41), A26–A27.

Tannen, D. (2002). Agonism in academic discourse. *Journal of Pragmatics, 34*(10), 1651–1669.

Taylor, S. K. (2012). *Workplace bullying in higher education: Faculty experiences and responses* (Unpublished doctoral dissertation). University of Minnesota, Minneapolis, Minnesota.

Twale, D. J., & De Luca, B. M. (2008). *Faculty incivility: The rise of the academic bully culture and what to do about it.* San Francisco, CA: Jossey-Bass.

University of South Carolina (USC). (2014). Workplace bullying (ACAF 1.80). Retrieved from http://www.sc.edu/policies

Vartia, M. (2001). Consequences of workplace bullying with respect to the well-being of its targets and the observers of bullying. *Scandinavian Journal of Work, Environment and Health, 27*(1), 63–69.

Wajngurt, C. (2014). Prevention of bullying on campus. Retrieved from https://www.aaup.org/article/prevention-bullying-campus#.V2Cl9TV8lm4

Westhues, K. (1998). *Eliminating professors: A guide to the dismissal process.* Lewiston, NY: Edwin Mellen Press.

Westhues, K. (2002). At the mercy of the mob. *Occupational Health and Safety Canada, 18*(8), 30–36.

Westhues, K. (Ed.). (2004). *Workplace mobbing in academe: Reports from twenty universities.* Lewiston, NY: Edwin Mellen Press.

Westhues, K. (2006). The unkindly art of mobbing. *Academic Matters: The Journal of Higher Education, 2006* (Fall), 18–19. Retrieved from http://www.kwesthues.com/unkindlyart.htm

Westhues, K. (2007). Before drafting your policy on workplace decency, compare these two alternatives. Retrieved from http://arts.uwaterloo.ca/~kwesthue/dignitypolicies01.htm

White, C. H., & Malkowski, J. (2014). Communicative challenges of bystander intervention: Impact of goals and message design logic on strategies college students use to intervene in drinking situations. *Health Communication, 29*(1), 93–104.

Williams, E. A., & Ruiz, Y. (2012). Workplace bullying survey: Final report. Retrieved from http://www.umass.edu/local1776/Flyers,%20Updates%20&%20Documents_files/WBS%20Final%20Report%202012%2010%2004.pdf

Williams, F. I., Campbell, C., & Denton, L. T. (2013). Incivility in academe: Strategies for managing high-performing instigators. *Journal of Business and Educational Leadership, 4*(1), 148–159.

Young, K., Anderson, M., & Stewart, S. (2015). Hierarchical microaggressions in higher education. *Journal of Diversity in Higher Education, 8*(1), 61–71.

Zabrodska, K., Linnell, S., Laws, C., & Davies, B. (2011). Bullying as intra-active process in neoliberals universities. *Qualitative Inquiry, 17*(8), 709–719.

23

Workplace Bullying and Mobbing in the Public Service Sector and the Role of Unions

Gregory Sorozan

Public sector workplaces are those federal, state, municipal, county, city, or town agencies, departments, commissions, or boards whose purpose and intent is defined by statute or regulation. They are typically funded by taxes and other forms of public revenue. Public sector workplaces are also more likely than their private sector counterparts to have unions and collective bargaining agreements. This mix renders public sector workplaces uniquely different from their private and nonprofit counterparts.

Unfortunately, bullying and mobbing behaviors are hardly strangers to the public sector workplace. In fact, they can be every bit as destructive as in the other employment sectors. Accordingly, this chapter will explore bullying and mobbing in public sector employment and the potential role of labor unions to be part of the solution. I will be drawing significantly upon my experience in public sector employment and public sector labor relations, informed by graduate training and professional experience in mental health counseling.

I have also been building a record of dealing with bullying and mobbing situations in my role as a senior union official. I have served since May 2000 as the president of a local union for the National Association of Government Employees (NAGE) with representation of approximately 4,000 bargaining unit members. What was first intended as an opportunity to fashion contract language designed to address bullying in the workplace has turned into a second career representing Massachusetts state employees in all manner of contract disputes and labor activities, including bullying complaints.

SETTING THE STAGE

As of this writing, there is currently no direct legal liability for workplace bullying and mobbing in the United States. Public sector employment systems, however, may address some of these behaviors through employer policies, collective bargaining, and the inclusion of antibullying language in union contract provisions. Although impacted by public laws, public policies, public procedures, and public funding, work practices that are hostile, humiliating, and intimidating continue to exist in federal, state, and municipal government workplaces. Numerous factors contribute to workplaces that may be abusive to the public servant, some of which are shared with for-profit workplaces. However, perhaps more overtly than in the private sector, politics and political will are inherently significant contributors to the day-to-day workings of public sector workplaces.

Public agencies often undergo changes in their missions and cultures as a result of the election of new public officials. The political will of the people is translated down by the elected official, agency head, or commissioner to the public servant, who must act in compliance with changes in policy, procedures, rules, and relationships. Between the victorious candidate and the public servant are layers of career administrators and managers who continue to be charged with the management of the agency. Their actions are not so easily observed, but they control the information to and from the public servant and back to the top administrator of the agency. They influence the relationships between different strata of employees within their agency.

Unions can play a key role in ensuring that the intended mission and goals of the agency are carried out in an efficient, transparent, and fair manner. In representation of their members, unions serve as a check and balance to unbridled ambitions of individuals that run contrary to contract, to labor laws, and to state and federal laws. Unions, by collective bargaining agreements, collectively bargain over the terms and conditions of employment through a negotiation process. The union is empowered by its members to represent their interests in the workplace. Bullying in the workplace can be understood to exist on the abusive end of the spectrum for power and control in the work environment. One fundamental interest of all working people is that of working in a healthy workplace.

OBLIGATIONS OF UNIONS

The National Labor Relations Act (2016) empowers unions to organize employees and negotiate for them with their employer. In its opening paragraph, the NLRA states, "Congress enacted the National Labor Relations Act (NLRA) in 1935 to protect the rights of employees and employers, to encourage collective bargaining, and to curtail certain private sector labor and management practices, which can harm the general welfare of workers, businesses and the U.S. economy" (para. 1).

Individual states have borrowed from the NLRA and forged their own collective bargaining laws. In Massachusetts, this appears in the form of Massachusetts General Law Chapter 150E (2016):

> Employees shall have the right of self-organization and the right to form, join, or assist any employee organization for the purpose of bargaining collectively through representatives of their own choosing on questions of wages, hours, and other terms and conditions of employment, and to engage in lawful, concerted activities for the purpose of collective bargaining or other mutual aid or protection, free from interference, restraint, or coercion. (para. 1)

Behaviors and practices at work that are hostile, humiliating, or intimidating and that adversely impact the job performance of the employee are exactly those practices that collective bargaining laws were meant to address. Unions may negotiate changes to the terms and conditions of employment that negatively impact their members. When such terms and conditions adversely impact the functioning of the agency in completing its stated mission and goals, there is even greater reason to intervene and to effect changes that are beneficial for both sides.

In 2009, NAGE, representing some 12,000 state employees in Massachusetts, successfully negotiated a "mutual respect" provision for its contract bargaining agreement (CBA) with the Commonwealth of Massachusetts. The author drafted and negotiated the provision, drawing upon the work of Suffolk University law professor David Yamada and working with NAGE's principle negotiator, Kevin Preston. Article 6A states,

> The Commonwealth and the Union agree that mutual respect between and among managers, employees, co-workers and supervisors is integral to the efficient conduct of the Commonwealth's business. Behaviors that contribute to a hostile, humiliating or intimidating work environment, including abusive language or behavior, are unacceptable and will not be tolerated. Employees who believe they are subject to such behavior, and who want to pursue the matter, shall raise their concerns with an appropriate manager or supervisor as soon as possible, but no later than ninety (90) days from the occurrence of the most recent incident(s). In the event the employee(s) concerns have been formally raised at the agency level and are not addressed within a reasonable period of time, the employee or the Union may file a grievance at step III of the grievance procedure as set forth in Article 23 (notice shall be sent concurrently to the Agency Head or designee). If an employee, or

the Union, requests a hearing at step III, such hearing shall be granted. Grievances filed under this section shall not be subject to the arbitration provisions set forth in Article 23. No employee shall be subject to discrimination for filing a complaint, giving a statement, or otherwise participating in the administration of this process. (National Association of Government Employees, 2014, p. 17)

Since adopting Article 6A, union intervention in instances of bullying in the workplace has proven to be a resounding success. The terms of the article caused the labor relations arm of state government to take seriously egregious and abusive behaviors and to follow through with investigations of complaints filed by bargaining unit members.

A complaint that factually explains the claimed hostility, humiliation, or intimidation is a key factor toward a successful investigation. Teasing out the specific behaviors, however, can often be complicated by the trauma experienced by the target. To some degree, discussing the behaviors opens up fresh wounds currently held in check to varying degrees, an experience clinically known as *retraumatization* (see chapter 13 for more information). When abusive behaviors are carefully enacted by a perpetrator, the target often lacks sufficient perspective or language to identify and describe the unexpected, often shocking, and uncalled-for mistreatment.

Targets' responses to abusive behaviors vary from case to case. One very common and maladaptive response to bullying in public sector employment is to go over the head of an abusive supervisor. This has sometimes proven to be a big mistake. Without specific recognition of abusive supervisory actions by management, and without policies, procedures, and practices to investigate those actions built into the day-to-day functioning of the agency, supervisors and managers quickly close ranks against the complainant. The target is often driven out of employment.

PUBLIC SECTOR WORKPLACES AND THEIR SYSTEMS

Public sector work encompasses federal, state, municipal, and county governmental entities. At each of these levels of government, there is a separation of power and an inherent system of checks and balances on the use of powers and authority, ideally for the benefit of citizens.

The executive, whether it be the president in the federal structure, a governor in the state structure, or a mayor in the city or town structure, oversees the executive branch agencies and has a direct line of authority to the administrator of the agency or department. In the federal government, the extension of authority can most easily be seen by the reporting nature of the cabinet secretaries to the president.

Such a grouping of agencies or functions under a direct appointee of the chief administrator may also be evidenced at the state level, as with the secretariat structure within state government. An example of this from Massachusetts is the Executive Office of Health and Human Services (EOHHS), headed by the secretary of the EOHHS and overseeing 14 state agencies. As of 2014, the number of public employees (public servants) employed within Massachusetts, and overseen by the governor, was approximately 63,000 (Governing, 2016). (To put this in some perspective, in 2014, the president of the United States oversaw approximately 2.66 million federal employees, exclusive of uniformed military personnel (Office of Personnel Management, n.d.).)

The legislature maintains oversight of the agency through the budget process and committee hearings. Ideally, each public agency is scrutinized to ensure its compliance with the enabling legislation, other applicable laws, and the demands of the public. Logic dictates that they all do their jobs as described, while communicating their actions up and down the chains of authority, contributing to an agency that functions smoothly, efficiently, and consistently with directives from the top. Of course, it does not necessarily work that way.

When necessary, the judicial branch interprets the pertinent laws. Because of this balance of power between the three branches of government, the theory holds that the will of the people will be more fairly carried out and that the power to control and influence the public will be more fairly distributed and used for the public good and not for individual glory or personal gain.

Public sector unions operate against this backdrop. Unions, enabled by collective bargaining laws, provide for the collective rights of individual working people to be brought to the attention of their management or administrators to bargain for fair and humane treatment while carrying out their work. Unions offer another balance to the power that may be misapplied by an individual supervisor who does not take into consideration the very real and human needs of those actually doing the work of the people. The checks and balances enacted through the process of negotiating a union collective bargaining agreement are intended to put labor and management on the same page within the four corners of the contract. The CBA codifies how employees are to be treated and how they may not be treated. The line between labor and management is more finely drawn when both sides of the labor and management equation are held to account for abuse.

GRIEVANCE PROCESSES

When labor and management disagree over the interpretation of contract language and its application to specific infractions, a grievance process is the normal practice for resolving the dispute. Most CBAs provide for informal resolution of grievances at the early stages. At this juncture, labor and management sit down together with the grievant to apply relevant contract language to the matter being grieved. Management may decide that the facts of the matter fall correctly within the agreed upon terms of the contract and change its decision, thereby finding in favor of the grievant. Potentially, facts brought out in a meeting between labor and management, applied to relevant provisions of the CBA, can lead to a changed workplace labor decision.

When dealing with public employers, the individual worker is often exposed to an ever-changing landscape of new people with differing degrees of knowledge, skills, and attitudes. Political, social, and cultural changes should influence what the agency does and how it achieves its ends. Again, in theory, in a democracy, those changes should be more quickly integrated due to the involvement of its citizens up and down the public service chain. Theory and reality do not always coincide.

CHALLENGES IN UNION REPRESENTATION OF BULLYING AND MOBBING TARGETS

As stated above, unions should be behaviorally specific when describing bullying for reporting purposes. Recognizing and teasing out the specific behaviors in such a way as to paint a moving picture with words, while staying away from jargonistic expressions that are conclusive and not behaviorally descriptive, is of primary importance to uncovering abusive supervisory behaviors. To develop this narrative, targets of bullying and mobbing quite often need a patient and accepting listener to discern the details through the pain, frustration, opinions, and other feelings engendered by the abuse they may have suffered. Such a quality of presence demands clarity of thinking and perceptual awareness on the part of the intervener. Skills in interviewing are tested by interviewees who are usually experiencing some degree of trauma.

Trust immediately becomes an issue upon engaging and interviewing a target. A common phenomenon after trust is established is for the target to begin spilling volumes of information in the form of a running dialogue: *He said, she said, then that person said and I reacted this way, and the next day, and my husband told me, and so forth.* It is usually during this stage that I find it most helpful to attend to the behavioral and factual details reported and to name a cluster or pattern of harmful behaviors for the reference of the interviewee. This helps to focus on the main factual points requiring investigation for the problem to be more thoroughly understood and ultimately remedied.

In one case involving six members of a personnel unit of a hospital, I heard story after story alleging how their manager of nine months had been mistreating them, micromanaging them, withholding sick and vacation leave benefits from employees, issuing orders contrary to established policies, and adding additional work to their already busy daily schedule by creating a daily checklist and accounting of work for the day. The manager expounded in staff meetings how she was going to rewrite the policy book for the hospital and that it would become a model for the state. This was not part of her job responsibilities. Despite the presence in the group of six experienced human service professionals who had won awards for their outstanding work performances, the new manager wanted to fix a work unit that was not really broken to prove that she was a really great manager. In fact, this was the first time she was managing or supervising others in her 20 plus years of work experience. It was also a new assignment after having worked in a specialty position with another state agency for most of her career. Her management style included

- Micromanaging generally;
- Not completing her actual responsibilities for signing off on personnel transactions;
- Creating duplicative and unnecessary work processes;
- Treating her staff harshly and speaking to them as though they were children;
- Finding fault in work products where there was none; and
- Ignoring longstanding policies of personnel practices and ordering her staff to do things differently.

In public sector work, union attempts to gain information about individual managers are often routinely resisted. The walls go up and lines are drawn at the hint of a problem. Despite these challenges, the outcome of the union grievance in this case was that the manager was ordered to go to training and to be tutored by a senior-level manager. Her abusive behaviors toward her staff diminished sufficiently according to reports of her unit members. Sick time usage was greatly reduced by the entire unit, and she was more closely watched by the administration of the agency. She ultimately left the agency approximately one year after the investigation.

BEHAVIORAL PATTERN RECOGNITION

Bullying behaviors usually emerge into patterns of control over time. The degree of abusiveness also emerges in relation to the degree to which the subordinate attempts to resist orders and directions that are contrary to past expectations and often contrary to the mission of the agency, as with the example above. Orders that are contrary to the goals and objectives of work should be a red flag to people more senior in the organization.

In public sector employment, it is not at all uncommon to find a superior making orders that are "busy making" or askew of a more direct approach toward getting the work done. For example, I became familiar with a situation in which one manager ordered an entire department of 60 experienced information technology (IT) professionals to take part in mandatory training in basic personnel topics, such as sexual harassment, violence in the workplace, and employee benefits, in lieu of the planned (and budgeted) "cross-training" in C++ and other Web and database programming skills needed for the IT staff to support the new Web-based architecture that was central to the new agency Web site. The human resources training was generic, expected to be completed yearly, and could have easily been done at a later time. Meanwhile, the entire IT department was working under a tight time frame with their consultants to tie the old databases into the new Web-based data servers.

The risk to the Commonwealth of Massachusetts was huge, in terms of both the loss of bond monies to pay for the development of the Web-based data services and the fact that the old system handled a quarterly flow of more than $200 million. This mandated basic training was used as a whip to force staff into scheduling conflicts and thereby further discredit them. This bully knew of his staff's dedication. They questioned being ordered to go to sexual harassment training when they had been pleading for a correctly developed cross-training schedule to participate in during the conversion crunch. Chaos and resentment were created by this assistant director and with the tacit approval of the director of the group. The harder they worked, the more they fell behind.

Two group meetings, numerous individual interviews, and a behavioral survey of union members revealed a truly Machiavellian pattern of authoritarian control. The manager could not have been further from the task at hand. The facts showed that he worked extra hard at creating conflicts and scheduling problems while trying to prove how state workers were not up to the task. The manager was seen giving a tour of the IT operations to a group of individuals and explaining how he knew how to handle state workers. It was later confirmed that the manager was attempting to drive the state workers out of their jobs to hire, in their place, former associates from a consulting group. His actions were oblivious to the threat of losing $11 million of contracted services based on achieving very specific database targets within a predetermined timeline for rolling out the new system. With all of the evidence gathered and presented to the administration of the agency, the manager was walked out of the building under police escort.

SYSTEMS WITHIN SYSTEMS

In my work, I take a systems approach to understanding problems brought to my attention. In public sector work, many differing systems impinge upon the day-to-day work of public employees. The political system is perhaps the largest influence. Politics translate to budget. Budget controls resources, people, technology, oversight, and most everything connected to the daily work of the public employee.

In the story shared above, a well-meaning political decision led to a very poorly written contract for Web site development and database conversion. The resulting confusion provided ample opportunity for the selection of an incompetent director, who in turn selected an incompetent and manipulative assistant director who wreaked havoc on an entire IT department. It took a behavioral survey to bring the problems to light and to the attention of the chief administrative staff. The survey, coupled with the threat of loss of $11 million in bond money, caused the assistant director to be literally walked out the front door. Also, the director ultimately left the agency after righting the IT contract and getting his group settled on a more correct course of action.

PUBLIC SYSTEM AND POLITICS

In public employment systems, many senior positions become open when the party in power changes. The new appointees, in turn, hire friends, and the friends hire friends. In many federal and state government agencies, civil service systems exist to maintain a competent core of midlevel managers and personnel with a sense of shared agency history and knowledge of fundamental agency practices. Civil service systems can also help to reduce the use of political patronage. Ideally, this core group is sufficiently qualified and experienced to educate new senior administrators and to help the agency avoid mistakes through an understanding of past trials and errors. In Massachusetts, civil service has helped to create a midlevel administrative core serving different state administrations going back to the 1970s.

This dual approach to making appointments creates factions in public workplaces and an ever-increasing cadre of higher-salaried managerial jobs. My particularly favorite scenario is when there is one bargaining unit professional being "supervised" by four or five highly paid managers. Yet, when problems in the workplace make it into the newspapers, subordinate bargaining unit members are invariably ridiculed and blamed for driving up the costs of state government. Either political party is complicit in driving up the costs for government through a political spoils system maintained by complicit agreement and exclusive of a more objective measure of competence. Whenever competency-based measures for the selection of managers are used at an agency level, the higher paid "rulers" are exempt. This is a perk of power. The default decider for agency efficacy is the election process. Should the malfunctioning of any agency make it to the level where that agency appears on the front page of the newspapers and then into the political debate, we see the lines drawn by the pundits, and political debate begins anew.

People presumably come to their work because they are qualified and have passed the scrutiny of their hiring authority. We are products of past experiences and systems. The education system and the family system leave their impact on the individual, whether that person is an administrator or manager or a subordinate employee. The screening done during the hiring process for a subordinate bargaining unit job is more likely to ensure competent performance. By contrast, a less formal process is often used to assess potential competence for a senior administrative or managerial job, especially if the individual has not worked his or her way up the ladder within the agency.

In a noteworthy case of rampant bullying of an entire small state agency, the newly appointed commissioner appeared to have convinced the new governor of his skills in managing people. He immediately began a reign of terror toward all 30 or so "do-nothing state employees." He treated everyone with an equal share of contempt, regardless of their years of service, age, sex, national origin, or sexual orientation. Because of the indiscriminate nature of his abusive behavior, the union was able to obtain corroborated testimony from virtually all of the staff about the horrible working conditions and tirades this man inflicted on them. Racial epithets were among his favorite forms of communication. He was known for saying out loud, "Hey! Send in the &#$%@!" My union attempted to present our detailed findings of numerous complaints to the governor's staff, but we were rebuffed. It was only when we threatened going to the press with the story that the commissioner was quickly removed from his appointed office. It was this case and another high-profile case that paved the way for contract negotiations over the antibullying Mutual Respect Article (6A) that eventually would be included in the NAGE (2014) CBA.

ENABLING BEHAVIORS THAT FAVOR THE BULLY

In public service, the bully does not work in a vacuum. Often the bully has an uncanny ability to read others' behavioral patterns and exploit those around them in the name of change. It is not at all uncommon for a new manager to quickly identify the most "successful" worker and use that target as a shining example for what is wrong at work. By taking down the best, the message very quickly becomes that the bully wields the power. Splitting off the target from past relationships on the job further isolates the target and plants a message for others to understand. Therefore, the single most destructive enabler of a bully in the workplace is the silence of witnesses to grave injustices.

One assistant director of an agency with 40 employees was an attorney who had a unique ability to keep herself in the position of arbiter and keeper of knowledge for the agency. Its structure was a hybrid between state agency and commission. A board of commissioners would be appointed by the sitting governor for terms not to exceed three years. This meant that each successive governor would be appointing several commissioners with little or no experience in the workings of this oversight agency. The agency director was appointed coterminus with the governor. This left the assistant director in a powerful position because she knew how to ingratiate herself with each newly appointed director by keeping the operation working without apparent incident. She also knew how to coerce her staff into working long hours without asking for due compensation. One of her newly hired attorneys was ready to prove herself and eagerly worked after hours and on weekends along with her in preparing cases for trial or for presentation to the commission. This agency had no complaints coming from any of our bargaining unit members. There was no union steward in place, and for all intents and purposes, it appeared there was no need to fix what was not broken.

Things began to unravel when the new attorney became pregnant and needed time to go for prenatal care. This high-performing attorney was quickly deemed unreliable. Use of leave time was denied. She became torn between her need for medical prenatal care and her demanding assistant director. The act of giving birth was deemed the final act of refusal to be the willing slave she had previously been. This attorney suddenly needed to do motherly things and to work normal hours and take sick time and parental leave as a normal and responsive human being.

She was denied the use of time, not paid for time, suspended for not complying with job orders, and reviewed on her performance evaluation as performing below expectations. The assistant director publicly advertised her sudden fall from grace, going from a chosen favorite to an outcast, among the entire office. She was used both as an example to the others of being a good employee when she was newly hired and working extraordinary hours and then easily portrayed as a bad employee for not doing what she was hired to do. Of course, the staff of the agency had little sympathy for the person they saw as being held up as an overly ambitious model for others to emulate.

The toll this took on the attorney was evidenced by numerous stress-related illnesses, the questioning of her own judgment, further isolation from colleagues in the agency, and, ultimately, the decision to quit the agency. By the time I was able to involve myself in her problems at work, I was only able to work out a settlement agreement protecting her credentials as an attorney and her professional reputation. It took her another year and a half and some therapy for her to find another job, one that she continues in successfully. The bully would drive three more people out of the agency. She was appointed acting director of the agency when the governor had some difficulty finding a permanent successor. She lasted two years in that position and retired from state service. Unfortunately, personalities and power struggles continue to play out at this agency, while the people who actually do the work cope as best they can.

It is a lot easier demonstrating an injustice when evidence abounds through the testimony or reports of colleagues and coworkers than by relying upon the report of the target alone. Isolation is a formidable technique for maintaining power and domination over others. In the example above, the workforce had been dominated and repeatedly threatened for years by a true master.

Isolation is further enhanced when the bully misrepresents facts to their superiors, thereby creating a context that places the bully as the hero in a drama about wrongful actions in the workplace. In all fairness to administrators and managers, many bullies are extremely good at their game. They have gotten far in life and worked their way toward the top over the broken backs of many people. They are experts at "kissing up and kicking down," a phrase invoked often by workplace antibullying advocates. Lack of awareness of these bullying behaviors is easy to maintain when vigilance and transparency of operations are lacking. The values that leaders hold often permit an anything goes atmosphere. In the public sector realm, values emerge through the political campaign.

RESILIENCE

The inevitable changes that can be expected over time in public service make resilience a valuable trait to possess. Resilience comes from having more successes in life than failures. If a person is told early in life that they are worthless and will amount to nothing, and if that statement is reinforced and internalized, the stage has been set for a pattern of rigidity at work and a heightened sense of defensiveness. Early patterns of inattentiveness and confused orientation toward social norms may minimize the likelihood of successes in subsequent education, training, or work experiences. All staff and managers, administrators, and leaders are influenced by their early development and subsequent education. We are all affected in different ways, and those internalized messages set the stage for how we respond to injustices perpetrated upon ourselves and others.

Because of the inevitability of change in public service work due to the many forces driving the work, normal stress is a part of everyday work life. Most employees learn to cope and perhaps even grow with the challenges by participating in training and even in the design of the work they do. A certain amount of perseverance is necessary. Such growth under pressure contributes to a sense of resilience. In my experience as a union president dealing with workplace situations, I have formulated this personal equation: Challenge + Knowledge/Action + Grit = Resilience.

People make mistakes. Bullying cuts short an employee's opportunities for trial and error, and the resultant learning contained therein. Bullying robs the employee of the ability to grow and to contribute to the team effort. It strips the employee of any sense of dignity by focusing on weaknesses or by turning positive attributes into deficits.

EXAMPLES OF INTERVENTIONS

Bullying by Proxy

Some bullies prefer to use others to do their dirty work while maintaining the illusion that they are fair-minded and ethically correct. Their abilities to tap into the darker side of others and exploit them in their dominance over subordinates can be confusing at first, when trying to get to the root cause of the problem. This leads to the challenge of identifying true aggressor participants in a given situation:

- The person who abuses their subordinates?
- The person who so readily follows the orders of the director?
- The director who appears to be following the mandate of the top administrator?
- The director and the bully who abuse all who pose a threat to their intentions?

Bullying by proxy requires an understanding of the relationships and enabling behaviors of the bullies. A successful intervention may be measured by reports from subordinates that the bullying has stopped, through measurements of peripheral indicators such as reduced sick leave usage, improved productivity, reduced time for completion of projects, and so on.

For example, I became familiar with a situation involving a high-ranking public agency administrator who held a grudge against one of the more competent information technology professionals because he believed that he was not being given enough attention for his IT needs compared to that provided to administrators in the other divisions. He ordered the director of IT, who was subordinate to the administrator, to review the IT professional harshly, refuse him vacation time, and change his job assignments more frequently. The director of IT complied and used the opportunity to attempt to drive the professional out of work to hire someone he knew personally. At no point did the director of the IT unit speak up for the professional, who had actually been following orders and attending to the priorities of the director for delivery of service to the five different divisions.

An investigation of the complaint brought under the mutual respect provision of the collective bargaining agreement was able to demonstrate that the bargaining unit IT professional was acting in accordance with his instructions. The complainant's sick time was restored to him, and he was no longer threatened with disciplinary action for doing his job. The administrator retired after about one year, and the director of IT was terminated for other larger reasons in addition to this instant matter.

Monitoring ordered change is particularly important when the origin of a bullying problem appears complex. The very process of intervention needs review and adjustment if the system is to change positively and in line with the mission of the agency. Often, the very mission of the agency is adversely affected by the actions of the bully.

The twist that a bully's behaviors are often at odds with the mission of the agency never ceases to amaze. The incongruence between the bully's actions and "good management" can be startling. For example, consider the case of a target who may have expected understanding and clarity of direction from the director in a child protection agency, but who instead was subjected to intimidation, humiliation, conflicting orders, and threats on a daily basis. This worker was sent the very clear message that abusive and dismissive treatment of staff is permissible, at least by the director.

Peer-to-Peer Bullying

According to a 2014 national scientific survey by the Workplace Bullying Institute (WBI), approximately 10 percent of bullying incidents in the general workplace population involve peer-to-peer abuse (Namie, 2014). In some of these cases, a bully will solicit others to harm and control a colleague, thereby creating a mobbing situation. Public service is not exempt from such dynamics. In a public service and union setting, such behaviors occasionally crop up. It is most unfortunate when the bully has volunteered to be a union shop steward and uses the resulting workplace relationships and positional power to cause harm toward fellow union members. This kind of behavior is and should be contrary to virtually any set of union bylaws and should be deemed antilabor at its core.

A great deal of faith is given to anyone who agrees to be of service to their colleagues through stewardship in a union. A union shop steward should be fair and objective to all members and must represent all members through the terms and conditions of the collective bargaining agreement. A steward should not act in a self-serving manner. A steward is expected to consult with the union president, national representative, or union executive board in determining how to handle situations involving members. In this way, problematic situations are better understood, and strategies for intervention and correction can be undertaken. Such oversight and guidance are all in the name of teamwork. Final accountability rests with the president of the union local. Hopefully, the president has not permitted a bully to take the role of steward, but it happens.

All too often, I have observed a reluctance on the part of certain union administrations to become involved in reports of peer-to-peer bullying, some of which suggest violations of the antibullying mutual respect provision in our CBA. A superficial and feigned confusion by management often accompanies directives to the local president to simply put a stop to the bullying behaviors.

On the surface, such an attitude seems somewhat logical; perhaps member-to-member bullying is not something management "should" be concerning itself about. Such an assumption cannot be further from reality. Union members are not employees of the union. In Massachusetts, they are agency employees with contractual protections, and they are obliged to uphold a code of conduct and the agency's personnel policies.

Suppose, then, that one member is seeking dominion over another. That member is creating the hostile, humiliating, or intimidating work environment within that workplace. The complaint begs for proper investigation and resolution, just like other forms of bullying. Accountability for violations of policy and codes of conduct is totally within the agency's domain as a public employer, to be handled through normal applications of corrective action and progressive discipline. The union is in the position of ensuring that the evidence gathered in the investigatory stage is properly weighted and applied and that the remedy is just and fair.

Subordinate-to-Manager Bullying

In rare instances, a subordinate (and union member) may act abusively and in a controlling manner toward his or her boss. In public service, this scenario is potentially more likely due to the political nature of public service. When governors and administrations change, other changes to the workforce trickle down, whereby sometimes positions are made or allocated for campaign "friends" of the administration assuming control. This patronage happens frequently enough to occasionally erupt into workplace issues. Often the patronage comes in with a sense of entitlement due to connections with the new administration, and the new hire proceeds to let people know it. Such attitudes may dissipate after the reality of the job demands sink in to the new arrival.

One such issue arose through a complaint filed under the mutual respect provision of the CBA by a union member against her manager. The crux of the problem centered on her being asked to comply with the standard start and end times for a workday. The new bargaining unit member alleged that the manager was treating everyone in the unit unfairly and in a hostile and controlling manner. The complaint appeared to be supported with evidence for the complainant's charges. She was articulate and had certain family obligations that allegedly were not being considered in scheduling her work.

However, my investigation and a survey of the entire 13-person work unit revealed that it was the union member who was acting in very hostile and intimidating manner toward all. She apparently could not get along with anyone in the unit. She wanted to come and go as she pleased and to decide what work she performed. The manager, upon being interviewed, could not have been a more accommodating and fair-minded person. He had demonstrated a six-month history of trying to accommodate her changing needs, provided training in topics she had identified, and held group meetings designed to better facilitate the working of the unit. The member resigned after realizing she could not manipulate her employer and her union into being allowed to come and go as she pleased and not be charged for the time taken. Apparently, she had been given her job because a relative was an elected state official and wanted to help her out.

A couple of points need to be raised about this misuse of contract provisions by a union member. First, it happens occasionally. A small subset of individuals can be extraordinarily narcissistic, manipulative, and quite capable of framing a situation to their personal advantage. A union can be drawn into disputes very easily. Second, managers in public service are mostly outside of the contract and are usually appointed to their positions after submitting to a cursory background check and resume review. If someone high up in the administration wants to appoint their person to a management position, they can do it. All managers are not equal, however. Third, those who intervene from the union's perspective must be sharply focused on the facts and not be captive to their individual beliefs and prejudices. Self-awareness does not come to all who work for a union or in an administrative or managerial capacity.

In this instance, although a union member had filed a complaint about a manager, the facts did not support the complaint. When confronted with the facts, the member chose to leave, following a tumultuous year on the job. The union was left with a complaint that could only be closed out. There remained nothing for the union to do. As it turned out, another person was hired into the position on the merits of her potential, and she fit in very nicely with the unit, performing her responsibilities reliably and competently while enjoying the safeguards of the CBA.

IMPACT OF SUCCESS

Public Services

Measuring success in ameliorating bullying in public service can be achieved with a before, during, and after snapshot assessment of events, behaviors, and work product. Testimony of affected individuals helps to round out an evaluation of an intervention or change.

For example, one new assistant commissioner remained unknown to his group of employees for six months. These employees were responsible for giving a double review of protective safety assessments in nursing facilities. During that time, he was charged with making changes to the system that ensured the safety of nursing home residents by streamlining the operations and shortening the review process. The current system had been backed up and overwhelmed with first and second reviews. The unit had lost a supervisor and several reviewers due to illnesses. Within two months of assuming his position, the assistant commissioner issued a memo with a directive changing the review process, dropping it from two reviews to one review. The unit supervisor never implemented the directives of the memo with her staff reviewers. The reviewers remained working feverishly to reduce the growing backlog of first reviews to move on to the second reviews.

At six months, the assistant commissioner saw no change in statistics and told his two managers and one supervisor that the unit was to have a meeting in which he would fix the problem. Eight reviewers, one supervisor, and two managers were called to a meeting. Staff members were not told what the meeting was about.

The meeting began without introductions. Staff had never met their new top administrator. They were not aware of his memo on changing the reviews. The assistant commissioner and managers chatted amicably as the group assembled. Then the assistant commissioner abruptly began to yell at the staff members for not doing their work. He blamed them for their alleged inefficiencies and shamed them for not earning their salaries. When staff tried to give their side—citing short staffing, lack of a supervisor, working through lunch and evenings without pay, coping with illnesses, and filling in for colleagues taking time off—they were told to shut up, work harder, and not make excuses.

The fact that the earlier memo never made it to the people who should have changed their work from two reviews to one review was never discussed in the meeting. Reviewers were in shock at having met the new assistant commissioner for the first time since his appointment. The union was contacted the next day. A meeting was held with the reviewers to clarify the facts, and a group complaint was filed against the assistant commissioner and his managers. The reasoning was simply that the workers did not want to be treated in this manner anymore.

The resulting investigation involved the testimony of reviewers, the supervisor, the managers, and the assistant commissioner. The investigator found that the complaints were founded, but this was only a single incident. A meeting was called between the assistant commissioner and his union subordinates, with the supposed intent of reviewing the outcome of the investigation and providing a remedy for moving forward, with the workers seeking a simple apology. However, at the meeting, the assistant commissioner offered no acknowledgment of any wrongful behavior. In fact, his apparent purpose in attending the immediate meeting was to impress upon all who attended the significant importance of his job in the agency. He declined to apologize for any of his actions or statements, and he continued to blame the reviewers for not doing their jobs properly. As the union representative, I challenged his accusations, and we ended the meeting. Consequently, the case had to be immediately moved to a grievance hearing, as prescribed by the contract language.

Upon receipt of the grievance and discussion of the facts with this union president and the agency investigator, the hearing officer remanded the case back to the agency for remediation of the complaint. The outcomes included the following: (1) the grievants were no longer threatened and intimidated and received an apology of sorts; (2) the bully was spoken with and kept under scrutiny; and (3) the work flow of the agency began to resolve with old reviews completed and a new process in place to expedite the reviews of abuse investigations in nursing facilities for the elderly. Staff had to be "borrowed" from other parts of the agency to help out with all the work.

Creativity and Responsiveness

A competent and experienced natural leader in a workplace makes for an ideal target when a new manager or administrator wants to quickly demonstrate power and authority. The choice for the organizational leader is whether past practices will be understood and modified to arrive at new goals or whether the people who are knowledgeable of the work and population will be vilified, punished, and treated as the problems they have been attempting to help resolve. In public employment, I have witnessed how the latter choice triggers a dark, downward spiral. It leads to an ever-increasing defensive workforce that may turn in upon itself in many dysfunctional ways. People are hurt, traumatized, and terminated. Representing members in such dark circumstances is difficult and not without a price.

But when a bully is found to be the root cause of such abuses at work, a potentially great opportunity exists for the organization and for the people who work in the organization. Accountability for agency malfunction is often thought of as a one-way street heading toward the lowest common denominator, the subordinate public employee. Bullies usually gravitate to positions of power and control over others. When their actions harm others and are reported, and they are held accountable by their own administration, they are left with a choice: *change or be changed.* The inherent creativeness within the work group may then return after some time and after dealing with the resultant trauma inflicted by the bully.

Finances

There is always a cost to an organization abusing its workforce. Collective bargaining laws almost always allow for good faith information requests by the union from the organization. Collecting before and after data about hiring rates, vacancies, and sick time usage in a distressed work unit shows not only some of the systemic impact of bullying in the workplace but also part of the financial cost to the organization. Productivity can usually be measured before and after the insertion of a bully into the workplace. Whenever a new person, be it a subordinate or manager, is added to a work unit, the unit changes in ways to accommodate the new person.

My experience of managers who resort to bullying tactics in pursuit of dominance and control of their respective work units is that they are lacking in ability to integrate the mission and goals of the organization into their behaviors for managing others in a humane and respectful manner. The impact of their mismanagement can be measured in medical costs for treating harmed personnel, time lost to sick time or time off the books, plans disrupted, and goals not achieved, as previously described in several examples. The output of the work unit is often severely curtailed by the time that people must take sick time or seriously consider quitting. Finding replacements for individuals who decide to leave the job takes time and the expense of interviewing and training new employees. Workplaces with high turnover, or higher than average turnover, could benefit from an objective exit interview of their personnel only if top administrators are willing to acknowledge the weaknesses in those they may have appointed to positions of authority. I know of very few agencies that solicit this feedback. This makes the role of a union even more crucial in the creation of a healthy workplace.

CONCLUSION

People who are allowed to assume power and control over others are often not fit for their responsibilities. In public service, the responsibility for recognizing these mistakes belongs to elected officials and agency heads, with some potential reckoning at the ballot box. In the Commonwealth of Massachusetts, this comes in the form of a gubernatorial election every four years.

As awareness of bullying in the workplace continues to increase and the impact of bullying is better recognized and understood, the workplace should slowly move toward an environment that does not tolerate abuses. In public employment, this, of course, presumes that agency leaders want an organization that functions with fewer abusive controls. Unions have an inherent role in helping the workplace to see what is actually going on and then to negotiate changes in practice that are more beneficial to both sides. Unions bring a needed balance of power to the table.

Contract language that calls for mutual respect and freedom from hostile, humiliating, and intimidating behaviors from anyone at work is a big step. Enacting the antibullying Healthy Workplace Bill (Yamada, 2013), which creates a civil legal claim for severe workplace bullying and offers liability-reducing incentives for employers to act preventively and responsively toward bullying at work, would actually make it easier for agency heads to promulgate and enforce policies that prevent bullying behaviors. In public sector workplaces, it could help to lessen partisan influence sometimes associated with abusive work situations.

The Healthy Workplace Bill would also assist unions in safeguarding their members in the workplace. Even without a negotiated contract provision addressing bullying or mutual respect, a union and the public agency would have to comply with the law, just as they must currently comply with existing sexual harassment and other discrimination laws. Those laws have helped the workplace to be better environments for working as one expects when one begins employment. So too would the law on healthy workplaces (Healthy Workplace Campaign, n.d.) bring the workplace up to a level where mutual respect and informed discourse would serve to guide people toward better achieving the goals determined by leaders.

Laws, public policies, rules, codes, and regulations govern public employment. The theory holds that they guide the actual behavior of those individuals hired to conduct the work. Codes of conduct, ethical principles, training, supervision, and management practices are, again theoretically, thought of as further means for guiding behaviors at work toward stated goals. Abusive work practices such as bullying circumvent the expected discourse in the workplace. These behaviors create a cognitive dissonance of sorts, removing a set of learned expectations for more normal behavior at work and replacing them with unexpected, hurtful, and arbitrary demands that frequently undermine the general mission of the agency.

REFERENCES

Governing. (2016). States with most government employees: Totals and per capita rates. Retrieved from http://www.governing.com/gov-data/public-workforce-salaries/states-most-government-workers-public-employees-by-job-type.html

Healthy Workplace Campaign. (n.d.). *Quick facts about the Healthy Workplace Bill.* Retrieved from http://healthyworkplacebill.org/bill

Massachusetts General Laws, Chapter 150 E, §2 (2016). Retrieved from https://malegislature.gov/Laws/GeneralLaws/PartI/TitleXXI/Chapter150e/Section2

Namie, G. (2014). *2014 WBI U.S. workplace bullying survey.* Retrieved from http://workplacebullying.org/multi/pdf/WBI-2014-US-Survey.pdf

National Association of Government Employees (NAGE). (2014). *Collective bargaining agreement between the Commonwealth of Massachusetts and the National Association of Government Employees, Unit 6, July 1, 2014–June 30, 2017.* Retrieved from http://www.nage.org/login/assets/images/nage%20unit%206.pdf

National Labor Relations Act of 1935, 29 U.S.C. §§ 151–169 (2016).

Office of Personnel Management. (n.d.). *Historical federal workforce tables.* Retrieved from https://www.opm.gov/policy-data-oversight/data-analysis-documentation/federal-employment-reports/historical-tables/total-government-employment-since-1962

Yamada, D. C. (2013). Emerging American legal responses to workplace bullying. *Temple Political & Civil Rights Law Review, 22*(2), 329–354.

24

Workplace Bullying and Mobbing in the Corporate Sector

Kelly H. Kolb and Mary Beth Ricke

Everyone has memories of the grade school bully and the associated dread of encountering the bully during lunch period, on the playground, or on the walk home from school. I [KHK] have memories of a *grade school* bully who had not materially improved his conduct as of my *high school's 20th reunion*. According to a number of studies, many of us are now suffering or seeing bullying in the workplace, and it is affecting employee health and workplace productivity—both issues of concern to employers (Harvey, Heames, Richey, & Leonard, 2006). As a result, bullying has come into increased focus for human resources professionals, particularly as recent surveys indicate that workplace bullying is more prevalent than sexual harassment (Namie, 2007).

This chapter will examine the phenomenon of workplace bullying in the U.S. corporate sector, its effects on bullying victims and employers, and its likely causes. Legislative efforts to address workplace bullying will be discussed, along with efforts by various corporate entities and human resource organizations to combat workplace bullying, and the obstacles those efforts are encountering.

WORKPLACE BULLYING GENERALLY

Since it was first studied in the 1980s (Leymann, 1990), workplace bullying (or mobbing) has been variously defined (see Appendix A). However it is defined, workplace bullying is generally regarded as deliberate and repeated physical or emotional mistreatment of a person that takes the form of verbal abuse, sabotage of work product, or aggressive conduct that is threatening humiliating, demeaning, or intimidating.

Typical Bullying Conduct

Bullying includes overt aggression (screaming, verbal threats, belittling in front of coworkers, physical contact, use of profanity, etc.) and passive-aggressive conduct (assigning demeaning tasks or undesirable work schedules, isolation, exclusion from critical meetings, denial of necessary resources, and taking credit for the victim's work; Koonin & Green, 2005; Leymann & Gustafsson, 1996).

Frequency of Workplace Bullying

Studies suggest that workplace bullying affects a majority of workers in the United States. A recent study suggested that upward of 75 percent of the American workforce suffered from or had witnessed workplace bullying (Fisher-Blando, 2008). A 2014 survey by the Workplace Bullying Institute (WBI), however, found that 27 percent of respondents self-identified as bullying victims and that 21 percent of respondents had witnessed workplace bullying firsthand (Namie, Christensen, & Phillips, 2014). A more recent compilation of studies found, consistent with Namie et al.'s (2014) survey, that 13–36 percent of U.S. employees reported working for a "dysfunctional" supervisor (Rose, Shuck, Twyford, & Bergman, 2015).

The Namie, Christensen, and Phillips (2014) and Rose et al. (2015) statistics are consistent with cross-country research conducted in New Zealand (Bentley et al., 2009). However, Bentley and his colleagues also found that the frequency of reported workplace bullying varied significantly from country to country, most likely because of the fluid nature of how workplace bullying is defined and measured. This variation, they concluded, precludes meaningful cross-country comparisons (Bentley et al., 2009).

Geographic and Industry Frequency

In the United States, workplace bullying has been found to vary by geographic region. The reported incidence of workplace bullying is highest in the West (41%), followed by the South (38%), the East (35%) and the Central and Great Lakes regions (26%; Namie, 2007). While the Namie (2007) study offers no explanation for these regional differences, it is instructive to note that the Western and Southern regions of the United States generally have the highest per capita number of discrimination charges filed with the U.S. Equal Employment Opportunity Commission (Equal Employment Opportunity Commission (EEOC), 2014). No U.S. studies have attempted to identify the factors contributing to the geographical variance in reported workplace bullying frequency. However, some researchers have suggested that the variation is due to increased awareness of the phenomenon of workplace bullying in certain regions of the country.

More detailed data has been generated with respect to the variation in reported frequencies of workplace bullying across industries. Specifically, U.S. studies reveal that the incidence of workplace bullying is highest in the health care (27%), education (23%), and public services (16%) sectors (Namie, 2013). Namie's findings are consistent with studies from other countries. Australia (which outlawed workplace bullying in 2014) has maintained detailed statistics on bullying complaints submitted to the Australian Fair Work Commission. Australian statistics reveal a remarkably consistent pattern (year over year) of bullying complaints. A majority of the complaints derived from the retail, home care, health care, and educational industries, and almost all complaints concerned managers, groups of managers, coworkers, or groups of coworkers (Australia Fair Work Commission, 2014, 2015).

Employer Size

No reliable studies have been conducted in the United States attempting to correlate workplace bullying frequency to the size of the employer. However, data from the Australian Fair Work Commission reveals a remarkably consistent pattern (year over year) of bullying complaints; 44–50 percent of all bullying complaints were lodged against large (more than 100 employees) employers, and 33 percent were lodged against small (1–50 employees) employers. (Australia Fair Work Commission, 2014, 2015). One possible explanation for these findings is that small employers are ill-equipped to recognize and combat workplace bullying, whereas large employers afford bullies organizational cover via diffusion of responsibility.

WORKPLACE BULLYING VICTIMS

Studies abound describing the "usual" or "typical" bullying victim. Some have suggested that workplace bullying victims tend to be women (60%), regardless of the gender of the bully (Namie et al., 2014); subordinates whose (perceived) competence poses a threat to superiors (Namie, 2014); or employees who are compassionate, cooperative, and agreeable (Namie et al., 2014). Many victims are simply people pleasers who do not have the desire or skill to defend themselves. For example, former Miami Dolphins offensive tackle Jonathan Martin texted his mother while he was being bullied by teammates: "I figured out a major source of my anxiety. I'm a pushover, a people pleaser. I avoid confrontation whenever I can, I always want everyone to like me. I let people talk about me, say anything to my face, and I just take it, laugh it off, even when I know they are intentionally trying to disrespect me" (Shpigel, 2014).

Other studies suggest that those at risk for succumbing to workplace bullies are younger or newer workers, workers returning to work from an injury or illness leave, or minorities (Safe Work Australia, 2013). Regardless of how one describes the "typical" victim, anecdotal evidence demonstrates that even employees trained to withstand mental abuse can be negatively affected by bullying. For example, the CIA's director of Iran operations was removed from his post for bullying his CIA subordinates (Loeb, 2014).

Physical, Emotional, and Employment Effects on Victims

A growing body of research suggests that victims of workplace bullying may suffer severe anxiety (76%), PTSD (47%), clinical depression (39%), impaired sleep (71%), impaired concentration (71%), panic attacks (32%), and suicidal thoughts (25%) (Namie, 2003a; Rafferty, Restubog, & Jimmieson, 2010; Safe Work Australia, 2013) and a host of physical ailments, including high blood pressure, cardiovascular disease, migraines, ulcers, and heart disease (Eisenberger, 2012; Safe Work Australia, 2013). Other victims are paralyzed by shame from being victimized and being unable to do anything about it (Lutgen-Sandvik, Tracy, & Alberts, 2007). By way of example, Jonathan Martin's e-mails to his mother acknowledged he was saddened and ashamed of being bullied: "I used to get verbally bullied every day in middle school and high school, by kids that are half my size. I would never fight back, just get sad & feel like no one wanted to be my friend" (Ley, 2014).

Qualitatively, the effect of workplace bullying on a victim has been equated to suddenly losing a loved one (Mikkelsen & Einarsen, 2002). Victims self-report that bullying made them feel maimed, beaten, abused, broken, scarred, and eviscerated (Tracy, Lutgen-Sandvik, & Alberts, 2006) and that they felt like a slave, a prisoner, or a heartbroken lover (Tracy et al., 2006). As stress is a contributing factor to 90 percent of all visits to primary care physicians (Atkinson, 2004), bullying victims are more than likely to seek health or mental health care benefits (driving up health care costs); take more sick leave; file workers' compensation or short-term or long-term disability claims; or simply quit (Daniel, 2006).

Moreover, the effects of prolonged workplace bullying are not limited to the targeted victim. Several studies have found that bullying victims bring their negative feelings, depression, and anxiety home, negatively affecting the victim's family (Hoobler & Brass, 2006). Thus, bullying has demonstrable negative effects far beyond the workplace, potentially affecting people with no relationship to the bully or his or her workplace.

Statistically, bullies have very little to lose by engaging in workplace bullying, as, generally, bullying victims lose their jobs at a much higher rate than bullies (82% vs. 18%) (Namie et al., 2014). Most workplace bullying victims (29%) voluntarily quit; others (19%) are forced to quit (i.e., are constructively discharged) because the conditions are intolerable; and still others (13%) are terminated (Namie et al., 2014). For unexplained reasons, women bullies suffer the highest job loss rate (30%; Namie et al., 2014). It is possible that this anomaly is attributable to sexual stereotypes disfavoring such aggressive conduct by women.

Response Mechanisms of Bullying Victims

Victims commonly respond to workplace bulling in one of two general ways—avoidance or confrontation. Avoidance can consist of seeking a medical or personal leave of absence or minimizing the situation (Zapf & Gross, 2001). However, in the vast majority of cases (87%), bullying victims simply quit or are fired (Namie, 2003a; Zapf & Gross, 2001).

Confrontation typically takes the form of confronting the bully directly or seeking assistance in doing so from supervisors or human resources professionals (Zapf & Gross, 2001). As noted in one study, however, employees usually lack the skills, hierarchical leverage, resources, or support to effectively combat workplace bullying (Vigoda-Gadot, 2006).

Whether regarded as avoidance or confrontation, the coping mechanism frequently utilized by victims of workplace bullying is to intentionally withdraw from their commitment to the employer (Rafferty et al., 2010). This reaction can take many forms, including discontinuing attempts to go above and beyond the victim's usual job duties and adopting the mind-set of "what's the point?" (Mitchell & Ambrose, 2007). In addition, bullying victims often exhibit aggression toward their own coworkers in what one study described as a "cascading effect of dysfunctional leadership" (Rose et al., 2015, p. 75) under the assumption that workplace bullies imprint their bullying techniques onto their subordinates, who simply repeat the supervisor's bullying behavior (Rafferty et al., 2010). Other victims may engage in retaliatory conduct directed at the employer (as opposed to the bully), who the victim perceives as an enabler of the bullying, if not the root cause (Bowling & Michel, 2011). Regardless of the particular mechanism utilized by a workplace bullying victim, it is clear that many victims respond to workplace bullying in ways that are broadly destructive to the employer's efficient functioning.

EFFECT OF WORKPLACE BULLYING ON EMPLOYERS

The harmful effects of prolonged, unchecked workplace bullying on an organization's well-being has been compared to organizational cancer. The litany of costs to employers is well established and is beyond the scope of this chapter (see chapter 9). However, in general, employers face a wide spectrum of negative consequences, most of which are easily and objectively quantifiable.

Quantifiable Costs

Because of the harmful physiological and emotional effects of workplace bullying, victims frequently seek medical attention through employer-sponsored health insurance plans, file claims for short- and long-term disability benefits, and file workers' compensation claims, raising the employer's premiums and costs for these benefits year over year (Namie et al., 2014).

Decreased Productivity

Employers incur less directly quantifiable costs in lost productivity due to a variety of circumstances. First, the physiological and emotional pain with which bullying victims are forced to cope and the mechanisms they utilize to cope with that pain distract them from performing their job duties, thereby reducing their productivity (Lim, Cortina, & Magley, 2008). Indeed, one study concluded that 25 percent of victims wasted time to avoid encountering the perpetrator or withdrew from projects involving the perpetrator, and 30 percent reported reducing their commitment to the employer (Burnes & Pope, 2007).

Second, this productivity malaise spills over to the victim's coworkers who observe the bullying (and, often, the employer's failure to intervene) and conclude that they could be next, so they become distracted with fear even though they are not the target (Lutgen-Sandvik et al., 2007). In smaller workplaces, this spillover effect is increased where the obviousness and effects of the bullying are magnified. The impact on the victim's coworkers is further magnified when they feel compelled (through bullying, peer pressure, etc.) to support the bully's efforts against the victim.

Third, victims who are absent on (extended) medical or personal leave, either to obtain treatment or to avoid the effects of workplace bullying, are no longer productive employees. Their absence further reduces productivity and, in the vast majority of cases, causes additional stress on the victim's coworkers, who are required to cover for the absent victim.

Employee Turnover and Replacement Costs

But perhaps the most harmful by-product of workplace bullying is rampant turnover of (usually) talented personnel. As previously discussed, a significant number of bullying victims are those who are actually or perceived as highly talented and thus threatening to their immediate superiors (Namie et al., 2014). These are the employees the employer likely spent significant sums recruiting and onboarding, and they are, therefore, the employees the employer can least afford to lose. However, workplace bullying is a principal cause of the loss of these employees (Mehdi, Raju, & Mukherji, 2012). The cost of this turnover is magnified if the bullying victim is a relatively new hire. New hires are less invested in the employer and have less to lose by leaving to avoid bullying (Tepper et al., 2009), and the employer has not been able to recoup any of its recruiting and onboarding costs when a new hire immediately quits. By some estimates, it costs between 90 percent and 200 percent of a departing employee's annual salary to recruit, train, and onboard that employee's replacement (Mitchell, Holtom, & Lee, 2001).

Litigation Costs and Risk

One must also add to this mix of costs the risk of litigation inherent in the reality that the typical bullying victim is a member of a protected class under Title VII of the Civil Rights Act and the typical bully is not. For example, the usual bully is a male (69%), the usual victim is female (60%), and 57 percent of all workplace bullying involves a male bully and a female victim (Namie et al., 2014). It does not strain logic to see how 57 percent of all workplace bullying incidents lend themselves to the filing of a sex discrimination claim by the victim. In addition, the physiological and psychological maladies suffered by most bullying victims are all covered disabilities under the Americans with Disabilities Act, lending those bullying incidents to the filing of a disability discrimination claim.

Despite these costs, the majority of employers do nothing to stop workplace bullying. For example, 31 percent of employers defend bullying as a necessary by-product of a competitive marketplace, 25 percent deny it occurs, and 16 percent discount its effects, whereas only 28 percent acknowledge the problem exists and attempt to address it (Namie et al., 2014). Employer inaction explains why (according to studies) bullies are not likely to face repercussion; only 13 percent of bullies were transferred, 11 percent were punished, 10 percent were fired, and 5 percent quit (Namie et al., 2014).

CAUSES OF WORKPLACE BULLYING

Significant efforts have been undertaken to identify the root causes of workplace bullying. The suggested causes range from societal norms and competitiveness in a capitalist system to psychiatric disorders such as narcissism. There is no consensus. It should be obvious, however, that the causes of workplace bullying must first be identified before preventative approaches can be identified or a remedy suggested. To that end, the leading theories for the root causes of workplace bullying are summarized in this section.

Capitalism

Could the basic structure of the corporate organization explain, in whole or in part, the presence of workplace bullying? One theory suggests that bullying is a simple but effective technique used by management to control the "lower classes" of workers. When viewed through this prism, workplace bullying *enhances* productivity (albeit in the short term) by forcing victims to work harder and more efficiently to save their self-image or their job (Vega & Comer, 2005). While perhaps appealing to the uninitiated, this theory ignores current data (summarized above) that just the opposite occurs in response to workplace bullying—the victim's attention, commitment, effort, and thus production decreases, usually resulting in termination or resignation—the ultimate loss of efficiency in production. An alternative (and less psychopathic) explanation is that bullies simply lack relevant social and management skills and are unaware of the impropriety of or harm caused by their conduct (Mattice, 2016).

A more intuitive explanation derives from the reality that American business culture has always been permeated—to various degrees—by social Darwinism, that is, only the strong survive. Some have suggested that the Darwinian essence of the American business culture, and its associated individual competition among coworkers to either rise up the corporate ladder or be escorted out the door, is the genesis of the workplace bullying phenomenon (Duffy, 2009). For example, several studies posit that victims suffering from anxiety, depression, and the other physiological and emotional harms discussed above are regarded as weak, defective, and "not up to the task" (Baillien, Neyens, De Witte, & De Cuyper, 2009). Other studies conclude that supervisors engaging in alleged bullying behavior are perceived as stronger and thus are routinely promoted and otherwise rewarded by the employer (Hutchinson & Jackson, 2014). It is in this survivalist-based paradigm where supervisors make statements such as "It's me against them [the employees] and I am going to win or die trying" (Harvey et al., 2006).

Dynamics of Particular Industries

Several studies have correlated higher frequencies of workplace bullying with various industries. For example, Namie (2013) suggests that the prevalence of workplace bullying is greatest in high-stress occupations such as commissioned sales and in altruistic industries such as health care, home care, and education. Foreign studies generally support Namie's conclusions

(Australia Fair Work Commission, 2014, 2015). While correlation does not establish causation, the correlations found by the foreign studies in several different countries (over varying time periods) are compelling evidence of a possible causative link.

The Australian government, in its 24-page *Guide for Preventing and Responding to Workplace Bullying*, warns that the presence of "workplace stressors" increases the risk (and thus the frequency) of workplace bullying (Safe Work Australia, 2013). The growth of the service sector in the United States means that employees are increasingly required to cooperatively interact with each other and also with clients and customers. This demand for personal interaction on a daily basis makes it difficult to mask the ongoing emotional and physiological trauma suffered by most workplace bullying victims, adding to their stress in a cycle of escalation.

In an attempt to explain the relatively higher frequency of workplace bullying in altruistic industries, Namie (2013) posits that victims in these industries are more vulnerable precisely because of their altruistic desire to help others, to see the best in others, and to not create conflict by opposing a workplace bully. Again, as altruistic employees have always existed in the health care sector, their mere presence today would not seem to explain the presence of explosive growth of reported workplace bullying incidents in that sector.

With respect to the higher incidence of bullying in the public sector, Namie (2013) suggests that lack of managerial training in interpersonal communication skills is to blame. However, the same could be said of the health care and educational industries. Perhaps an alternative explanation is the insular rigidity of public sector workplaces (relative to the private sector) characterized by formal and inflexible promotional paths (i.e., promotions premised principally on tenure or longevity) and union protectionism, which combine to preclude prompt and efficient discipline or the termination of bullies (Aryee, Sun, Chen & Debrah, 2008). This dynamic, which effectively insulates the bully from any meaningful negative consequences of his or her behavior, is not lost on the bully, who perceives he or she can act out with impunity.

Absence of Corporate Leadership

Several studies, both in the United States and abroad, have identified corporate leadership styles as a recurring theme in bullying environments. Bullies reported that their upper-level managers were not outgoing or dynamic (Hepworth & Towler, 2004); they were abusive (Mitchell & Ambrose, 2007) or tyrannical or laissez-faire (Hauge, Skogstad, & Einarsen, 2007). These leadership styles apparently foster a sense of uncontrolled chaos characterized by role confusion and conflicts, a lack of clear lines of authority or responsibility, and weak relationships between employees and supervisors.

An interesting paradox is presented by the narcissistic manager—someone who is perceived by upper management as outgoing and confident but simultaneously perceived by subordinates as a selfish "kiss-ass" willing to step on anyone he or she must to rise up the corporate ladder. From upper management's point of view, the narcissist is "management material," possessing the fundamental management traits of individualism, competitiveness, and unbridled ambition (Burgemeester, 2013). From a subordinate's point of view, narcissists lack the ability to see the viewpoint of or empathize with others, and they are hypersensitive to criticism (Burgemeester, 2013). "They tend to be bullies" and often exploit subordinates and discard them, regarding them as disposable tools to achieve a personal goal (Burgemeester, 2013, para. 1). It would appear, therefore, that narcissists are initially embraced by upper management as "go getters" who get things done and strive to achieve. Whether that perception changes (and management reins in the narcissist)—with the onset of employee absenteeism, decreased production, and the turnover discussed above—may depend on the level of success the narcissist has achieved, the extent to which that success offsets the quantifiable harm his or her conduct has caused, and the willingness of upper management to recognize that harm and address it.

Workplace Dynamics

Rather than identifying a single or principal cause of workplace bullying, intriguing studies point to a combination of causes. Van Heugten (2010), who conducted an admittedly small survey of 17 bullied social workers, found that survey participants identified a spectrum of root causes for the bullying they experienced. The identified causes included the following: (1) lack of job control and thus uncertainty as to the longevity of their continued employment; (2) the desire of supervisors to avoid competition from subordinates they perceived to be higher performing or more capable and thus a threat to the supervisors' continued employment; (3) increased economic pressures on employers to reduce headcounts and get more done with less; (4) the absence of workplace policies and procedures prohibiting bullying and identifying how victims are to respond to bullying, particularly by supervisors; and (5) a lack of training and ineffective management.

This spectrum approach has been validated in part by Namie (2014), who surveyed employees and found that they reported a variety of perceived causes for workplace bullying. The leading cause identified was the defective personality of the bully (41%), followed by the failure of the employer to discipline the bully or otherwise protect the victim (28%), and 20 percent blamed the victims for not defending themselves.

The takeaway from these studies is that victims and others in the workplace reported that workplace bullying was not caused by a single factor, but by a spectrum of factors over which the victim had no control (Namie, 2014). This spectrum of causes presents a significant challenge to identifying and implementing measures to prevent workplace bullying.

RESPONSES TO WORKPLACE BULLYING

Several approaches have been tried in an effort to curb the rising tide of workplace bullying, none of which has met with much success. Those that have achieved success have been based on a corporate commitment at the highest levels of management to foster a corporate culture inimical to workplace bullying.

Legislative Efforts

The United States is the last of the Western democracies not to have a law against workplace bullying. Following model legislation drafted by the WBI in 2003 and the Healthy Workplace Campaign, 26 states, the U.S. Virgin Islands, and Puerto Rico have attempted, unsuccessfully, to pass and sign into law anti–workplace bullying legislation.

Critics of the WBI model legislation claim it amounts to the sort of "general civility code" that the U.S. Supreme Court warned against (*Oncale v. Sundowner Offshore Services, Inc.*, 1998). Most state legislatures appear hesitant to enact such a general civility code. There is also a concern that such "be nice" legislation will, because of its subjective definitions, be impossible to enforce, at best, or unconstitutional, at worst. Accordingly, several states have passed significantly watered-down versions of the Healthy Workplace Bill:

- Tennessee: The Tennessee Healthy Workplace Act is limited to public sector employers and does not bar workplace bullying or create a cause of action for employees suffering workplace bullying. Rather, the act provides immunity from certain civil lawsuits for public sector employers who implement the state's model antibullying policy (Tennessee Healthy Workplace Act, 2014).
- California: The California bullying statute is limited to employers with 50 or more employees and requires those employers to provide "classroom or other effective interactive training and education" regarding "abusive conduct," but only to supervisory personnel. The statute does not create a cause of action for workplace bullying or make such conduct actionable under existing nondiscrimination laws. Notably, the statute makes no effort to delineate prohibited bullying conduct and

normal supervisory practices such as discipline, performance improvement programs, etc. (California Government Code §12950.1).
- Utah: Utah's act is applicable only to state executive branch agencies, does not prohibit bullying, does not create a cause of action for workplace bullying, and only requires state agencies to train state supervisors and employees about how to prevent bullying (Utah Code §67-19-44, 2015).
- Minnesota: The Respectful Workplace Policy applies only to state executive branch agencies and state contractors and excepts normal supervisory actions from the definition of prohibited bullying.

Thus, legislative efforts to curb workplace bullying have not and (as discussed in the next section) likely will not succeed.

Employer Efforts

Rather than wait for the legislatures to address workplace bullying, many employers are establishing procedures for investigating complaints of workplace bullying utilizing their existing hostile work environment policies and procedures. The WBI recommends employers adopt and implement an antibullying policy that (1) mandates zero tolerance; (2) treats bullying as a workplace safety issue (i.e., in the same realm as OSHA safety matters); (3) requires investigation of bullying complaints; (4) imposes prompt remedial action for confirmed complaints; (5) requires intervention and counseling for bullies, victims, and witnesses; and (6) requires training on how to recognize and report bullying (Namie, 2003b). In the author's experience, the majority of the WBI's suggestions are appropriate, as discussed below.

Zero-Tolerance Policies

Anecdotal evidence and a fair number of studies have demonstrated that zero-tolerance policies, while easy to implement, rarely yield reasonable, sensible, or fair results in practice. Witness the eight-year-old student threatened with expulsion under a zero-tolerance gun policy for *drawing* a ninja, a soldier, and a Star Wars character with a gun as possible Halloween costumes. (CBS5, 2013).

Zero-tolerance policies may be particularly inappropriate in the workplace, where several federal laws (including the Americans with Disabilities Act) *require individualized assessment* of circumstances (EEOC, 2000). Further, typical zero-tolerance policies require all employees, under threat of termination, to report every other coworker's violations, regardless of the severity of the violation, history of previous violations, and so on. If these policies accomplish anything, it is to create an Orwellian environment filled with fear and distrust resembling the Soviet bloc's East Germany.

More importantly, however, a recent Canadian study (albeit of student cyberbullying) suggests that a zero-tolerance policy may be counterproductive and actually result in *fewer* reported incidents of bullying (Steeves, 2014). Steeves (2014) found that students were reluctant to follow a zero-tolerance policy because it effectively transferred control of the situation from the student to a school official and because students abhorred the stigma associated with causing the expulsion of a classmate by reporting a violation of the zero-tolerance policy. The parallels to the workplace are obvious.

Further, zero-tolerance policies preclude utilization of an employer's single most valuable asset in dealing with workplace conflict—the human resources (HR) professional. In every other aspect of workplace discord and conflict, the HR professional has flexibility in dealing with the perpetrator and the victim and fashioning an appropriate remedial course of action based on the unique circumstances presented, often with input from the victim. Indeed, studies suggest that while many bullying victims experience a harsher work environment after complaining about bullying, employees who reported bullying to an HR professional did not suffer the same negative response (Namie et al., 2014).

Elements of a Proper Bullying Policy

According to a 2012 workplace bullying survey by the Society for Human Resource Management, 40 percent of employers already have an antibullying policy (Society for Human Resource Management, 2012). Adopting an antibullying policy can be as simple as adding verbiage to existing policies prohibiting sexual harassment.

Define the prohibited conduct. Define workplace bullying and include examples of what is and is not bullying. To dissuade employees from using the policy to preemptively head off anticipated discipline, it is critical to state that bullying does not include performance reviews, constructive criticism, being held to reasonable performance parameters, and the like.

Declare that bullying is prohibited and why. State in clear terms that workplace bullying is destructive to coworkers and the company and thus is prohibited. Identify the consequences of confirmed instances of bullying—that is, discipline up to and including termination.

Provide a complaint mechanism. Encourage victims to report bullying and require employees witnessing bullying to report it. Clearly identify how and to whom complaints should be addressed. Suggest that the complaint and investigation will be kept confidential to the extent practical.

Promise prompt investigations. The policy should outline the same basic investigation procedures contained in the sexual harassment policy, including documenting the victim's complaint, interviewing witnesses, reviewing relevant e-mails and performance evaluations, and so on. Do not allow the complaint to be investigated by someone close to or in the direct line of reporting of the victim or bully.

Prohibit retaliation. The best policy in the world is useless if employees are afraid to use it. Any complaint mechanism must clearly and unequivocally prohibit retaliation against those filing complaints or participating in investigations.

Statement of prompt remedial action. The policy should not promise any action other than that warranted by the factual investigation. Whether remedial action is taken or not, both the bully and the victim should be advised, in general terms, of the results of the investigation and whether discipline will occur.

Implement training. It is not enough to create a paper policy. The policy must be communicated to employees and supervisors and reinforced with training, similar to sexual harassment training provided on an annual or biannual basis.

Revise job descriptions. Job descriptions should be revised to require acceptable coworker interaction and interpersonal skills. In addition, this performance metric should be included on all annual performance reviews. By clearly defining expectations in this manner, it will be much easier for employers to discipline or terminate toxic employees.

Model Policies

Several companies and governmental entities have written their own bullying policies. Care should be taken, however, to craft a policy that is consistent with the employer's existing policies and reflects the company's desired culture. A one-size-fits-all approach is not recommended. The following sample polices appear in the appendix:

- Tennessee Model Bullying Policy—Appendix B-1
- American Bar Association Model Bullying Policy–Appendix B-2
- Corporate harassment policy incorporating bullying as additional prohibited conduct—Appendix B-3

OBSTACLES TO ANTIBULLYING EFFORTS

Some employers are declining to adopt broad antibullying policies out of fear they will be misused. Just as some employees use existing antidiscrimination, harassment, and retaliation policies to file preemptive claims against legitimate supervisory criticism, employers fear employees will use antibullying policies to do the same. Given the vague definition of bullying, there is a very fine line (in the real world) between legitimate supervisory criticism and bullying (Canadian Centre for Occupational Health and Safety, 2014). For example, an employee working for a new (more demanding) supervisor and anticipating a reprimand or other discipline for poor performance could file a preemptive complaint against the supervisor asserting that the supervisor's critical comments are bullying.

In a particularly noteworthy case, a special needs assistant (SNA) at a national school in Ireland asserted a claim of bullying and harassing treatment after she was given a final written warning for improperly completing paperwork and for locking a student in a "sensory room" during a test the SNA was administering to the student. Following the school's (admittedly perfunctory) investigation into both incidents, the school's board voted to discipline the SNA but provided her a final written warning, which she claimed was inconsistent with the verbal discipline she had received from the school's principal. The court found that the school had engaged in bullying in that its investigation was inadequate, biased, and premised on falsehoods and that the board effectively denied the SNA a viable appellate remedy because the board would only allow her to appeal to the original decision maker. The court was satisfied with the evidence the employee presented that she suffered anxiety, a depressive disorder, loss of confidence and self-esteem, and an inability to cope with everyday life because of what happened to her at work from September 2009 to September 2010. Thus, the court awarded her €75,000 for psychiatric injury to date, €40,000 for psychiatric injury for the future, and loss of earnings of €140,276 for both past and future earnings, for a total award of €255,276 in damages (Carolan, 2016). The award, however, was reversed on appeal by the Irish Appellate Court, which found that even the "hopelessly flawed" and "botched" disciplinary process did not fit the definition of bullying, for if it did, it would expand the legal definition of bullying "to all kinds of situations it was never intended to cover" (*Ruffley v. The Board of Management of St. Anne's School*, 2015).

Perhaps the biggest obstacle to antibullying legislation and policies is the National Labor Relations Board's (NLRB) assault on workplace policies mandating civility. The NLRB enforces the National Labor Relations Act (NLRA), which principally governs relations between unionized workers and management but also governs nonunionized workplaces. However, continuing under the Obama administration, the NLRB has aggressively applied the NLRA to nonunionized workplaces, enforcing NLRA Section 7 rights of nonunionized employees to engage in "protected concerted activity"—that is, discussions of wages, working conditions, and workers' rights. The NLRB has pursued unfair labor practice charges against nonunionized employers with fairly standard employee handbook policies prohibiting employees from mistreating coworkers, arguing that the mere existence of such policies (even if not enforced) "chills" the Section 7 rights of employees. For example, the NLRB has found the following employee handbook policies chill, and thus violate, NLRA Section 7 rights:

- Prohibitions against "making false, vicious, profane or malicious statements towards or concerning the [employer] or any employee."[1]
- Prohibitions against "verbal comments or physical gestures directed to others that exceed the bounds of fair criticism and behavior that is counter to promoting teamwork."[2]
- Prohibitions of "behavior that is disruptive to maintaining a safe and healing environment or that is counter to promoting teamwork."[3]
- Prohibiting "loud, abusive or foul language."[4]
- Allowing discipline for "the inability or unwillingness to work harmoniously with other employees."[5]
- Prohibiting "negative conversations" about employees or managers.[6]

A cursory comparison of these policies challenged by the NLRB as violative of the NLRA to those suggested by the WBI or implemented by various employers leads inexorably to the conclusion that many antibullying polices violate the NLRA because they arguably "chill" the Section 7 rights of employees. Thus, an employer wishing to curtail workplace bullying is faced with a Hobson's choice: adopt an antibullying policy and risk being sued by the NLRB for unfair labor practices, or do not adopt such a policy and suffer the lack of productivity and decreased competitiveness likely to result from workplace bullying.

Further, assuming state legislatures ever pass true antibullying legislation, it is doubtful that the legislation will be enforceable in light of the supremacy of federal laws (including the NLRA) over inconsistent state laws. Many of the proposed state antibullying statutes track the WBI's antibullying legislation, which is modeled after the WBI's antibullying policies. Because, as discussed above, those policies may run afoul of the NLRA, the statutes modeled after those policies may also violate Section 7 of the NLRA. While there are differences between simple workplace incivility and workplace bullying, those differences typically never enter into the equation in an NLRA enforcement action because those actions are (at least to date) focused not on any *actual conduct* but rather on the *mere existence of policies* that chill the Section 7 rights of employees. Further, the fact that the NLRA is inapplicable to management and supervisors is of little solace to employers who (like most employers) do not have one set of personnel policies applicable to management and a separate set applicable to rank-and-file employees. As a result, the federal NLRA will preempt and thus preclude enforcement of any state antibullying statutes.

CONCLUSION

Workplace bullying is present in most American workplaces. The harmful effects of workplace bullying on targeted employees and the employer are well documented and undeniable. If left unchecked, workplace bullying will spread throughout a company like a cancer, causing widespread economic and competitive harm in quantifiable and unquantifiable ways.

The causes of workplace bullying are varied and most likely dependent on workplace dynamics unique to each workplace, but it is clear that a lack of corporate leadership allows bullying to flourish and spread. Legislative efforts to outlaw workplace bullying have not yielded useful results and may be preempted by the NLRB's current vision of the NLRA, thus precluding enforcement, assuming the NLRB's current vision of the NLRA continues indefinitely.

The likely remaining avenue to address the bullying phenomenon (apart from employees organizing to oppose bullying) is for employers to adopt their own antibullying policies prohibiting bullying, following the model of their existing antidiscrimination and retaliation policies. However, employers may have to resist efforts by the NLRB to void such antibullying policies. Given the costs of not adopting a bullying policy, it is recommended that employers adopt a properly worded antibullying policy and take their chances with the NLRB.

NOTES

1. *Lafayette Park Hotel*, 326 N.L.R.B. No. 69 (1998) (the Hotel Employees Local 2850 brought an unfair labor practices charge against the hotel and alleged that 7 of the 42 "unacceptable conduct" rules listed in the hotel's Employee Handbook "interfere[ed] with, restrain[ed], or coerc[ed]" the hotel employees in violation of the NLRA, even though no employee had ever been disciplined under any of the seven rules).

2. *William Beaumont Hospital & Jeri Antilla*, 363 NLRB No. 162 (2014) (the NLRB ordered a nonunionized hospital to rescind this provision in its Code of Conduct, finding the prohibitions to be unfair labor practices).

3. *Valley Health System LLC*, 363 NLRB No. 178 (2016) (striking provisions of a health care facility's conduct rules, finding that it chills employees' exercise of their Section 7 rights to engage in protected, concerted activity).

4. *Flamingo Hilton-Laughlin*, 330 NLRB No. 287 (1999) (finding that the rule in the Employee Handbook violated the NLRA because it did not define abusive or foul language and could be interpreted as barring lawful union-organizing propaganda).

5. *2 Sisters Food Group Inc.*, 357 No. 168 (2011) (finding this provision in the Employee Handbook to be unlawful because, according to the NLRB, the rule was too imprecise that it could encompass any disagreement or conflict among employees, including discussions and interactions protected by Section 7).

6. *Claremont Resort and Spa*, 344 NLRB No. 832 (2005) (finding the non-union employer violated the NLRA by maintaining a work rule prohibiting employees from having negative conversations about their managers because the NLRB believed that employees could construe the rule to "bar them from discussing with their co-workers complaints about their managers that affect working conditions, thereby causing employees to refrain from engaging in protected activities.")

7. Model Abusive Conduct Prevention Policy Pursuant to Public Chapter 997, the Healthy Workplace Act, *Report of the Tennessee Advisory Commission on Intergovernmental Relations*, pp. 13–17, https://tn.gov/assets/entities/tacir/attachments/2015Tab_4HealthyWorkplace.pdf.

8. Give Me Your Lunch Money! Dealing with Bullies in Today's Workplace, American Bar Association Model Anti-Bullying Policy, http://www.americanbar.org/content/dam/aba/events/labor_law/2012/03/national_conference_on_equal_employment_opportunity_law/mw2012eeo_eisenberg2.authcheckdam.pdf (last visited Aug. 1, 2016). Used by permission of Sue Ellen Eisenberg.

REFERENCES

Aryee, S., Sun, L. Y., Chen, Z. X. G., & Debrah, Y. A. (2008). Abusive supervision and contextual performance: The mediating role of emotional exhaustion and the moderating role of work unit structure. *Management and Organization Review, 4*(3), 393–411.

Atkinson, W. (2004). Stress: Risk management's most serious challenge? *Risk Management, 51*(6), 20–24.

Australia Fair Work Commission. (2014). Quarterly anti-bullying reports. Retrieved from https://www.fwc.gov.au/about-us/reports-publications/quarterly-reports

Australia Fair Work Commission. (2015). Quarterly anti-bullying reports. Retrieved from https://www.fwc.gov.au/about-us/reports-publications/quarterly-reports

Baillien, E., Neyens, I., De Witte, H., & De Cuyper, N. (2009). A qualitative study on the development of workplace bullying: Towards a three way model. *Journal of Community & Applied Social Psychology, 19*(1), 1–16.

Bentley, T., Catley, B., Cooper, H., Gardner, D., O'Driscoll, M., & Trenberth, L. (2009, December 17). *Understanding stress and bullying in New Zealand workplaces: Final report to OH&S steering committee*. Retrieved from http://www.massey.ac.nz/massey/fms/Massey%20News/2010/04/docs/Bentley-et-al-report.pdf

Bowling, N. A., & Michel, J. S. (2011). Why do you treat me badly? The role of attributions regarding the cause of abuse in subordinates' responses to abusive supervision. *Work & Stress, 25*(4), 309–320. doi:10.1080/02678373.2011.634281

Burgemeester, A. (2013, April 21). The narcissist in the workplace: Tips for working with a narcissist. Retrieved from http://thenarcissisticlife.com/the-narcissist-in-the-workplace-tips-for-working-with-a-narcissist

Burnes, B., & Pope, R. (2007). Negative behaviours in the workplace: A study of two primary care trusts in the NHS. *International Journal of the Public Sector Management, 20*(4), 285–303.

California Government Code §12950.1.

Canadian Centre for Occupational Health and Safety (2014). OSH answers fact sheet: Bullying in the workplace. Retrieved from https://www.ccohs.ca/oshanswers/psychosocial/bullying.html

Carolan, M. (2016, May 10). Court to hear appeal on overturning of SNA's €255,000 award. *Irish Times*. Retrieved from http://www.irishtimes.com/news/crime-and-law/courts/supreme-court/court-to-hear-appeal-on-overturning-of-sna-s-255-000-award-1.2642381

CBS5. (2013, November 15). 8-year-old threatened with expulsion for drawings. Retrieved from http://www.cbs5az.com/story/23847600/8-year-old-threated-with-expulsion-for- drawings

Daniel, T. A. (2006). *Bullies in the workplace: A focus on the "abuse disrespect" of employees*. Retrieved from http://noworkplacebullies.com/assets/docs/BulliesintheWorkplace1_HR_Magazine.23410 1040.pdf

Duffy, M. (2009). Preventing workplace mobbing and bullying with effective organizational consultation, policies and legislation. *Consulting Psychology Journal: Practice and Research, 61*(3), 242–262.

Eisenberger, N. (2012). The pain of social disconnection: Examining the shared neural underpinnings of physical and social pain. *Nature Reviews Neuroscience, 13*(6), 421–434. doi:10.1038/nrn3231

Equal Employment Opportunity Commission (EEOC). (2000, July 27). *EEOC enforcement guidance: Disability-related inquiries and medical examinations of employees under the Americans with Disabilities Act*. Retrieved from https://www.eeoc.gov/policy/docs/guidance-inquiries.html

Equal Employment Opportunity Commission (EEOC). (2014). EEOC charge receipts by state. Retrieved from https://www1.eeoc.gov/eeoc/statistics/enforcement/state_14.cfm

Fisher-Blando, J. (2008, February). *Aggressive behavior: Workplace bullying and its effect on job satisfaction and productivity* (Unpublished doctoral dissertation). University of Phoenix, Phoenix, Arizona.

Harvey, M. G., Heames, J. T., Richey, R. G., & Leonard, N. (2006). Bullying: From the playground to the boardroom. *Journal of Leadership and Organizational Studies, 12*(4), 1–11.

Hauge, L. J., Skogstad, A. & Einarsen, S. (2007). Relationships between stressful work environments and bullying: Results of a large representative study. *Work and Stress, 21*(3), 220–242.

Hepworth, W., & Towler, A. (2004). The effects of individual differences and charismatic leadership on work aggression. *Journal of Occupational Health Psychology, 9*(2), 176–185.

Hoobler, J. M., & Brass, D. J. (2006). Abusive supervision and family undermining as displaced aggression. *Journal of Applied Psychology, 91*(5), 1125–1133.

Hutchinson, M., & Jackson D. (2014). The construction and legitimation of workplace bullying in the public sector: Insight into power dynamics and organizational failures in health and social care. *Nursing Inquiry, 22*(1), 13–26.

Koonin, M., & Green, T. (2005). The emotionally abusive workplace. *Journal of Emotional Abuse, 3*(3–4), 71–79.

Ley, T. (2014, February 14). Messages between Jonathan Martin and his parents are heartbreaking. Retrieved from http://deadspin.com/the-messages-from-jonathan-martin-to-his-parents-are-he-1522865373

Leymann, H. (1990). Mobbing and psychological terror at workplaces. *Violence and Victims, 5*(2), 119–126.

Leymann, H., & Gustafsson, A. (1996). Mobbing at work and the development of post-traumatic stress disorders. *European Journal of Work and Organizational, 5*(2), 119–126.

Lim, S., Cortina, L. M., & Magley, V. J. (2008). Personal and workgroup incivility: Impact on work and health outcomes. *Journal of Applied Psychology, 93*(1), 95–107.

Loeb, S. (2014, June 10). CIA cites officers for "bullying" and other harassment. *CBS News*. Retrieved from http://www.cbsnews.com/news/cia-cites-officers-for-bullying-and-other-harassment

Lutgen-Sandvik, P., Tracy, S. J., & Alberts, J. K. (2007). Burned by bullying in the American workplace: Prevalence, perception, degree and impact. *Journal of Management Studies, 44*(6), 837–862.

Mattice, C. (2016, June). *The real world: Case studies of real organizations who solved their workplace bullying problems*. Presentation at the Society for Human Resource Management 2016 Annual Conference and Exposition, Washington, D.C.

Mehdi, A., Raju, R. M., & Mukherji, A. (2012). Abusive supervision and employee attrition: A study of executives in the Indian high technology sector. *Competition Forum, 10*(2), 42–48.

Mikkelsen, E. G., & Einarsen, S. (2002). Basic assumptions and symptoms of post-traumatic stress among victims of bullying at work. *European Journal of Work and Organizational Psychology, 11*(1), 87–111.

Mitchell, M. S., & Ambrose, M. L. (2007). Abusive supervision and workplace deviance and the moderating effects of negative reciprocity beliefs. *Journal of Applied Psychology, 92*(4), 1159–1168. doi:10.1037/0021-9010.92.4.1159

Mitchell, T. R., Holtom, B. C., & Lee, T. W. (2001). How to keep your best employees: Developing and effective retention policy. *Academy of Management Executives, 15*(4), 96–108.

Namie, G. (2003a, October). *2003 Report on abusive workplaces*. Retrieved from http://www.workplacebullying.org/multi/pdf/N-N-2003C.pdf

Namie, G. (2003b). Workplace bullying: Escalated incivility. *Ivey Business Journal Online, 68*(2), 1–6. Retrieved from http://iveybusinessjournal.com/publication/workplace-bullying-escalated-incivility

Namie, G. (2007, September). *U.S. workplace bullying survey*. Retrieved from http://workplacebullying.org/multi/pdf/WBIsurvey2007.pdf

Namie, G. (2013). *2013 WBI survey: Bullying by industry*. Retrieved from http://www.workplacebullying.org/multi/pdf/WBI-2013-Industry.pdf

Namie, G. (2014). *The WBI website 2014 instant poll-F—believe it or not: Impugning the integrity of the targets of workplace bullying*. Retrieved from http://www.workplacebullying.org/multi/pdf/WBI-2014-IP-F.pdf

Namie, G., Christensen, D., & Phillips, D. (2014). *2014 WBI U.S. workforce bullying survey*. Retrieved from http://workplacebullying.org/multi/pdf/WBI-2014-US-Survey.pdf

Oncale v. Sundowner Offshore Services, Inc., 83 F. 3d 118 (U.S., 1998).

Rafferty, A. E., Restubog, S. L. D., & Jimmieson, N. L. (2010). Losing sleep: Examining the cascading effects of supervisors' experience of injustice on subordinates' psychological health. *Work & Stress*, 24(1), 36–55. doi:10.1080/02678371003715135

Rose, K., Shuck, B., Twyford, D., & Bergman, M. (2015). Skunked: An integrative review exploring the consequences of the dysfunctional leader and implications for those employees who work for them. *Human Resource Development Review*, 14(1), 64–90. doi:10.1177/1534484314552437

Ruffley v. The Board of Management of St. Anne's School, IECA 287 (2015).

Safe Work Australia. (2013, November). *Guide for preventing and responding to workplace bullying*. Retrieved from http://www.safeworkaustralia.gov.au/sites/SWA/about/Publications/Documents/827/Guide-preventing-responding-workplace-bullying.pdf

Shpigel, B. (2014, February 14). "A classic case of bullying" on the Dolphins, report finds. *New York Times*. Retrieved from http://www.nytimes.com/2014/02/15/sports/football/investigation-finds-pattern-of-harassment-in-dolphins-locker-room.html?_r=0

Society for Human Resource Management. (2012, February 28). Workplace bullying survey. Retrieved from https://www.shrm.org/research/surveyfindings/articles/pages/workplacebullying.aspx

Steeves, V. (2014). *Young Canadians in a wired world, phase III: Cyberbullying: Dealing with online meanness, cruelty and threats*. Retrieved from http://mediasmarts.ca/sites/mediasmarts/files/pdfs/publication-report/full/YCWWIII_CyberbullyingFullReport.pdf

Tennessee Healthy Workplace Act, Tenn. Code Annot. §50-1-501 et seq. (2014).

Tepper, B. J., Carr, J. C., Breaux, D. M., Geider, S., Hu, C., & Hua, W. (2009). Abusive supervision, intentions to quit, and employees' workplace deviance: A power/dependence analysis. *Organizational Behavior and Human Decision Processes*, 109(2), 156–167.

Tracy, S. J., Lutgen-Sandvik, P., and Alberts, J. K. (2006). Nightmares, demons, and slaves: Exploring the painful metaphors of workplace bullying. *Management Communication Quarterly*, 20(2), 148–185.

Utah Code §67-19-44 (2015).

van Heugten, K. (2010). Bullying of social workers: Outcomes of a grounded study into impacts and interventions. *British Journal of Social Work*, 40(2), 638–655.

Vega, G., & Comer, D. (2005). Sticks and stones may break you bones, but words can break your spirit: Bullying in the workplace. *Journal of Business Ethics, 58*(1–3), 101–109.

Vigoda-Gadot, E. (2006). Compulsory citizenship behavior: Theorizing some dark sides of the good soldier syndrome in organizations. *Journal for the Theory of Social Behaviour, 36*(1), 77–93. doi:10.1111/j.1468-5914.2006.00297.x

Workplace Bullying Institute. (2014). Definition of bullying. Retrieved from http://www.workplacebullying.org/individuals/problem/definition

Zapf, D. & Gross, C. (2001). Conflict escalation and coping with workplace bullying: A replication and extension. *European Journal of Work and Organizational Psychology, 10*(4), 497–522.

APPENDIX A

Sample Definitions of Workplace Bullying

Workplace Bullying Institute

"Workplace bullying is repeated, health-harming mistreatment of one or more persons (the targets) by one or more perpetrators. It is abusive conduct that is (1) threatening, humiliating, or intimidating; or (2) work interference—sabotage—that prevents work from getting done; or (3) verbal abuse" (Workplace Bullying Institute, 2014, para. 1).

California Code

"Abusive conduct" is defined as,

> conduct of an employer or employee in the workplace, with malice, that a reasonable person would find hostile, offensive, and unrelated to an employer's legitimate business interests. Abusive conduct may include repeated infliction of verbal abuse, such as the use of derogatory remarks, insults, . . . verbal or physical conduct that a reasonable person would find threatening, intimidating, or humiliating, or the gratuitous sabotage or undermining of a person's work performance. A single act shall not constitute abusive conduct, unless especially severe and egregious. (California Government Code §12950.1.)

APPENDIX B-1

Tennessee Model Bullying Policy*[7]

The [Insert Entity Name] is firmly committed to a workplace free from abusive conduct as defined herein. We strive to provide high quality products and services in an atmosphere of respect, collaboration, openness, safety and equality. All employees have the right to be treated with dignity and respect. All complaints of negative and inappropriate workplace behaviors will be taken seriously and followed through to resolution. Employees who file complaints will not suffer negative consequences for reporting others for inappropriate behavior.

This policy applies to all full-time and part-time employees of [Insert Entity Name] including interns. It does not apply to independent contractors, but other contract employees are included. This policy applies to any sponsored program, event or activity including, but not limited to, sponsored recreation programs and activities; and the performance by officers and employees of their employment related duties. The policy includes electronic communications by any employee.

Abusive conduct includes acts or omissions that would cause a reasonable person, based on the severity, nature, and frequency of the conduct, to believe that an employee was subject to an abusive work environment, which can include but is not limited to: 1) Repeated verbal abuse in the workplace, including derogatory remarks, insults, and epithets; 2) Verbal, nonverbal, or physical conduct of a threatening, intimidating, or humiliating nature in the workplace; or 3) The sabotage or undermining of an employee's work performance in the workplace. A single act generally will not constitute abusive conduct, unless such conduct is determined to be severe and egregious.

Abusive conduct does not include: 1) Disciplinary procedures in accordance with adopted policies of [Insert Entity Name]; 2) Routine coaching and counseling, including feedback about and correction of work performance; 3) Reasonable work assignments, including shift, post, and overtime assignments; 4) Individual differences in styles of personal expression; 5) Passionate, loud expression with no intent to harm others; 6) Differences of opinion on work-related concerns; or 7) The non-abusive exercise of managerial prerogative.

Supervisors and others in positions of authority have a particular responsibility to ensure that healthy and appropriate behaviors are exhibited at all times and that complaints to the contrary are addressed in a timely manner. Supervisors will: 1) Provide a working environment as safe as possible by having preventative measures in place and by dealing immediately with threatening or potentially violent situations; 2) Provide good examples by treating all with courtesy and respect; 3) Insure that all employees have access to and are aware of the abusive conduct prevention policy and explain the procedures to be followed if a complaint of inappropriate behavior at work is made; 4) Be vigilant for signs of inappropriate behaviors at work through observation and information seeking, and take action to resolve the behavior before it escalates; and 5) Respond promptly, sensitively and confidentially to all situations where abusive behavior is observed or alleged to have occurred.

Employees shall treat all other employees with dignity and respect. No employee shall engage in threatening, violent, intimidating or other abusive conduct or behaviors. Employees are expected to assume personal responsibility to promote fairness and equity in the workplace and report any incidents of abusive conduct in accordance with this policy.

Employees should co-operate with preventative measures introduced by supervisors and recognize that a finding of unacceptable behaviors at work will be dealt with through appropriate disciplinary procedures.

Retaliation is a violation of this policy. Retaliation is any act of reprisal, interference, restraint, penalty, discrimination, intimidation, or harassment against an individual or individuals exercising rights under this policy.

All supervisors and employees are encouraged to undergo training on abusive conduct prevention conduct as directed by [Insert Entity Name]. Training should identify factors that contribute to a respectful workplace, familiarize participants with responsibilities under this policy, and provide steps to address an abusive conduct incident.

Any employee who feels he or she has been subjected to abusive conduct is encouraged to report the matter orally or in writing to a supervisor including his or her supervisor, manager, appointing authority, elected official, or to the human resources office. Employees should not feel obligated to report their complaints to their immediate supervisor first before bringing the matter to the attention of one of the representatives identified above. Any employee seeking to file a complaint should ensure the complaint consists of precise details of each incident of abusive conduct including dates, times, locations and any witnesses. Formal complaints should be documented in writing, but are not required to be in writing.

An employee who witnesses or is made aware of behavior that may satisfy the definition of abusive conduct (as defined herein) should report any and all incidents as set forth herein.

Supervisors must timely report known incidents involving workplace abuse, intimidation, or violence to the [HR, appointing authority or investigator]. Supervisors and appointing authorities are required to take reasonable steps to protect the complainant, including, but not limited to, separation of employees involved. The person complained against will be notified that an allegation has been made against him or her and informed of the investigative procedure.

Investigations of abusive conduct shall be conducted as soon as practicable and in accordance with the policies and practices of [Insert Entity Name].

In the event of a finding of abusive conduct, the employer will take immediate and appropriate corrective action. Remedies may be determined by weighing the severity and frequency of the incidences of abusive conduct and in accordance with existing disciplinary policies of [Insert Entity Name]. Such corrective action may include but is not limited to participation in counseling, training, and disciplinary action up to and including termination, or changes in job duties or location.

Supervisory personnel who allow abusive conduct to continue or fail to take appropriate action upon learning of such conduct will be subject to corrective action. Such corrective action may include but is not limited to participation in counseling, training, or disciplinary action up to and including termination, or changes in job duties or location.

Any employees exhibiting continuing emotional or physical effects from the incident in question should be informed of established employee assistance programs or other available resources. When abusive conduct has been confirmed, the employer will continue to keep the situation under review and may take additional corrective actions if necessary. Preventative measures may also be taken to reduce the reoccurrence of similar behavior or action.

To the extent permitted by law, the [Insert Entity Name] will maintain the confidentiality of each party involved in an abusive conduct investigation, complaint or charge, provided it does not interfere with the ability to investigate the allegations or to take corrective action. However, state law may prevent the employer from maintaining confidentiality of public records. Therefore, the [Insert Entity Name] cannot guarantee confidentiality.

Note: The Tennessee Advisory Commission charged with creating this model policy refused to accept this policy.

APPENDIX B-2

American Bar Association Model Bullying Policy[8]

Company, Inc. considers workplace bullying unacceptable and will not tolerate it under any circumstances. This policy shall apply to all employees, regardless of his or her employee status (i.e. managerial vs. hourly, full-time vs. part-time, employee vs. independent contractor).

Any employee found in violation of this policy will be disciplined, up to and including immediate termination. Independent contractors found to be in violation of this policy may be subject to contract cancellation.

Company, Inc. defines bullying as persistent, malicious, unwelcome, severe and pervasive mistreatment that harms, intimidates, offends, degrades or humiliates an employee, whether verbal, physical or otherwise, at the place of work and/or in the course of employment.

Company, Inc. promotes a healthy workplace culture where all employees are able to work in an environment free of bullying behavior.

Company, Inc. encourages all employees to report any instance of bullying behavior. Any reports of this type will be treated seriously, investigated promptly and impartially. Company, Inc. further encourages all employees to formally report any concerns of assault, battery, or other bullying behavior of a criminal nature to the local Police Department. Company, Inc. requires any supervisor who witnesses any bullying, irrespective of reporting relationship, to immediately report this conduct to the Human Resources Director.

Company, Inc. will protect an employee who reports bullying conduct from retaliation or reprisal.

Company, Inc. considers the following types of behavior to constitute workplace bullying. Please note, this list is not meant to be exhaustive and is only offered by way of example:

Staring, glaring or other nonverbal demonstrations of hostility;
Exclusion or social isolation;
Excessive monitoring or micro-managing;
Work-related harassment (work-overload, unrealistic deadlines, meaningless tasks);
Being held to a different standard than the rest of an employee's work group;
Consistent ignoring or interrupting of an employee in front of co-workers;
Personal attacks (angry outbursts, excessive profanity, or name-calling);
Encouragement of others to turn against the targeted employee;
Sabotage of a co-worker's work product or undermining of an employee's work performance.

APPENDIX B-3

Sample Corporate Policy Incorporating Bullying Prohibition into Sexual Harassment Policy

Definition

Harassment or bullying can take the form of a number of different behaviors, including persistent comments, actions, jokes, or suggestions, which are unwanted by the recipient and create an intimidating environment.

Other forms of harassment or bullying may include:

- Physical contact, sexual or otherwise;
- Offensive language, gossip, or slander;
- Posters, graffiti, obscene gestures;
- Abuse of internal e-mail systems, the Internet or intranet;
- Pestering, spying, and stalking;
- Persistent undermining of confidence, competence, and self-esteem;
- Failing to acknowledge the rights or needs of people with different views or practices;
- Undignified treatment or exclusion of people with disabilities or on the grounds of gender, age, sexual orientation, or race;
- Request for sexual favors;
- Express/implied threat of dismissal/loss of promotion on racial grounds or for refusal of sexual favors.

Harassment can occur on the grounds of

- Race
- Sex
- Sexual orientation
- Age
- Disability
- Bullying generally
- Policy

The Company fully supports the rights and opportunities of all people to seek, obtain, and hold employment without harassment. Harassment is conduct that is unwanted or offensive to the recipient, whether on the basis of sex, race, or disability or whether it takes the form of bullying generally. Harassment is a form of unlawful direct discrimination, which may expose the company as well as culpable employees to proceedings in the Employment Tribunal.

Appropriate disciplinary action, in accordance with the Company's Disciplinary Procedure, including dismissal for serious offenses, will be taken against any employee who violates this policy.

25

Workplace Bullying and Mobbing in the Nonprofit Sector

Vega Subramaniam

The nonprofit sector shares some similarities with its public and for-profit counterparts. Like the public sector, nonprofit organizations seek to benefit society, not to make profits that benefit private shareholders. Like the for-profit sector, the nonprofit sector is not publicly accountable in a closely transparent way. Unlike the public sector, management behaviors and decisions in nonprofits are not subject to greater public scrutiny, despite the public tax benefits nonprofits accrue. The unique characteristics of the nonprofit sector require a separate examination of the topic of workplace bullying and mobbing within the sector.

This chapter offers an introduction to the nonprofit sector, a statement of the problem of toxic leadership (as defined in Lipman-Blumen, 2005) in the nonprofit sector, and a summary of research to date. This is followed with a synopsis of manifestations of toxic leadership in the sector and the impact workplace bullying has on individual organizations as well as on the sector as a whole. The chapter concludes with a discussion of causes of and possible solutions to toxic leadership in the sector.

INTRODUCTION TO THE NONPROFIT SECTOR

A nonprofit organization is an entity established for member or community benefit and for which any funds and surpluses must be used to further its mission or organizational purpose. The nonprofit sector is a major contributor to the economy. As of June 2016, the IRS reported almost 1.6 million nonprofit organizations, and in 2015, the public gave a record $373.25 billion to public charities (Internal Revenue Service, 2016; Pon, 2016). In 2013, public charities reported $1.74 trillion in revenues, $1.63 trillion in expenses, and over $3 trillion in assets (National Center for Charitable Statistics, 2016).

In 2012, the sector accounted for more than 11 million jobs and generated $532 billion in wages alone (U.S. Bureau of Labor Statistics, 2014, 2016).

While workplace bullying likely manifests the same everywhere, the nonprofit sector is worth considering separately. In particular, three unique characteristics affect the nature of workplace bullying in the sector: its purpose, its funding structure, and its governance.

Purpose

A defining characteristic of nonprofit organizations is that they do not exist to make money but to serve a purpose. Individuals are thus drawn to working for nonprofit organizations because they are inspired by the mission. In this context, where both the organization and the employee seem to hold similar values, encountering toxic leadership perhaps as widely as in other workplaces seems surprising. Violations of principles of equity, fairness, and dignity feel like a greater betrayal for new staff than similar violations at for-profit or government workplaces.

Funding Structure

To operate their organizations, nonprofits rely on charitable funding from individuals, foundations, the government, and corporations. For funders, grantee success indicates that they are mindful stewards of their donations. Currently, "mindful stewardship" is associated with low administrative (or overhead) costs (Bedsworth, Gregory, & Howard, 2008; Josephson, 2015; Klein, 2003; Le, 2014; Masaoka and Zimmerman, 2014; Pettijohn, Boris, De Vita, & Fyffe, 2013; Snibe, 2006; Song, 2014).

Underinvesting in administrative costs, and indeed seeing administrative costs as "wasteful," is unique to the nonprofit sector. While the for-profit sector recognizes the need to invest in staff development and safer working conditions, nonprofits struggle to raise money for these same things (Brandt, 2013; Francis & Talansky, 2012; International Labour Organization & International Finance Corporation, 2013). Nonprofit staff are thus underpaid (relative to their qualifications and to the for-profit sector) and overworked (relative to their job descriptions, employee policies, overtime regulations, and federal holiday schedules; Alexander, 2013; Cohen, 2010; GuideStar, Better Business Bureau Wise Giving Alliance, & Charity Navigator, 2013; Manzo, 2004; Schmidt, 2016).

Governance

Nonprofit organizations are governed by volunteer boards of directors. Too often, people selected for board service have little to no experience with or knowledge about running a nonprofit (No Bullying: Let's Stop Cruelty @ Work, 2013). Quite often, they are friends of the executive director (ED) and recruited to the board by the ED (La Piana Consulting, 2003; Straughan, 2003). Board members are thus too often ill-equipped to vet potential EDs or to provide or require the training necessary to develop management skills.

STATEMENT OF THE PROBLEM

There appears to be an explosion of toxic leadership in the nonprofit sector (Bloom & Farragher, 2010; Eisenberg, 2002). Nonprofit sector magazines and online industry sites increasingly report stories of staff experiences with abusive or exploitative supervisors. Simultaneously, capacity-building attention is increasingly directed at building healthier organizations and shifting organizational cultures. This increased focus on "healthier organizations" is a tacit implication that current organizations are not "healthy." Bloom (2006) suggests that toxic leaders emerge from unhealthy environments:

> Such an unhealthy environment lends itself to the emergence of what have been described as "toxic leaders." Toxic leaders are subtly or overtly abusive, violating the basic standards of human respect, courtesy, and rights of the people who report to them. They tend to be power-hungry and appear to feed off of the use and abuse of the power they have. They play to people's basest fears, stifle criticism, and teach followers never to question their judgment or actions. They lie to meet their own ends and tend to subvert processes of the system that are intended to generate a more honest and open environment. They compete with rather than nurture other leaders, including potential successors, and tend to use divide-and-conquer strategies to set people against each other. Toxic leaders will not hesitate to identify scapegoats and then direct followers' aggression against the designated scapegoat rather than themselves. They frequently promote incompetence, corruption, and cronyism and exploit systems for personal gain (p. 47).

LITERATURE REVIEW

The past decade has seen a proliferation of management literature on toxic leadership and workplace bullying. The literature can be categorized based on their target audience: the victim of abuse, the manager, and a broader field of people interested in systemic issues such as organizational culture and health.

Self-Help

Literature targeting victimized individuals comes in the form of self-help support. Self-help literature mostly assume the leadership cannot be held accountable and cannot change because the leader is truly certifiable with a personality disorder; the systems and institutions at play will never address the victim's needs or provide a remedy; and the reader should focus on what is in his or her control to change.

Self-help literature is designed to help individuals recognize and handle their toxic situations (Cavaiola & Lavender, 2000; Maravelas, 2005; Weinstein, 1998). Management consultants might offer individual behavior-based solutions to achieve higher-functioning workplace cultures. Other texts review profiles of personality disorders: narcissists, sociopaths, and others. The emphasis is on what workers can do to respond differently and how to navigate toxic coworker interactions. Such literature typically does not tackle broader causes or solutions of toxic workplaces; nor does it offer insights into the nonprofit sector specifically.

People-Centered management

Literature targeting managers focuses on skills development and centers on greater self-awareness and interpersonal effectiveness. Such literature assumes leaders can change with the right motivation and new skills. People-centered management literature focuses on positive intervention in supervision, management, and leadership (Pfeffer, 1998; Plas, 2013; Williams, 2015). This literature offers leaders resources on how to manage oneself, how to manage people in organizations and in projects, and how to create employee-centered workplaces (DeCarlo, 2004).

People-centered management literature tends to promote self-management: taking self-assessments or employing practices for mindfulness, self-regulation, behavior-modification, and resilience. Topics on managing people include increasing employee engagement, conducting performance management, engaging in participatory decision making, and building communication skills, such as giving and receiving feedback (Carbonara, 2012).

Organizational Health

Literature targeting the field of organizational health and culture focuses on systemic dynamics and effects on organizational health and culture. This literature typically assumes that many complex factors combine to create toxic leadership and workplaces, and it focuses on identifying the context and root causes of workplace bullying.

Organizational health and culture interventions include developing positive organizational cultures; establishing fair workplace policies, processes, and procedures; and addressing systemic issues around organizational health, trauma and healing, and trauma-informed organizations (Bloom & Farragher, 2013; Clarke, 2012; Kanter & Sherman, 2016; School of Unity and Liberation (SOUL), 2006; Vivian & Hormann, 2013).

Beyond anecdotal evidence of toxic leadership, formal research specific to the nonprofit sector is scant. As nonprofit consultants with expertise in leadership development and human resources who have heard stories of workplace bullying with alarming frequency, we saw an urgent need to better understand this problem. We therefore undertook a research project that offers a systematic exploration of the problem of toxic leadership in the nonprofit sector. We examine how toxic leadership practices affect leadership development and retention in the sector and the resultant impact on organizations' effectiveness in fulfilling their missions.

OUR RESEARCH

Our research is a qualitative study based on one-hour structured interviews. We interviewed 35 nonprofit staff members, 5 nonprofit leaders, 5 organizational consultants, and 3 nonprofit funders. Interview participants were recruited through snowball sampling, and the 48 interviewees represent dozens of organizations and geographic locations throughout the United States. Despite the fact that we anticipated minimal risk to our subjects through our interview process, and that our subjects did not constitute a vulnerable population, we took every precaution to maintain our interviewees' well-being and confidentiality. We received informed consent prior to each interview in the form of signed consent forms outlining the purpose and form of our research; the risks involved to the interviewee (who were all willing adults interested in sharing their stories for the sake of bringing the topic of workplace bullying in the nonprofit sector to light); the assurance that interviewees were at liberty to withdraw from the interview at any time; and the assurance of confidentiality and our methods of handling confidential information. At the start of each interview, informed consent was received again by verbally outlining the above procedures and receiving verbal assent from each interviewee, which are preserved in each transcription. Interview transcriptions are kept confidential through a secured, password-protected local file.

Our results are based on the qualitative analysis of these interviews, using standard thematic analysis methods. Below is a summary of our findings regarding manifestations of workplace bullying in nonprofit organizations. All quotes within boxes represent actual quotations from research participants. Given the small sample size and nonrepresentative nature of our sample, these findings should be seen as tentative rather than definitive and as a foundation for future research.

MANIFESTATIONS OF WORKPLACE BULLYING IN NONPROFIT ORGANIZATIONS

Problems in the Hiring and Onboarding Processes

When asked what excites them about joining a nonprofit organization, new staff note how important it is for them to work on causes they "believe in," on a mission "so from the bottom up," in an organization that "intersects" with their values and interests. They mention how organizations appear to celebrate their social, racial and ethnic, gender, and religious identities; to reflect strong, balanced, and diverse leadership; and to welcome the value that new staff will add. New staff start, by and large, with great expectations and a desire to contribute meaningfully.

Red flags emerge very early on, even during the hiring process: job descriptions seek a superhero. Job responsibilities exceed what could reasonably be expected from one person and include a combination of skill sets that are rare, such as financial duties combined with fund-raising.

Red flags continue to surface during the selection process: Interview dates are shifted with little notice. Applicants are told they will be interviewed by one person, but they show up to find a panel of five interviewers. Applicants do not hear from an organization for weeks and then get a call asking if they are available the following morning for an interview with the ED. That level of chaos suggests a leader who is controlling and who keeps everyone around them continually guessing.

Once new staff are hired, signs of a toxic workplace also emerge relatively early on. An early warning sign is that supervisors fail to offer new staff guidance, structure, onboarding, training, or strategic vision. Also, actual job responsibilities are largely unrelated to the posted position descriptions. Thus, new staff struggle to cobble together the training and guidance they need to do their jobs, in a context where they cannot even be sure what their job responsibilities are.

> "The job description had nothing to do with what I did. My job title had nothing to do with what I did. Nothing I have ever done has been sourced from my job description. Or the job description is so vague that it could cover anything, like 'help with stuff, assist with organizational efforts.'"
>
> "My peers were my main source of support. But as far as training goes, there was none. I asked for it; I repeatedly asked for more information. They were like, 'Why are you asking so many questions?' It seemed ridiculous to me that they didn't train people, like, there was no training."

Common Patterns of Toxic Behaviors

Workplace bullying behaviors that staff experience over time can be grouped into the following six categories: (1) creating an atmosphere of mistrust, (2) micromanagement, (3) capriciousness, (4) blaming and criticism, (5) exploitation and violation of labor laws, (6) ethical violations.

Toxic leaders deliberately create an atmosphere of mistrust. They talk about staff behind their backs to other staff members. They also falsely tell one staff member that they are disliked or distrusted by their colleagues.

> "My boss would go to my colleagues and complain about me. She would also talk about colleagues behind their backs in a common area."
> "She would try to pin people against one another. . . . Her goal was to say this about this person so you wouldn't trust that person. So then people didn't know if they could trust you with whatever they were doing or whatever they were saying."

Toxic supervisors also micromanage. They tell staff in excruciating detail how to do something and require approval of every step, however small and however skilled or experienced the staff member is. Leaders perceive themselves to excel at everything and find it difficult to delegate. They cause long, unnecessary delays by demanding to approve each step and creating a bottleneck. They insist on tracking every minute of staff's time and demand frequent updates, requiring unnecessary meetings under the guise of staying in the loop. They demand to be copied on all e-mails.

> "We had leadership that based their leadership on fear and people were afraid to do anything other than what she wanted you to do. Or, you know, 'Got to run this by that person first.'"
> "It was a joke, but he could not stop himself. Meetings meetings meetings. Every little thing turns into a meeting. And then reports. Reports about every little single thing. Every day."

Toxic supervisors are typically capricious and unpredictable. They make new decisions on the fly and without connection to strategy or agreed-upon goals. They change their minds about priorities at a moment's notice and with no communication.

> "Whatever the job description says, it was decided on a per-week/per-month basis. 'Oh this is how we're going to do it.' . . . That allowed this sense in which the goal posts were always moving, so it was hard to tell what I was being evaluated by."

"She would also be changing the rules of the game. She would make a major change, and people were in the dark. There would be major changes, and people were like, 'Oh, we're supposed to do *what* now?'"

A common complaint about workplace bullies involved public, unfair, and often false blaming and criticism. The blaming and criticism negatively affected performance by instilling an environment of fear and secrecy.

"One time, a coworker and I were preparing for our major event, and we were playing music, so we had the door closed so we wouldn't disturb the rest of the office. And instead of coming to talk to us about it, the ED sent around an email—to *all* of us—and the tone of it was so *nasty*. 'I don't know if you guys are keeping the door closed to camouflage the fact that you're working on other things or just chatting. We have all this work to be doing.' And I'm here in my free time for hours and hours."

"I wasn't doing enough or I wasn't smart enough or she was constantly criticizing me and not recognizing the things that I do well."

"She would yell, swear words, every other word was the f-bomb. She would just flare up."

Nonprofit staff, especially those working at small organizations, typically work well beyond a full-time 40-hour work week. For many, this is a choice they willingly make, at least for short bursts of time (for example, before a major event), because of their passion for the mission. However, while functional leaders encourage their staff to take time off, leave work at a reasonable time, and minimize evening and weekend work, this is not so in toxic workplaces. Toxic leaders make workers feel guilty for leaving work at a reasonable time, expect staff to regularly work evenings and weekends, and require staff to work during time off or over federal holidays.

"I worked a lot of extra hours from the very, very beginning."

"If I would question, 'Why do we work so many hours?' 'Well, this is what it takes; this is what it means to care about our communities and to care about this work.'"

"She slammed the door open and yelled at the both of us. She was like, 'You guys are just watching YouTube videos.' And I was like, 'Yeah, my best friend *is* watching YouTube videos. Because she's *here*, because it's *hours* after I was supposed to leave work, and she's very nicely keeping me company.'"

"If you tried to leave at the stated hour, she would be like, 'Oh, do you have plans?' like that's the only reason that you could be leaving at 6:00.

She would say, 'Sometimes I wonder about the commitment of you and the people in this organization to this work.' And I'm like, *REALLY?!*"

A particularly egregious sign of a toxic leader is their willingness to cross ethical lines that comes from feeling so important or superior that rules sometimes need to be ignored for the greater good. A typical example is EDs requiring staff to misrepresent organizational work on grant reports.

"We weren't being honest with our funders. When I would be exposed to our grant documents, I was like, we are not doing this stuff. We're just not. We promised to do this stuff and we're not doing them. And I always felt very, very uncomfortable with that."

"I always wondered how honest we were being with funders. If I had access, I would feel like it was my ethical responsibility to tell them. But I had no access."

Responsive Actions by Staff

Nonprofit staff try to address bullying at their organizations in various ways, such as responding directly to the bully, going up the chain of command (including seeking support from their direct supervisor), unionizing, and disengaging or leaving.

A reality that staff who respond directly learn swiftly is that workplace bullies cannot accept negative feedback. They do not believe they are doing anything wrong or that they need to change. If someone who works for them points out a problem, workplace bullies immediately make the problem the other person.

"I tried to follow the grievance procedure. I wrote her a letter, I asked for a meeting. But I can't really do anything through this grievance process because I can't really prove anything."

"My boss refused to listen to the feedback offered by my predecessor, me. She had that reputation: that you cannot give her feedback because she would get very defensive and she would turn against you personally."

"I know my life will be harder if I try to fight [her]. So let me just stop bothering. It is just so much easier to let you be the way that you want to be. Because I will never win. It will only make you retaliate more and more."

Staff who went up the chain of command or observed other staff doing so found that to be ineffective and demoralizing.

"I tried to talk to [the VP] about that. . . . So the VP checked in with my boss: 'Is this true?' My boss says, 'Of course it's not true.' My boss is the VP's friend. The VP is going to take my boss's word."

"I do happen to know a person that took action. I don't know all the specifics, but I do know that our lawyer was involved and I don't think much came of it, to be honest. As far as I know. Which is really unfortunate because it is almost like people don't feel like there is any kind of support."

"I couldn't find a way to hold him accountable. The board liked him; they were his friends."

Occasionally, staff attempt to unionize. Some staff reported discussions among themselves to explore the route of unionization.

"The best experiences have been when colleagues have come together to talk about their experiences and create spaces, this power structure be damned, we're going to think of the best interests of ourselves and our colleagues and our clients. There's so much empowerment and strength in that. The odds may be stacked too high against you. But once that happens, it makes everything so much better. We have to start building alliances in our workplaces that are based on mutual trust."

Absenteeism and presenteeism are rampant at nonprofit organizations with toxic EDs.

"I would do things reluctantly and with minimal effort."

"If I am going to have to be here until 9:00 p.m. every night anyway, and I will never satisfy you anyway, then I am going to spend a significant number of hours doing whatever the f* I want to."

"You know, when I first started, I had a theory that was like, 'first one in, last one out.' So, I was trying to get in earlier than everyone else and work and leave after—just really show that I was really committed. But after that [last incident], I get to work when I'm supposed to get to work. And at 4:59, I have my purse and I'm ready to go."

Impacts on Staff

Bullying has repercussions on the lives of staff members. For most, the bullying consumes their personal, interpersonal, emotional and physical, and professional lives. Eventually, staff leave (or are pushed out of) the organization.

As a result of being bullied at work, staff members stop doing things they enjoy. They have no energy to get together with people. They have no energy for hobbies. They spend their weekends recovering, and they spend Sundays dreading Monday.

> "I didn't realize it was happening, but at a certain point I realized that so much of my mental real estate was taken up by this one person, and their reaction to everything, everything that I did: how I was dressed, how I was walking, how I was talking, who I talked to, what I said when I talked to them, how I addressed them, how I addressed her, how I addressed other people in front of her."
>
> "I felt under so much pressure that it was difficult for me to sleep at night, but I was at the same time working very long hours. I was constantly in a state of stress while at work. I was sick frequently. I was not eating. It crowded out time for me to have a personal life."
>
> "My hair started to fall out. I was miserable. It was a misery-making kind of job."

Once staff "come out" to each other about their experiences, they find that the bullying is all they can talk about, both in and out of the office. Their intimate partners and loved ones, while wanting to support them, feel helpless to do so, and at the end of their rope: "You need to stop talking about this."

> "You do not want to spend time with friends because soon people get turned off by your negativity."
>
> "My partner just kept saying, 'You have to stop bringing that home. You have to stop bringing that home. All we do is talk about her. You have to stop bringing that home.' It was all I could do to get any joy out of [my friendships and rest of my life]."

Staff experience emotional and physical effects as well, including depression, dread, anxiety, anger, and trauma. Physically, individuals gain or lose weight, drink heavily, and experience hair loss, rashes, and other physical changes.

> "I remember having this terrible conversation with my coworkers because all of us hated Sundays. Because Sundays reminded us it was going to be Monday soon. And Monday means 'reckoning.'"
>
> "One of my coworkers: her hair was falling out. She was all splotchy and broken out."
>
> "You don't want to exercise. You put on weight."
>
> "I drink too much because of my work."

"It was devastating. After the campaign, I basically went to my home country for six months and slept, and got my spirit back. Because my spirit had disappeared."

"I will never be the person that I was before I met [my ED]."

Professionally, people lose their sense of competency. They also lose valuable years of their lives because they are not able to use their professional competencies in their jobs. When they apply for new jobs, they have few or no relevant experiences to point to. Small nonprofit organizations are notorious for hiring young people out of college or with few years of experience. Without a long track record, losing two, three, or four years of professional development leaves staff with a hole in their resume, a spotty track record to have to explain to potential employers, and few professional references. Often, personnel policies explicitly state that only the ED is allowed to serve as a reference for anyone in the organization, even those who report to others. While this policy is supposed to "protect" the organization, it also means staff either lose a reference or must go behind the ED's and organization's back.

Finally, people leave or are terminated from their positions, leaving them professionally and financially vulnerable.

"Everybody left . . . due to mismanagement."

"After this incident, I sat at my desk and I thought about my experiences. And something dawned on me, and I said, I don't want to be part of an organization where I have to spend my whole time on internal political fights. So I wrote a one-sentence letter of resignation. They were very shocked. And I left. And I got a job for 10% more than the original raise that I had asked for."

"The biggest thing I tell people is not to go work at nonprofits."

"I'm never working for a nonprofit again. At least at a for-profit company, I'll get paid well even if I'm exploited."

"This? This is a cesspool. It's like a rapist trap. It's a workplace bullying trap. I think there's another workplace bullying trap in the for-profit sector, but I think that there's a *little bit* of ability to push back there. But here there is none at all. So all we're going to do is keep attracting these sociopaths into this work. And so I don't know what we're doing about that as a sector. And I take myself out of that, what you and others are doing, because I'm not in the sector, and I don't want to be in the sector, because I see it as a cesspool of predators."

Our research finds clear patterns in how toxic leadership is manifested in the nonprofit sector and the impact of such toxic leadership on nonprofit staff. Workplace bullying not only causes harm to individuals, but it also ruptures the nonprofit ecosystem. Our research, however, does not explicitly address these larger, sector-wide impacts.

IMPACTS OF TOXIC LEADERSHIP ON THE NONPROFIT SECTOR

The section below outlines the current state of the literature regarding the impact of bullying and mobbing at the organizational, movement-building, and sector-wide levels. While this research is in its nascent stages, some patterns are emerging.

At the *organizational level*, staff turnover results in increased costs to replace staff, delays in project outcomes, and perhaps, most importantly, loss of talent. The loss of talent also results in a loss in the leadership pipeline: those who would otherwise have become leaders in their organizations. Team productivity also suffers; toxic leadership leads to team members losing trust in one another, avoiding conflict, and feeling disengaged from projects and outcomes. Finally, in toxic organizational cultures, staff are disempowered and discouraged from challenging ineffective ideas or practices of the ED (Davis, 2007; Kim & Kunreuther, 2016; Landles-Cobb, Kramer, & Smith Milway, 2015; Opportunity Knocks, 2010; Solomon & Sandahl, 2007).

At the *movement-building level*, toxic leadership negatively affects the ability of nonprofit coalitions and collaborations to make progress on their joint missions (Truit, 2012). For example, micromanaged staff who attend coalition meetings are not empowered to commit to actions or activities without reporting back to their supervisors, thus slowing down the coalition's forward progress (Blackney, 2013; McAndrews, 2010). Likewise, staff turnover in individual organizations within coalitions means that new relationships must be built over and over again, and institutional knowledge is continuously lost (Center for Community Change, 2014; TCC Group, 2011). As Herold (2012) puts it,

> Everyone knows that organization A has an executive director who's a megalomaniac. Everyone knows that two particular organizations bully other smaller organizations. Everyone knows that organization B likes to fire (almost) everyone every couple of years. Everyone knows that certain national organizations have less than cordial relationships with their local affiliates (para. 2).

At the *sector-wide level*, there are also impacts worth noting. Funding and resources are misused or underused: when turnover is frequent, programs are not delivered, or are not delivered effectively or in a timely fashion. Parties who witness the bullying are reluctant to talk publicly about the issue. Such publicity puts organizations at risk, and staff remain loyal to the organization and the mission, regardless of the toxicity of the leader. Finally, public distrust of not only individual nonprofit organizations but of the nonprofit sector as a whole increases (Berman, 2016).

Manifestations of toxic leadership in the nonprofit sector and the resulting negative effects on staff, organizations, and the sector are clear and require urgent attention. It is therefore imperative to understand the conditions that lead to or allow for toxic leadership in the sector and possible solutions that could be derived from those conditions. The following sections explore the causes and consequences of toxic leadership in the nonprofit sector.

CAUSES OF TOXIC LEADERSHIP IN THE NONPROFIT SECTOR

While some toxic leaders may truly suffer from a personality disorder (e.g., narcissistic personality disorder), most experts feel that toxic leadership in nonprofit organizations is caused by structural, not personality, factors (Lipsky, 2009; Vivian & Hormann, 2013). Structural causes exist at the organizational level as well as at the sector-wide level.

Organization-level causes include the lack of clear qualifications required of EDs; the lack of managerial accountability and board oversight; the notion ingrained in the culture that the noble cause of the mission trumps employee mistreatment; and the lack of resources and concomitant stresses placed on organizations. These factors are described in greater detail below.

The process by which individuals become EDs is haphazard. Frequently, people become EDs merely by virtue of passion for a cause. While passion for a cause is necessary, it is not sufficient for effective leadership, management, or supervision (Carver, 1997). Indeed, sometimes, the two are incompatible. When leaders' egos and identities become enmeshed with the nonprofits at which they work, organizational effectiveness is at risk (Dobbs, 2004; Vivian & Hormann, 2013).

Managerial accountability is a challenge in nonprofit organizations. For example, funders operate with limited information, receiving much of their information through the EDs of the organizations they fund. EDs monitor and control staff relationships with funders, affecting the flow of complete and accurate information. Likewise, boards of directors, charged with evaluating EDs, are ill-equipped for this function, and they rarely require 360-degree evaluations. The 360-degree evaluations are a challenge in any case; the small size of the vast majority of nonprofits makes anonymity almost impossible. Staff are unlikely to feel comfortable giving honest feedback in such circumstances.

As mentioned earlier, people often become EDs based on the passion that they have for a cause. Passion for a cause is not sufficient for effective leadership, management, or supervision. Passion for a cause does, however, lead to unrealistic expectations of what their employees can and should be willing to do and tolerate. Nonprofit EDs often expect that "passion for a cause" must be proven through unending service, and "working for the cause" is considered payment enough. Therefore, when staff express needs for time off, professional development, employment benefits, or work-life balance, it is not uncommon for them to be told they are betraying the cause or are not taking their jobs seriously. The mission of the organization is glorified at the expense of the staff's mental and physical well-being. Recent trends in accountability and high performance in the nonprofit sector have predominantly focused on being mission-focused and data-driven, but there is scant attention paid to what kind of productive workplaces and healthy employees are needed to make that sustainable.

Because nonprofits are expected to do more with less, bullying results from leaders feeling squeezed. Funder demands to minimize administrative costs and focus on programming puts EDs in a position of exaggerating their organization's successes and understating their administrative costs (Barden, 2015). Low annual budgets result in leaders operating with a mind-set of scarcity. This scarcity mind-set is a fertile ground for exploiting labor and minimizing staff salaries and benefits, all under the guise of the urgency of the organization's mission: "There is often a general understanding that if you don't accept the way you're being treated, you aren't truly committed to the movement" (Kacere, 2015, para. 12). Relatedly, lack of unrestricted funding also leads to a form of exploitation in which EDs improperly use interns and contractors to essentially do employee work.

Some *sector-wide causes* of toxic leadership in the nonprofit sector include the increased urgency caused by economic decline and the obsession with short-term results. In economic decline, wealthy donors hold onto their money or shift more of their funding to direct services. This reduction and shift creates greater pressure on nonprofits, a greater sense of scarcity, and greater stress on the ED to raise funds—all of which increase the likelihood of toxic leadership.

Nonprofits are increasingly expected to run like businesses. And the business sector has increasingly become obsessed with short-term results. That obsession with short-term, data-driven results is misplaced in a sector in which societal changes may take years or even decades to observe. In addition, societal change efforts require collective action, so EDs cannot necessarily splice apart exactly which parts of the collective impact result from their specific organization's efforts. Still, it is not uncommon for funders to expect unrealistic short-term results and clear organizational outcomes tracked to their funding. Naturally, the pressure EDs face from these unrealistic requirements has trickle-down negative effects on their organizational culture.

POSSIBLE SOLUTIONS

Researchers are just beginning to address the problem of toxic leadership in the nonprofit sector and are therefore at very preliminary stages regarding prevention and interventions. The following discussion is therefore an exploration of possible solutions.

One set of solutions is *preventive*. These measures are designed to minimize the possibility of toxic leadership. A more rigorous hiring process could incorporate preventive measures, such as including a requirement in the job description that ED applicants have had formal management training and using assessment tools to gauge emotional intelligence (Brightman, 2014). A promising sign in the sector is that organizations are starting to value managerial experience (Kim & Kunreuther, 2016).

Measures could also be put into place outside of the hiring process to prevent or minimize the potential for toxic leadership. For example, boards of directors could tie ED salaries to staff salaries, effectively reducing the large power inequity between them. We know that increased income inequality leads to increased narcissism (Wilkinson & Pickett, 2014).

Intervention measures are measures taken after toxicity manifests. These interventions include performance management, professional development, and termination or exit.

Some suggest traditional approaches to address the issue, using effective performance management (Eisenberg, 2002; Mitnick, n.d.). Some have suggested using 360-degree behavioral assessments (Brightman, 2013). However, if 360-degree assessments are not administered or interpreted properly, they can be ineffective. For example, boards may not recognize the need to use a third-party entity to administer the 360, to keep responses confidential, or to solicit multiple perspectives and not just the respondents identified by the leader. Interpreting 360 results requires looking at the results with respect to the leader-respondent power relationship and the divergence between the leader's self-evaluation and the respondent's. Also, in small organizations, 360s require particular care in administering, especially with regard to confidentiality. Some advocate for keeping open avenues for subordinates to give feedback, maintaining checks and balances, and moderating toxic behaviors immediately to reduce their harmful effects (Aubrey, 2012). Others recommend that 360s be used solely for development or coaching purposes and not for annual performance evaluations (Grote, 2011).

Professional development includes executive coaching and leadership development opportunities (Herman & Wilson, 2016). It is not clear whether professional development is effective in reducing toxic behavior in leaders. In fact, some leaders who have had management training, executive coaching, mentorship, or other professional development simply become more adept at manipulating and abusing their power in more subtle nonpublic ways. In our research, capacity builders and staff reported limited success with coaching and mentorship. First, leaders must be open to receiving critical feedback. Second, the approach must disarm the defensiveness, resistance, and aggression that arises when leaders consider feedback threatening. Each personality type requires a different approach and coaching strategy, and leaders seem to respond more positively by having mentorship from more seasoned leaders with a similar personality type to themselves. Third, the coach or mentor must be able to report results to the board (Kets de Vries, 2014; Williams, 2016).

Coupling executive coaching or other professional development with staff support mechanisms, anonymous 360-degree evaluations, and exit interviews is a fruitful avenue to explore, as together these strategies are likely to yield more positive results than an individual strategy on its own (Johnson, 2016; Kets de Vries, 2014). When all else fails, it is possible to terminate the leader (although nonprofits have also been known to simply wait, knowing the leader will eventually depart). While this may seem to offer a temporary fix to the problem, toxic leadership leaves dysfunctional organizations in its wake. Even with a new leader, the organization continues to operate under the same conditions as the previous ED. Staff continue to be demoralized and suspicious (Vivian & Hormann, 2013). Firing may also just migrate the issue to another organization. To effectively use the firing of an ED to set the stage for healing and recovery, those working in or with the organization need to give attention to staff recovery and healing the organizational culture (Taylor, 2014).

Funders have a potential role to play as well. They could offer professional development funding for entire teams rather than only leadership, helping to level the playing field and create leadership pipelines; they could test for toxic leadership with appropriate questions in grant applications; or they could actively intervene with technical assistance. In egregious cases (such as misappropriation of funds), funders have been known to require their grantees to accept technical assistance. And as a final resort, they could (and some have chosen to) defund an organization. When that happens, organizations dissolve (Cohen, 2012; Heintz, 2013). This is an outcome everyone in the sector works to avoid and is one reason that staff are hesitant to come forward about their experiences. The damage to the organization, the mission, and even the sector overall are potentially very costly indeed (Harshbarger & Crafts, 2007).

CONCLUSION

The unique characteristics of the nonprofit sector both strengthen organizations in the sector as well as create the conditions in which toxic leadership is difficult to prevent, observe, or stop. We are still at the initial stages of understanding the full extent and impacts of workplace bullying on individuals, organizations, and employment sectors overall. Nevertheless, emerging research offers more information about the effects of workplace bullying and toxic leadership in the nonprofit sector. And emerging best practices offer insights and tools toward building healthy organizational cultures and supporting healthy, emotionally intelligent leadership.

REFERENCES

Alexander, D. (2013, March 21). Inequitable salaries at nonprofits are a kind of bullying. *Chronicle of Philanthropy*. Retrieved from https://www.philanthropy.com/article/Inequitable-Salaries-at/196071

Aubrey, D. W. (2012). *Strategy research project: The effective of toxic leadership* (Master's strategy research project). United States Army War College, Carlisle Barracks, Pennsylvania.

Barden, P. (2015, April 20). Overhead: Time to pull our heads out of the sand? [Blog post]. Retrieved from http://npengage.com/nonprofit-management/overhead-time-to-pull-our-heads-out-of-the-sand

Bedsworth, W., Gregory, A. G., & Howard, D. (2008, April). Nonprofit overhead costs: Breaking the vicious cycle of misleading reporting, unrealistic expectations, and pressure to conform. *Bridgespan Group*. Retrieved from http://www.bridgespan.org/getattachment/93a03c17-154b-4cea-b7e7-5020f1c1ffec/Nonprofit-Overhead-Costs-Break-the-Vicious-Cycle.aspx

Berman, R. (2016, March 21). Wounded trust in charities: High overhead costs indicate a wasteful approach to helping. *Washington Times*. Retrieved from http://www.washingtontimes.com/news/2016/mar/21/richard-berman-wounded-trust-in-charities

Blackney, B. (2013, August 6). The debilitating effects of micromanagement [Blog post]. Retrieved from http://www.portical.org/blog/micromanagement/2459.htm

Bloom, S. (2006). *Organizational stress as a barrier to trauma-sensitive change and system transformation*. NASMHPD Publications. Retrieved from http://www.nasmhpd.org/sites/default/files/Bloom%20Organizational%20Stress%20FINAL%20121806.pdf

Bloom, S. L., & Farragher, B. (2010). *Destroying sanctuary: The crisis in human service delivery systems*. New York: Oxford University Press.

Bloom, S. L., & Farragher, B. (2013). *Restoring sanctuary: A new operating system for trauma-informed systems of care*. New York: Oxford University Press.

Brandt, J. (2013, October 3). Overhead costs: The obsession must stop [Blog post]. Retrieved from http://ssir.org/articles/entry/overhead_costs_the_obsession_must_stop

Brightman, B. (2013, December 12). How to overcome the 6 most toxic employee behaviors. *Fast Company: Leadership Now*. Retrieved from http://www.fastcompany.com/3023318/leadership-now/how-to-overcome-the-6-most-toxic-employee-behaviors

Brightman, B. (2014, October 2). Preventing toxic behavior at work [Blogpost]. Retrieved from http://bairdbrightman.blogspot.com/2014/10/preventing-toxic-behavior-at-work.html

Carbonara, S. (2012). *Manager's guide to employee engagement*. Columbus, OH: McGraw-Hill Education.

Carver, J. (1997). *Boards that make a difference: A new design for leadership in nonprofit and public organizations* (2nd ed.). San Francisco, CA: Jossey-Bass.

Cavaiola, A. A., & Lavender, N. J. (2000). *Toxic coworkers*. Oakland, CA: New Harbinger Publications.

Center for Community Change. (2014). Change starts here: A report on the center for community change and its continuing journey to individual and organizational transformation. Retrieved from http://www.communitychange.org/wp-content/uploads/2014/11/CCC_Future_Report.pdf

Clarke, M. (Ed.). (2012). *People practices for sustainable organizations: Social justice approaches to human resources management*. Retrieved from http://www.roadmapconsulting.org

Cohen, R. (2010, June 21). Nonprofit salaries: Achieving parity with the private sector. *Nonprofit Quarterly*. Retrieved from https://nonprofitquarterly.org/2010/06/21/nonprofit-salaries-achieving-parity-with-the-private-sector

Cohen, R. (2012, August 29). Faces of the fallen: Nonprofits folding after federal cuts. *Nonprofit Quarterly*. Retrieved from https://nonprofitquarterly.org/2012/08/29/faces-of-the-fallen-nonprofits-folding-after-federal-cuts

Davis, E. (2007). *Young nonprofit professionals: Preparing the path for leadership*. Retrieved from http://download.2164.net/PDF-newsletters/preparingthepath.pdf

DeCarlo, D. (2004). *eXtreme project management: Using leadership, principles, and tools to deliver value in the face of volatility*. Hoboken, NJ: John Wiley & Sons.

Dobbs, S. M. (2004). Some thoughts about nonprofit leadership. In R. E. Riggio & S. S. Orr (Eds.), *Improving leadership in nonprofit organizations* (pp. 11–18). San Francisco, CA: Jossey-Bass.

Eisenberg, P. (2002, October 17). The buck stops with the board of directors—or at least it should. *Chronicle of Philanthropy, 15*(1). Retrieved from http://www.eisenhowerfoundation.org/docs/ChroniclePhilanthropy_Buckstops_021017.pdf

Francis, A., & Talansky, J. (2012). *Small nonprofits solving big problems*. Retrieved from http://www.nonprofitfinancefund.org/sites/default/files/ccer_final12-12.pdf

Grote, D. (2011). *How to be good at performance appraisals: Simple, effective, done right*. Brighton, MA: Harvard Business Review Press.

GuideStar, Better Business Bureau Wise Giving Alliance, & Charity Navigator. (2013). The overhead myth [Open letter]. Retrieved from http://overheadmyth.com

Harshbarger, S., & Crafts, A. (2007, December 21). The whistle-blower: Policy challenges for nonprofits. *Nonprofit Quarterly*. Retrieved from https://nonprofitquarterly.org/2007/12/21/the-whistle-blower-policy-challenges-for-nonprofits/

Heintz, P. (2013, September 17). After Feds pull funding, Vermont health co-op folds. *Seven Days*. Retrieved from http://www.sevendaysvt.com/OffMessage/archives/2013/09/17/after-feds-pull-funding-vermont-health-co-op-folds

Herman, M. L., & Wilson, E. (2016, May 10). The dark side of leadership. *Center for Nonprofit Studies at Austin Community College*. Retrieved from http://sites.austincc.edu/npo/the-dark-side-of-leadership

Herold, S. (2012, April 25). Toxic work environments in the reproductive health, rights, and justice world [Blog post]. Retrieved from http://abortiongang.org/2012/04/25/toxic-work-environments-in-the-reproductive-health-rights-and-justice-world

Internal Revenue Service. (2016). *Exempt organizations business master file extract* [Data file]. Retrieved from https://www.irs.gov/charities-non-profits/exempt-organizations-business-master-file-extract-eo-bmf

International Labour Organization, & International Finance Corporation. (2013, December). *Improving business outcomes by understanding what matters to workers*. Retrieved from http://betterwork.org/global/wp-content/uploads/Research-Brief-What-Matters-to-Workers-LR.pdf

Johnson, K. (2016, June 28). Toxic leadership 2: Its impact and how to address it. *Training Journal*. Retrieved from https://www.trainingjournal.com/articles/feature/toxic-leadership-2-its-impact-and-how-address-it

Josephson, B. (2015, March 22). Nonprofit overhead doesn't matter: Except when it does [Blog post]. Retrieved from http://www.huffingtonpost.com/brady-josephson/nonprofit-overhead-doesnt_b_6508830.html

Kacere, L. (2015, May 6). 6 things to do if your social justice job is a toxic environment [Blog post]. Retrieved from http://everydayfeminism.com/2014/09/social-justice-job-toxic

Kanter, B., & Sherman, A. (2016). *The happy, healthy nonprofit: Strategies for impact without burnout*. Hoboken, NJ: Wiley & Sons.

Kets de Vries, M. (2014, April). Coaching the toxic leader. *Harvard Business Review*. Retrieved from https://hbr.org/2014/04/coaching-the-toxic-leader

Kim, H., & Kunreuther, F. (2016). *Vision for change: A new wave of social justice leadership*. Retrieved from http://www.buildingmovement.org/pdf/FINALVisionForChange.pdf

Klein, K. (2003). "Outing" overhead. *Grassroots Fundraising Journal*, November/December. Retrieved from http://www.grassrootsfundraising.org/wp-content/uploads/2014/03/22_6_OutingOverhead.pdf

Landles-Cobb, L., Kramer, K., & Smith Milway, K. (2015, October 22). The nonprofit leadership development deficit. *Stanford Social Innovation Review*. Retrieved from http://ssir.org/articles/entry/the_nonprofit_leadership_development_deficit

La Piana Consulting, Inc. (2003). *Tool for assessing startup organizations: A due diligence supplement for grantmakers*. Retrieved from http://www.lapiana.org/portals/0/documents/tool%20for%20assessing%20startup%20organizations.pdf

Le, V. (2014, December 8). Can we all just admit there is no such thing as nonprofit sustainability? [Blog post]. Retrieved from http://nonprofitwithballs.com/tag/nonprofit-funding

Lipman-Blumen, J. (2005). *The allure of toxic leaders: Why we follow destructive bosses and corrupt politicians—and how we can survive them*. New York: Oxford University Press.

Lipsky, L. (2009). *Trauma stewardship: An everyday guide to caring for self while caring for others*. San Francisco, CA: Berrett-Koehler Publishers.

Manzo, P. (2004). The real salary scandal. *Stanford Social Innovation Review*. Retrieved from http://ssir.org/articles/entry/the_real_salary_scandal

Maravelas, A. (2005). *How to reduce workplace conflict and stress*. Wayne, NJ: Career Press.

Masaoka, J., & Zimmerman, S. (2014). A board member's guide to nonprofit overhead [Blog post]. Retrieved from http://blueavocado.org/content/board-members-guide-nonprofit-overhead

McAndrews, C. (2010). *What works: Developing successful multigenerational leadership*. Retrieved from http://www.buildingmovement.org/pdf/what_works.pdf

Mitnick, E. R. (n.d.). *Transforming toxic employees into positive performers: Essential and effective management skills to improve employee performance* [PowerPoint slides]. Retrieved from https://www.mma.org/resources-mainmenu-182/doc_view/293-transforming-toxic-employees-into-positive-performers

National Center for Charitable Statistics. (2016). *Quick facts about nonprofits*. Retrieved from http://nccs.urban.org/statistics/quickfacts.cfm

No Bullying: Let's Stop Cruelty @ Work. (2013, May 22). Workplace bullying in nonprofit organizations [Blog post]. Retrieved from http://www.nblsc.org/?p=94

Opportunity Knocks. (2010). *Opportunity Knocks nonprofit retention and vacancy report 2010*. Retrieved from http://commongoodcareers.org/assets/pdf/Retention_Vacancy_Report.pdf

Pettijohn, S. L., Boris, E. T., De Vita, C. J., & Fyffe, S. D. (2013, December). *Nonprofit-government contracts and grants: Findings from the 2013 national survey*. Retrieved from http://www.urban.org/sites/default/files/alfresco/publication-pdfs/412962-Nonprofit-Government-Contracts-and-Grants-Findings-from-the-National-Survey.PDF

Pfeffer, J. (1998). *The human equation: Building profits by putting people first*. Brighton, MA: Harvard Business Press.

Plas, J. M. (2013). *Person-centered leadership: An American approach to participatory management*. Thousand Oaks, CA: Sage Publications.

Pon, S. (2016, June 22). Giving USA 2016 report: $1B+ given each day in 2015 [Blog post]. Retrieved from http://grantspace.org/blog/giving-usa-2016-1b-given-each-day-in-2015

Schmidt, A. (2016, May 19). Is exploiting workers key to your nonprofit enterprise model? The new overtime requirements. *Nonprofit Quarterly*. Retrieved from https://nonprofitquarterly.org/2016/05/19/is-exploiting-workers-key-to-your-enterprise-model-nonprofits-and-the-new-overhead-requirements/#

School of Unity and Liberation (SOUL). (2006). *Support and accountability manual: SOUL's organizational development and supervision model*. Retrieved from http://www.schoolofunityandliberation.org/soul_sec/resources/re-shp_manuals.html

Snibe, A. C. (2006, Fall). Overhead isn't everything. *Stanford Social Innovation Review*. Retrieved from http://ssir.org/articles/entry/overhead_isnt_everything

Solomon, J., & Sandahl, Y. (2007). *Stepping up or stepping out: A report on the readiness of next generation nonprofit leaders.* Retrieved from http://www.ynpn.org/stepping_up_or_stepping_out

Song, U. (2014, April). A funder's message to other funders about overhead [Blog post]. Retrieved from http://blueavocado.org/content/funders-message-other-funders-about-overhead

Straughan, B. (2003). *Managing in hard times.* Retrieved from http://www.rmnat.org/wp-content/uploads/2013/04/Managing_in_Hard_Times_full_000.pdf

Taylor, G. T. (2014). *Transformation and reconciliation in the toxic workplace* (Unpublished master's thesis). Fresno Pacific University, Fresno, California.

TCC Group. (2011, July). *Strengthening organizations to mobilize Californians: Lessons learned from a major initiative to build the capacity of civic engagement nonprofits.* Retrieved from http://www.tccgrp.com/pdfs/Strengthening_Organizations-Lessons_Learned.pdf

Truit, J. (2012, April 25). Quick hit: Toxic workplaces in the reproductive health, rights, and justice fields [Blog post]. Retrieved from http://feministing.com/2012/04/25/quick-hit-toxic-workplaces-in-the-reproductive-health-rights-and-justice-fields/

U.S. Bureau of Labor Statistics. (2014, October 21). Nonprofits account for 11.4 million jobs, 10.3 percent of all private sector employment. *Economics Daily.* Retrieved from http://www.bls.gov/opub/ted/2014/ted_20141021.htm

U.S. Bureau of Labor Statistics. (2016, February). Nonprofits in America: New research data on employment, wages, and establishments. *Monthly Labor Review.* Retrieved from http://www.bls.gov/opub/mlr/2016/article/nonprofits-in-america.htm

Vivian, P., & Hormann, S. (2013). *Organizational trauma and healing.* North Charleston, NC: Author.

Weinstein, B. (1998). *I hate my boss!: How to survive and get ahead when your boss is a tyrant, control freak, or just plain nuts!* New York: McGraw-Hill.

Wilkinson, R., & Pickett, K. (2014, February 2). How inequality hollows out the soul. *New York Times.* Retrieved from http://opinionator.blogs.nytimes.com/2014/02/02/how-inequality-hollows-out-the-soul/?_r=0

Williams, R. (2015). *Eye of the storm: How mindful leaders can transform chaotic workplaces.* Vancouver, Canada: Author.

Williams, R. (2016, February 15). The rise of toxic leaders [Blog post]. Retrieved from https://coachfederation.org/blog/index.php/5797

Epilogue

An Agenda for Moving Forward

David C. Yamada and Maureen Duffy

This project has been rooted in the presumption that research, analysis, and practice join together in understanding, preventing, and responding to workplace mobbing and bullying. We hope that the preceding chapters have reinforced that conviction in ways that are helpful and informative to our readers.

This epilogue gives us an opportunity to suggest where we go from here, by offering a proposed agenda that builds on the contents of these volumes. Systems of employment relations, mental health care, law and dispute resolution, and research and public education all play important roles in preventing and responding to mobbing and bullying behaviors. We offer the following comments as food for thought on how they operate as individual and component parts.

ORGANIZATIONAL PREVENTION AND RESPONSE

Overall, we are encouraged by the growing attention now being devoted to mobbing and bullying behaviors by scholars and practitioners in fields such as industrial and organizational psychology, occupational health psychology, business management and human resources, and labor relations. Professional and academic conferences and seminars regularly cover workplace bullying, mobbing, and incivility, joined by a burgeoning number of journal articles and books—many of which are cited in these volumes.

However, we still have a long way to go. Survey data discussed in the preceding chapters clearly show that bullying and mobbing are serious problems in the American workplace, that too many employers are not adequately responding to these behaviors, and that workers and organizations are suffering the consequences. Furthermore, merely adopting policies and establishing procedures are not enough. As David Yamada wrote in an article applying principles of ethical leadership to workplace bullying (Yamada, 2008),

The real test appears, however, when leaders who profess to abhor bullying are asked to address specific, inconvenient occurrences of such behavior.... For example:
- What does a manager do when she learns that one of her best friends in the office has been a serial bully and most recently was responsible for the departure of an excellent worker who resigned to avoid facing further mistreatment?
- How does an organization respond to an administrative assistant who is suffering from depression because of bullying and retaliation that occurred after she rightfully accused her highly-productive supervisor of engaging in an unethical business practice?
- What does a human resources director do when confronted with a socially quirky, adequately performing employee who fears going to work because he is being bullied and ostracized by productive, more popular co-workers? (p. 59).

In the United States, since the 1980s, when the early research about workplace bullying and mobbing started to get the attention of stakeholders, the focus necessarily has been on identifying and acknowledging the nature and scope of the problem. In boardrooms and in courtrooms around the country, there is still active resistance to acknowledging that the problem of workplace bullying and mobbing exists, accompanied by a propensity to deny its significance by blaming individual workers for their misperceptions of it or for having allegedly difficult personalities that invite aggression toward them.

Yet, the body of research and practice documented in these volumes is overwhelming with respect to the nature of the negative behaviors involved in workplace bullying and mobbing, the social and organizational processes that fuel it, and the significant health and psychosocial harm to targets and their families that result from it. Healthy organizations will either begin or continue to address workplace bullying and mobbing by policy development and education about what it looks like and how it harms workers and the organization.

The key variable in determining organizational response will be leadership buy-in and support of efforts to reduce and prevent workplace bullying and mobbing. With leadership acknowledgment and buy-in, the sticky questions about how to manage the inevitably complicated interpersonal dynamics reflected in the questions above will be easier to address. Leadership acknowledgment and buy-in create a conversational space within organizations to talk about how we expect to treat each other in the workplace and how we might respond when our expectations and standards are not met. In terms of protection of health in the workplace, the future is here, and it unquestionably includes organizational responsibility and accountability for the protection not only of the physical health of workers but also of their psychological health.

MENTAL HEALTH AND COACHING

Building a larger cadre of trauma-informed mental health treatment providers who are familiar with workplace bullying and mobbing must be a top priority. Among the unmet stakeholder needs in terms of responding to workplace bullying and mobbing, mental health treatment ranks with the highest. Over and again, we have encountered individuals who have not been able to find counselors and therapists who comprehend the traumatic impacts of their abusive work experiences.

This is ironic but not surprising. Back in 1998, when Gary and Ruth Namie wrote their first prototype edition (Namie & Namie, 1998) of what would evolve into the leading informational and self-help guide on workplace bullying, their overwhelming focus was on the experiences of targets and how to help them. Over the past two decades, both research and countless individual accounts have documented the health-harming effects of bullying and mobbing behaviors. However, any casual survey of professional conference agendas for mental health providers reveals a paucity of educational programming devoted to working with clients and patients who are seeking this kind of help. In addition, the psychological literature concerning mobbing and bullying is much richer in the organizational realm as opposed to clinical interventions.

But perhaps we are seeing signs of positive change. For example, in the spring of 2016, *Counseling Today* ran a cover story on bullying behaviors, including the workplace, urging that "counselors need to increase their understanding of bullying in all of its forms" (Meyers, 2016). The piece extensively profiled the counseling and coaching work of Jessi Eden Brown, who coauthored chapters 13 and 14 to this book project. Also, later that year, Maureen Duffy presented a keynote address about counseling targets of workplace mobbing and bullying at the annual conference of the American Mental Health Counselors Association. Both of these developments indicate that the mental health community is placing greater importance on offering services to those who are suffering from the effects of abusive work environments.

Nonetheless, the current reality is that very few mental health professionals have an understanding of the dynamics of workplace bullying and mobbing or experience in working with targets and their families. There is an urgent need for formalized training for mental health professionals in the area of workplace bullying and mobbing to increase the number of professionals with the requisite skills to assess and treat targets and their families. Given the prevalence rates for workplace bullying and mobbing in the United States, the absence of skilled mental health providers in this area is glaring and represents a public health challenge that needs to be addressed as a top priority.

Although the field of coaching remains something of a cottage industry, this modality holds promise for helping targets in at least three ways: First, coaching can serve a triage function by helping targets to assess their situations and to identify potentially helpful resources. Second, coaching can help those who are well into the recovery stages from their abusive work experiences and are now ready to make more affirmative choices for the future. Third, and finally, the niche specialty of career coaching can help targets transition into new jobs and vocations.

We offer more tempered enthusiasm regarding therapeutic and coaching interventions for individuals who engage in mobbing and bullying behaviors. For those whose psychological profiles suggest psychopathic, sociopathic, or severely narcissistic traits, psychotherapy or coaching may be of limited application, at least as a realistic workplace intervention tool. Unfortunately, such individuals can be the main drivers of some of the most virulent, targeted bullying and mobbing actions.

However, plenty of workers who engage in such behaviors are not suffering from a clinically diagnosable personality disorder. Samples of the general population indicate that only about 1 percent of females and 3 percent of males have antisocial personality disorder, the kind of personality associated with disregard for the feelings and rights of others (American Psychiatric Association, 2000). Thus, the vast majority of workers who participate in abusive and aggressive behaviors toward others in the workplace do not suffer from the personality disorder most associated with a willingness to trample on the rights of others. As Maureen Duffy and Len Sperry (2014) put it, "Most people who display aggressive, mobbing-type behaviors in the workplace are 'normal'" (p. 182).

Accordingly, individual psychopathology is but one factor that potentially contributes to workplace mobbing and bullying behaviors, and in most instances, it is likely not relevant at all. Overall, in the case of the proverbial "bad boss" or "nightmare coworker," the usefulness of therapy or coaching depends on how receptive those individuals are to potential interventions and how determined the organization is to promote a fair-minded, dignity-embracing, and safe workplace by finding solutions for abusive behavior.

LAW AND PUBLIC POLICY

American legislatures are slowly becoming more hospitable to Healthy Workplace laws that respond to bullying and mobbing behaviors. For now, however, the lack of comprehensive legal protections against workplace bullying and mobbing leaves workers vulnerable to psychological abuse.

America lags behind many countries around the world in not having direct legal protections against workplace bullying and mobbing. Canada, Australia, and many European nations are among the jurisdictions that have enacted laws, regulations, and codes in response to these forms of workplace mistreatment.

Widespread adoption of the Healthy Workplace Bill or similar legislation would not only provide targets of severe workplace bullying with a legal claim for damages, but also provide employers with legal incentives to prevent and effectively respond to these behaviors. This, in turn, would prompt greater attention by organizational leaders and employees, including, hopefully, the adoption and actual implementation of policies and practices designed to address bullying and mobbing behaviors. Furthermore, by proclaiming that the law should intervene when these behaviors become targeted and health harming, we would be affirming, as a populace, that a decent society does not condone these behaviors.

In addition to enacting Healthy Workplace legislation, at least two additional areas need to be addressed in the law and public policy realm. First, targets of bullying and mobbing need a stronger, nonlitigious safety net of employee and public benefits to provide income replacement and health care to help them cope with their situations and to make necessary job transitions. Paid family and medical leave, workers' compensation, and unemployment benefits and comprehensive, affordable health care are chief among them.

Second, and concededly this is a much larger topic, our systems of resolving legal disputes need to reduce the stress and anxiety of employment litigation, especially for those who have already experienced severe mistreatment at work and face daunting odds toward obtaining relief:

> Although the creation of individual employment protections was spurred in part by civil rights advocacy backed by the solidarity of social movements, workers often must effectuate these rights in solitary fashion, pursuing stressful, lengthy, and expensive legal proceedings, typically without the benefit of large group or union support. . . . Modern employment litigation all too often encompasses the David vs. Goliath scenario of an aggrieved worker and a small plaintiffs' law firm vying against a large company armed with an overstaffed team of attorneys. (Yamada, 2009, p. 535)

CHANGING WORKPLACE STANDARDS

While responsibility for initiating organizational change to prevent workplace bullying and mobbing rests squarely on the shoulders of leadership, all organizational members must ultimately be involved in organizational culture change that will lead to psychologically safe workplaces for all. Responsibility for treating one's coworkers, supervisors, and subordinates appropriately and with dignity is a shared responsibility that binds each member of an organization. Accountable workplaces in which every person takes seriously the obligation to communicate ethically and to behave appropriately requires that the model or schema in use within the organization is one in which all members are regarded as responsible adults, not as demanding parents or as wayward children. The templates of parent-child relationships and all the approval-seeking and rebellious behavior that goes along with them have long ceased to be useful models for workplace relationships.

An emerging model for workplace practices and relationships is the values-driven workplace, also variously referred to as a conscious culture, an intentional workplace, a high-performing workplace, a mindful workplace, or an employee-driven workplace. The key standard in such workplaces is that organizational values are spelled out and that actions are aligned with those values and the degree of alignment between values and actions is routinely assessed. For an organization to be truly values-driven, the match between values and actions has to be real and in practice, not just on paper. In a values-driven workplace that upholds the values of respect and care, for example, it would not be acceptable behavior to engage in negative gossip about a coworker, to gang up on someone, to exclude a coworker from workplace conversations or interactions, to not give credit where credit is due, or to shut someone out of information loops necessary for that person to get the job done. The responsibility for behaving consciously and respectfully cuts across the entire organization at every level.

What are acceptable and unacceptable standards for workplace behavior change over time. Prior to changes in the law and in levels of personal awareness, it was common for jokes and comments of a sexist and homophobic nature to be shared openly and repeated. These kinds of comments have not been wholly eliminated from the workplace, but their utterance has been reduced and brings with them the risk of personal sanctions such as discipline or firing and legal actions such as discrimination lawsuits. As awareness of the nature of the abusive actions involved in workplace bullying and mobbing and of the harm inflicted on targets by them increases, these bullying and mobbing behaviors will also change from being tolerated to being unacceptable, especially if laws like the Healthy Workplace Bill are adopted.

TOWARD A "DIGNITARIAN" SOCIETY

In terms of the bigger picture, the concept of human dignity relates strongly to workplace mobbing and bullying. For example, Robert Fuller, a physicist and former college president, has called upon us to create a "dignitarian" movement devoted to advancing individual dignity (Fuller, 2006). Fuller believes that the ongoing presence of "rankism," which he defines as "abuses of power associated with rank," presents the main obstacle to building such a society (Fuller, 2006, p. 7). He has placed workplace bullying squarely within a dignitarian framework—calling it a form of "archetypal rankism"—while expressing optimism that we are "approaching a tipping point" in responding to it (Fuller, 2006, p. 65).

Robert Fuller's work dovetails comfortably with that of Human Dignity and Humiliation Studies (HumanDHS), a "global, transdisciplinary fellowship of researchers, practitioners, activists, artists, and others who collaborate in a spirit of mutual support to understand the complex dynamics of humiliation, especially as it relates to violence" (Hartling, Lindner, Britton, & Spalthoff, 2013, p. 134). Founded by Evelin Lindner, a physician and psychologist, HumanDHS is dedicated to advancing human dignity and to understanding the experience of humiliation as a root cause of aggression and violence.

At first glance, even the most horrific mobbing and bullying behaviors may not appear to rise to the level of global human rights abuses that concern many members of the HumanDHS community. However, David Yamada, a HumanDHS board member, has found a very receptive audience for his work on workplace bullying at the organization's annual workshops, sounding consistent messages of abuse, injustice, and trauma.

Simply put, workplace bullying and mobbing are dignity violations that create enormous human carnage. Workplace aggressors often intend to shame and humiliate their targets and drive them out of the organization. These reasons alone underscore why we must pursue all effective ways to reduce the frequency and severity of these abusive behaviors and help those who have been wounded by them.

REFERENCES

American Psychiatric Association. (2000). *Diagnostic and statistical manual of mental disorders* (4th ed., text revision). Washington, D.C.: American Psychiatric Association.

Duffy, M., & Sperry, L. (2014). *Overcoming mobbing: A recovery guide for workplace aggression and bullying*. New York: Oxford University Press.

Fuller, R. W. (2006). *All rise: Somebodies, nobodies, and the politics of dignity*. San Francisco, CA: Berrett-Koehler Publishers.

Hartling, L. M., Lindner, E. G., Britton, M., & Spalthoff, U. (2013). Beyond humiliation: Toward learning that dignifies the lives of all people. In G. P. Hampson, M. Rich-Tolsma (Eds.), *Studies, reflections, questions* (Vol. 2 of *Leading transformative higher education*, pp. 134–146). Olomouc, Czech Republic: Palacký University Olomouc Press.

Meyers, L. (2016, April 21). Fertile grounds for bullying. *Counseling Today*. Retrieved from http://ct.counseling.org/2016/04/fertile-grounds-for-bullying

Namie, G., & Namie, R. (1998). *Bullyproof yourself at work!: Personal strategies to recognize & stop the hurt from harassment.* Benicia, CA: DoubleDoc Press.

Yamada, D. C. (2008). Workplace bullying and ethical leadership. *Journal of Values-Based Leadership, 1*(2), 49–62.

Yamada, D. C. (2009). Human dignity and American employment law. *University of Richmond Law Review, 43*(2), 523–569.

About the Editors and Contributors

EDITORS

MAUREEN DUFFY, PhD, is a workplace consultant to organizations and individuals and a preeminent authority on workplace mobbing behaviors. She is coauthor of *Mobbing: Causes, Consequences, and Solutions* and *Overcoming Mobbing: A Recovery Guide for Workplace Aggression and Bullying.* She is also a family therapist who works with targets and their families. Her clinical and consulting work focuses on workplace mobbing and bullying. Maureen has been a frequent featured speaker at national conferences addressing workplace issues.

DAVID C. YAMADA, JD, is a professor of law and director of the New Workplace Institute at Suffolk University Law School in Boston. David is an internationally recognized authority on the legal, public policy, and organizational implications of workplace bullying. He wrote the first comprehensive analysis of workplace bullying and American employment law (*Georgetown Law Journal*, 2000), and his antibullying Healthy Workplace Bill is the template for American law reform efforts in this realm. He is a frequent speaker and presenter at regional, national, and international conferences and is widely quoted and cited in articles on workplace bullying and employee relations generally. His *Minding the Workplace* blog is a popular source of commentary on work, workers, and workplaces. David received his JD degree from New York University School of Law in 1985.

CONTRIBUTORS

TONY BELAK, JD, was ombuds at the University of Louisville and a cofounder of the International Center for Compassionate Organizations (http://compassionate.center), which currently has initiatives in leadership, conflict management, policing and peacekeeping, and public information. He is also cofounder of the 4Civility Institute (http://4civility.com) established to prevent and correct incivility and bullying. He was senior dispute resolution counsel for the Department of Veterans Affairs and established a shared neutral program among all federal agencies in the region, which was instrumental in the creation of the U.S. Postal Service's internal EEO mediation program (REDRESS), where he continues to serve as a mediator, and he was an initial member of the Civil Justice Reform Act Committee for the Western District of Kentucky, a former assistant commonwealth attorney, a special assistant U.S. attorney, and president of the Federal Bar Association, Kentucky Chapter. He is an arbitrator for the Financial Industry Regulatory Authority (FINRA).

PEGGY ANN BERRY, PhD, MSN, RN, is the CEO of Thrive_At_Life: Working Solutions, providing occupational services and training to employers and individuals regarding physically and psychologically safe workplaces. She received a National Institutes of Occupational Safety and Health Education Resource Center grant and stipend for her master's in nursing and PhD through the University of Cincinnati as well as internal and external grants to study workplace bullying. She is an American Nurses Foundation Scholar and a founding fellow of the Workplace Bullying Academy. Novice nurse productivity following workplace bullying (2012), her first research-based article as co- and first author was awarded the 2013 Best of Journal of Nursing Scholarship for Profession, World Health, and Health Systems. She was a commentator in Dellasega and Volpe's (2013) *Toxic Nursing*. She continues collaboration and publication on her dissertation research in workplace bullying.

JO BLASE, PhD, is research professor emerita of educational administration and leadership at the University of Georgia and a former school administrator. Since receiving her PhD from the University of Colorado, her research has focused on instructional and transformational leadership, school governance and reform, professional development, the principalship, and discourse analysis of principal-teacher communications. She also conducts research on discourse among physicians and consults with physicians in U.S. medical centers. Professor Blase has received research and teaching awards, is an expert witness, and holds international doctoral faculty appointments. She has published over 100 academic articles, chapters, and books. Her nine book editions include such best sellers as *Handbook of Instructional Leadership*. With Joseph Blase, she conducted seminal studies of administrative mistreatment of teachers and coauthored *Breaking the Silence: Overcoming the Problem of Principal Mistreatment of Teachers*.

JOSEPH BLASE, PhD, is research professor emeritus of educational administration and leadership at the University of Georgia. Since receiving his PhD from Syracuse University, his research has focused on educational micropolitics, school reform, transformational leadership, the principalship, principal-teacher relationships, and principal mistreatment. His work on school-level micropolitics received the Davis Memorial Award given by the University Council for Educational Administration, and he is recognized as an elite scholar among the *Most Productive and Influential Scholars of Educational Administration* in the world. Professor Blase has published over 120 academic articles, chapters, and books. His 13 book editions include the winner of the Critic's Choice Award of the American Education Studies Association and several best sellers, such as *Bringing Out the Best in Teachers*. He is coauthor, with Jo Blase, of seminal studies of administrative mistreatment of teachers and the book *Breaking the Silence: Overcoming the Problem of Principal Mistreatment of Teachers*.

JESSI EDEN BROWN, MS, LMHC, LPC, NCC, is a licensed psychotherapist in private practice in Seattle, Washington. As the professional coach and former administrator of the Workplace Bullying Institute, Jessi has garnered national recognition as a counselor-expert in the area of workplace bullying. She works with hundreds of bullied targets annually through professional counseling and coaching services offered in the United States and worldwide.

ELLEN PINKOS COBB, JD, is the author of *Workplace Bullying and Harassment: New Developments in International Law* (2017). She is a senior regulatory and legal analyst at the Isosceles Group, an environmental health and safety consultancy, in Boston, Massachusetts, and a founding fellow of the Workplace Bullying Academy. Ellen also has years of experience in the employment discrimination field as a neutral fact finder for state and federal agencies and is a certified Equal Employment Opportunity investigator. She has been tracking international laws and developments in workplace bullying, violence, harassment, discrimination, and stress since 2010. A magna cum laude graduate of Bowdoin College, she received her JD from the University of Connecticut School of Law.

RENEE L. COWAN, PhD, is an affiliate assistant professor of communication at Queens University of Charlotte. She has published numerous journal articles on workplace bullying in journals such as *Management Communication Quarterly*, *Human Resource Management Journal*, *Personnel Review*, and others. She cochairs the National Communication Association's Anti-Bullying Task Force.

JOHN-ROBERT CURTIN, PhD, is a senior fellow and executive director of the 4Civility Institute, Louisville, Kentucky, and is the author of *An Exploratory Study of Existing State Anti-Bullying Statutes* (2016), Lambert Academic Press. The 4Civility Institute provides mediation training, ombuds training, certifications, software reporting systems, restorative justice, and behavioral transition practice solutions to schools, businesses, and organizations. He has extensive experience in alternative dispute resolution, restorative justice, education, training, and in antibullying efforts. He also the founded the Connected Learning Network, an education-based company, that has provided online services to over 120 schools, colleges, businesses, and organizations worldwide. John-Robert is also known for his work in public television, as an Emmy award-winning producer and station president. His PhD is from the University of Louisville in alternative dispute resolution. His academic background also includes degrees in creative writing and oceanography. He describes himself as a "serial social entrepreneur with an overcommitment addiction."

TERESA A. DANIEL, JD, PhD, serves as dean of the Human Resource Leadership Program at Sullivan University, based in Louisville, Kentucky. She is also chair of the HRL concentration in the university's PhD in management program. Her growing body of work on toxic leadership and workplace bullying has been actively supported by the Society for Human Resource Management through numerous interviews about her research and its implications and the publication of two of her books. She is the coauthor of *Stop Bullying at Work: Strategies and Tools for HR, Legal, & Risk Management Professionals* (2016) and was named as an initial fellow of the International Academy on Workplace Bullying, Mobbing, and Abuse in 2014.

CAROL FEHNER, BA, is a retired American Federation of Government Employees (AFGE) officer with the Social Security Administration. She received a Hammer Award for her work on the first benchmarking study under the government reinvention initiative. She teaches union members about workplace bullying.

SUSAN JOHNSON, RN, PhD, is an assistant professor of nursing and health care leadership at the University of Washington Tacoma. After working as a hospital staff nurse for over 20 years, she obtained her doctoral degree from the University of Washington Seattle in 2013. Her dissertation research was on managerial and organizational discourses of workplace bullying. For this work, Susan was honored with the Dissertation Award from the UW School of Nursing and was named March of Dimes Nurse of the Year (2012) in the category of "New Generation." Susan has written numerous journal articles and book chapters and has given presentations locally, nationally, and internationally on the subject of workplace bullying among nurses. She is a member of the American Nurses Association, and as a member of the Steering Committee on Workplace Violence and Incivility, she helped draft a position statement that also covers the topic of workplace bullying.

MELODY M. KAWAMOTO, MD, MS, is a retired occupational medicine and public health specialist with more than 25 years' experience in evaluating workplaces for health hazards.

LORALEIGH KEASHLY, PhD, is an associate professor in the Department of Communication and associate dean for Student and Curricular Affairs for the College of Fine, Performing and Communication Arts, Wayne State University, Detroit, Michigan. She is intrigued by workplace relationships because of how they affect the quality of our work, the meaning and identity we derive from it, and the overall workplace climate and culture. In her research and consulting, she has focused on tough and difficult relationships, for example, conflict and bullying with an eye to taking our understanding of the "why" and "how" and translating that into ways to ameliorate at the individual and organizational levels. Most recently, she has developed training in building bystander efficacy to take constructive action in challenging work situations. Her works in progress focus on the power of relationships at work and (in)civility in academia. She has published over 40 articles and book chapters.

KELLY H. KOLB, JD, is a shareholder in the Labor & Employment Section at Buchanan Ingersoll & Rooney PC. He received his undergraduate degree at Vanderbilt University and his JD degree from Washington University School of Law in St. Louis, Missouri. He is a frequent author, contributor, and lecturer on employment issues for publications and audiences across the country. He has been selected for inclusion in the Florida Super Lawyers list and was selected by his peers for inclusion in the 20th–23rd editions of *The Best Lawyers in America* list under the Employment Law–Management and Litigation–Labor and Employment category. Mr. Kolb currently serves on the board of directors for Habitat for Humanity of Broward County. He also serves as chair of the Business First Sub-Committee for the Greater Fort Lauderdale Chamber of Commerce and is on the Chamber's board of directors.

PAMELA LUTGEN-SANDVIK, PhD, is an associate professor at North Dakota State University–Fargo, teaching and researching organizational communication. She is the author of *Adult Bullying—A Nasty Piece of Work* and coeditor of *Destructive Organizational Communication*. She has published numerous monographs in such top-tier journals as *Journal of Management Studies, Organization,* and *Management Communication Quarterly.* National, Western States, and Central States Communication Associations have conferred to her research *Top Book* and numerous *Top Articles* and *Top Papers* awards. She has studied workplace bullying since the early 2000s, examining U.S. prevalence, effect on identity, worker emotions, sensemaking or trying to explain abuse, and a host of related topics. Dr. Lutgen-Sandvik's work has branched out to examine positive communication at work, especially the power of positive managerial communication on employees and organizations. Prior to working in academia, she was an administrator of nonprofit agencies dealing with domestic violence, sexual assault, and alcoholism–drug addiction treatment.

GARY NAMIE, PhD, and **RUTH NAMIE, PhD,** are pioneers of the U.S. Workplace Bullying movement begun in response to Ruth's abuse by a bullying woman supervisor. In 1997, they founded the Workplace Bullying Institute (workplacebullying.org), the first and only organization to combine help for targeted individuals; empirical research; books; public education; training for professionals, unions, and employers; legislative advocacy; expert witness services; and consulting to organizations. WBI's national scientific prevalence surveys are the most cited workplace bullying statistics in America. WBI is also the lead advocacy organization in U.S. states to enact the antibullying Healthy Workplace Bill. Together, the Drs. Namie authored the books *The Bully-Free Workplace* (2011) and *The Bully At Work,* 2nd ed. (2009). Gary serves as expert witness in litigation and arbitrations. He is a social psychologist and former university professor of management and psychology. Ruth holds a doctorate in clinical psychology.

JOEL H. NEUMAN, PhD, is emeritus associate professor of management and organizational behavior in the School of Business, State University of New York at New Paltz. His research and consulting activities focus on workplace aggression and bullying. His work has appeared in publications such as the *Journal of Applied Behavioral Science, Journal of Management, Journal of Vocational Behavior, Public Administration Quarterly, Employee Rights and Employment Policy Journal, Aggressive Behavior, Journal of Healthcare Management,* and the *Journal of Management & Organization.* His book chapters have been included in *Antisocial Behavior in Organizations, Bullying and Emotional Abuse in the Workplace, The Dark Side of Organizational Behavior, Counterproductive Work Behavior, The Destructive Side of Organizational Communication, Insidious Workplace Behavior,* the *Handbook of Unethical Work Behavior, Gender and the Dysfunctional Workplace, Work and Quality of Life,* and *Bullying in*

Higher Education. He is currently retired and living a nonaggressive life of travel and leisure.

MARY BETH RICKE, JD, is an associate attorney in the Labor & Employment Section at Buchanan Ingersoll & Rooney PC. She received her undergraduate degree from Rhodes College in Memphis, Tennessee, and her JD degree from Washington University School of Law in St. Louis, Missouri, in 2013. She was selected as a 2016 Florida Rising Star and included in the 2016 Florida Super Lawyers list. She routinely contributes articles to the Broward County Bar Association publication *The Barrister*. She is active in the charitable organization of the Junior League of Greater Fort Lauderdale.

PIETER J. ROSSOUW, PhD, is director of Mediros Clinical Solutions, the BRAINGro Institute, and the Neuropsychotherapy Institute—companies that provide training and conduct research in neurobiology and neuropsychotherapy. Pieter is professor in brain-based education at Central Queensland University and president of the International Association of Clinical Neuropsychotherapy. He conducts teaching and research in the fields of neurobiology and neuropsychotherapy as well as clinical training for clinicians, psychologists, and general practitioners. Pieter's latest books—*The Predictive 6 Factor Resilience Scale: Clinical Guidelines and Applications*, with Jurie Rossouw, and *Bullying: Taking Control*, with Melisa Kaya—were published in 2016. His other major works in applied neuroscience are *Neuropsychotherapy: Theoretical Underpinnings and Clinical Applications* and *BrainWise Leadership* (coauthored with Connie Henson). He is chief editor of the *International Journal for Neuropsychotherapy* and a member of the editorial boards of the *Journal of Psychiatry*, the *Journal of Psychology and Clinical Psychiatry*, and *The Neuropsychotherapist*.

GREGORY SOROZAN, MEd, is president of SEIU/NAGE Local R1-282 in Quincy, Massachusetts. Greg has served as president since the year 2000 and represents more than 3,000 professional-level state employees. Greg also serves as national vice president to SEIU/NAGE, representing more than 60,000 members. As president, he negotiated one of the first antibullying clauses in the nation into the NAGE Contract Bargaining Agreement in 2009. Greg is a licensed certified social worker and is experienced in child welfare practices. Knowledge of interactional patterns of behavior connects family and work. Greg has served as a consultant and trainer for the National Resource Center on Family Based Services and has served on the Professional Advisory Committee for the Workplace Bullying Institute. He is an experienced trainer and interventionist. "Each day brings its own rewards."

LEN SPERRY, MD, PhD, is professor of mental health counseling at Florida Atlantic University and clinical professor of psychiatry and behavioral medicine at the Medical College of Wisconsin. He is coauthor of *Mobbing: Causes, Consequences, and Solutions* and *Overcoming Mobbing: A Recovery Guide for Workplace Aggression and Bullying*.

VEGA SUBRAMANIAM, MA, is a nonprofit consultant and leadership coach at Vega Mala Consulting in the Washington, D.C., metropolitan area. She holds an associate certified coach certification through the International Coach Federation. She is a member of the RoadMap consultant team and Maryland Nonprofits and serves as the board president of Training for Change.

BENJAMIN M. WALSH, PhD, is assistant professor of management at the University of Illinois at Springfield. His research program addresses interpersonal treatment in organizations, with a focus on understanding antecedents and outcomes of mistreatment experiences and the effectiveness of interventions designed to prevent workplace mistreatment. His research is published in outlets such as *Journal of Occupational Health Psychology*, *Applied Psychology: An International Review*, *Journal of Managerial Psychology*, *Stress and Health*, *Journal of Business and Psychology*, and *International Journal of Selection and Assessment*.

Index

Italicized numbers refer to figures and tables.

Absenteeism, 120, 204–205, 208, 210–211, 249, 359, 393, 395, 491, 570, 598. *See also* Presenteeism
Abuse. *See* Abusive supervision; Emotional abuse; Work abuse
Abusive supervision, 10, 66, 338, 482; definitions of, 12; effects of, 202; and labor union members, 428–429; perpetrators' characteristics, 63–65; and target personalities, 54; and teachers, 490
Abusive work environment: and bullying policies, 583; definitions of, 11, 16–17, 416, 498; effects of, 180, 204, 210; and family/medical leave, 426; and Healthy Workplace Bill, 11, 230, 415–416; and legislation, 415–416, 426, 430, 436, 498; and mental health services, 613
Adams, Andrea, 5, 16, 18, 381
Addiction. *See* Alcohol and drug abuse
Aggression. *See* Workplace aggression
Alcohol and drug abuse, 65, 171, 181, 182–183, 292, 309
Alvesson, Mats, 133
American Counseling Association, 318
American Psychiatric Association (APA), 224, 318, 342. *See also* *Diagnostic and Statistical Manual of Mental Disorders* (DSM)
Andersson, Lynne, 207, 368
Anxiety, 5, 88, 105–108, 111–112, 140, 145–146, 179, 184, 209, 292–293, 307, 309, 322, 347, 369, 391, 422, 481, 490, 563–564, 568, 575, 615
Arkansas Supreme Court, 422
Australian Human Rights Commission, 153

Balducci, Cristian, 114
Banas, Kasia, 137
Barling, Julian, 203, 205
Baron, Robert, 201
Batsche, George M., 153
Behavior classification and inventories, 36–39
Behavioral consequences of bullying, 204–206
Behaviors of bullying and mobbing, 14–16; and definitions, 3–13; measuring, 36–38; person-related, 36, 38; physical intimidation, 36, 38; work-related, 36, 38
Bergen, Daniel E., 213
Bergen Bullying Research Group (University of Bergen, Norway), 55
Bergman, Matt, 203, 207, 562

Bonfiglioli, Roberta, 114
Book, Angela S., 64–65
Breland, Jacob W., 63
Brodsky, Carroll M., 10
Brown, Jessi Eden, 71, 613
Bullying. *See* Workplace bullying; entries under Workplace bullying and mobbing
Burnazi, Laurela, 39, 41
Bystander action, 35
Bystander effect, 56, 377
Bystanders and witnesses: and conflict resolution, 266–267, 271, 273–275, 277, 279–280, 282–283; education of, 249, 399, 472, 529–530; and education sector, 517, 525, 529–530; and impact of bullying and mobbing, 205–207, 211; and vicarious and secondary victimization, 172–177, 181, 186, 188

Califano, Joseph A., 35, 41, 42
Camilleri, Joseph A., 64–65
Campaign Against Workplace Bullying, 5, 414
CareerBuilder, 33, 41, 42, 44
Chen, Serena, 63
Chesler, Phyllis, 57
Choi, Bongkyoo, 120
Civil rights, 57–58, 366, 370, 615
Civil Rights Act (1924), Title VII, 13–14, 212, 416–417, 423–424, 567
Coaching, 145, 227, 275; for aggressors and offenders, 276–277, 335–351; for bystanders, 279–280; case example, 326–329; coaching versus psychotherapy, 315–318; definitions of, 336–337; effectiveness of, 337; and human resources, 237, 238, 239, 245, 250–253; licensing and credentials, 317–318, 325–326; International Coach Federation (ICF), 316–317, 320; legal and regulatory issues, 325–326; practitioner skills, 323–325; process of coaching, 318–323; for targets, 278–279, 315–330. *See also* Consultants
Cognitive behavioral therapy, 307, 309, 337, 348–349
Cognitive processing therapy, 121
Cole, Richard T., 213
Comorbidities: definition of, 105; and PTSD, 107, 111, 116
Conflict resolution, 21, 70, 137, 264–286, 365; and bystanders and supporters, 279–280; and civility, 284–285; coaching offenders, 276–277; conflict roles, 266–267; and human resources, 243, 250, 252; and ombuds, 283–284, 388–393, 399–401; positive and negative conflict, 266; restorative justice myths and realities, 275–276; restorative justice steps, 273–275; restorative practices, 265–286; safe reporting, 270, 280–284, 286; and social pain, 137; and targets, 278–279; three-party system, 280–283
Consultants, 357–383; American employer attitudes and reactions, 362–363; antecedents to traditional consulting, 357–362; goals, 373–375; indirect alternatives to, 364–370; and legal system, 381–383; and policies, 370–373; and unions, 380–381. *See also* Coaching
Cooper, Cary, 5, 6, 9, 17, 18, 34, 207
Corporate sector, bullying and mobbing in, 561–577; causes of, 567–571; effect on employers, 565–567; obstacles to antibullying efforts, 575–577; prevalence, 562–563; responses to, 571–574; victims, 563–565
Costello, Kimberly, 64–65
Counterdependency, 86. *See also* Dependency
Crawshaw, Laura, 338, 341, 343, 345, 346–348, 351, 377
Critical incident model of workplace mobbing, 7, 9, 15

Cubela Adoric, Vera, 143, 144
Cyberbullying, 280; and Brodie's Law (Australia), 445; definition of, 115; and education sector, 514, 521; workplace, 36, 267; and zero-tolerance policy, 573

Daniel, Teresa, 17
Darwinism, 156. *See also* Social Darwinism
Davenport, Noa: definition of workplace mobbing, 6, 7–8, 18; effects of workplace mobbing on friendships, 190; effects on performance and productivity, 205, 207; prevention of workplace mobbing, 213
D'Cruz, Premilla, 56, 186, 241
Denmark, 438–440, 450. *See also* Scandinavia
Dependency, 86–87, 90
Depression, 88, 105–112, 137, 140, 143, 147, 171, 182–184, 204–205, 209–210, 277–278, 292, 309, 322, 337, 366, 428, 430, 489–490, 564, 568, 599, 612
Derks, Belle, 57
Dewey, John, 4
Diagnostic and Statistical Manual of Mental Disorders (DSM): DSM-III, 103, 106–107; DSM IV, 107–109; DSM-5, 88, 107–109, 293–295; and narcissistic personality disorder, 88; and "neurosis," 103; and PTSD, 106–109, 293–295
Dignitarian society, 616–617. *See also* Future agendas and visions
Displaced aggression, 179
Displaced workers, 60, 62, 68–69, 71, 359
Disruptive behaviors, 10, 102, 458–463, 469–473
Diversity, 284, 366–367, 370, 399, 431
Dollard, Maureen, 203
Dopamine, 157, 161, 163. *See also* Neuroscience
Dormann, Christian, 203

Drug abuse. *See* Alcohol and drug abuse
DSM. *See Diagnostic and Statistical Manual of Mental Disorders* (DSM)
Duffy, Maureen: on aggressors, 614; American Mental Health Counselors Association keynote, 613; definition of workplace mobbing, 7, 8–10, 16, 17, 18; intent as element of bullying and mobbing, 26; isomorphism, 177; mental health of aggressors, 614; negative acts, 16; negative impacts, 17; psychological impacts, 144–145; restorative justice, 213; vicarious and secondary victimization, 171, 172, 177, 178, 180–182, 189–190

Education sector, bullying and mobbing in: higher education, 507–351; mistreatment and abuse by administrators, 482–483; prevalence of, 481, 516–517; principal mistreatment and abuse of teachers, 481–501; studies and research, 492–500
Egocentrism, 88. *See also* Narcissism
Einarsen, Stale, definition of workplace bullying, 5, 6, 9, 17, 18, 33, 55, 203, 295, 369
Eisenberger, Naomi I., 137
Ellemers Naomi, 57
Elliott, Gail, 6, 7–8, 18
Elliott, Ray, 317
Embitterment disorder, 68, 109–111
Emotional abuse, 61, 118, 509; cycle of, 206; definitions of, 11, 16; emotional and psychological consequences of, 59, 66; and mobbing syndrome, 7; performance and productivity consequences of, 205; spousal, 66; use of the term, 10, 391, 509
Emotional intelligence (EQ), 61; assessment of, 604; and coaching, 345, 347; and leadership, 249, 250, 347, 349, 387, 392, 393, 604; and perpetrators, 63, 341; and soft skills

training, 251, 399; and states of
    being, 269
Empathy, 64, 137–138, 159, 174,
    184–185, 227, 230, 237–238,
    250–251, 265, 273–274, 323,
    341–342, 345, 347–349, 398, 489,
    497, 570
Employability, 17, 131, 132, 139–140,
    145
Epigenetics, 113, 152, 157
Epstein, Seymour, 161, 162
Equal Employment Opportunity (EEO),
    58, 67
Equal Employment Opportunity
    Commission (EEOC), 249, 300,
    497, 562
Eye movement desensitization and
    reprocessing, 121–122, 307
Exposure therapy, 306–307; prolonged
    exposure therapy, 121

Family and Medical Leave Act (FMLA),
    426–427
Fast, Nathanael J., 63
Fix, Bryan, 138
Flannery, Raymond, 12
French Supreme Court (Court of
    Cassation), 442
Fryers, Tom, 135, 136
Fuller, Robert, 616–617
Fundamental attribution error, 55, 375
Future agendas and visions, 611–617;
    dignitarian society, 616–617; law
    and public policy, 614–615; mental
    health and coaching, 613–614;
    organizational prevention and
    response, 611–613; workplace
    standards, 615–616

Gallup, Inc., 119–120, 394
Garcia, Patrick Raymund James M., 63
General affective aggression model, 201
General Social Survey (GSS), 25, 34,
    41
Generalized Workplace Harassment, 36

Generalized workplace harassment, 40,
    369, 508–509. *See also* Workplace
    harassment
Glambek, Mats, 205
Glaso, Lars, 55
"Going postal," 45, 223. *See also* United
    States Postal Service
Gok, Sibel, 68
Grawe, Klaus, 161
Guglielmi, Dina, 114
Guilt: of aggressors, 191, 404; of
    bystanders, 172, 175, 186, 530;
    and clinical evaluations, 121; and
    coaching, 321, 322; shame versus,
    66; of targets, 66, 68, 107, 321, 322;
    and toxic leadership, 596. *See also*
    Shame
Gustafsson, Annelie, 105, 106

Harassment. *See* Students: harassment
    of; Workplace harassment
Hare, Chauncey, 10–11
Hare, Robert, 64
Hart, Vicki, 318
Health, World Health Organization
    definition of, 101, 105, 118, 122
Health care sector, bullying and
    mobbing in, 457–474; contributing
    factors, 463–468; current responses
    to, 468–473; use of labels, 458–460;
    prevalence of, 460–463
Health Insurance Portability and
    Accountability Act (HIPPA), 108
Health outcomes, definition of, 104
Healthy Workplace Bill (HWB), 11,
    213, 223–225, 229–230, 246, 395,
    414, 415–421, 431, 492, 615, 616;
    antiretaliation protection, 417;
    damages, 417; definition of abusive
    conduct, 11, 229, 416, 419–420,
    498; definition of abusive work
    environment, 11, 230, 415–416;
    and educational settings, 492, 495,
    497, 499–500; features of, 415–418;
    influences on, 424; liability, 416–417;

Index

primary cause of action, 415–416; state versions of, 499, 571; support for, 421, 429, 497–499, 500; and unions, 497, 558
Healthy workplace legislation: California, 418; Georgia, 420; Tennessee, 418–419; Utah, 419–420. *See also* Healthy Workplace Bill (HWB)
Heath, Renee G., 138
Henle, Christine A., 53
Hershcovis, M. Sandy, 203, 205
Hetland, Jorn, 205
Hoel, Helge, 5, 6, 9, 17, 18, 34, 58, 207, 369, 397
Hollis, Leah P., 202, 203, 210, 513
Horizontal violence. *See* Lateral (horizontal) violence
Hostile work environment, 43, 45, 340, 572; definitions of, 13–14, 102, 416, 423–424; and harassment, 416, 423–424, 438; neck pain caused by, 114; and workplace bullying, 13–14, 35, 114, 340
Human Dignity and Humiliation Studies, 617
Human resources (HR), 56, 81, 91, 208, 357, 397, 429, 435, 437, 546, 561, 565, 573; accountability strategies, 252–254; identifying bullying and mobbing, 244–247; intervention strategies, 249–251; organizational roles of HR professionals, 235–239, 283; organizational strategies, 247–254; perceptions of HR's role and performance, 239–244; prevention strategies, 247–249; responsibilities of, 236, 240, 243, 246; restoration and recovery strategies, 251–252; and safe reporting, 212, 280; workplace relationships, 254–255
Hutchinson, Marie, 78, 81, 83, 90
Hypothalamus-pituitary-adrenal (HPA) axis, 157–158, 161. *See also* Neuroscience

ICD-10 (World Health Organization diagnostic manual), 103, 108–111. *See also* World Health Organization (WHO)
ICD-11, 108–109, 111
Illness, definition of, 104
Incivility. *See* Workplace incivility
Indiana Supreme Court, 229, 382
Injury, definition of, 104
Institute of Medicine (IOM), 107
Intentionality: and definitions of workplace bullying and mobbing, 16–17, 18, 26, 153, 246, 494; in education sector, 487, 490, 527; and legal system, 381–382, 404, 407, 415, 419, 422; and power harassment (Japan), 447; and tort law, 415, 422
Intentional Infliction of Emotional Distress (IIED), 212, 381–382, 415, 422
Intentional workplace, 616
International Labour Organization, 13
Intervention studies in the United States, Australia, and Finland, 165
Isolation. *See* Social isolation

Jagatic, Karen, 39, 41, 482
Janoff-Bulman, Ronnie, 60, 61
Jeffrey Johnston Stand Up for All Students Act, 498
Job strain, 88, 113–116, 205. *See also* Stress and stressors; Work stress
Job strain model, 113–114, 116
Job stress, 80, 360. *See also* Job strain; Stress and stressors; Work stress
Johns, Gary, 204
Johnson, Susan L., 206
Just-world beliefs, 141–144

Kandel, Eric, 156, 158, 160
Karasek, Robert A., Jr., 113–114
Karatuna, Isil, 68
Keashly, Loraleigh, 39, 41, 206, 428; bystander training, 377, 529; definition of emotional abuse, 10, 11, 16, 17, 18

Keeney, Bradford P., 3
Kiewitz, Christian, 63
Knoff, Howard M., 153
Kvartuc, Tina, 143, 144

Labor unions, 324, 615; and consultants, 357, 371, 372, 374, 380–381; corporate sector, 561, 569, 575–576; education sector, 305, 488–489, 493–494, 497; health care sector, 464; and legal system, 421, 425, 428–429; mobilizing support for, 361–362; nonprofit sector, 597–598; public service sector, 540, 544–546, 548–549, 551–558
Lamarck, Jean-Baptiste, 157
Lambert, Lisa Schurer, 53
Lambert, Ronald D., 524
Lateral (horizontal) violence, 10, 57, 458–459, 471–472
Law, Rebecca, 203
Leadership: definition of, 82–83; and emotional intelligence, 249, 250, 347, 349, 387, 392, 393, 604; instructional leadership, 499–500; toxic leadership, 337, 342, 589–593, 595–597, 600–606; transactional leadership, 83; transformational leadership, 83, 499–500
Legal system and legislation: antiretaliation provisions, 417, 424; Australia, 444–445; Belgium, 441–442; Canada, 446–447; collective bargaining laws, 424–425; and consultants, 361; cultural influences, 448–450; damages, 395, 415, 417, 498, 575, 615; Denmark, 440; and diversity, 431; employee handbooks, 425; and employees' lawyers, 428; and employers and their lawyers, 429; employment discrimination law, 423–424; Europe, 436–444; France, 442–443; Germany, 444; and intentional infliction of emotional distress (IIED), 212, 381–382, 415, 422; international, 435–450; Ireland, 443–444; Japan, 447–448; and labor unions, 428–429; liability, 326, 359, 370, 395, 416, 419, 422, 428–429, 435, 442, 450, 498, 539, 558; and mental health providers, 430; occupational safety and health laws, 425; policy objectives, 414–415; public benefit programs, 426–427; redress and liability, 413–432; Slovenia, 441; Sweden, 439; therapeutic jurisprudence, 431–432; tort law, 212, 272, 415, 417, 422–423, 426, 444; United Kingdom, 444; whistle-blower provisions, 424. *See also* Civil Rights Act (1964); Healthy Workplace Bill
Leymann, Heinz, 71–72, 119, 206; critical incident model, 7, 9, 15; definition of workplace mobbing, 6, 17, 18, 37, 369; psychological effects of workplace bullying, 105, 106, 121, 292
Liability, 326, 359, 370, 395, 416, 419, 422, 428–429, 435, 442, 450, 498, 539, 558. *See also* Legal system and legislation
Lieberman, Matthew D., 137
Lind, Karina 55
Linden, Michael, 68, 109–110
Lindner, Evelin, 617
Lipscomb, Jane, 33, 38, 40, 41, 42
Lorenz, Konrad, 7
Lutgen-Sandvik, Pamela, 33, 34, 38, 40, 41, 134, 144, 202, 205–208, 213, 482

MacDonald, Geoff, 137
Machiavellianism, 61, 230, 546
Malice, 14, 576; and abusive conduct (California), 418, 582; definition of, 17; and distinction between bullying and tough management, 17; and moral harassment (France), 442; and negative acts, 16; and workplace bullying and mobbing, 5, 7, 17, 242–243, 246, 586

Martin, Brian, 9
Martin, Jonathan, 366–367, 564
Matthiesen, Stig Berge, 205
McEwen, Bruce, 112
McGinley, Meredith, 40
Meditation, 307. *See also* Mindfulness
Metcalf, Gary, 17
Mindfulness, 307, 309, 592
Mobbing. *See entries under* Workplace bullying and mobbing; Workplace mobbing
Moral exclusion theory, 54
Moser, Klaus, 141

Namie, Gary, 40; *BullyProof Yourself at Work*, 414, 613; Campaign Against Workplace Bullying, 5, 414; "communal character" of bullying, 207; definition of workplace bullying, 5–6, 13, 16–17; effects of workplace bullying on organizations, 206–208, 211, 212, 213; as expert witness, 229, 382; psychological violence, 13; role of human resources, 254; Workplace Bullying Institute, 6, 221, 495; workplace bullying in the corporate sector, 562–563, 568–570; Workplace Bullying Survey, 495
Namie, Ruth: *BullyProof Yourself at Work*, 414, 613; Campaign Against Workplace Bullying, 5, 414; definition of workplace bullying, 5–6, 13, 16–17; effects of workplace bullying on organizations, 211, 212, 213; psychological violence, 13; role of human resources, 254; Workplace Bullying Institute, 6, 221
Narcissism, 66, 88, 230, 493, 554, 567, 592; and coaching, 342, 348–349, 614; and disrespect, 368; and education sector, 489; and group cohesiveness 90; and income inequality, 604; and management, 570
Narcissistic personality disorder, 88, 602
Narrative therapy, 307–308

National Academies of Sciences, Engineering, and Medicine: *Preventing Bullying through Science, Policy, and Practice*, 77
National Education Association (NEA), 77
National Health Interview Survey (NHIS), 25, 41–43, 292
National Institute for Occupational Safety and Health, 12, 25, 43, 120
Natural selection, 156
Negative acts: and behavior classification, 36–38; and coaching, 277; and critical incident model, 7, 15; and definitions of workplace bullying and mobbing, 16, 18, 37, 153, 389, 461; definitions of, 16; and gender, 58; and restorative justice, 275, 405; and self-labeling, 33, 58; and social capital, 141; and states of being, 269; and strain theory, 268; and victimization, 439; withholding or denial of job references, 147
Negative Acts Questionnaire (NAQ), 36, 38, 369, 460–461, 464, 471
Negative Acts Questionnaire–Revised (NAQ-R), 27, 29, 34, 36–37, 516
Negative affectivity (NA), 53–54
Neuman, Joel H., 201
Nielsen, Morten Birkeland, 37, 202–203
Nelson, E. D., 524
Nelson, Eric, 346
Neurobiology of pathology, 155–156
Neurofeedback, 308
Neuroplasticity, 155–156, 159
Neuropsychotherapy, 160–166
Neuroscience, 121, 151–160; brain development and genetics, 156–157; bullying and neural structures, 158–160; bullying and neurochemicals, 157–158; and conflict management, 402; dopamine, 157, 161, 163; and emotions, 396; and health care professionals, 465; neural development and connectivity, 154–156; and neuropsychotherapy,

160–166; and ostracism and exclusion, 137, 146; serotonin, 157, 161

Neurosis, 103, 106

Nonprofit sector, workplace bullying and mobbing in, 589–606; impacts on staff, 598–601; literature review, 591–593; responsive actions by staff, 597–598; toxic behavior patterns, 595–597; and toxic leadership, 601–605

Nordgren, Loran F., 137

Noronha, Ernesto, 56, 186, 241

Norway: education sector, 222, 483; surveys and research, 55, 449, 483; workplace bullying and mobbing laws, 212, 439, 440. *See also* Scandinavia

Obsessiveness, 66–68, 106, 486

Occupational Safety and Health Administration. *See* U.S. Occupational Safety and Health Administration (OSHA)

Oppressed group behavior, 10

Occupational Safety and Health Act, 425

Occupational Safety and Health Administration (OSHA), 120, 360, 497; *Preventing Workplace Violence: A Road Map for Healthcare Facilities*, 468–469; on workplace violence, 12, 465, 468–469

Olweus, Dan, 153, 222

Ombuds, 387–407; advanced skills for, 402–405; historical perspective, 388; office of ombuds, 396–397; role of, 389–391; strategies for, 397–402; as trust leader, 391–393; and workplace culture, 393–394; and workplace trust, 394–396

Organizational climate, 119, 300, 404, 405; and bystanders, 172, 517; climate surveys, 249; and coaching, 338–341, 351; definition of, 82; and definitions of bullying and mobbing, 9; and education sector, 491–494, 497, 517, 522, 525, 528; negative impacts of bullying and mobbing on, 35, 208–209, 212, 213; and organization development, 86; and prevention of bullying and mobbing, 247–249; and psychological safety, 360. *See also* "Climate of fear" 207, 23

Organizational culture, 119, 393, 615; and bystanders, 172; definition of, 81–82; and definitions of bullying and mobbing, 9, 18; negative impacts of bullying and mobbing on, 176, 207–209, 213, 254, 284; and nonprofit sector, 591, 593, 601–606; and organization development, 85–86; as precedent to mistreatment and abuse, 493

Organizational developmental trajectory, 84–87; consolidation, 85–86; early bureaucratization, 86; expansion, 85; late bureaucratization, 86–87; new venture, 84–85; professionalization, 85

Organizational responsibility, 18, 45, 68, 71, 223, 254, 363, 372–373, 522, 612, 615–616. *See also* Human resources (HR): responsibilities of

Organizational risk factors for bullying and mobbing, 75–95; case study, 91–94; and individual dynamics, 87–89; and integrative model of prevention, 78–79; and organizational dynamics, 79–87; and work team dynamics, 89–90; zero-tolerance policies, 76–78

Organizational shame, 69. *See also* Shame

Ostracism, 19, 612; as behavior of bullying or mobbing, 65, 68, 82, 144, 240, 245; and education sector, 222, 496; effects of, 65, 137, 144, 178, 179; and incivility, 368; and leadership, 82; neuroscience of, 146; and power harassment, 447; and prevention policy, 371; and "social death," 137. See also Social isolation

Pallesen, Stale, 55
Panic attacks, 106, 322, 481, 564. See also Anxiety
Passive-aggression, 86, 174, 285, 459
Pearson, Christine, 13, 207, 209, 368
Peña Saint Martin, Florencia, 9
Perceived injustice, 66–67, 68, 110, 495, 524–525
Perfectionism, 62–63
Perry, Tara, 138
Political intelligence, 61
Porath, Christine, 13, 209, 240
Postal workers. See United States Postal Service
Posttraumatic embitterment disorder (PTED), 68, 109–111
Posttraumatic stress disorders, 105–111, 121, 292–296; and bullying and mobbing, 8, 111, 171, 181, 184, 209, 292–293, 295–296, 391, 428, 430, 564; complex PTSD, 108–109; diagnostic criteria for posttraumatic stress disorder (PTSD), 108–109, 116, 293–297; posttraumatic embitterment disorder (PTED), 68, 109–111. See also Trauma; Trauma-informed care
Power, healthy, 404–405
Power distance, 449
Power harassment (Japan), 436, 447–448
Power imbalances and differentials, 63, 387; and administration, 482–483; and conflict resolution, 21, 58, 266, 267, 286, 365, 402–404; contrapower bullying, 515, 517; and counseling and coaching, 300, 302–303; and definitions of bullying and mobbing, 5, 11, 12, 18–19, 153, 244; and education sector, 341, 493–495, 501, 509, 515, 517–519, 524–526; and gender, 58; and health care sector, 464–470; and hierarchy, 464, 468, 515; and mediation, 365; measurement of, 26, 33; mirroring strategy for, 403–404; and political intelligence, 61; power swapping strategy for, 403–404; and public service sector, 548–550, 552, 556–558; and rankism, 617; and recovery from bullying and mobbing, 144; and toxic leadership, 591, 598, 601, 604–605
Powerlessness, 56, 58, 300, 302, 305, 501
Presenteeism, 204–207, 210–211, 271, 277, 395, 598. See also Absenteeism
Prolonged exposure therapy, 121. See also Exposure therapy
Protected class status, 11, 13–14, 370, 416, 418, 423–424, 428, 431, 436, 567
Psychological safety, 66, 69, 71, 301, 306, 360, 382
Psychological violence, 6, 12–13, 57, 66, 364, 372, 398. See also Violence; Workplace violence
Psychopathology, 64–65, 106, 158, 159, 230, 273, 568, 614
Psychosocial, definition of, 131
Psychosomatic illness, definitions of, 103–104
Psychotherapy: best practices, 291–310; coaching versus psychotherapy, 315–318; posttraumatic stress disorder, 292–296; specific treatment modalities for trauma, 306–309; trauma-informed care, 296–309
Public service sector, bullying and mobbing in, 539–558; bullying behaviors 545–546; enabling behaviors, 548–560; examples of interventions, 551–554; grievance processes, 543–544; impact of success, 555–557; politics of,

547–548; public sector workplaces and systems, 542–543; and resilience, 550–551; and unions, 540, 544–545

Queen bee phenomenon, 57

Rape, 12, 59. *See also* Sexual assault
Rea, Ruth, 206
Reeves, Maiyuwai, 63
Reintegrative shame, 273. *See also* Shame
Reio, Thomas G., 203
Relaxation therapy, 307
Resilience, 113; and coaching, 324, 337; definitions of, 120–121, 154; and employability, 139; and neuropsychotherapy, 154, 162, 164, 166; as protective factor, 120–121; and public service sector, 550–551; and recovery, 139–140, 162, 164, 166, 324, 337, 592; and self-management, 592; training for, 252
Restorative justice, 265–286; myths and realities, 275–276; practices, 265–286; safe reporting, 270, 280–284, 286; steps and procedures, 252–273–275; and victims, 272–280
Restubog, Simon Lloyd D., 63
Richman, Judy, 40, 369
Rose, Kevin, 203, 207, 562
Rospenda, Kathleen M., 41, 369

Safe reporting, 265, 270, 280–284, 286, 399
Sakmann, Bert, 156
Salin, Denise, 58, 495, 524
Sanders-Reio, Joanne, 203
Scaer, Robert, 292
Scandinavia, 34, 37, 436, 448–449. *See also* Denmark; Norway; Sweden
Schat, Aaron, 41
Schwartz, Ruth Distler, 6, 7–8, 18
Schwartz, Tony, 346
Scott, Kristin L., 63
Sebastian, Catherine, 159

Self-harm, 65, 326. *See also* Suicide and suicidal ideation
Sensky, Tom, 110, 111
Sensorimotor psychotherapy, 308
Serotonin, 157, 161. *See also* Neuroscience
Sexual assault, 59, 64, 107, 624
Sexual harassment, 11, 39, 56, 115, 246, 295, 450; anti–sexual harassment policy, 79, 93, 212, 573–574, 586–587; and bullying, 367, 368–369, 371, 561; and California, 418; in education sector, 487; prevalence of, 14; and Title VII of the Civil Rights Act, 13–14, 416, 424; and tort law, 422; use and impact of the term, 19, 20; and workplace mobbing, 8; and workplace training, 546, 574. *See also* Workplace harassment
Selye, Hans, 103, 112, 115
Shame, 555; of aggressors, 273; and coaching, 321, 322; destigmatizing, 69; and education sector, 489; as intent of bullying and mobbing, 617; guilt versus, 66; organizational shame, 69; and public education, 226–227; reintegrative shame, 273; of targets, 66, 107, 226, 321, 322, 564. *See also* Guilt; Stigma
Shaughnessy, Brooke A., 63
Shuck, Brad, 203, 207, 562
Sias, Patricia, 138
Silva, Deborah, 138
Social Darwinism, 568
Social isolation, 65–66, 105, 136, 322; as behavior of bullying or mobbing, 15, 65, 134, 201, 267, 397–398, 485, 520, 527, 562, 586; and coaching, 322, 323; and education sector, 485, 486, 487, 489–491, 494; effects of, 146, 163; as enabling bullying and mobbing, 548–550; and general workplace harassment, 369; and mistrust, 299; and power harassment,

447; and prevention policy, 371; as response to bullying or mobbing, 65, 105, 136–138, 163; and suicide, 65. *See also* Ostracism
Social pain, 132, 136–138, 145–146, 159
Social rejection, 159. *See also* Ostracism; Social isolation
Society for Human Resource Management, 42–45, 236–237, 239–240, 243–244, 248, 254, 573; SHRM *Body of Competency and Knowledge*, 254
Somatoform disorders, definitions of, 103–104
Sperry, Len: definition of workplace mobbing, 7, 8–10, 16, 17, 18; isomorphism, 177; mental health of aggressors, 614; negative act and negative impacts, 16, 17; psychological impacts, 144–145; restorative justice, 213; vicarious and secondary victimization, 171, 172, 177, 178, 180–182, 189–190
Stigma, 15, 19, 58, 69, 105, 229, 572. *See also* Shame
Stress resilience, 121. *See also* Resilience
Stressors and stress: definitions of, 103; Intentional Infliction of Emotional Distress (IIED), 212, 381–382, 415, 422; *karoushi* (stress-related suicide), 448; and physical health, 112–115; work stress, 10–11, 342, 347, 489. *See also* Posttraumatic stress disorders
Substance Abuse and Mental Health Services Administration (SAMHSA), 296–298, 309
Sugden, Karen, 153
Suicide and suicidal ideation, 366, 442; case of Brodie Panlock (Australia), 445; case of Phoebe Prince (Massachusetts), 281; and children of divorce, 185; France Telecom suicides, 443; *karoushi* (stress-related suicide), 448; media coverage of suicide, 222, 223; risk for targets of bullying and mobbing, 65–66, 105–106, 111, 171, 222–223, 369, 564; and social isolation, 65; and traumatic brain injury, 160; and work orientation, 89
Supreme Court. *See* United States Supreme Court
Sutton, Robert, 76
Sveningsson, Stefan, 133
Sweden: ombudsman, 388; surveys and research, 105, 113, 483; workplace bullying and mobbing laws, 361, 439, 439–440. *See also* Scandinavia
Symptoms, definition of, 104
Syndromes, definition of, 104

Tang, Robert L., 63
Targets of workplace bullying and mobbing: anger and embitterment, 67; behavioral antecedents to targethood, 62–63; behaviors as predictors, 60; and blaming victims, 55; and coaching, 278–279, 315–330; and conflict resolution, 278–279; and gender, 56–58; high self-disclosers, 62; and personalities, 53–55; and fighting back, 56; history of prior abuse, 59–60; negative affectivity (NA), 53–54; obsessiveness, 66–68, 106, 486; ostracism, isolation, and self-harm, 65–66; perceived injustice and obsessiveness, 66–68; and perpetrators' characteristics, 63–65; and race, 58–59; as representing our "better nature," 70–71; risk factors, 53–72; shame and guilt, 66; strengths as liabilities, 60–62; unwanted and uninvited assault, 56. *See also* Victims and victimization
Telomeres, 112–113
Tepper, Ben, 12, 53–55, 202, 482
Terkel, Studs, 70

Tort law, 212, 272, 415, 417, 422–423, 426, 444. *See also* Legal system and legislation
Tracy, Sarah J., 213, 482
Transactional leadership, 83
Transactional stress theory, 489
Transformational leadership, 83, 499–500
Transformative prescriptions, 277, 279
Trauma: and neuroscience, 156; and nonprofit sector, 593, 599; retraumatization, 59, 487, 542; and service sector, 569; trauma-informed care, 146, 291, 296–310 (*see also separate entry*); traumatization theory, 60, 61; treatments, 121 (*see also* Trauma-informed care); work trauma, 10, 330; and workplace friendships, 138. *See also* Posttraumatic stress disorders (PTSD)
Trauma-informed care, 146, 291, 296–297, 315, 378; case illustration, 304–306; and coaching, 319–330, 613; and cognitive behavioral therapy, 306; and exposure therapy, 306–307; and eye movement desensitization and reprocessing, 121–122, 307; and mindfulness and meditation, 307; and narrative therapy, 307–308; and neurofeedback, 308; principles of, 297–298; from principles to practice, 298–304; and relaxation therapy, 307; and sensorimotor psychotherapy, 308; and somatic experiencing, 308–309
Traumatic brain injury, 160
Treadway, Darren C., 63
Tuckey, Michelle, 203
Twyford, Devon, 203, 207, 562

Unemployment benefits, 427
Unions. *See* Labor unions
United States Postal Office, 35, 42, 45, 223, 620

United States Supreme Court: *Burlington Industries v. Ellerth*, 416; definition of hostile work environment, 13, 416; *Harris v. Forklift Systems, Inc.*, 416, 423–424; *Oncale v. Sundowner Offshore Services, Inc.*, 571

Van Laar, Colette, 57
Vicarious and secondary victimization, 171–192; aggressor allies, 173–174; children and parenting, 180–185; coworkers and bystanders, 172–177; friendships, 185–187; future research, 188–191; intimate partners, children, and friends, 177–188; silent bystanders, 175–176; target allies, 174–175; target-partners, 176–180; witness bystanders, 173
Victim blaming, 55–56, 142–143, 147, 297
Victim-perpetrator interactions, 494–495
Victim precipitation, 53–55
Victims and victimization, 35, 38–39, 42, 45, 64, 153, 366; "bullied/nonvictim" category, 40; criminal victimization, 54; definitions of, 439–440; in education sector, 487, 500, 515; and human resources, 241; and self-labeling, 33–34, 38–39; and social pain, 137; vicarious and secondary, 171–192. *See also* Restorative justice: and victims; Targets of workplace bullying and mobbing
Victimology, 118
Vignoli, Michela, 114
Violence: against children, 59, 115; conflict resolution as violence, 365–366; domestic or partner violence, 54, 59, 108, 115, 120, 226, 229, 336, 365–366; Domestic Violence Awareness Month, 226; humiliation as cause of, 617;

lateral (horizontal) violence, 10, 57, 458–459, 471–472; and posttraumatic stress disorder, 293; prevention of, 371–372; psychological violence, 6, 12–13, 57, 66, 364, 372, 398; sexual violence, 59, 293, 529; suicide as violence, 369; symbolic violence, 240; witness bystanders to, 173, 181; work as violence, 70. *See also* Workplace violence
VitalSmarts, 35, 36, 40, 45

Westhues, Kenneth, 7, 292, 519, 521, 527
Whistle-blowing, 71, 284, 424
Whitehall studies, 113
WHO. *See* World Health Organization (WHO)
Williams, Patrick, 316
Witnesses. *See* Bystanders and witnesses
Wolff, Hans-Georg, 141
Work abuse, use of the term, 10–11
Work orientation, 89, 94
Work pressure, 80
Work stress, 10–11, 342, 347, 489. *See also* Job strain; Job stress; Stress and stressors
Work trauma, 10, 330. *See also* Posttraumatic stress disorders (PTSD); Trauma; Trauma-informed care
Workplace aggression, 391; and bullying, 9, 40, 43, 45, 153, 171–173, 208, 209, 267, 346, 561–562; and bystanders, 173–174, 176, 377; and chronic stress, 466; displaced, 179, 401; effects and costs of, 160, 176–177, 203, 205, 208–209; and embitterment disorder, 110; and emotional abuse, 11; family origins of, 63, 182; general affective aggression model, 201–202; and generalized workplace harassment, 369; and gender, 57, 565; group, 9; in higher education, 507–508, 524, 531; humiliation as cause of, 617; and incivility, 368; and individual dynamics and differences, 87–88, 341–342, 612; indirect, relational, and social, 10; and leadership, 82; levels of, 484, 485–487; and mobbing, 9, 40, 43, 45, 171; and narcissism, 230; and negative affectivity, 64; and norm violations, 524; occasional, 26, 34; one-on-one, 9, 57; passive-aggression, 86, 174, 285, 459; physical, 12, 229, 423; prevalence of in the workplace, 25, 38, 45–46; psychological, 25; and PTSD, 294; reciprocal, 180, 565; relational, 10; vicarious, 34–35; workplace aggression defined, 369. *See also* Workplace incivility

Workplace bullying, definitions of, 5–6, 9–10, 16–21, 102–103

Workplace bullying and mobbing, definitions and concepts: abusive work environment, 11, 16–17, 416, 498; actors, 18; frequency and duration, 17; implications of terms and definitions, 19–21; intentionality, 16–17, 18, 26, 153, 246, 494; malice, 17–18; negative acts, 16, 18, 37, 153, 389, 461; negative impacts, 17–18; power imbalances and differentials, 5, 11, 12, 18–19, 153, 244

Workplace bullying and mobbing, impacts of, 101–102; attitudinal and affective consequences, 202–204; cardiovascular disorders, 113–114; and childhood adversity, 113, 115; exclusion, 136–139; and just-world beliefs, 141–144; latency of, 116; loss of work relationships, 136–139; mental health outcomes, 105–112; musculoskeletal disorders, 114; organizational impacts, 201–214; organization-level consequences,

208–213; physical health outcomes, 112–115; posttraumatic disorders, 106–112; professional reputation, 139–141; protective factors, 120–121; psychosocial impact, 131–147; public and occupational health, 117–122; and recovery, 144–146; reemployability, 139–141; research and clinical issues, 115–117; and resilience, 120–121; role of clinicians and health care system, 121–121; social pain, 136–139; symptoms and diagnoses, 105–106; terms and definitions, 102–105; work and personal identities, 133–136; workplace behavioral consequences, 204–206; workplace group-level consequences, 206–207

Workplace bullying and mobbing, research and measurement: actors and targets, 43–44; behavioral classification, 36–40; industries and occupations, 42; intentionality, 26, 33; measurement, 25–26, 33–46; prevalence, 25–46; sampling, 41–42; self-labeling, 33–35, 38–40; time frames, 40–41; U.S. studies, 27–32

Workplace Bullying Institute (WBI), 5–6, 28, 33; definition of workplace bullying, 57, 102–103; WBI Blueprint, 374, 376, 378–379

Workplace harassment, 9, 92; anti-harassment policy and procedures, 91, 208, 284, 286, 425, 574, 586–587; and bullying, 102, 118, 153, 370–371, 398, 586; and cultural influences, 448–450; and disability, 424; and educational sector, 40, 495, 497–498, 507; effects of, 113, 117, 266; generalized workplace harassment, 36, 40, 369, 508–509; and health care sector, 461; and hostile work environment, 13–14, 423–424; and independent investigators, 67; international terms and policies, 435–444, 446–450; legal protections against, 11, 13–14, 212, 416–417, 423–424, 431, 437; and leadership, 83; and mobbing, 7–8, 398; moral harassment (Belgium and France), 435, 441–443; and organizational culture, 82; perpetrators of, 268–269, 275–276; power harassment (Japan), 436, 447–448; prevalence of, 34; psychological harassment (Canada), 435, 446–447; status-blind harassment, 66, 498; and target personalities, 88; and verbal violence, 12, 118; and workplace training, 93. *See also* Hostile work environment; Protected class status; Sexual harassment; Students: harassment of

Workplace incivility, 391, 471, 472; and bad bosses, 394; bullying or mobbing versus, 13, 34, 45, 102, 367, 368, 368–370, 509, 576–577; and coaching, 341, 351; definitions of, 13, 367–369; effects of, 203, 286; and federal legislation, 576–577; multiplier effect of, 207, 209; prevention of, 611, 620; school climate predictors of, 491–492; and workplace aggression, 203, 209, 369; and working conditions, 365–366; and workplace restorative practice, 286

Workplace mobbing: definitions of, 6–8; workplace bullying versus, 9–10. *See also entries under* Workplace bullying and mobbing

Workplace violence: and bullying and mobbing, 15, 66, 75–76, 118, 367, 398; and bullying policy, 583–584; and bystanders, 181; and Canada, 446; definitions of, 12–13, 118, 446; and education sector, 489; and Europe, 437–441, 449; and health care sector, 458–459, 465, 469, 471–473; and human resources, 240;

prevalence of, 25; prevention of, 371–372, 488–489; and regulatory agencies, 468–469; and working conditions, 465; and zero-tolerance policies, 77. *See also* Violence
World Health Organization (WHO): definition of health, 101, 105, 118, 122; *ICD-10* (diagnostic manual), 103, 108–111; on psychological violence, 13; on workplace conditions, 120
Wyatt, Judith, 10–11

Yamada, David, 541; definition of abusive work environment, 11, 16–17; employment litigation, 615; ethical leadership, 611–612; Healthy Workplace Bill, 11, 213, 229, 395, 498; HumanDHS board member, 617; human resources (HR) role, 237–238, 243, 255; intent as element of bullying and mobbing, 26; *Minding the Workplace* (blog), 224. *See also* Healthy Workplace Bill (HWB)
Yang, Haiou, 114
Yang, Jun, 63

Zero-tolerance policies, 76–78, 93, 94, 335, 471, 572–573
Zogby Analytics (was Zogby International), 6, 14, 421, 482, 483, 495